Bedouin Poets of the Nafūd Desert

Letter from the General Editor

The Library of Arabic Literature makes available Arabic editions and English translations of significant works of Arabic literature, with an emphasis on the seventh to nineteenth centuries. The Library of Arabic Literature thus includes texts from the pre-Islamic era to the cusp of the modern period, and encompasses a wide range of genres, including poetry, poetics, fiction, religion, philosophy, law, science, travel writing, history, and historiography.

Books in the series are edited and translated by internationally recognized scholars. They are published as hardcovers in parallel-text format with Arabic and English on facing pages, as English-only paperbacks, and as downloadable Arabic editions. For some texts, the series also publishes separate scholarly editions with full critical apparatus.

The Library encourages scholars to produce authoritative Arabic editions, accompanied by modern, lucid English translations, with the ultimate goal of introducing Arabic's rich literary heritage to a general audience of readers as well as to scholars and students.

The publications of the Library of Arabic Literature are generously supported by Tamkeen under the NYU Abu Dhabi Research Institute Award G1003 and are published by NYU Press.

Philip F. Kennedy
General Editor, Library of Arabic Literature

شعـراء النفود

خـلف أبو زويّد وعـدوان ابن راشـد الهِربيـد
وعجـلان ابن رمـال

LIBRARY OF
المكتبة
ARABIC
العربية
LITERATURE

Bedouin Poets of the Nafūd Desert

Khalaf Abū Zwayyid, ʿAdwān al-Hirbīd, and ʿAjlān ibn Rmāl

Edited and translated by
Marcel Kurpershoek

Volume editor
Philip F. Kennedy

NEW YORK UNIVERSITY PRESS
New York

NEW YORK UNIVERSITY PRESS
New York

Library of Congress Cataloging-in-Publication Data

Names: Kurpershoek, P. M., editor, translator. | Abū Zūwayd, Khalf, 1844-1942, author. | Hirbīd, ʻAdwān, -1896, author. | Ibn Rmāl, ʻAjlān, author.
Title: Bedouin poets of the Nafūd desert / by Khalaf Abū Zwayyid, ʻAdwān al-Hirbīd, ʻAjlān ibn Rmāl ; edited and translated by Marcel Kurpershoek.
Description: New York : New York University Press, 2024. | Series: Library of Arabic literature | Includes bibliographical references and index. | Summary: "Bedouin Poets of the Nafūd Desert features poetry from three poets of the Ibn Rashīd dynasty-the highwater mark of Bedouin culture in the nineteenth century. Khalaf Abū Zwayyid, 'Adwān al-Hirbīd, and 'Ajlān ibn Rmāl belonged to tribes based around the area of Jabal Shammar in northern Arabia. A cultural and political center for the region, Jabal Shammar attracted caravans of traders and pilgrims, tribal shaykhs, European travelers (including T.E. Lawrence), illiterate Bedouin poets, and learned Arabs. All three poets lived at the inception of or during modernity's accelerating encroachment. New inventions and firearms spread throughout the region, and these poets captured Bedouin life in changing times. Their poems and the accompanying narratives showcase the beauty and complexity of Bedouin culture, while also grappling with the upheaval brought about by the rise of the House of Saud and Wahhabism. The poems featured in Bedouin Poets of the Nafūd Desert are often humorous and witty, yet also sentimental, wistful, and romantic. They vividly describe journeys on camelback, stories of family and marriage, thrilling raids, and beautiful nature scenes, offering a window into Bedouin culture and society in the nineteenth and early twentieth centuries"-- Provided by publisher.
Identifiers: LCCN 2023043686 | ISBN 9781479826155 (hardback) | ISBN 9781479826162 (ebook) | ISBN 9781479826209 (ebook other)
Subjects: LCSH: Dialect poetry, Arabic--Saudi Arabia--Translations into English. | Arabic poetry--Bedouin authors--Translations into English. | Arabic poetry--19th century--Translations into English. | Arabic poetry--20th century--Translations into English. | LCGFT: Poetry.
Classification: LCC PJ8005.65.E54 B43 2024 | DDC 892.7/1508089272--dc23/eng/20240130
LC record available at https://lccn.loc.gov/2023043686.

New York University Press books are printed on acid-free paper, and their binding materials are chosen for strength and durability.

Series design by Titus Nemeth.

Typeset in Tasmeem, using DecoType Naskh and Emiri.

Typesetting and digitization by Stuart Brown.

Manufactured in the United States of America
c10 9 8 7 6 5 4 3 2 1

Table of Contents

To my brothers, Ernest Kurpershoek and Eric Kurpershoek

Abbreviations

CA	classical Arabic
cf.	compare
f. pl.	feminine plural
HA*	Hess Archive
lit.	literally
n.	noun
pl.	plural
sg.	singular
v., vv.	verse(s) (a single line of Arabic, translated as a couplet)

Acknowledgments

The fieldwork and research that went into this edition and translation would not have been possible without a Humanities Research Fellowship offered by the New York University Abu Dhabi Institute. I am deeply grateful for the imaginative commitment shown by the institute's leadership of Dr. Reindert Falkenburg and Dr. Martin Klimke, and the program's associate director, Alexandra Sandu.

Dr. Saad Sowayan is not only the foremost authority on Arabian culture, but also a dear friend and a source of inspiration and guidance. As the collector, editor, and interpreter of a vast amount of oral Bedouin heritage, including this volume's Arabic text, he has unfailingly and with enviable patience answered my countless questions regarding interpretation. His scholarly presence has enabled my efforts to come to fruition. During my years of research in 2015–22, I was overwhelmed by the famous hospitality and ready interest shown to visitors by the people of the Nafūd Desert. This edition would not have been possible without the learned help of my principal informant, Ibrāhīm ibn Suʿayyid al-Hamazānī of the Aslam division of Shammar. We have been close friends since a visit to Ḥāʾil in 1988, when his father, the renowned poet and transmitter Suʿayyid ibn Fuhayd al-Dūkhī al-Hamazānī, asked me to explain a poem with a particularly difficult rhyme, composed for the occasion to test my seriousness of purpose. I always found a warm welcome in the majlis of Nazzāl ibn Muḥammad ibn Suʿayyid al-Shammarī and his friend Aḥmad ʿAbdallah Khalaf al-Shaghdalī, who in their turn enlisted the assistance of other aficionados through Twitter. I am also grateful to Dr. Khalif al-Shammarī of Ḥāʾil University for sharing his expertise in modern history and taking me to visit one of the last surviving sources of Sowayan's recordings, the Bedouin poet and transmitter Riḍā ibn Ṭārif al-Shammarī at the ancient wells of Līnah, before he passed away in 2016.

Through these years, I was fortunate to find in the King Faisal Center for Research and Islamic Studies in Riyadh a home away from home, and I formed an abiding attachment to this deeply humanist scholarly institution.

Introduction

Ensconced behind vast deserts and the granite barrier of the Ajā mountain range, the town of Ḥā'il in northern Arabia, the capital of the Ibn Rashīd dynasty (1834–1921), was a magnet for visitors of every kind.[1] A hub of long-distance desert transportation, the province's core area of Jabal Shammar (Shammar Mountain) offered safety and a spirit of tolerance and civility. Its strategic location and influence attracted caravans of traders and pilgrims, tribal shaykhs, lords of Najdī oasis towns, European travelers and scholars, illiterate Bedouin poets, and learned Arabs. Marvelously attuned to the customs and way of life of the Bedouin, the majlis of the princely court, described with excitement by European explorers, was an arena of choice for poets vying for preeminence and favor with the rulers. Poetic excellence was rewarded, and performing for a discriminating and critical audience stirred competitors to give it their all. Many of the Ibn Rashīd princes were poets in their own right and some are counted among Arabia's greatest bards, their verses cited with admiration by aficionados until today. For these reasons, the court's culture radiated over many hundreds of miles, and the role of the Ibn Rashīd in the domain of Arabian tribal and Bedouin culture was similar to that of the court of al-Ḥīrah for poetry in pre-Islamic times.

Over the centuries, tribes have come and gone, merged, and transformed. Critically, though, the ecosystem; pastoral and oasis economy; means of cultivation, irrigation, and transportation; and traditions and customs embodied in the so-called desert code have in their essentials continued as before. In the nineteenth century, much of the fighting was still done with matchlocks and cold weapons. Storytellers dwell on quaint habits such as the poet Abū Zwayyid walking about armed with a sword. Toward the end of the century, the pace of change picked up markedly. The three Bedouin poets whose verse and lore are presented in this volume lived to see, or at least hear of, modernity's accelerating encroachment. Deadly firearms made raiding less entertaining as a chivalrous sport.[2] Muḥammad ibn Rashīd, in whose time the principality expanded to include the dominions of the House of Saud in Riyadh and the Bedouin culture of the north, had seen how a telegraph machine functioned in Baghdad.[3] The text makes mention of the extension of the Ottoman railway from Damascus to

Medina in Hejaz Province and the possession of automobiles by some shaykhs in Syria and Mesopotamia in the run-up to the First World War. New anxieties crept in, and more than ever the sands of the Nafūd Desert seemed a refuge from unwelcome events beyond, summed up in the poet ʿAjlān ibn Rmāl's nostalgic sigh (§52.6, v. 1):

> My home, sanctuary from telegraph and rail:
> I am not cut out to be a maker of bombs.[4]

Even more profound was the impact of another development that shook Bedouin society, and its poets in particular. The Ikhwān, "the Brothers," the religiously motivated armed vanguard that laid the ground for the restoration of Saudi supremacy, created deep fissures in tribal society, pitting clans and even family members against one another.[5] The easygoing old ways of the Bedouin were frowned upon and adherence to the strict tenets of puritanical Wahhabism were harshly enforced. Tobacco, men's long tresses, music, poetry, and a certain tolerance for more informal religious practices fell by the wayside. Traditional social distinctions and respect for inherited or conventionally acquired prestige were scoffed at and spurned.[6] ʿAjlān's despair at being witness to this cultural devastation is echoed by transmitters decades later in nostalgic offhand remarks about "times when truthfulness still counted for something" (§2.3).[7] In poetry, the hallowed motif of a world gone topsy-turvy gained a new poignancy (§49.8, v. 2):

> Ibn Saʿūd has curbed warhorses and chiefs;
> nobles became servants; bastards went on a spree.

Unable to conceal his disgust, ʿAjlān burst out (§52.6, vv. 4–5):

> Escaping riffraff, shirt hems smeared with shit,
> blockheads wrapped about with pompous turbans,
> I put ten days of riding between me and them,
> marching at a grueling pace deep into the night.

And in derision of a purportedly religious thuggery that trampled over the old Bedouin virtues, he added: "Ugh, God help you, conflicted by double ancestry" (§52.6, v. 8)—that is, the generous-spirited ancestors of the bloodline and those who inculcated the new doctrine and "seek Paradise by slaughtering their relatives" (§52.7, v. 9).[8] Like many in the Arabian north, who were close to areas that remained outside the Saudi reach and were already in the habit of migrating and traveling there, ʿAjlān took his family first to the Nafūd sands ("lofty dunes, our hideout from those fanatics"), and from there toward the Syrian desert (§52.5, v. 3).

ʿAjlān, the third poet in this volume, whose oeuvre is slighter than those of his two fellow poets, has left us with the most explicit denunciations and descriptions of the havoc wreaked on traditional Bedouin society, an imposition of homegrown modernity more fatal than any other blow it received since the pre-Islamic Kingdom of al-Ḥīrah. Yet, in the end, he grudgingly makes his peace and pays obeisance to the new governor of Ḥāʾil, a member of the House of Saud, as had Abū Zwayyid. Implicit in their conversations with the new ruler is the notion that Ibn Saud has the final word. Also, given the fact that the House of Saud had a broader understanding of society and dictated how far the Ikhwān were allowed to go, these poets and others recognized that its princes might offer some protection against excesses deemed harmful to social harmony. It is impossible to tell whether the measure of forbearance shown by the Saudi governor is a gloss put on events by transmitters of the lore, or whether it was truly experienced by the poets at the time.[9] In any case, it chimes with a widespread opinion in Saudi Arabia concerning the existence of an unwritten compact between rulers and society. Differences with the Ikhwān came to a head in the Saudi showdown with their most hardline elements, who rebelled against the limits imposed on them in 1929.

ʿAdwān al-Hirbīd

The poet ʿAdwān al-Hirbīd cuts a very different figure from Abū Zwayyid and ʿAjlān, hewing closer to the poets of the "Romantic School," grouped around Ibn Sbayyil in the small town of Nifī and other parts of ʿĀliyat Najd (the High Najd), south of Ḥāʾil, beyond al-Qasīm Province. More modest in attitude and ambition than his two fellow poets, yet more subtle and intricate in his verse, al-Hirbīd demands to be seen as an ordinary person, someone who has no business ingratiating himself with the high and mighty. On one occasion, he was chided by the members of his tribe for turning a deaf ear to an invitation by Muḥammad ibn Rashīd. The excuse he gave was that answering the call might not go down well with the ruler at the time, Bandar ibn Ṭalāl.[10]

Yet al-Hirbīd shows no trace of timidity when slugging it out in verbal matches with other poets. In such duels, he invariably comes out as the hardest hitter, whose final punch flattens his opponent with a knockout. The pièce de résistance is a section that starts with his ire at a poem mocking how he treated his palm trees. His detractor speaks scathingly of him for giving his palms female names. A concatenation of events leads to a climax that gives birth to one of the most famous poems in northern Arabia, which goes by the name of al-Shēkhah, "Lady Shaykh" (§49). It opens with a furious outburst against two camel nomads of his clan, one of them the poet who had impersonated his disconsolate palm trees. They accuse him of cowardice because he, as a sheepherder whose animals have little tolerance for water deprivation, urges the shaykh to lead the tribe and herds home from the spring pastures in the Nafūd at the onset of the hot season. Adding insult to injury, they call him out for being a tobacco addict who hankers after a smoke at home, and a poet who, like all poets, is only talk and no action, conveniently forgetting that they are poets themselves. Al-Shēkhah is especially significant and unique for including a kind of *fihrist* of Arabian oral culture: a catalog of famous poets who were also respected men of action, be they early classical or Nabaṭī poets, Bedouin or oasis dwellers (§49.19, vv. 16–31).[11]

Apart from the gripping histrionics of dueling poets, the narrative leaves no doubt that the episode stems from a pastoral divide that runs through much of the lore connected with al-Hirbīd and others. In the class-conscious society of Arabian Bedouin, camel nomads are regarded as superior to herders of sheep and goats.[12] Al-Hirbīd is pictured as belonging to the latter category. It is at the root of all his troubles: in the transmitters' masterful telling, whenever he joins the true Bedouin on a migration to a pastoral idyll of desert meadows, carpeted with herbage after plentiful rains, his rhapsodic elation gives way to melancholy. It bursts into crisis, then ends in sobering catharsis and poise regained: his powerful artistic and intellectual voice overcomes his lower status in the group. In the lead-up to al-Shēkhah and another episode of migration to spring pastures, he and his adopted son Jrēs keep falling behind, unnerved and exhausted, while his camel-owning fellow tribesmen cover the distance in a breeze, are having a good time and doing some falcon hunting as the women set up camp in late afternoon, easily making do with camels' milk in the absence of water. At the same time, al-Hirbīd seems particularly attached to his groves of date palms, and he has been loaned sheep by his better-off kinsmen. The pros and cons of raising camels versus small cattle and of Bedouin mobility versus the settled existence of palm cultivation are spun out in detail in his poems and lore.

In the oral tradition, such differences in lifestyle make for never-ending exchanges of poetry comparing one to the other and discussing their respective merits and disadvantages. In this case, one also suspects that al-Hirbīd's camel-versus-sheep predicament has been emphasized as part of his poetic persona: a struggling, hard-pressed underdog who against all odds employs his acumen, imaginative art, and psychological insight to emerge victorious—or at least with his aura of deeply felt humanism enhanced. For these poets, preserving one's moral integrity is an overriding concern.[13] Al-Hirbīd's skinny sheep are part of a running gag, including his orphan child's disdain for taking care of the lowly animals and al-Hirbīd's lines of verse with an impersonation of his adoptive son's point of view.

The setting for the sheep motif is thrown into sharp relief in his opening selections. Having married the sole surviving wife of his murdered brothers from a sense of duty, the poet takes it upon himself to care for and educate her child, Jrēs. His efforts come to naught. When Jrēs is old enough to herd the sheep given on loan by fellow clansmen, he is taunted by boys pasturing camels—sheep and goats are traditionally tended by girls—and as a result refuses to carry out this chore. Obdurate and thickheaded, he asks for the impossible—camels—and from that moment on leaves it to his uncle to drive the sheep out in the morning. The poet, seeing his careful child-rearing and character-building efforts in shambles, pours his heart out. As in other instances of initially failed parenting in Nabaṭī poetry, the son will later emerge as his father's pillar of strength on a journey with camel nomads in the Nafūd Desert, as mentioned above. In al-Hirbīd's humorous impersonation of poetic dialogue, Jrēs turns the tables on his stepfather, whom he mocks for his fruitless amorous pursuit of much younger girls.

As a lyrical poet, al-Hirbīd is held in special esteem for his ghazals, or love poetry, with many original touches inspired by the desert and oasis environment. His style is noteworthy for its shorter versions of the extended simile, or "submerged similes," in which the subject underlying the comparison is not even mentioned: the poet counts on the audience recognizing it from the imagery of the comparison (for example, §17.5, v. 6). One poem, §41, is composed in a unique long meter. The poet shows a philosophical bent in his contemplation of Creation when, an avid hunter, he opens the belly of a bustard and finds other creatures, each smaller than the previous one, like a set of matryoshka dolls: the Lord has made "eat or be eaten" the rule of His universe (§43).

As the narrative progresses, the poet fights his gloom regarding his project to educate his son, and shows a combative side. Jrēs soon comes in for biting sarcasm and scathing remarks. More serious skirmishes ensue when the poet locks horns with his equals, tearing into poetic opponents with rebuttals that leave their reputations in shreds—figuratively speaking, because the verbal rough-and-tumble might be in jest. From the picture given by the storytellers, al-Hirbīd emerges as a complex, multifaceted artistic personality. No dashing raider, he appears genuinely, and sometimes jokingly, introspective, and self-critical to an extent rarely seen in Arabian poetry. In a modest way, he cuts a fatherly figure. Though generally unassuming, he jealously guards his pride and self-esteem, yet he is also pleasure-loving and intensely social. Romantically inclined, he sensually and delicately warbles of his love when he is at ease. In a pensive mood, he gives free rein to his wandering thoughts. In his dialogues, he engages in tongue-in-cheek and lighthearted banter, punctuated with melodramatic touches. When slighted or made the butt of flippant remarks, he is capable of devilish outbursts of fury. His lyrical verse keeps historical events at bay and is free from Abū Zwayyid's penchant for name-dropping. Faced with the dilemmas common to all humanity, the likable al-Hirbīd finds his way, whether cheerful or saddened, always forging ahead with unfailing psychological insight, and guided by his art.

Khalaf Abū Zwayyid

Khalaf Abū Zwayyid is the most famous of the three poets in the volume. Some of his poetry has been preserved in manuscript, whereas the works of the other two poets have survived exclusively in oral tradition.[14] His artistic persona stands in stark contrast to the portrayal of al-Hirbīd. Throughout his career, Abū Zwayyid consorted with the highest aristocracy of tribal shaykhs and frequented their majlises. He gained notoriety for his barbs aimed at the most powerful prince of Arabia in his time, Muḥammad ibn Rashīd. The insults were prickly because of his unabashed flattery of Ibn Shaʿlān, head of the clan of chiefs of the Rwalah tribe (who, according to the narrative, murdered al-Hirbīd's brothers and their families).[15] As a relative of the Ibn Rakhīṣ shaykhs of Shammar, who had played a pivotal role in establishing the rule of Ibn Rashīd, moving in the corridors of power came naturally to Abū Zwayyid. Though not himself one of the clan's shaykhs, belonging to the Ibn Rakhīṣ was sufficient claim to desert nobility.

In Abū Zwayyid's poems, set within the narratives, history unfolds, from the pinnacle of political grandeur and flourishing of Bedouin culture during Muḥammad ibn Rashīd's reign to the sordid, cruel, and at times tragicomical spectacle of prolonged decline, and finally to the House of Ibn Rashīd's demise without a whimper at the hands of Ibn Saud. Abū Zwayyid is shown sparring and jesting with the great on familiar terms. The circles in which he moves include not only Ibn Rashīd, but some of the brightest luminaries in the Bedouin universe: the shaykhs of the ʿAnazah confederation, Ibn Shaʿlān of the Rwalah and Ibn Hadhdhāl of the ʿAmārāt; he also eulogizes the Jarbā shaykhs of Shammar in Iraq. Embedded in his ode to Ibn Shaʿlān is a reference to his "uselessness" to women craving real men, a none-too-subtle allusion to Muḥammad ibn Rashīd's infertility. This broadside was especially injurious as it came in the context of gushing praise for his host, Ibn Shaʿlān, a "stud," dreamt of by beauties (§4.1, v. 12), and for Ibn Mhēd, the shaykh of the Fidʿān of ʿAnazah, the father of Ibn Shaʿlān's wife Turkiyyah. For this reason, the poem earned him an outpouring of scorn from his opponents, all well-known poets, who rushed to the defense of Ibn Rashīd.[16] But when Abū Zwayyid was staying with Ibn Hadhdhāl, and Ibn Shaʿlān came on a visit, he told them that he rated Ibn Hadhdhāl's hospitality higher than that of the visitor. On his return from Ibn Hadhdhāl, and through the good offices of Ibn Rakhīṣ, he made his entry into the courtyard of the Barzān castle, dressed in a white shroud, to the astonishment of the crowds of visitors.[17] Once Ibn Rashīd and his brutal cousin Ḥmūd became aware of the weird visitor's identity, they flew into a rage. Ḥmūd demanded his execution on the spot, wishing to "taste [his] blood" (§10.3).[18] But Abū Zwayyid pleaded that his key verse had been distorted and made offensive by his enemies. As proof, he produced the correct wording of the verse that extolled the virtues of Ibn Rashīd beyond even those of Ibn Shaʿlān.[19] A slave cut off his forelock and Ibn Rashīd dismissed him.[20]

Again and again, Abū Zwayyid is shown pushing his luck and displaying a fondness for verbal brinkmanship. The narrators portray him as a gambler who is tempted to see how far he can go, relying on his quick wit and powers of repartee. It is not necessarily the case that he had such an irreverent attitude toward shaykhs generally held in awe. Rather, as can often be seen in the anecdotes of the tenth-century *Book of Songs* (*Kitāb al-Aghānī*), his effrontery has become a trademark of his poetic persona, as has his ugliness, which seemed to have made him even more attractive to many Bedouin women of high birth. As a poet, he has the knack of using women's fascination with him to advantage—and women are shown by the transmitters as being better at perceiving truth behind outward appearances than men.[21] Both Ibn Shaʿlān and Ibn Hadhdhāl call on him to persuade their runaway wives, who are sisters, to return to them and their children and accept a reconciliation (§§6–7). He is richly rewarded by both women for his adulation of their beauty and, especially, for his paeans to their father, whose name is synonymous with boundless generosity in the desert interior of Arabia, Syria, and Iraq. Abū Zwayyid's powers of persuasion and extensive knowledge of precedent also make him an invincible opponent in cases brought before tribal judges who give opinions in accordance with Bedouin customary law. While at Ibn Shaʿlān's camp, he was called upon as a legal expert in his own right to solve a case that threatened to descend into an armed brawl between sons of Ibn Shaʿlān (§5).

As in the chain of events leading to the composition of al-Hirbīd's al-Shēkhah poem, an unintentional slight, here prompted by Abū Zwayyid's repellent physiognomy, sets in motion a sequence of poems and attracts female attention until his future wife comes in search of him. At her suggestion, she and the poet are given permission by her father to marry and spend three nights together in a small wedding tent on condition that the marriage will be dissolved if she is not pregnant after their days of seclusion. She becomes the mother of his son Dikhīl, who causes as much disappointment to his father as Jrēs to al-Hirbīd. The counsel and exhortations in Abū Zwayyid's verses to Dikhīl do not bear fruit. The son brings shame to his father by losing a case in a court of customary law, whereas Abū Zwayyid had always won his legal battles. Again, none of this is to be taken literally. Like Māniʿ, the son of the early-eighteenth-century poet Ḥmēdān al-Shwēʿir, the characters of Jrēs and Dikhīl serve as foils that allow their makers to present verses of wisdom and spew their anger at the world's iniquities.[22]

Abū Zwayyid's poetry often brings material gain, though that is rarely stated as the principal aim. For example, he is showered with costly presents for his successful practice of marriage counseling. In the general tableau sketched by the transmitters, it is a by-product of his struggle to make ends meet. Following a severe spell of drought in which his camels perished, he and his family are rescued by a friend with whom he goes raiding. Rewarded for the dangerous job of scouting for enemy herds, he is gifted with the most beautiful she-camel and sings the animal's and his friend's praises in verse (§21).[23]

Abū Zwayyid is regarded as the foremost master of camel description—a genre hardly touched by al-Hirbīd, just as Abū Zwayyid has very few pure ghazals to his name. Often looked upon as the most boring part of Arabian poetry, the camel sections of Abū Zwayyid come alive in vibrant scenes. They are not catalogs of animal parts, as in the best-known pre-Islamic examples. For those familiar with the animal as a mount, his camel sections are instantly recognizable: the animal's behavior and movements under all kinds of conditions are sharply observed. Real-life experience and riding enthusiasm combine with sympathetic insight and artistic mastery to produce exhilarating scenes. For that reason, Abū Zwayyid's red-hued she-camel, his messenger's fiery mount for swift delivery of a poem to the addressee, has become a trademark of his poetry.[24]

Abū Zwayyid and al-Hirbīd, arguably the greatest north Arabian Bedouin poets, draw on the same vast repository of motifs, imagery, and literary conventions accumulated over more than a thousand years in the Arabian ecosystem of deserts, arid lands, and oases. However, they differ markedly when it comes to their approach to chiaroscuro, the pervasive and stark binary oppositions in Bedouin poetry. Al-Hirbīd draws his contrasts to enhance his lyricism; Abū Zwayyid does so to boost his bravado. If one goes by the narrative lore, such aspects of style often come down to personal characteristics and philosophy of life. Intensely competitive, Abū Zwayyid delights in confounding opponents and friends with saucy remarks and bold feints to come out on top, in spite of an initial perceived disadvantage. The third poet, ʿAjlān, the owner of famed herds of white camels, seems much better off than the hard-bitten Abū Zwayyid. But in a tight situation, as happens on their approach to Ibn Shaʿlān's camp, ʿAjlān panics, whereas Abū Zwayyid keeps his cool and deftly handles the situation. ʿAjlān fumbles for excuses to dodge Ibn Shaʿlān's request to go and mollify his estranged wife; Abū Zwayyid, on the other hand, lambasts Ibn Shaʿlān for his mistakes and clumsiness, then waits for the right moment to flatter his wife, who against her husband's will rewards him with a coffer full of riches she had received as the price of her reconciliation. ʿAjlān is left empty-handed, reduced to begging Abū Zwayyid for part of his haul.

Turnarounds and upsets against all expectations, crafted to make the underdogs come out on top thanks to their savviness and temerity, are standard fare in oral narrative entertainment. In the guise of realism and historicity, a wondrous tale is served up in the anecdotal style of the classical *Book of Songs*. Abū Zwayyid is presented as a picaresque poet-hero by storytellers and transmitters, who find in him a connection to their own forebears, either through tribal lineage or because of his praise of their ancestors. From its place of origin, the lore moves into the overall domain of Arabian literary taste: once an audience is rooting for the poet-hero, it will naturally fall into the time-hallowed pattern of sympathy for the lesser party who, in defiance of the odds, stages a surprise victory. Therefore, such tales should not be taken literally but rather as organic outgrowths of the interplay of individual talent and personality, literary and cultural convention, and networks of audiences with common interests and backgrounds.

These narratives-cum-poetry are of relatively recent date. Bedouin poetry, as preserved in oral tradition, probably had its heyday in the second half or last quarter of the nineteenth century. Around 1982, this lore was recorded from storytellers who were born not long after that time, some of whom were close to the dramatis personae. Grafted onto events that took place within the purview of modern history, these traditions already show manifold signs of transformation from more or less factual reports into legend. In contrast to even earlier periods, however, there are many more reasonably reliable accounts against which facts can be checked: northern Arabia features in numerous nineteenth-century descriptions of travelers, while Saudi historians and ethnographers have compiled even better-informed studies, though without some of the vivid color and detail added by visitors from outside the area.[25]

ʿAjlān ibn Rmāl

Like Abū Zwayyid, ʿAjlān is the winner who comes from behind. From this perspective, ʿAjlān and Abū Zwayyid have more in common with each other than either does with al-Hirbīd. Both belong to the upper ranks of Bedouin society. For them, love of camels is bred in the bone. They consort with the most venerated tribal leaders. Wherever they appear, they are in high demand for their wit, their amusing tales that walk the fine line between acceptable and outrageous, and their beautiful poetry on issues of abiding interest to the audience. Their vast knowledge of desert lore is appreciated both for its educational value and for its utility in identifying relevant precedent for issues that fall within the remit of customary law and the ethics of the desert code. There has always been a connection between customary law and poetry. Abū Zwayyid is an example of those Bedouin poets who distinguish themselves "in the defense of their tribal rights in law courts when pleadings and counter pleadings are exchanged back and forth between intense, resolute adversaries."[26] When asked for an opinion on a case, his role approaches that of a tribal judge.[27] With respect to a story in the genre of narratives-cum-poetry, verses of poetry are compared to witnesses giving evidence in customary law proceedings; the section on ʿAjlān demonstrates that poetry may also literally serve as evidence in such cases.[28]

ʿAjlān ibn Rmāl belongs to the tribe of al-Rmāl (which means "the sands"), whose main base is the village and oasis of Jubbah, situated at the southern edge of the Great Nafūd Desert, Arabia's second-greatest sea of sand after the Empty Quarter in the south, bordering Oman and Yemen. Jubbah, despite its minuscule size, is one of the most fabled locations in the Arabian desert. For generations of European travelers, heading to the court of Ibn Rashīd armed with letters of recommendation from his notional sovereign, the Ottoman sultan in distant Istanbul, Jubbah would be the first vista of greenery and human habitation after five days on camelback from al-Jawf oasis. Without exception, they describe in their travelogues their jubilation at the delightful contrast upon their arrival.

More practical than these romantically inclined travelers, the tribespeople of al-Rmāl looked to the sands, and their rich growth of perennials and cover of plants after spring rains, as a source of firewood and fodder for their animals, as a barrier against raiders, and as a safe refuge when pressed by their enemies.[29] Therefore, it comes as no surprise that the Nafūd, and in particular its strategic and political importance, looms larger in ʿAjlān's oral traditions than in the lore of the other two poets. The exception are episodes that show al-Hirbīd acceding to the request of the Rmāl clans to accompany them on their spring migration into the desert in order to have the benefit of his entertainment around their campfires in the evening.[30] To procure themselves that pleasure, they went as far as to offer baskets suspended over the humps of their camels as transport for his sheep when they were too fatigued to walk.

Al-Hirbīd plays no role in the lore of ʿAjlān and Abū Zwayyid. On the other hand, the latter pitched in with a composition of his own in the exchanges between ʿAjlān and the famous desert knight Khalaf al-Idhn, a member of the Ibn Shaʿlān clan of the Rwalah tribe. The story illustrates how, in the pantheon of tribal luminaries, everyone was caught in the web of drama and soap opera. Khalaf al-Idhn is the poet–knight who in close combat killed the chivalrous chief Ibn Mhēd, the warlike father-in-law of Saṭṭām bin Shaʿlān, on both of whom Abū Zwayyid heaped praise in a poem that aroused the ire of Ibn Rashīd and made him swear to shed the poet's blood. Abū Zwayyid and ʿAjlān seem to have regularly run into one another at the tents of Bedouin shaykhs, who were so grand that they were called princes by the European visitors. Perhaps their sparring and teasing buffoonery worked to the advantage of both, as it did for poets who slugged it out for wowed crowds in the days of early classical poetry. In the telling of the transmitters, they were therefore probably friendly competitors, in a camaraderie of peers, who occasionally met on the trail of gatherings, attracted by hospitality provided at the tents of desert lords.

Not long after the capture of Ḥāʾil by the Ikhwān, ʿAjlān and Abū Zwayyid were separately received—somewhat condescendingly, but not in an unfriendly way—by the Saudi governor, Ibn Musāʿid. Though the poets adopted a contrite tone, they did not hide from him that faced with a fait accompli, and for lack of an alternative, they had felt compelled to make their peace and offer allegiance to the new masters. While careful to exhibit a demeanor of proper deference, and an awareness of being at the new ruler's mercy, they kept their dignity and even showed flashes of their trademark wit. Similarly, Ibn Musāʿid's words hint at a wry understanding of the old men's plight and former station, and possibly even a glimmer of nostalgia at the spectacle of obeisance paid, albeit reluctantly, by such unassuming, humanist, and cultured representatives of the ancien régime. Though other reports suggest that the scene may have been spiced up by the narrators, it may well be a fair rendering of what happened at the transfer of political loyalty and the atmospherics surrounding it.[31]

Though advanced in age by the time of Ḥā'il's fall, ʿAjlān and Abū Zwayyid had remained involved in desert politics almost to the very end. Abū Zwayyid's longest poem, a masterpiece of panegyric, ended with a request to Sʿūd ibn ʿAbd al-ʿAzīz, nicknamed Abū Khashm ("Father of the Nose"; that is, "Big Nose"), who had ascended the Rashīdī throne at the age of twelve, to pay off the debts he owed to one of the ruler's slaves.[32] He was prompted to do so when he discerned an opportunity at the Rashīdī capture of rich spoils in the battle of al-Jawf in 1920. He might have already been blind by that time.

Following the example of many Shammar clans, ʿAjlān fled north, beyond the reach of the Ikhwān. There he attached himself to one of the most influential shaykhs, Fahd ibn Hadhdhāl, a leader of astounding political longevity (see §53.1). Addicted to the poet's art of conversation, the shaykh did everything possible to keep ʿAjlān in his company. At that time, Ibn Hadhdhāl and the Jarbā shaykhs of Shammar in Mesopotamia quarreled about their respective rights to levy protection money from the ʿAnazah and Shammar tribes. When matters came to a head, they were called to the Ottoman-Turkish authorities in Baghdad to argue their case. Both parties agreed on ʿAjlān as their arbiter. ʿAjlān had not been informed and, unaware of what was happening, was brought to Baghdad by Ibn Hadhdhāl's son, driving across the Syrian desert in one of the first automobiles to appear there. Initially reluctant to become embroiled in a tribal hornet's nest, ʿAjlān laid down his conditions. The parties accepted and duly signed an Ottoman document to that effect. With that security, ʿAjlān decided the case by reference to an earlier poem on fights for territory between ʿAnazah and Shammar. No one contested the verses' authenticity and ʿAjlān's ruling was adopted without demur. Ibn Hadhdhāl's son had expected otherwise, but the evidence presented by ʿAjlān showed that the claims of his host, Ibn Hadhdhāl himself, were ill-founded.[33]

Having followed his conscience, ʿAjlān decided, notwithstanding the old shaykh's desperate pleas, that it was time to pack up. Home was in or near the Nafūd. In Ḥā'il, he asked the Saudi prince, "Grant me protection against those who pretend to be devout, whereas in fact they are not true men of religion in any sense. And by now the gates of poetry have been slammed shut" (§54.4). Likewise, Ibn Musāʿid informed Abū Zwayyid on his arrival: "Look, Abū Zwayyid, we are in a session devoted to the study of the Prophet's sayings. This nonsense of verses is over" (§1.4).

It is not known if al-Hirbīd was still there to witness the dawn of the new age. If so, he must have kept silent, as did a like-minded ghazal poet, Ibn Sbayyil, though the latter lived into the 1930s.[34] By and large, this style of playful, tongue-in-cheek poetry that is both tender and boisterous—the hallmark of inner Arabia's largely secular culture—went underground. But in private the embers were kept alive until the flames were fanned again and leapt up as things gradually eased some decades later.

Tolerance and Freedom in Rashīdī Ḥā'il

The late-eighteenth- and early-nineteenth-century dynasties of Ibn Rashīd and their predecessors, known as Ibn ʿAlī, had their origins in appointments as governors by the Ibn Saud rulers, known as imams, in the first Wahhabi capital of al-Dirʿiyyah. Following the Wahhabi campaigns and violent excesses in the holy cities of the Hejaz, Mecca and Medina, and the destruction of Shiʿi shrines in Iraq, al-Dirʿiyyah was razed in 1819 by troops at the orders of the Egyptian ruler Muḥammad ʿAlī, thus ending the first Saudi state. Restored in the new capital of Riyadh in 1824, Saudi power was much diminished. Thanks to his closeness to the Saudi imam, Fayṣal, ʿAbdallah ibn Rashīd was appointed the Saudi governor in Ḥā'il in 1835, with a short interruption when the Ibn ʿAlī family was reinstated. With the help of the Ibn Rakhīṣ chief, ʿAbdallah returned as Ḥā'il's ruler, an episode that was spun into a romantic legend, fueled by his own verses. When Abū Zwayyid took the risk of setting the record straight with Muḥammad ibn Rashīd, who had sworn to have him killed—no idle threat from someone who had murdered scores of his relatives on accession to power—he subtly reminded him of this assistance by his Ibn Rakhīṣ relatives. ʿAbdallah ibn Rashīd was particularly gifted in the art of poetry, and was the first of many Ibn Rashīd poets. At the Rashīdī court, poetry was held in as high esteem as skill in warfare and statecraft.

ʿAbdallah's brother ʿUbayd (ʿBēd) sealed the fate of Ibn ʿAlī by force of arms. He achieved recognition for his brother's rule by convincing the Ottoman-Egyptian commander in the Hejaz that Ibn Rashīd would be more useful to him than the ousted governors, in particular by providing baggage camels from Shammar and other tribes in their orbit. ʿAbdallah and ʿUbayd made a compact according to which ʿAbdallah's descendants would succeed him as emir of the fledgling state, while the descendants of ʿUbayd would be the commanders-in-chief of the armed forces.[35] ʿAbdallah and ʿUbayd, though of very different character, were inseparable, and so were Muḥammad ibn Rashīd and ʿUbayd's son Ḥmūd, under whose stewardship the dynasty reached its apogee. ʿUbayd and Ḥmūd were the most prolific poets of the House of Ibn Rashīd, and some of ʿUbayd's verses remain popular today.[36] Their numerous battles were celebrated in their compositions and their panache vaunted. No event of political note passed without being recorded in verse. Tireless in their public relations, they were in regular correspondence with numerous tribal poets and shaykhs. Thus, they acted as the prince's ministers of propaganda and information, of defense, and of home affairs.

In addition, the Ibn Rashīd rulers maintained a legion of poets who followed them on the campaign trail and who were in attendance at the court to brag about their masters' achievements. The three poets in this volume did not belong to this group of eulogists: they were true artists who valued their independence above anything else, though they did freely interact and joust with colleagues in the rulers' retinue.[37] Practically state functionaries, the court poets were no mere hacks; some were even of considerable note. As a result, a significant part of the military and political fortunes of the Rashīdī state was reflected in poetry. And despite the obvious bias, these compositions tell us much about the inner workings of the system and the general outlook at a court that became the measure of things in large swaths of Arabia.

ʿUbayd and his son Ḥmūd were more closely aligned with the dynasty's Wahhabi roots. But even such displays of devoutness were diluted by Ḥāʾil's proximity to the more diverse areas north of the Nafūd and by the town's significance as a station on the east-to-west pilgrim and trade routes. Though austerity was not a façade, neither was it imposed or considered an incontrovertible standard of behavior.[38] Politically, this was useful in relations with Riyadh and in keeping the more fervent believers among the population from becoming too uncomfortable with the regime. ʿAbdallah's successor, Ṭalāl, inherited an established dominion that left him free to concentrate on peaceful pursuits such as the expansion of trade and attending to the general welfare. In connection with the latter, he allowed Shiʿi merchants from Iraq and Persia to set up shop. Though despised even more than Christians by many, they flourished economically and, thanks to the protection they received, were not bothered. General safety was one of the most valued features of Rashīdī rule. The Finnish traveler Georg August Wallin wrote: "There is a common saying among the present inhabitants, that one may go from one end of their land to another, bearing his gold on his head without being troubled with any questions."[39] No wonder Ḥā'il became a magnet for European visitors attracted to Arabia.

European Eyewitness Accounts and the Nafūd Poets

With the xenophobic Wahhabi capital Riyadh mostly out of bounds to travelers, nineteenth-century explorers of Arabia headed in increasing numbers to the Hejaz, and also to Ḥā'il, a capital in the Arabian desert. Most wrote observant, detailed, learned, and highly readable accounts of their impressions, such as Charles M. Doughty's two-volume *Travels in Arabia Deserta*, a source of inspiration for T. E. Lawrence (Lawrence of Arabia) and his *The Seven Pillars of Wisdom*.[40]

Religion as such, other than commonly practiced rituals, hardly features in the lore and poetry of Abū Zwayyid and al-Hirbīd. This undoubtedly reflects the general situation in northern tribal circles. Abū Zwayyid takes an inclusive view of the Lord's compassion (§25.5, v. 2):

> Creator of the Shiʿah, of Unbelievers and Islam,
> all equally desirous of noble conduct's rewards,

and of his fellow tribesmen's international linguistic orientation: "Eloquent in Arabic and proficient in Turkish" (§25.2, v. 21). From travelers' reports we know that these are no vain boasts. Doughty writes that Muḥammad ibn Rashīd knew Turkish, "and he knew [. . .] Persian; Mohammed, formerly conductor of the pilgrimage, can also speak in that language."[41] In 1883, the prince enjoyed a reading from al-Qaṣṭallānī's *Life of Muhammad*, brought by Julius Euting from Cairo, and selections from the pre-Islamic *Muʿallaqāt* poems, "recited in an impermissible singsong manner."[42] In another session, the prince gave Euting a manuscript of the *Muʿallaqāt* and "a beautiful manuscript with poems and commentary of al-Mutanabbī."[43] Clearly, classical secular literary culture and native Nabaṭī tradition were much in vogue at the Rashīdī court. Among the population at large, however, classical poetry was practically unknown and the oral tradition reigned supreme. In this domain, interest in literate circles remained overwhelmingly confined to religious writings.

The parallels between the lore of the three Nafūd poets and the sizable travel literature concerning the Rashīdī court and northern Arabia would need a separate study. Reports from both sides, foreign and indigenous, are hardly ever contradictory, but perspectives and emphases naturally differ depending on the culture of the observers. Sometimes they share an uncanny resemblance, even in minute details. One extraordinary example is the description of Doughty's efforts to bring about a reconciliation between a chief of the Fugarā tribe of ʿAnazah and his young runaway wife, who was the daughter of a shaykh.[44] The manner in which the chief makes his request to Doughty; his speech and the telltale signs of his deep depression; the scene of the young woman with her relatives in a tent, surrounded by a big circle of sympathizing gossips; the artful means of persuasion employed; her eventual quasi-reluctant return; and the elation and gratitude of her husband are a choreographed performance, each step reflected in the stories of Abū Zwayyid's role as marriage counselor to the preeminent Bedouin shaykhs of the Arabian north, Ibn Shaʿlān and Ibn Hadhdhāl. The principal wife of Saṭṭām ibn Shaʿlān, Turkiyyah, daughter of Ibn Mhēd, and her love marriage to Saṭṭām, feature realistically and romantically in Alois Musil's study of the Rwalah tribe, in which he takes Bedouin poetry as his point of departure (see §6.1 and §7.1). While in the service of the Austrian-Hungarian government, Musil made the most of his time as a reconnaissance agent to study the customs and poetry of these Bedouin. An important source for the oral Bedouin poetry noted by Musil, including a charming poem by al-Hirbīd, was Ṭrād, one of the sons of Saṭṭām. His mother belonged to the Sirḥān tribe, and she instructed Ṭrād in committing to memory a vast cache of oral Bedouin poetry. Ṭrād features in the chapter of Abū Zwayyid as one of two sons of Saṭṭām who had mobilized their armed followings to battle it out over the rights of their respective clients, one a camel trader of the ʿUqayl (ʿGēl), a commercial guild mainly based in al-Qasīm, the other a Bedouin of the tribe of the Sharārāt, famous for breeding premium riding camels.[45] When matters threatened to spiral out of control, Abū Zwayyid saved the situation with a solution that set a precedent under tribal law among Shammar.

Gender Relations in the Arabian North

Women are ubiquitous in the lore relating to all three poets. In poetry, they are mostly portrayed in line with (male) convention, in the sense that they are the object of male admiration of their beauty. The poets enumerate their physical features and exult at the stunning sum total of their parts, much as in the traditional camel description. This volume includes some unusual, and occasionally astonishingly candid, scenes of physical and spiritual give-and-take between Bedouin poet and female companion (see, for instance, §18.3). As with other aspects of the orally transmitted texts, it is difficult to determine with any degree of precision where convention ends and lived experience begins.

Convention dates back to the beginnings of Arabic poetry, which even in the early Islamic era is to a considerable degree an extension of poetry originating in the Arabian Peninsula. The closest stylistic parallel to the lore in this volume, the narratives-cum-poetry of *The Book of Songs*, provides many early examples of a pervasive feature in the Abū Zwayyid and al-Hirbīd material: the all-consuming eagerness of Bedouin women to have their praises sung by renowned bards. Poets pursue women and women pursue poets. *The Book of Songs* describes, for example, how Nuṣayb, on a visit to the Holy Mosque in Mecca, overheard a circle of high-born, literarily inclined women reciting verses of their favorite composers of love poetry, himself one of them, and how he was avidly questioned when he revealed his identity.[46] Abū Zwayyid and al-Hirbīd were similarly sought after.

Sometimes women ask for more, as a matter of pride. Laylā, the mother of ʻAbd al-ʻAzīz ibn Marwān, the Umayyad governor of Egypt, stood in the way of Nuṣayb's recompense until he mentioned her by name in his verses.[47] A girl called Mnīrah refused to accept a poem of al-Hirbīd because he only extolled her charms in the final verses and had not devoted the entire poem to her (see §35.1). Renowned poets are charmed and cajoled into singing women's praises, or persuaded to do so by niceties, a means of spreading word of their ravishing looks, thereby attracting suitors. Having requested a drink of water from a servant girl, Nuṣayb is asked to glorify her good looks in verse. He asks her to tell him her name (Hind) and the name of a nearby mountainous outcrop (Qanā), and on the spot rhapsodizes in verse that he would forever love the Qanā outcrop because of a girl named Hind living at its foot. The verses spread like wildfire. The girl's wishes were fulfilled and she was offered a suitable marriage prospect.[48] In the same fashion, a recently divorced woman contrived to have al-Hirbīd all to herself, away from other women, by dolling herself up and expertly packing and loading the dates for which he had come. Like Hind, she was rewarded with charming verses (see §36.1).

Women who interact with the Nafūd poets are mentioned by name, and often with the name of their father, in marked contrast to the anonymous and more stereotyped women one encounters in the verses of ghazal poets in the Najdī oasis towns. Though the latter pretend to be at the mercy of ladies who enjoy nothing more than toying with their delicate souls, they seem mostly oblivious to any kind of real-life personality behind a woman's bewitching shape. Abū Zwayyid, by contrast, engages in lively discussions with female members of households. And he seems mightily pleased when Bedouin women take the initiative and act as if in command of the situation. Al-Hirbīd is shown making detours simply for the pleasure of chatting with a shepherdess who loves conversation and anecdotes.[49] Sowayan explains that "Bedouin ghazal is about real love stories because Bedouin society, unlike the settled communities, does not lock up women and does not regard love as blameworthy," and Musil notes that it was not rare for Bedouin to have love marriages.[50]

In some narrative sections, the teller of the story makes no secret of his distaste for the restrictive norms introduced in the post-Rashīd era and laments the pervasive social distrust regarding gender relations. The text is interspersed with comments such as: "This was in the olden days, before Bedouin girls began to cover up and act bashfully, when they still consorted freely with men and spent time in their company [. . .]. The nice olden ways, free of whispers and base gossip" (§17.5). Or: "Yes, in those days the girls had their role to play" (§33.1). Indeed, the female members of the House of Ibn Rashīd were taught to read and write, and were instructed in the Qur'an.[51] And from 1908 until the collapse of the Rashīdī state, real power in Ḥā'il rested with Fāṭimah, the daughter of Zāmil al-Sibhān, from a family that had intermarried with the Ibn Rashīd rulers.[52]

The Three Poets in Society

While the impression of each poet's station in society and appearance varies depending on the narrator, the details mostly match. The stories about ʿAjlān are limited to his deeds and his tactics. The sources of his income are not mentioned, but as the owner of sizable herds of the famous white camels of the Rmāl tribe, he must have been fairly well-to-do. Al-Hirbīd and Abū Zwayyid, on the other hand, are repeatedly portrayed as hard-pressed to make ends meet, and occasionally as destitute—that is, until their poetic skills result in a sudden windfall. Al-Hirbīd, after the misfortune that befell his family, scrapes together a living by keeping sheep loaned to him by fellow tribesmen, but his distaste for playing nice and cozying up to the rich and powerful worked against him. Somewhat incongruous with these portrayals are stories and poetry of the prominent part played by his productive groves of date palms in the open spaces between the granite rocks of Ajā Mountain.[53]

Abū Zwayyid is the closest to being seen as a poet wedded to his vocation, someone who "made a living from his tongue. He composed poems as he followed the trail of shaykhs who gave him presents" (§10.1). [54] Likewise, al-Hirbīd "entertained people with his stories and accompanied his recitations with tunes from his rebab" (§32.1). ʿAjlān was "a conversationalist in the majlis, someone whom shaykhs liked to have around them, and a poet who also entertained at his own tent" (§50.1). Conversation is key, especially narratives-cum-poetry, the *giṣṣah w-giṣīdah* genre in Najd.[55]

Occasionally, Abū Zwayyid is shown supplementing his income by taking part in the Bedouin for-profit sport of raiding other tribes for their camels. The expression for going on a raid used in these texts is "to try one's luck in stocking up with God-given booty" (*ytarazzag allāh*, CA *rizq*: "subsistence granted by God"). Interestingly, the poet participates both in private expeditions of plunder and in the "official" large-scale robbing tours yearly launched by Muḥammad ibn Rashīd.[56] By joining the latter, the poet took part in a state-sponsored activity that contributed significantly to the budget and thus kept the wheels of finance and the local economy turning. A unique example of a state based mainly on one Bedouin tribe, Shammar, the Ibn Rashīd principality maintained its position and popularity through daily lavish hospitality to all comers.[57] Every day, hundreds were fed a substantial meal in the courtyard of the Barzān palace.[58] Some loot from successful raids, such as thoroughbred horses from the House's fabled stables, was given to visitors of importance, tribal shaykhs and headmen of towns, and sent to solidify friendship with the Saudi princes in Riyadh, the Great Sharif in Mecca, the Ottoman-Turkish sultan and the Ottoman representatives in the Hejaz, and other neighboring powers.

Income was principally generated from zakat levied on the subjects of Ibn Rashīd, from trade and transport, and from the pilgrim caravans from Iraq that passed through Rashīdī territory to the Hejaz and back. Tribes around the periphery of the Shammar territory were liable to attack and despoilment of their herds if they refused to pay taxes similar to those levied in the core area of Jabal Shammar. The tribes roaming the desert areas from northern Syria and Iraq to Najrān in the south, bordering Yemen, remained by and large outside the writ of town-based political centers. By that excuse, they were considered legitimate targets for plunder, the more so because the attackers did not have to fear reprisals. During the nineteenth century, the scope for this Rashīdī practice was considerably expanded thanks to the destructive infighting within the House of Saud and to the sharp erosion of its reach, even in its native Najd. Muḥammad ibn Rashīd is said to have led more than forty raiding expeditions against the confederation of ʿUtaybah tribes alone.[59] The Shammar Bedouin were not able to hide their wealth from the Rashīdī tax collectors. One ruse employed to mislead the tax collectors through the intervention of al-Hirbīd on behalf of his fellow tribesmen is included in this volume (see §44.2).

In addition to his frequently straitened circumstances, Abū Zwayyid labored under the disadvantage of his unappealing appearance. Hyperbole used in description of his face became proverbial. He was walleyed and his eyes were said to be bulbous and positioned toward the side of his face, like the eyes of a locust (see §10.3 and §18.5). His self-descriptions include "the wolf-faced bane of his pursuers, a mangy camel in a pen made of thorny bushes where those infected with smallpox are quarantined" (§17.2).[60] However, the combination of hideous looks, artistic renown, unshakable composure, pluck, and savviness proved irresistible to the ladies of Shammar and beyond. He was tracked down by his future wife, who had sworn to kiss him if she found him after hearing his poem about a beautiful woman. What she saw, as she came splashing toward him through the shallow water of a desert pond of rainwater, was "the snout of a hyena and watery eyes that made for poor vision. He stood there squinting and straining his eyes to have a good look at the girl as she hurried toward him, with her skirt lifted from the surface of the water and her shiny legs like lamps illuminated from below" (§18.3).

Al-Hirbīd's deadly invective poetry described the repulsive appearance of rival poets (§48.5, v. 2 and §48.9, vv. 19–20). In his comments, the transmitter adds that one of these opponents "had suffered the loss of his eyelashes" and another "had rheumy eyes, messy with white discharge," and "was capable of wolfing down two trays of food and still have appetite for more" (§48.7).

Judging the Poetry

If much poetry was composed with a specific purpose and subject in mind, such practicality was not judged off-putting by the audience. On the contrary, one transmitter of this oral poetry lauds Abū Zwayyid's poetry precisely because "every verse is spot on: it hits the target and pierces through its target." Contrasting it with much modern Arabic poetry, he opines that his "poems are about matters that are very recognizable. Every single word is to the point and deals with a real subject" (§5.1).

Hitting the mark was what early classical poets like al-Farazdaq strove to achieve in fashioning their verses. The Bedouin poet thinks like Ibn Mayyādah, who, when criticized for some metrical flaws, said, "Listen, Ibn Jundab, poetry is like an arrow in your quiver, made to hit the target, rising and falling, straying and on target."[61] It is assumed that in pre-Islamic times, some poets specialized in invective poetry and that their audience regarded this as an effective instrument in real-world contests. These poets had powers associated with sorcerers.[62] In al-Hirbīd's poetry, however, one detects signs that the original animist belief in poetry's power as a curse may have retained a measure of credibility. In one instance, the poet, aggravated by the departure of his beloved, considers that he does not want to hurt her father, who is a decent man, and instead might cripple her camel, forcing her return. In another instance, following an exchange of invective, his competitor's palm grove, near to his own, inexplicably burns down. By the late nineteenth century, poetic conventions and practices dating back to pre-Islamic times, even if not used in all seriousness, were recognized by the audience for what they were.

Style, Imagery, Technique

The poets' individual characters as portrayed in the narratives also come through in their poetry. Often, certain details in lines of verse have been woven into the narrative thread simply as a matter of fact, sometimes with the purpose of elucidating an allusion or an elliptical remark. But stories and poems are not always evenly matched. On the way back from a failed raid, Abū Zwayyid and other camel riders indulge in pranks and race their mounts at a gallop. Counter to expectation, his poem about their lighthearted capers starts out in a grave and somber tone, bemoaning that the "era has saddled us with woeful leaders" (§13.2, v. 8) and that all traditional values and virtues have been upended. The opening verses reflect the poet's distress at the anarchy and rot that rapidly eroded the Rashīdī edifice of government when Muḥammad ibn Rashīd passed away. Nine verses later, without transition, the poet celebrates the wild ride on "the mount of [his] dreams" (§13.2, v. 10) and the lightning-fast successful capture of booty.[63]

The great majority of Abū Zwayyid's poems open with a messenger dispatched on a spirited, at times impetuous she-camel. This trademark red-hued beast, kept in check by a skilled and daring rider, might be taken as a metaphor for the poet's pugnacious and fiery temper. Up to the end of his life, Abū Zwayyid appears as an enterprising, cheeky Bedouin hero. Even old, blind, and frail, when he is led to the vaguely menacing presence of the new ruler, a prince of the House of Saud, he gently and half teasingly succeeds in drawing him out. He may well have been the only poet to leave the new court and its grim circle of turbaned Ikhwān with the gift of a camel for use as a draft animal.[64] Here, style and content match to perfection.

Almost none of the poems by al-Hirbīd feature a camel prelude. The wistful, slightly elegiac tone of his chapter's first poems, lamenting the loss of his brothers and their families at the hands of Ibn Shaʿlān Bedouin raiders, draws on the imagery of the early classical poet's laments at an abandoned campsite. Al-Hirbīd's poetry hits the mark too, but in a subtler manner, by exploring the twisted pathways and unexpected detours of sentiment and wandering thoughts. Tribal pride is celebrated, but the dominant impression is one of personal feeling, from joyful passion to raging anger and sad resignation.

Devoted to his sheep, which are half-mockingly contrasted with camel herding, and to his palm groves, al-Hirbīd comes across as tribal but only partially Bedouin, even as he treks and consorts with the camel nomads. Abū Zwayyid, for instance, hardly mentions date palms in his poetry, whereas al-Hirbīd weaves the details of the tree's efflorescence intricately into his ghazal (see §34.2, vv. 12–14).[65] If he speaks about Bedouin life, he often does so in a mode of self-deprecation, comparable to Ibn Sbayyil lowering himself to the position of a villager as he looks up to the towering Bedouin. Ibn Sbayyil's "I am just a villager—they, redoubtable Bedouin"[66] is mirrored in al-Hirbīd's "Breathless, we pant after camels and horsemen / who raid for sport . . ." (§32.10, v. 5). And yet, even he cannot escape camel imagery for the similes and metaphors of his ghazal. The lore of the Nafūd poets aptly underscores Doughty's observation that "camels, the only substance of the nomads, are the occasion of all their contending."[67] From the beginning, the camel was a metaphor used to describe certain aspects of poetry itself. The seventh-century Dhū l-Rummah, for instance, tells one of his poem's addressees that he will soon receive rhymes like a beautifully adorned, broken-in camel, to be followed by likewise tamed and well-trained poetry.[68] In Bedouin poetry, the metaphor is taken further: the camel stands for the poem itself, as in the standard expression "I mounted and dispatched a poem" (*arkabt lī giṣīdah*). The next step in the development of the metaphor is to do away entirely with the object of comparison and speak of a camel in lieu of a poem.[69] On his marriage-saving excursion to the estranged wife of Ibn Hadhdhāl, al-Hirbīd tells her about the fast camel he has readied for her. "Let me hear it," she says, and in the poem she is likened to a nicely caparisoned white she-camel. Among the presents she gives him as a reward for his camel/poem are a real camel loaded with goods and an even more valuable mare (§7).

The most egregious and comical example of full identification of poem and camel occurs in a conversation between Abū Zwayyid, who is accompanied by a Rwēlī companion,[70] and Muḥammad ibn Rashīd during a raiding expedition. Abū Zwayyid lodges a complaint with the prince about his Rwēlī friend, accusing him of acting like a stupid, undiscriminating young male camel trying to cover a pregnant female; that is, of plagiarizing one of his poems. He goes on to say that he found one of his camels with his Rwēlī mate, while all of his camels (that is, poems) are truly his own. The prince, himself a poet steeped in desert lore, at once deciphers the code language: the verses have been composed by Abū Zwayyid but he did his Rwēlī friend a favor by allowing him to claim the lines as his own. "Let's have it, then!" he says with a straight face (§15.1). The Rwēlī recites it and the prince asks if it is a stand-alone composition or has any "sisters"—a group of pedigree riding camels of the same color and strain are called "sisters." On being informed that these lines are all there is, the prince orders his servants to let the Rwēlī pick one of the camels. To the astonishment of the attendants, the ugliest beast in the herd is chosen: walleyed like the poet, a long navel cord dangling from its belly, chewing on a bone.[71] Like the ugly poet, it is an example of a recurring motif in oral lore: smart heroes who deceive but are not deceived by appearances. The Rwēlī, a crack cameleer, knows what he is doing. With his training, the beast metamorphoses into a champion long-distance desert cruiser.[72] He thanks Abū Zwayyid for helping him with the ruse in verses that this time might be his own.

The text presumes an audience steeped in this oral poetry's conventions. Just as the audience knows that a "camel" may stand for a poem, mention of certain objects evokes associations of the thing to which it refers, and that need not be explicitly identified. From the context, it should be obvious that the sparkle of a sword's blade is the finely chiseled straight nose of the woman haunting the poet (§17.5, v. 6). The nose does not need to be mentioned; its omission introduces an element of speed, excitement, and enjoyment at being able to decipher these small riddles delivered staccato-like, in rapid succession. Virtually all the features of this oral poetry are designed to enhance the addictive pleasures of conversation and verbal entertainment in the majlis.

Abū Zwayyid's camel-shaped, marriage-saving poem (§7) that persuaded Nūrah to give Shaykh Ibn Hadhdhāl another chance is a masterpiece of deft turns and twists. Scenes switch in rapid succession to create an exhilarating impression of speed and daring. The camel itself, "towering on giraffe-like legs," is "God's favored racer." Its pace seamlessly transitions to the exploits of Nūrah's father. Some men of the "shaykh's raiding group" are welcomed at home by an unattractive mate who "yells and shouts with abandon," and the more fortunate, people like the shaykh, are welcomed by sweet smiles. The daughter of this "shaykh of shaykhs," the most alluring of camels, "Insouciant, she strides in scented fur dyed yellow." With a final flourish, Nūrah is crowned as the equal of Ibn Sha'lān:

> Never did I see Nūrah's like among kin or friends,
> or ever hear of her equal from anyone.[73]

In a further example, warned in a dream by the daughter of the chief of the Rmāl, al-Hijhūj, he extols her father, sends his verse with "a skittish camel that hates getting hit," praises him, and then seemingly deviates into scenes of camel robbery and hot pursuit. Next comes an imagined dialogue of a young man who announces his intention to raid, expecting his tribal elders to caution him against it. However, he is encouraged to prove his mettle—a backhanded way of paying a compliment to his sweetheart's father, al-Hijhūj.[74] Surprisingly, the poem ends with a diatribe against a pastoralist who is ridiculed for "fattening his sheep and churning butter," an inveterate miser, the opposite of camel nomads born to be noble and generous (§17.6).[75] Stripped of its plumage, the piece's aim is simply to praise al-Hijhūj as a champion among his tribal competitors: chief of tribesmen who habitually and without a care send their sons on the warpath. Valuing prestige above all else, they pour scorn on a life of profit-making for its own sake. For the poet, achieving similar success for himself not only depends on the praised shaykh's real-life status, but also on artful delivery. He endeavors to stand out from the crowd of poets and dazzle the audience with amazing swerves and dashes—a technique at which Abū Zwayyid excels. Similarly, al-Hirbīd's ghazal depicts a buxom girl who helps a cousin and promised future husband to hoist water from a well. Rope in hand, she is distracted by the appearance of the poet, and the future husband punishes her with a hard pull on the rope that makes her fall to the ground. Al-Hirbīd's poem curses the jealous fiancé, then without further explanation transforms the girl into a tender young she-camel forced to join a raiding expedition and keep pace with "pitiless, hard-bitten mounts / ridden by boisterous, hookah-smoking toughs" (§39.3).

For the uninitiated, such abrupt transitions might be disorienting. The technique's building blocks are miniature set pieces, borrowed from convention and molded into the poet's personal style to be turned into short and dense vignettes. Related to similes and extended similes, these are not merely figures of speech: pried loose from the poem's frame, they can run to several verses and can be quasi-independent units. Delivered in a spirited performance, the recitation assumes the presence of an audience so steeped in the lore that they can effortlessly grasp the meaning and scope. Preservation in oral transmission is testimony to the collective experience and intimate knowledge of the environment that underlies this kind of highly stylized speech. In this way, all observers, indigenous and foreign, reckon poetry itself to be an inextricable part of Arabian desert life. This poetry summarizes and puts a slant on events and thought in this arid land, at once fertilized and brought forth by it, and at times exercising considerable influence on developments in its habitat.

This may explain one of the most remarkable features of the poetry: the systematic reduction of matters to values and imagery characterized by stark, binary opposition. A warrior comes home to "a wife like a hissing snake" (§7.2, v. 9) and another to the "sweet smiles of a dazzling beauty" (§7.2, v. 13); some camels "stagger across wastes like invalids" (§7.2, v. 4); for others, "uphill stretches serve to make her run faster still" (§7.2, v. 7); and so on (see also §18.8, v. 1 and §19.5, v. 2). Routine use of hyperbole in Bedouin and early classical poetry are part of the poet's aspiration to sharpen such oppositions to the utmost. But if poet and transmitter stretch credulity, they do so in accordance with the taste of an audience rooting for the poem's subject to overcome all odds and countervailing forces. Ultimately, the tendency toward binary opposition can be traced to the poetry's harsh natural setting. In a vast wilderness crisscrossed by a patchwork of tribal hostility, one might be faced at any moment with life-or-death situations, severe droughts, and other blows of Fate; or be given sudden relief by rain or good fortune. Like the desert itself, such an environment is inhospitable to softer tones and nuanced speculation. Either/or situations and the lack of forewarning require quick decisions, carried out with unwavering determination. Born in the desert, the three poets are among the last representatives of nineteenth- and early-twentieth-century Bedouin life. Having inherited verbal art and imagery from the earliest classical poetry of Arabia, their spirited performances illuminate the circumstances in which the tradition is rooted in pre-Islamic times, and indeed, their poetry and technique are best understood against that historical background.

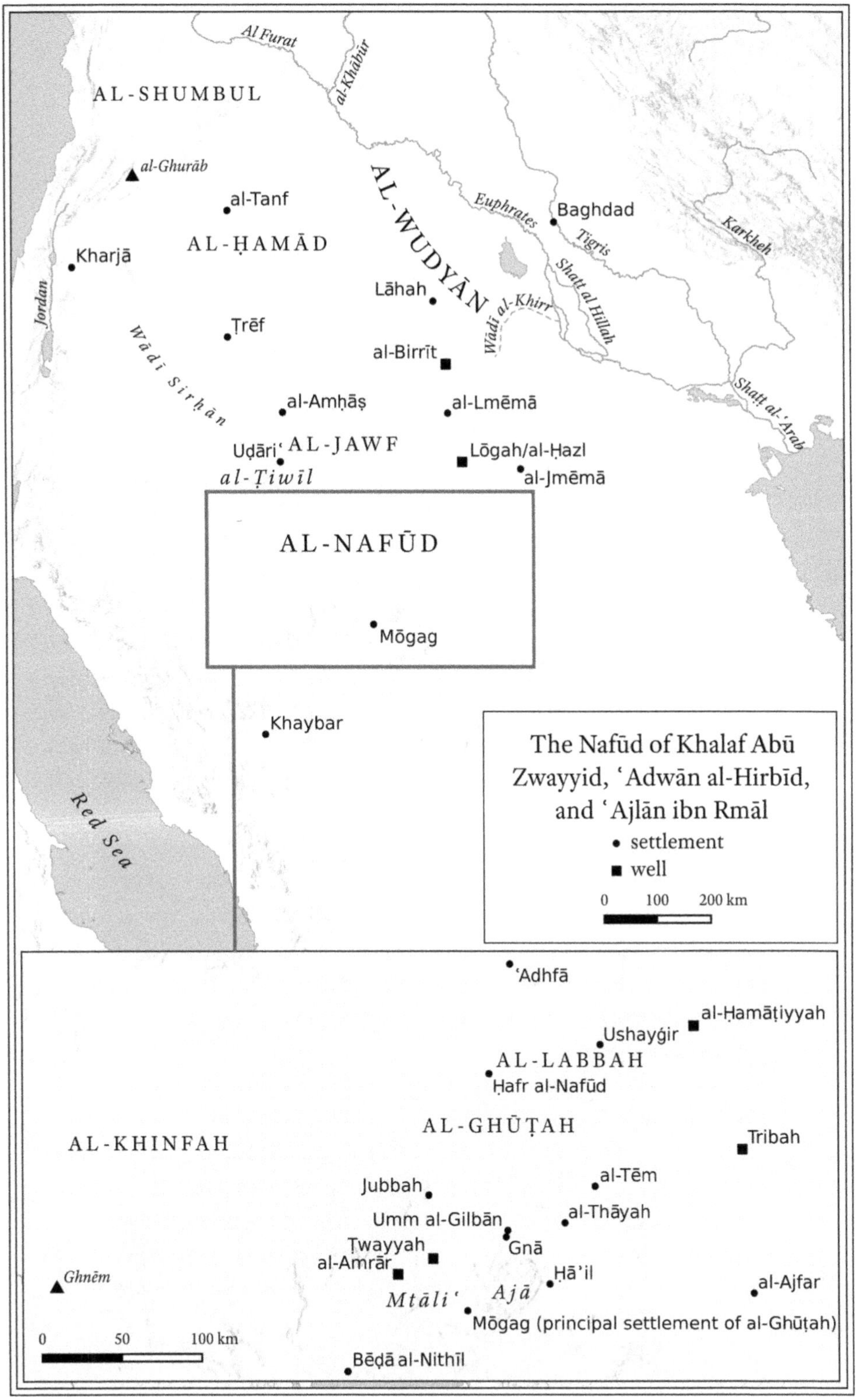
Al Furat
al-Khābūr
AL-SHUMBUL
al-Ghurāb
al-Tanf
AL-WUDYĀN
Euphrates
Baghdad
Tigris
Karkheh
AL-ḤAMĀD
Kharjā
Jordan
Lāhah
Shaṭṭ al Hillah
Wādī al-Khirr
Ṭrēf
Wādi Sirḥān
al-Birrīt
Shaṭṭ al-ʻArab
al-Amḥāṣ
al-Lmēmā
Uḍāriʻ
AL-JAWF
Lōgah/al-Ḥazl
al-Jmēmā
al-Ṭiwīl
AL-NAFŪD
Mōgag
Khaybar
The Nafūd of Khalaf Abū Zwayyid, ʻAdwān al-Hirbīd, and ʻAjlān ibn Rmāl
settlement
well
0 100 200 km
Red Sea
ʻAdhfā
al-Ḥamāṭiyyah
Ushayġir
AL-LABBAH
Ḥafr al-Nafūd
AL-GHŪṬAH
AL-KHINFAH
Tribah
al-Tēm
Jubbah
Umm al-Gilbān
al-Thāyah
Ṭwayyah
Gnā
al-Amrār
Ḥā'il
Ghnēm
al-Ajfar
Mtāliʻ
Ajā
Mōgag (principal settlement of al-Ghūṭah)
0 50 100 km
Bēḍā al-Nithīl

Note on the Text

The Edition

The text has many contributors. Only a few poems by Abū Zwayyid have been preserved in manuscript, and then probably only because he belonged to a lineage that played a political role in the Rashīdī state, personally interacted with Muḥammad ibn Rashīd, and prompted other poets to respond to his daring forays into the realm of tribal power and influence. The ones preserved in manuscript are noteworthy for their wisdom verses, a popular genre with literate settlers. Except for these poems, the oeuvre of the three Nafūd poets has been passed down solely in oral tradition, recorded at a time when oil wealth had started to transform life and the economy in ways that would have been unimaginable to these poets and their society. By then, the transmitters and storytellers who had kept the tradition alive, many of whom had been personally familiar and in touch with others who witnessed the events of the period, were of an advanced age. They had retained stories and verses replete with celebrations of practices, amusement, and expression that had gone quiet once the third Saudi state established the strict imposition of the Wahhabi doctrines. After the fall of Ḥā'il to the Saudi Ikhwān, opprobrium was heaped on this "heathenish" past of the Rashīdī era, and by implication the thousand years or more before, during which the tradition had been kept alive. Intimidated by the Ikhwān, many burned their manuscripts containing the poetic heritage of their families, tribes, and others with whom they came into contact. Even under these new circumstances, the lore must have circulated in oral performance, albeit at more or less private social occasions.

The restrictive severity of the Ikhwān had relaxed to a considerable extent by the time of recording. The influx of petrodollars in the 1970s transformed the country's infrastructure, way of life, and commerce. By comparison, the "primitive" oral past seemed a trifling concern. But, despite the feverish modernization, old taboos had not ceased to exist. The state, the religious establishment, and much of society continued to regard this oral heritage as unworthy of official recognition. Partly, this stemmed from a fear of resuscitating the old ghosts of divisive tribalism that had been kept at bay or dormant, which was key to maintaining national unity in a large and diverse country that had never been unified in this manner before.

The "lawless" Bedouin tribes were targeted for subjection by the first Saudi state, based on the eighteenth-century compact between the House of Saud and the Islamic reformer Muḥammad ibn ʿAbd al-Wahhāb, the father of "Wahhabism." Early in the nineteenth century, the second Saudi state weakened, and as a result efforts to bring the Bedouin to heel suffered a setback that lasted for more than a century. The former Saudi stronghold of Arabia's central provinces, the region of Najd, fell under the sway of the unashamedly tribal rule of Ibn Rashīd, based on the confederation of Shammar. Initially, its influence was limited to a part of northern Arabia known as Jabal Shammar (Shammar Mountain). The first Rashīdī prince, ʿAbdallah, had befriended the Saudi imam Faysal and been appointed by him governor in Ḥā'il. Though Najd was nominally a vassal province committed to Wahhabism, the ebbing of Saudi influence was reason for Ibn Rashīd to recalibrate his loyalties to include the Ottoman empire to the north and its Egyptian proconsuls in the Hejaz, home to the holy cities of Mecca and Medina. In and around Ḥā'il, Wahhabi doctrine was honored often in the breach, and to a large extent became a façade of dwindling importance. Religion as a subject in its own right is apparently not considered sufficiently interesting to be given much attention in the traditions collected here. The three poets flourished during the rule of Muḥammad ibn Rashīd, the heyday of the Rashīdī emirate, when practically all of Najd, inner Arabia, and many areas beyond looked to Ḥā'il as the center of power. The leaders of the House of Saud had fled to Kuwait, and Bedouin spirit and culture, anathema to the Wahhabi clergy and their supporters, were given free rein.

While at the time of recording the old mindset was still at work—in some respects more fired up than ever thanks to financial empowerment and marks of respect from the state—the country's modernists likewise took umbrage at an oral past they would rather not be reminded of. They looked upon the Bedouin tradition with bemusement at its almost comical "primitiveness" and with exasperation at the unreconstructed attitudes that were obstacles to even more rapid transformation. Nevertheless, the tradition was resilient enough to make something of a comeback through radio programs such as *Story and Verses* (*Qiṣṣah wa-Abyāt*); magazines and books devoted to popular culture, albeit stripped of its more controversial aspects; and a general resurgence of Nabaṭī poetry, also for semiofficial purposes.

For these reasons, the recording project was timely and benefited from space created by the Saudi state's need to balance the various social forces at play. Still, it coincided with an uptick in tribal sentiment, inflamed by old and new poetry. This showed itself in sometimes angry responses to content of scholarly publications such as the source of the present edition, even though these were meant to stay above the fray. One reason was the conviction that whatever appeared in print in the kingdom had the stamp of official approval, meaning that it was "true." At the same time, passages such as the poetry and narratives of ʿAjlān in this volume could never have been published by the government-controlled press and publishing houses. These thorny issues explain the ambiguous status of an oral heritage that abounds in sensitive material and gives a more unvarnished picture of history than the official narrative. As Saad Sowayan notes, the oral traditions are riddled with explosive material.[76]

This volume's edition is based on the Arabic transcription and edition of the audio recordings in Sowayan's monumental *The Days of the Latter Arabs* (*Ayyām al-ʿarab al-awākhir*). Running to 1,143 densely printed pages, it is the edited repository of the largest collection of oral tradition and literature from northern Arabia in existence. In it, chapters are devoted to each of the three poets included here. These poets were chosen, in consultation with Sowayan, for their literary qualities, reputations that have stood the test of time, and inherent interest.

In his Introduction, Sowayan explains his method and the nature of the recorded materials:

> Recording started in 1982 and continued over a number of years. A vast amount of material, hundreds of hours of recordings on cassette tapes, was digitized for computer use in preparation of the production of thousands of pages: the written version of the text as spoken in the original vernacular of the transmitters. Most of the oral material stems from northern Arabia, in particular the tribe of Shammar, and the tribes of ʿAnazah, Banū Rashīd, al-Ṭarfā, and al-Bannāq; and transmitters from al-Jawf, Baqʿā, and villages in the general area of Jabal Shammar and al-Jawf.[77]

By the time of the work's publication in 2010, almost all the transmitters from whom the material was recorded had passed away. Subsequently, linguistic changes and the transformation of the desert and cultural environment made many elements of the spoken text less readily understood by the younger Saudi readership. Thus, preservation was an objective in its own right.

In *The Days of the Latter Arabs*, the chapters devoted to the three poets comprise 7 percent of the work. Abū Zwayyid's section runs to thirty-three pages based on recordings from twenty-two transmitters, together with seven more pages under various headings. Al-Hirbīd's runs to twenty-nine pages from thirteen transmitters, and ʿAjlān's to nine pages from six transmitters. Each transmitter tells the story in his own way. As Sowayan explains, he constructed a text as complete, detailed, and well-told as possible, drawing on versions to fill gaps and clear up obscurities in other versions.

> As a general rule, I have not introduced any element of my own making, but only used the words spoken by the transmitters. One might say that I have made myself the "super-transmitter," which is a legitimate procedure because each and every transmitter goes about it in this manner. After all, the only way to learn the stories and poetry, and commit them to memory, is by hearing them a number of times from several transmitters and different sources before embarking on the construction of one's own particular version based on these elements.

In the decades before the appearance of *The Days of the Latter Arabs*, other authors and collectors published many of these poems, sometimes accompanied by a bowdlerized version of a background story, invariably rendered in Modern Standard Arabic and stripped of its most expressive and colorful elements. In the editions of ʿAbd al-Raḥmān al-Suwaydāʾ, whom I met during my research visits to the area in May and July of 1988, I first noted the outstanding qualities of these poets. Transmitters from whom I recorded are also among those listed in *The Days of the Latter Arabs*. These recordings included famous pieces such as al-Hirbīd's al-Shēkhah poem and Abū Zwayyid's ode in praise of Ibn Shaʿlān. Thirty years later, while in the Nafūd area for research and a documentary on oral poetry for the Al Arabiya TV channel, including Abū Zwayyid and Ḥmedān al-Shwēʿir, some of my informants were the sons of my hosts during the earlier visit. Foremost among them was Ibrāhīm al-Hamazānī, the son of the poet Sʿayyid al-Hamazanī. His generous assistance was crucial in clarifying countless obscure or not fully understood parts of the text. My impression from yearly research visits to the area between 2015 and 2019 was that interest in this heritage was still strong. However, detailed knowledge of the technical vocabulary has become limited to an ever-dwindling circle of aficionados. None of the earlier material and publications came close to matching the edition of *The Days of the Latter Arabs.*

Sowayan's volume is dedicated to the memory of the early Arabic philologist Abū 'Ubaydah, who likewise traveled to Bedouin tribes in the desert in search of material close in nature and style to that collected by Sowayan. *The Days of the Latter Arabs* remains the standard for this lore, and this edition and translation are solely based on it. The original edition is mostly pure text, without explanatory notes, except for the glosses put by the transmitters themselves during recording, and critical apparatus. Sowayan refers readers to his earlier publications, which may assist in better understanding the text of *The Days of the Latter Arabs.* For Arabists and general readership alike, *The Arabian Oral Historical Narrative: An Ethnographic and Linguistic Analysis* (1992) is key. Its Arabic text, fully vocalized and included in *The Days of the Latter Arabs*, has been translated and annotated; an extensive Introduction and Glossary assist in interpreting the Arabic and English text. This work and Sowayan's *Nabaṭi Poetry: The Oral Poetry of Arabia* (1985) offer everything an Arabist and nonspecialist might wish to know about the subject, and in addition make for delightful reading. A more demanding study, the Arabic *Nabaṭī Poetry: Popular Taste and the Authority of the Text* (*Al-Shiʿr al-Nabaṭī, dhāʾiqat al-shaʿb wa-sulṭat al-naṣṣ*, 2000), covers and analyzes Nabaṭī poetry's history, linguistics and prosody, manuscripts, and other aspects in great detail. A comprehensive catalog of poets and poems is Sowayan's *Catalog of Nabaṭī Poetry* (*Fihrist al-shiʿr al-nabaṭī*, 2001). Finally, a cultural, social, and anthropological overview of the material in this book, and the Najdī tradition in general, is found in *The Arabian Desert: Its Culture and Poetry over the Centuries; An Anthropological Reading* (*Al-Ṣaḥrāʾ al-ʿarabiyyah: Thaqāfatuhā wa-shiʿruhā ʿabra al-ʿuṣūr, qirāʾah anthrūbūlūjiyyah*, 2010).

In the Introduction to *The Days of the Latter Arabs*, Sowayan refers the reader specifically to his *The Arabian Desert* as a compendium with the requisite background to *Ayyām al-ʿarab*. I had the opportunity to meet with Dr. Sowayan a number of times and we remained in touch, often almost daily, by WhatsApp to discuss this edition's text. However, the final responsibility for the text, including its shortcomings, rests solely with me. Explanatory communications of informants are preceded by "explained," and in Sowayan's case either with his name added, or between quotation marks without reference.

At the level of language, features discussed in *The Arabian Oral Historical Narrative*'s chapters "The Oral Narrative Style and Technique" and "Syntax of the Oral Narrative" are illustrated in the Introduction to *The Days of the Latter Arabs*, with examples drawn from its Arabic text. Both works stem from the same cultural and linguistic environment, and these chapters of the earlier work fully apply to this edition's text as well. The examples illustrate well-known characteristics of the oral narrative style and linguistics, such as repetition and other redundancies; the enlivening of the storytelling by use of narrative imperative; gestures and other body language accompanied by matching words; direct address to the audience meant to better involve it in the imagined action of the story, and direct address to the narrative's subject as if the person were present; devices for disambiguation, making sure the audience does not lose the plot and understands whom the narrator is talking about; the use of what Sowayan has termed the *-k* of courtesy, the second-person pronoun suffix, used as if the narrator addresses one listener in particular, but in fact a narrative routine even in large gatherings; and the use of the pseudo-dative when the preposition *l-* is followed by a pronominal suffix that might be doubled (for example, *luh luh* or *buh luh*).

One of the pitfalls in approaching these texts is to proceed on the assumption that the Arabic can be read in the same way as classical Arabic. Knowledge of classical Arabic, especially early poetry from the Arabian desert, is a great advantage in trying to understand it. In addition to lending depth to the reading, it offers a bridge to the later poetic idiom. Arabists wishing to take a closer look at the Arabic text might familiarize themselves with features of most frequent occurrence. For instance, *ilā*, also *lā*, *lyā*, and *yā*, is used as a particle with a subordinate function equivalent to CA *idhā*, "when, if"; and *yōm* not only as CA *yawm*, "day," but frequently as a conjunction introducing a subordinate clause, "when." Noteworthy is the ubiquitous occurrence of the internal passive, resembling CA usage, in the verbal forms.

In the Introduction to *The Days of the Latter Arabs*, Sowayan briefly lists linguistic aspects peculiar to the northern dialect of the Shammar tribe and explains how these and other more general vernacular characteristics of the text are reflected in his Arabic notation. For instance, the equivalent of the classical diphthong *-aw* is pronounced as *-ō*, and the presence of this diphthong is highlighted in the notation by a vowel *fatḥah* over the preceding consonant. The letter *yā'* is written as *alif maqṣūrah* if it is pronounced that way. For example, *wālī al-aqdār* ("the Lord of Destiny") is pronounced *wāl al-agdār*, written والى الاقدار, but the *qāf*, though not pronounced as in CA, is still written with the classical *qāf*. In the Arabic text, the word for "son of," *ibn*, is pronounced and written as such, where in standard Arabic it is written as بن. Except for text included from Sowayan's *The Arabian Oral Historical Narrative*, the Arabic text of *The Days of the Latter Arabs* has been voweled sparingly and selectively. In the present edition, I have added a modest number of short vowel signs, *sukūn*, *tashdīd*, and *tanwīn*, mostly in the poetry, to assist reading. Some of the vocabulary has been explained with the help of an unpublished dictionary of Bedouin language by the Swiss scholar J. J. Hess in the Archive of the Orient Institute of the University of Zurich, with the reference "HA" (for "Hess Archive"). For further information on the linguistic and prosodic aspects of the text, readers are referred to the works of Sowayan.

Note on the Translation

None of this volume's poems and stories have appeared in English translation, with the exception of one poem by al-Hirbīd (§35.3) in Musil, *The Manners and Customs of the Rwala Bedouins*, 321–23.

Not all courtesy expressions used by the transmitters in addressing the audience are included in the translation. Sometimes the transmitter or narrator departs from the narrative thread and directly addresses his audience or interpolates observations of his own. These moments should be easily recognizable in the translation and serve as a reminder of the text's origin in oral performance.

Because the oeuvre of the three poets is in the idiom of Najdī vernacular poetry, called Nabaṭī poetry, their names and those of others are transliterated in a way that more closely reflects the pronunciation of this predominantly oral poetry (recited on social occasions), and accepted among specialists. Names like ʿAbdallah (ʿAbd Allāh) and Ḍēfallah (Ḍayf Allāh) are written as they are spoken and in accordance with meter. Najdī Nabaṭī poetry has its own idiom, much of it borrowed from conventions that date back to the pre-Islamic beginnings of Arabic poetry.

The classical spelling of a name is used where this is more convenient or recognizable for readers. In this Introduction and elsewhere, some personal names, names of towns, and other geographical features mentioned in the poetry are transliterated according to the standard classical Arabic spelling or according to common spelling in English. For instance, Wahhabi, not Wahhābī, and Saud, as in the House of Saud. If names are commonly spelled in a certain way in English—for example, Ibn Rashīd, Ibn Rakhīṣ, Turkī, and Turkiyyah—that spelling is followed, rather than the vernacular Ibn Rishīd, Ibn Rikhīṣ, Tirkī, and Tirkiyyah. This applies to tribal names, which are also often spelled in a great variety of ways: ʿUtaybah, ʿAnazah, and Muṭayr, and not, as in the vernacular, ʿTēbah, ʿNizah, and Mṭēr. Occasionally, as appropriate, names and words that occur in the vernacular text may be given in the Introduction and the endnotes (for example, if they occur in book titles or as official family names) according to the classical Arabic transliteration. For instance, the name Ibn Musāʿid, which is Ibn Msāʿid according to the vernacular, is written throughout in accordance with the classical spelling. In transliteration of vernacular text and notes to the text, the assimilation of the sun letters in pronunciation is shown.

In the Arabic text, names of sections of tribes—for instance, "al-Hirbīd's clan"—are referred to with the English definite article in lieu of the Arabic article "al-": "the Swēd" rather than "al-Swēd." Tribal names such as Shammar are not used with the Arabic definite article, and thus do not appear with "the" in English. "Shammar" is also used as a collective for the entire tribal confederation or a group of tribespeople. Furthermore, it occurs as an adjective, such as Shammar division, Shammar troops; the word "Shammarī" refers to an individual from the tribe. In "Shammar made a run for it," the reference is not to the entire tribe, but to a group or small number of individuals of the tribe. In case of the indefinite "Shammar," the translation may add "tribespeople" or similar so as not to make it appear as the name of an individual.

Riding camels, frequently described in a poem's opening verses as part of the messenger motif, are always female, and a single riding camel will be referred to as "she;" the same applies to date palms. Likewise, in the Arabic text, f. pl. verb endings and the f. pl. suffix pronoun often refer to she-camels or date palms. In this edition and in the original text, words ending in classical Arabic with *tāʾ marbūṭah* are written with *-h* (ـه); they are only written with *tāʾ marbūṭah* (ـة) if the word is in construct with the following word or should be read with *tanwīn*, which may not be written but can be deduced. In the dialect of Shammar, the f. sg. suffix pronoun is *-ah*, not *-hā*, and indicated by a *fatḥah* over the preceding consonant; the m. sg. suffix pronoun is *-uh*.

The transliteration in these parts of the volume will hew closer to the classical Arabic practice in other respects and details: the *nisbah* of Shammar will be written as Shammarī, with a macron on the final vowel, and not as Shammari, as is common in the transliteration of the vernacular where all final vowels are long by definition, thus obviating the need for a macron. In the notes, transliterated verses in the Najdī vernacular show the affricated *g* (CA *qāf*) and *k* as, respectively, *ǵ* and *ć*. In this domain, it is not possible in a script developed to represent classical Arabic to render features such as the merging of the phonemes *ẓ* and *ḍ*: in this edition, the distinction between the two is made according to the classical Arabic root.

Notes to the Introduction

1 Ḥā'il is the spelling in classical Arabic (hereafter CA). In the spoken language, it is pronounced Ḥāyil, which is the spelling adopted in this volume.

2 The ʿUtaybah chief Mnāḥī al-Hēḏal lamented that firearms did away with chivalry, making "silly nobodies and good noblemen equals" (Sowayan, *al-Ṣaḥrāʾ al-ʿarabiyyah*, 469).

3 As Muḥammad ibn Rashīd told Doughty (*Arabia Deserta*, 1:651).

4 The waterless Great Nafūd sand desert, forbidding in the hot season, is also rhapsodized as a paradise following rains of spring.

5 The Ikhwān, "Brothers," not to be confused with the later Society of the Muslim Brothers (*Jamāʿat al-Ikhwān al-Muslimīn*), was shorthand for *Ikhwān man ṭāʿa Allāh*, "Brothers of Those Obedient to God." This was the name given to the religiously inspired troops, mostly composed of recently settled Bedouin, that played a crucial role in the conquests of the later king ʿAbd al-ʿAzīz (or Ibn Saud) in laying the foundations for the creation of the Kingdom of Saudi Arabia.

6 As another contemporary put it: "The Ikhwān took a very different course and were hostile to our time-honored, hallowed norms (*salm*, pl. *slum*)" (Sowayan, *Ayyām al-ʿarab al-awākhir*, 510). By 1918, "almost one-fourth of the Shammar had become *Ikhwan* and allied themselves with Ibn Saud" (Al-Rasheed, *Politics in an Arabian Oasis: The Rashidi Tribal Dynasty*, 225).

7 This seems to have been the general opinion among transmitters in the area: "It is said that a captured raider at that time never lied, always told the truth" (Sowayan, *The Arabian Oral Historical Narrative*, 111).

8 "The Wahhabi call had managed to split tribal coalitions and many loyal sections entered the battle against their own tribesmen," an aggravation of the divided loyalty between tribe and state (al-Fahad, "The *ʿImama* vs. the *ʿIqal*: Hadari-Bedouin Conflict and the Formation of the Saudi State," 74, nn114, 118). ʿAjlān mentions some examples of such religiously inspired killings (§52.6 and §52.7). Initially, old tribal feuds spilled over into the new age in a new guise (e.g., Sowayan, *al-Ṣaḥrāʾ al-ʿarabiyyah*, 546; Von Oppenheim, *Die Beduinen*, 1:107–8).

9 The long rule of Ibn Musāʿid in Ḥāʾil, a member of the Jluwī branch of the House of Saud, known for its severity, lasted with some interruptions until his death in 1970.

10 The birth and death dates of the three poets are unknown. From this detail, it might be surmised that al-Hirbīd flourished slightly earlier than the other two poets, whose texts make no mention of a ruler before Muḥammad ibn Rashīd (r. 1873–97). However, Abū Zwayyid composed a poem on ʿAbd al-Karīm al-Jarbā, who was executed by the Ottoman Turks in 1871, and therefore this poem must date from before the short rule of Bandar ibn Ṭalāl (r. 1869–73). Unlike Abū Zwayyid and ʿAjlān, al-Hirbīd is not shown as having witnessed the transition from Rashīdī to Saudi rule in Ḥāʾil in 1921.

11 The expression "knight and poet" (*fāris wa-shāʿir*) corresponds to the pre-Islamic notion of "the perfect man" (*al-kāmil*, pl. *al-kamalah*); i.e., a poet who is also remarkable for bravery. Dhū l-Iṣbaʿ is similarly named "knight and poet, someone who frequently went raiding and took part in famous battles" (al-Isfahānī, *al-Aghānī*, 3:25, 89). ʿAbdallah, the first Rashīdī ruler, and his brother ʿUbayd are among the poets listed in al-Hirbīd's al-Shēkhah poem.

12 "Both camel nomads and cultivators of date palm groves look down their noses at herders of sheep and goats" (Sowayan, *al-Ṣaḥrāʾ al-ʿarabiyyah*, 380).

13 Likewise, the main issue for ʿAjlān is not to act against his conscience, thereby keeping his honor and integrity.

14 Steeped in oral tradition, these illiterate poets were acutely aware of the view posterity would take of them and are shown keeping an eye on their legacy. Al-Hirbīd, who listed the immortal names in his al-Shēkhah poem, casually said of his compositions: "verses sown and waiting for future generations" (§48.9, v. 7). A century or so later, this elicited the transmitter's admiring comment: "Where is ʿAdwān now? And we are still reciting his poetry!" Poetry is more valuable than possessions such as camels, clothes, and money because "praise sung in poetry remains and paeans go from mouth to mouth" (al-Iṣfahānī, *al-Aghānī*, 1:343).

15 When the poet Rāshid al-Hijlī praised Saṭṭām ibn Shaʿlān, Muḥammad ibn Rashīd threatened to kill him and had him thrown in jail until he apologized in a poem (al-Suwaydāʾ, *Manṭiqat Ḥāʾil ʿabra al-tārīkh*, 425–27). ʿAbd al-ʿAzīz ibn Rashīd ordered the assassination of the poet Shāyish al-Ṣalj for having declined an invitation to pay allegiance and for his response to his earlier persecution (Musil, *Northern Neğd*, 136–37).

16 See also Sowayan, "Studying Nabaṭi Poetry," on this passage.

17 The poet had put on a white shroud in preparation for his burial, signaling that he was ready to face his execution (and, one suspects, in the hope that it would soften the heart of the irate ruler).

18 The expression "I only want a mouthful of your blood," as Sowayan explains, does not need to be taken literally, though it points to an intention to kill, but it did happen that a

warrior would drink the warm blood of a felled opponent if he was slain for revenge (*The Arabian Oral Historical Narrative*, 145, 316).

19 For similar ruses employed by early classical poets, see n. 74 of the translation.

20 In pre-Islamic times, it was customary to cut off the forelock of a released prisoner and keep it as a souvenir; see Jacob, *Altarabisches Beduinenleben*, 137.

21 Similarly, the poet Ibn Ẓāhir, "an old man dressed in rags and carrying a bundle of firewood [. . .] knows how to hide his identity while roaming his lands like a king on an incognito inspection tour" (Kurpershoek, *Love, Death, Fame: Poetry and Lore from the Emirati Oral Tradition; Al-Māyidī ibn Ẓāhir*, xxxiv).

22 See Kurpershoek, *Arabian Satire: Poetry from 18th Century Najd: Ḥmēdān al-Shwēʿir*, xxi–xxii. This is made explicit in the verses where al-Hirbīd impersonates the verses of Jrēs (§37.3).

23 For instance, in 1884 the Saudi ruler ʿAbdallah ibn Fayṣal sent thirty-five riders to reconnoiter. They were all surrounded and killed by Ibn Rashīd (Musil, *Northern Neǧd*, 277).

24 The great majority of Abū Zwayyid's poems open with a camel description embedded in the messenger motif, the poet's words addressed to the conveyor of his verses to their destination, *yā-rāćib illī*: "O rider of (a camel of such-and-such description)"; see n. 17 of the translation.

25 Al-Suwaydā', *The Region of Ḥā'il in History* (*Manṭiqat Ḥā'il ʿabra al-tārīkh*), is especially informative and, despite its general title, is principally a detailed account of all aspects of life during the rule of Ibn Rashīd.

26 Sowayan, "Customary Law in Arabia: An Ethnohistorical Perspective." Blunt observed that "disputants bring their cases to the Emir, who settles them in open court, not on the basis of Islamic law, but rather Arabian custom, an authority far older than the Mussulman code" (*A Pilgrimage to Nejd*, 266). Similarly, Sowayan: "Poetry in tribal society practically takes the place of Quran and *ḥadīth* in urban society." In tribal societies, legal and poetic functions overlap and can be complementary (Sowayan, "Tonight My Gun Is Loaded: Poetic Dueling in Arabia.").

27 See §5 on how to deal with a conflict between a neighbor and a guest if both are under the same family's protection.

28 See also Sowayan, *The Arabian Oral Historical Narrative*, 25, and "Customary Law in Arabia."

29 Expert surveys of all aspects of the Nafūd and its ecosystem are given in Watts and Al-Nafie, *Vegetation and Biogeography of the Sand Seas of Saudi Arabia*, and James Mandaville, *Bedouin Ethnobotany*.

30 Whereas Rmāl is a section of the Ghfēlah branch of the Sinjārah division of Shammar, al-Hirbīd belongs to the Swēd branch of the same division, and they "are considered

the closest to each other" (Sowayan, *The Arabian Oral Historical Narrative*, 15). This explains al-Hirbīd's sojourns with the Rmāl. In his poem on the camel nomads of the Ghfēlah (and, by implication, the Rmāl), he vaunts their superiority compared to a miserable shepherd like himself (§32.10, v. 10).

31 A similar, but politically more consequential, pledge of loyalty is given to Ibn Musāʿid by the shaykh and raid leader (*ʿaǵīd*) of the Rmāl tribe, Ghaḍbān ibn Rmāl, implausibly with the condition that it should not be at the expense of his loyalty to Shammar (Sowayan, *Ayyām al-ʿarab*, 338).

32 A time-honored gesture of Arab rulers. For example, in the Umayyad period, ʿAbd al-Malik ibn Bishr paid off debts accumulated by the poet al-Ḥakam ibn ʿAbdal, and ʿAbd al-ʿAzīz ibn Marwān paid those of Nuṣayb (al-Iṣfahānī, *al-Aghānī*, 2:425, 1:376).

33 In pre-Islamic times, essentially the same procedure was followed to negotiate an end to the war between the tribes of Aws and Khazraj. The aggrieved party agreed on the choice of an arbiter, who stipulated that the parties should give solemn pledges and commitments in writing, stating that they would abide by the outcome of his ruling, whether it was agreeable to them or not (al-Iṣfahānī, *al-Aghānī*, 3: 25–26, 40–41).

34 See Kurpershoek, *Arabian Romantic: Poems on Bedouin Life and Love; ʿAbdallāh ibn Sbayyil*, xvi.

35 This division of responsibilities corresponds to the one followed by many Bedouin tribes: armed expeditions were led by a commander regarded as successful (mostly phrased by the Bedouin as "lucky") in capturing rich spoils. The same division existed in pre-Islamic Arabia: a tribe's leader (*sayyid*) would leave leadership in armed conflict to a commander, corresponding to the *ʿaǵīd* at the time of this edition's poets (Jacob, *Altarabisches Beduinenleben*, 224–25). One poet said of an *ʿaǵīd*: "Fortune favored him, and he was numbered among the brave men" (Musil, *Rwala*, 606).

36 Doughty calls ʿUbayd "a martial man [...], a master of Arabian warfare [...], an excellent kassād [poet], he indited of all his desert warfare; his boastful rimes, known wide in the wilderness, were ofttimes sung for me, in the nomad booths" (*Arabia Deserta*, 2:41–42).

37 The retinue included known families of poets: al-Tbēnāwī, al-Jhēlī, Khḍēr ibn Ṣʿēlīć (see §28 for his riposte to Abū Zwayyid), and many others (al-Suwaydāʾ, *Manṭiqat Ḥāʾil*, 487–88). According to one opinion, the five preeminent poets of Shammar are Mbērīć al-Tbēnāwī, ʿAdwān al-Hirbīd, Khalaf Abū Zwayyid, ʿAjlān ibn Rmāl, and Khḍēr ibn Ṣʿēlīć (al-Ẓafīrī, *Dīwān al-shāʿir Abū Zuwayyid, ḥakīm Shammar wa-shāʿirūhā*, 19).

38 Ṭalāl ibn Rashīd, for instance, though married to one of the Saudi imam Fayṣal's daughters, was "liberal even to profusion," and was "rumoured to indulge in the heretical pleasure of tobacco, to wear silk, and to be very seldom seen in the mosque." His uncle ʿUbayd balanced matters by being "so devout, so far from the abominations" as to

"almost atone for and cover the scandals given by his nephew" (Palgrave, *Narrative of a Year's Journey through Central and Eastern Arabia*, 93–95, 121).

39 Wallin, *Travels in Arabia*, 158.

40 "It is inconceivable for a Najdī *Hadari* (non-Bedouin, settled) to name his son after a Christian. For a Bedouin, so long as such person possessed the requisite 'manliness' (*marjilah*), religion was of no importance; thus, the chiefly family of the Ruwala tribe named their son Orans, after the famous Lawrence of Arabia, who had died only recently" (Al-Fahad, "The *'Imama* vs. the *'Iqal*," 75).

41 Doughty, *Arabia Deserta*, 2:26–27. Eduard Nolde was surprised to learn that Ibn Rashīd was well-informed about Alsace and French-German tensions. Nolde noted that the emir received "a mass of Arabic and Turkish newspapers from Egypt, Syria and Istanbul and keeps up an extensive correspondence. During my presence, every day at least one camel messenger, and sometimes two or three, arrived in the camp from various regions" (Nolde, *Reise nach Innerarabien, Kurdistan und Armenien, 1892*, 44, 89).

42 The poem was possibly rendered in the Nabaṭī meter *al-masḥūb*.

43 Julius Euting, *Tagebuch einer Reise in Inner-Arabien*, 2:58, 24. The reference must be to the Cairene Shāfiʿī scholar Abū al-ʿAbbās al-Qasṭallānī (1448–1517) and his popular history of the Prophet, *al-Mawāhib al-laduniyyah fī al-minaḥ al-Muḥammadiyyah* (published in 1474 and reprinted in Cairo in 1864–65, not long before Euting's visit). According to Steinberg, "Ecology, Knowledge, and Trade in Central Arabia (Najd) during the Nineteenth and Early Twentieth Centuries," 97, the second half of the nineteenth century saw "the first massive influx of printed books into Central Arabia."

44 Doughty understood "that this is the guest's honourable office"; i.e., to urge an aggrieved Bedouin woman to return to her husband. He adds that there are "nearly none who continue in their first husband's household" (*Arabia Deserta*, 1:276–78). See §6.4 and §7.1 and n. 42 of the translation for the passages in question.

45 On ʿUqayl, see Sowayan, "al-ʿUqaylāt" in *al-Ṣaḥrāʾ al-ʿarabiyyah*, 367–72; Musil, *Rwala*, 278–81; and the Glossary.

46 Al-Isfahānī, *al-Aghānī*, 1:377.

47 Al-Isfahānī, *al-Aghānī*, 1:340.

48 Al-Isfahānī, *al-Aghānī*, 1:353.

49 "Bedouin women are renowned for their sweet conversation" (Sowayan, *al-Ṣaḥrāʾ al-ʿarabiyyah*, 442).

50 Sowayan, *al-Ṣaḥrāʾ al-ʿarabiyyah*, 433; Musil, *Northern Neğd*, 112–13.

51 Al-Suwaydāʾ, *Manṭiqat Ḥāʾil*, 530.

52 Al-Suwaydāʾ, *Manṭiqat Ḥāʾil*, 717.

53 At the time, these groves inside the rock formations of Jabal Shammar were numerous and represented an important source of income (al-Suwaydāʾ, *Manṭiqat Ḥāʾil*, 537, 553).

54 Burckhardt emphasizes the importance of the art of conversation for the Bedouin, and his own enchantment with it (e.g., *Notes on the Bedouins and Wahabys*, 366–67). See also Doughty, *Arabia Deserta*, 1:305–7.

55 For instance, al-Isfahānī, *al-Aghānī*, 2: 313, 327.

56 The entire area between Jabal Shammar and Urfa, today in southeastern Turkey, was subject to raids by ʿAnazah and Shammar (Von Oppenheim, *Die Beduinen*, 1:71). Abū Zwayyid sends a poem to Muḥammad ibn Rashīd from the Khābūr River, a northern tributary of the Euphrates (§10.4, v. 7). The ruler's good fortune showed in the long period of plentiful rains during his reign (al-Suwaydāʾ, *Manṭiqat Ḥāʾil*, 599, 607). Under his successor, years of drought followed, and "the power of the Shamar emir, Eben Rashīd, had collapsed in 1906" (Musil, *Rwala*, 517).

57 "Until recently, the Shammar of Najd were not only a Bedouin tribe, but also the mainstay of a state, the Shammar dominions of Ḥāʾil" (Von Oppenheim, *Die Beduinen*, 3:37).

58 Unanimously described with awe by European visitors (Wallin, Palgrave, Doughty, Blunt, Huber, Euting) and Arabic sources (in particular, the details in al-Suwaydāʾ, *Manṭiqat Ḥāʾil*); see also ʿAjlān's lament, "where the staffs tapping on laden royal trays, loud invitations to paupers waiting for food" (§52.1, v. 3).

59 Palgrave mentions that ʿUbayd ibn Rashīd took to the field with his troops forty times (*Narrative*, 92), and al-Suwaydāʾ quotes Muḥammad ibn Rashīd boasting that he had raided the ʿUtaybah tribe forty-seven times (*Manṭiqat Ḥāʾil*, 399–400).

60 Al-Suwaydāʾ, *al-Amthāl al-shaʿbiyyah fī manṭiqat Ḥāʾil*, 474, 434. The expression is part of the poets' predilection for super-hyperbole, making the incredibly bad even worse or taking the magnificent to even greater heights (e.g., Abu Zwayyid §§6:13, 13, 16:3–4, 48:41, 49:9, 49:13; al-Hirbīd §21:3, 25:4).

61 Al-Isfahānī, *al-Aghānī*, 2:269.

62 Goldziher, *Abhandlungen zur Arabischen Philologie*, section "Über die Vorgeschichte der Hijâʾ-Poesie," 13.

63 There is a strong possibility, of course, that the order of verses changed in the course of transmission and that verses went missing.

64 This is the only episode in which Abū Zwayyid is mentioned as an owner of palm trees.

65 On original touches not found in classical poetry, see al-Suwaydāʾ, *al-Nakhlah al-ʿarabiyyah adabiyyan wa-ʿilmiyyan wa-iqtisādiyyan*, 86, 88, and Sowayan, *al-Ṣaḥrāʾ al-ʿarabiyyah*, 379. In two of the three brief references to palm trees in Abū Zwayyid's poetry, two are part of a camel description and one occurs as a simile for a girl's beauty (§5.5, v. 13, §25.8, v. 6).

66 Kurpershoek, *Arabian Romantic*, 117.

67 Doughty, *Arabia Deserta*, 1:261.

68 Dhū l-Rummah, *Dīwān*, 2:715–16.

69 Also, "he dispatched a *giʿūd* (male camel) to so-and-so" (i.e., a poem), and *ʿād jāhum giʿūd abūhum*, "they received a poem from their father." When Shaykh al-ʿAwājī called on ʿAnazah to mobilize against Shammar, and Shammar heard his poem, the latter said, "Listen, folk! Which of you is going to send a camel (*giʿūd*) that overtakes and catches the camel of al-ʿAwājī?" (Sowayan, *al-Ṣaḥrāʾ al-ʿarabiyyah*, 236–37).

70 A Rwēlī is a member of the Rwalah tribe.

71 If camels have a salt deficit, generally because they have not been grazing on saltbushes for an extended period, "they become weak and thin and have a tendency to eat bones and carrion" (Mandaville, *Bedouin Ethnobotany*, 87).

72 The story resembles the poet Ibn Ẓāhir's choice of a young, not very good-looking camel as wages for his service as a camel herd, but the beast grows into an unrivaled racer (Kurpershoek, *Love, Death, Fame*, 153).

73 The line parallels the verse quoted by Ibn Rashīd that almost cost Abū Zwayyid his life. It is a common cliché used for flattery. Musil was honored with almost the same expression in verse: "To another like him no chaste beauty ever gave birth; and of all Bedouin chiefs none equals him" (Musil, *Rwala*, 291).

74 "When a son attains maturity, his father generally gives him a mare or a camel, that he may try his fortune in plundering excursions" (Burckhardt, *Notes*, 114).

75 The verses are a replica of a story about the sixth-century poet ʿUrwah ibn al-Ward (al-Isfahānī, *al-Aghānī*, 3:81–83).

76 In the magazine *al-Quṭūf*, 52, "al-Adab al-shaʿbī mawādd mutafajjirah"; and Sowayan, *al-Ṣaḥrāʾ al-ʿarabiyyah*, 319–20.

77 Sowayan, *Ayyām al-ʿarab*, 19; similarly, *The Arabian Oral Historical Narrative*, xi.

خلف ابو زويّد

Khalaf Abū Zwayyid

حياته

١،١ خلف ابن دخيل ابن خلف ابن فارس ابن زويد ابن خلف ابن رخيص جده خلف اخوٍ لضيف الله وصالح الرخيص شيوخ النبهان من الزميل من شمر. يقال ان جده خلف نِصى ابن سعود وقِصد بُه قصيدة ما اعرفه بَسّ مَنه اللي يقول

٢،١ اخوتي سبعـه وانا اكبـرهـم كلوا رمش العين وحَتّوا هِذبَه
ابيك تواعـدن لو ما عـطيـتن العَوين اللي يتـــرجى الاذبه

٣،١ وَعيّتُه انا الله يرحمه والله وانا كبرها الوغيد شوَيّبٍ عمى معُه لُه واحدٍ يقودُه. رجّال عَديم وضِرّس وطويل. له من العيال دخيل وعامش وفضل. عامش عقّب ولدٍ هالحين هو وعيالُه سكّان الرخيصيه. اما دخيل وفضل فهم ذِبحَوا بكون العامريه بين الشعلان والنبهان. ابو زويد عمرُه يوم يموت فوق ميّة سنه. توفى عام ١٣٦١ ه عقب سقوط حائل ويقال أن له قصايد يمدح به الأمير عبد العزيز ابن مساعد. عمر ابو زويد يوم سقوط حايل ٨٦.

٤،١ سَيّر على عبد العزيز ابن مساعد بحايل جابُه بْناخيٍ لُه يقودُه وعنده الاخوان ملفلفينٍ عمايمهم ويتضرّسون ولا يدانون ابو زويد ولا قصيده. يوم ان ابو زويد سلم على الامير قال الرُخصه يا طويل العمر عندي لي قصيدة ابْسَمّعَك اياه. قال يا بو زويد حنا هالحين مجلس حديث وراحت خرابيط القصيد. قال شعر شعر يالامير ما هو

His Life

His full name is Khalaf ibn Dikhīl ibn Khalaf ibn Fāris ibn Zwayyid ibn Khalaf ibn Rakhīṣ. His grandfather was a brother of Ḍēfallah and Ṣāliḥ al-Rakhīṣ, the shaykhs of the Nabhān of the Zmēl of Shammar. I heard that his grandfather Khalaf went to see Ibn Saʿūd with verses he had composed in his honor. I only know these two lines: 1.1

I am the oldest of seven brothers: 1.2
  they ate my eyelids, lashes dropped.
If not a gift, I crave then for a pledge,
  as a farmhand awaits a promised meal.[1]

I vaguely remember having seen him, God show him mercy, when I was a little kid: a frail and blind old man being led by the hand. Yet he was known as a bold, gritty, and outstanding individual. His sons were Dikhīl, ʿĀmish, and Faḍl. ʿĀmish had a son, who currently lives in al-Rakhīṣiyyah with his children. Dikhīl and Faḍl died in the battle of al-ʿĀmiriyyah between the Shaʿlān and the Nabhān. When Abū Zwayyid passed away, he was over a hundred years old. He died in the year 1361 [1942], long after the Saudi conquest of Ḥāyil [1921]. I was told that he composed poems in praise of Prince ʿAbd al-ʿAzīz ibn Musāʿid. At the time of the Saudi conquest of Ḥāyil, he was eighty-six years old.[2] 1.3

He went to call on ʿAbd al-ʿAzīz ibn Musāʿid in Ḥāʾil and was brought to him by some of his relatives. He found the prince in the company of the Ikhwān,[3] turbans wrapped around their heads, gnashing their teeth at the sight of this new entrant. They could not stand Abū Zwayyid and his poems. 1.4

Abū Zwayyid greeted the prince and said, "With your permission, may you live long, I would like to recite some verses I have composed in your honor."

The prince said, "Look, Abū Zwayyid, we are in a session devoted to the study of the Prophet's sayings. This nonsense of verses is over."

"Poetry, prince! It is poetry, not just some verses."

The prince said, "Well, if it is poetry, then go ahead!"

قصيد. قال ايه شعر ما يخالف. يوم ان ابو زويد قال قصيدته سكت ابن مساعد ما قال شي. ما هو يَخَبَر قَبِل يشجَّع ويقال له صَح لسانك. الناس هذي سكتت. وهو كهيف ولا يشوف وجيه الرجال واشْتَكّ من السكّته هذي.

قال الله يجعلَه على حظ الشوف يالامير اللي ما خلاني اشوف وجهك. قال طيّب ٥،١
وش تبي تسوي يا شفت وجهي. قال ابراعي انت من اللي الى مِنُّه مَدح يِقْعِد حجاجُه ويفتل شاربُه والا من اللي يدنق ويحك شْعَرات عِلْباوه. قال لا بالله انا ابو عبد الله من اللي يقعد حجاجه ويفتل شاربه. قال والله انك من مقامينه يا ولد تركي. قال زاد انا المعيد ماتت والنخلات ذِبَحْهن العطش واهْشمَن وابي لي لي مْعيدٍ لهن. قال رح رح يا علي عطوه له معيد. ويِطّلعون له من حوش المعاويد هكالاملح اللي هذا كبر رِكبه. يالله حصّله منه والا ما يعطي ابن مساعد.

When Abū Zwayyid had finished his recitation, Ibn Musāʿid remained silent. He did not utter a word. Abū Zwayyid had never experienced such a thing before. He was accustomed to praise and encouragement from an audience that showed its appreciation at the end of a poetry recital with the words "Well spoken!"[4] But these people uttered not a single word! And he was blind. He did not see the expression on the faces of the men gathered there. The ominous silence made him feel uneasy.

Abū Zwayyid said, "I wish God would grant me sight, Prince, since He made it impossible for me to see your face." 1.5

"Tell me, what would you do if you could see my face?"

"I would like to see for myself if you are of those who on being praised lift their eyebrows and twist the ends of their mustache or of those who lower their chin and scratch the hairs on their nape."

The prince said, "As sure as I am Abū ʿAbdallah! I belong to those who lift their eyebrows and twist their mustache."

"By God, you are truly deserving, son of Turkī!" he said, and added, "Let me just mention that my camel for drawing water from the well has died. My palm trees are thirsting and may turn into dead wood. For their sake, I need another camel as a replacement."

The prince issued orders to one of his servants: "Go, go at once, ʿAlī! Give him a camel strong enough to draw water from his well to irrigate his grove!"

His men took a camel from the courtyard where the draft camels were kept, a dark-gray beast with huge knee joints. It was God's will to provide for him. Ibn Musāʿid made an exception for him, as he was not in the habit of giving anyone presents.

ولده دخيل

١،٢ دخيل وَلَد ابو زوِيّد يرّكبن على الاجناب ويغزي معه ناس ما هي كثير من العشرين الى الثلاثين. مَدّ بعض المدّات غزى معه له رْبيع ما هم كثير ومد معه له حربي خَوي له من البيضان. قال الشايب يا وليدي يا دخيل وداعتك خويك. واقصد به قصيده. وجابوا البل. دخيل كسب البل وخذى ناقتين قبل يقسم البل على خوياوه شطّرهن وضّحاوين قال هذولي لخوِيّ اللي وصّان عليه ابوي. وجسم البل على خوياوه وعزل لخويّه مثل جسم خوياوه وناقتين زود ما طَبّن القسم لخويه. عِقْبٍ رايس ابن رخيص قال ابي هالنياق اللي عندك يالحربي. قال دخيل لا يا عمي خويي. قال يا منّك تعيقَدْت طَلّع خويك. وخَذه من الحربي وازعل انت يا دخيل. قال ابوه

٢،٢ دخِيل خِذ من والِدك لك مساله   مسالةٍ ما يفهمه كل رجالـ
احشـم خويّك عن دروب الرزاله   ترى الخوي عند الاجاويد له حالـ
خويك الداني الى شفت حاله   احمل عليك من المعاليق ما شالـ
والمرجله بالك تـرخّي حباله   وبالك تِعيل وْلا تراخى لمن عالـ
يا صار دَلْوِك ما تموحه شماله   ترى الرجال يطوّحونه على الجالـ
يا صار لك من عوص الانضا زْماله   حمرا تْوَرّد بك إلى سرّب اللالـ

His Son Dikhīl

Dikhīl, Abū Zwayyid's son, joined a group of raiders who rode out with the aim of despoiling one of the other tribes. They were a small bunch, twenty or at most thirty riders. He took part in a few such robbing expeditions. One of those who also joined belonged to the tribe of Ḥarb, the Bīḍān section. His old father said, "Dikhīl, my boy, I impress on you to keep an eye on your companion and take good care of him." For emphasis, he repeated his advice in a poem. They returned home with their booty and Dikhīl took his share of the robbed camels. Before the booty was divided among his fellow raiders, he put aside two she-camels, beautiful white ones. He explained, "These are reserved for my dear companion, the one my father entrusted to my care." So, over and above those he allotted to every raider, he set aside two more she-camels for his Ḥarbī ward. A little later, Ibn Rakhīṣ came to inspect the booty and supervise the division of the spoils.[5] He said, "Listen, you Ḥarbī! I want to take these camels of yours for myself." Dikhīl protested: "Dear Uncle, he is a companion entrusted to my care." Ibn Rakhīṣ said, "When you have grown up to become a real raid leader, who knows, then you may grant such favors to your friend." He took the camels from the Ḥarbī, leaving Dikhīl to stew in his anger. On that occasion, Abū Zwayyid composed the following verses: 2.1

Dikhīl, listen closely to your father's counsel: 2.2
it takes a man of sound mind to grasp its thrust.
Be considerate with a friend, stay away from dirt!
Don't forget that gentlemen treasure companions!
If you find him down and out, in dire straits,
lift a load off his back, help him carry it.
Do not let the cords of noble striving slacken!
Beware of hurting others, be firm with violators!
With your left, heave mightily at the ropes
lest others smash the bucket against the casing.
Always keep a hardy mount close at hand,
a reddish camel to cut through simmering air:

تِمْـرِس كما تمـرس خطـاة المحـاله   مع سَهْلةٍ عَمّال من جا معه ذالـــ
خــــلّه مع الدّيّان تمشي لحـالَه   يا صار ما انت لَلْمَسَة الخَشِم حمّالـــ
يا صـار ما تِحْسَب الى صـار قـاله   تصير من حِسْبَة هَدومٍ به ازوالـــ
يا عـل رَجْـلٍ شوفتـه قـدّ حـالَه   عسى تـدَوّر زوجته بيه الابدالـــ
الحِمِّرة تِـدْرِك معوشـة عْـياله   والا الرجل يِبغي مِنه بعض الاحوالـــ
تـرْ رِبع يومٍ مـقعـدك بالجلاله   تسوى حـياةٍ عـايشينٍ به انـذالـــ

ما يِفْلَح هو ابو زويد. هذا ولده دخيل غَبَش عليه له واحد راعي ناقةٍ كاسبينه. ٣٠٢
والرجّال اللي خذى الناقة هو اللي كاسبه ما هو دخيل ولد ابو زويد ومشهّد شهود على انه هو اللي طَقّ الناقه اللي كِسِبَه. وغبش عليه ولد ابو زويد دخيل. قال والله ان ربحك سوقك لَه مع الفِرْجه. يقوله الرجال هذاك اللي كسب الناقه. ويوم الْفَوا ويورّد الشهود انه هو اللي كسب الناقه وخَذاه خذاه من دخيل ولد ابو زويد. وِكِنُّه انغلب ابو زويد على انه ما عمره فِلِح هو قبل لأنه ما يعد الا الصِقّ (= الصدق) هو يوم الصق له وقت. ويزعل دخيل عقب هذي وينحر العليّان ويأخذ بنت لابن غازي انت يا دخيل. وينصحه ابوه

Hooves spinning like unhinged pulley wheels
hurtle across fearsome desert wastes.
Let it whisk you off into lonely plains:
better than to stay, your nose rubbed in dust.
Be first to volunteer at calls to heavy lifting,
or risk being counted a mere shred of cloth.
Sluggards hanging back have it coming:
may their wives send them packing.
Sparrows find sustenance for their brood;
humans must overcome greater hurdles.
Hey! One session seated in a seat of honor
equals a bastard's life spent in humiliation.

In court cases, Abū Zwayyid always came out the winner.[6] Now, one time 2.3
his son Dikhīl quarreled unfairly with another raider about a captured she-camel. The man who had seized the camel and could rightfully claim its ownership was not Dikhīl, the son of Abū Zwayyid. Plenty of witnesses had seen that the other man touched the animal first with his staff. Therefore, his right to the booty was not in question.[7] Dikhīl protested and argued, but the other merely said, "Well, do as you wish, but be aware that your only gain will be the trouble of driving the camel across this stretch of desert." These were the words of the man who had first touched the she-camel. On their return, witnesses from among the other raiders had testified that they had seen the other man making the she-camel his own. As a result, he took the animal back from Dikhīl. Abū Zwayyid was disconcerted by this verdict. He resented it as a personal defeat. It came as a blow to him since he had never lost a case in court. He had a solid reputation for being someone who spoke the truth and nothing but the truth. Those were times when truthfulness still counted for something. Dikhīl took it badly too. In response, he went off in a huff to stay with the ʿLayyān, and married the daughter of Ibn Ghāzī. That was Dikhīl's response. Thereupon, his father advised him:

٤،٢ أبديت انا هولاس قلبي بقيلي   ما هن هواليس القلوب الهبايل
هرجات ما هولس بهنّ الهبيلِ   ولا هو لهن بيرمْعَة العقل قايل
دخيل كان انك لهرجي تشيلِ   هرجي يِدِلّ اللي يِتِيه القوايل
وداعتك يا ويلدي يا دخيلِ   وداعة اللي ما يبوق الرسايل
يا ويلدي حذراك تنسى الجميل   ما تنفع اليمنى بليا شمايل
وداعتك يا مسندي لا تِعيل   ولا تْمَضّي العيلة لمن جاك عايل
خويك اللي بالخلا لك وكيل   لو زلّ عندك زلّةٍ لا تسايل
وحذراك عن رِفْقَة خطاة الرِذيل   ما ينْبِذِر به طِيب هافى الحمايل
صديقك اللي قبل جيلك وجيلي   صديق جدّك بالوقوت الاوايل
لا تْطيع به حكْي العرب والنقيلي   عَدّل مِعُه شَيله الى صار مايل
وافطن ترى باقى العرب ما يِظيل   يا وَيْلدي ما عقب رَبْعك صمايل
وعدوك اللي من قديمٍ محيلِ   تاتيك لو صافاك منه النقايل
والكدّ يصلح بالحصان الاصيل   اللي يشبّي بالمهار الاصايل
واصبر تصير بعين رَبْعك جليلِ   صبرك يجنّبك الدروب الرزايل
الصبر يُودِع باب خَطّك طويل   وخلّ الهبال لتايهين الدلايل

My troubled heart pours forth its verses— 2.4
not a whining dullard's petty complaints.
A dimwit is a stranger to tempestuous feeling:
clueless, his mind is at a loss to understand.
Dikhīl, if you care to weigh my words, take them:
they will guide you through midday's blistering heat;
This counsel, dear boy, I entrust to your care
with an appeal: "Stay faithful to its message!"
Never forget, my boy, to requite good with good:
what use is a right hand forsaken by its left?
I beseech you, apple of my eye, do no harm,
and let no one get away with wrongful deeds!
In empty deserts you depend on your friend:
overlook his misstep if he has offended you!
Beware of befriending gutless poltroons:
They are a rotten breed, profligate in evil ways.
Friends have been bequeathed to you:
your ancestors' friends from olden days.
Ignore what people say—insidious gossip;
adjust old friends' loads if they go askew.
Be smart, expect no benefit from other folks,
my boy, except from kinsmen: stout defenders
Against wily enemies lying in wait for ages,
waggling tongues to entice with honeyed words.
Put yourself out for a noble horse—it pays:
a stud to beget fillies from pedigree mares.
Bear up! Fortitude fills your kin with awe;
patient endurance staves off ignominy.
Patience is the key to reputation and salvation:
let foolish dimwits flounder in ignorance!

٥،٢

ويقول ابو زويد يسنّد على دخيل

برّقت بالدنيا وانا قبل غافل   ثري له موارد ومساقي وقليب
يسني على بيره ثمانين عِدّه   وكل عدةٍ تفرغ لها بشعيب
عسى اول ما يِخْضَرّ وادي هل الندى   وهل القهاوي وادي عشيب
اهل دلال تاعبينٍ بْشَبّهن   اربع دلال ومِنْشِياتٍ طيب
ونِجْرٍ الى جا الليل دلّى يدادي   يشدى مذيرة صياح رعيب
اوصي هل الخوّات بمدالى الخوا   عمل الرزاله بالرفيق يعيب
ورَدّ الثنا حقٍّ لكسابة الثنا   الفعل سيف والمديح نصيب

السيف يعني الفعل

الاشوار لو تصديرهن مثل وردهن   ما دير لهن عند الرجال طبيب
ترى ليا صافيت رجلٍ خيّر   يعطيك من اشوار الرجال صليب
لا تشرّف الرجل الرذيل بغَيبتك   من عاشر الرجل الرذيل يعيب
دخيل يا بني يا سلايل والدي   لا تصير لِلحِصْني سواة لعيب
تَرْمن عاشر الحصني يطيح بمذهبه   ما يعاشر الحصني نضايض ذيب
ولا تصقر وقت الهداد الا بهيلع   الدم من مضرب مِخْلَبه صبيب
لا ترافق الا رجلٍ صميدع   مَحَصٍ تدلي به بكل قليب
ان جت بالحيلات رجلٍ حيلي   وان جت بما يرضي الاله خطيب
ولا تعاشر الا كل رجلٍ طيّب   عجلٍ لى دعاه الفريق يجيب

In the following verses, Abū Zwayyid addresses Dikhīl: 2.5

Once heedless, I looked closer at the world,
a plethora of springs, water holes, and wells:
Eighty pulleys empty buckets into basins;
from each basin the water runs into a gully.
May big spenders' valleys turn green first,
carpeted with grass for generous entertainers,
Unflagging servers of coffee kept on the boil,
deliciously scented in four long-beaked pots;
Peals from beans pounded in brass mortars ring
all night long, like terrifying anguished shrieks.
Fellow seeker, I tell you, fraternizing means
you're despised for doing a bad turn to a friend.
Laudable deeds should be rewarded with praise:
reputations shine if glory is won by sword.[8]

—By sword, he means noble acts.

If wise counsel was as much applied as sought,
other men would not be needed to save the day.[9]
If you open your mind to a dependable man,
be confident he proffers advice solid as rock;
Never entrust your inner thoughts to wretches:
consort with rogues and you end up maimed.
Dikhīl, my dearest son, my ancestors' scion,
don't get chummy with foxes playing games!
Hanging with foxes will bring you down;
fennecs aren't on par with young wolves.[10]
In hunting season choose a peregrine,
talons dripping with blood from a strike.
Keep company with stalwart braves—
friends like ropes fit to haul from deepest wells—
If things get dicey, they're crafty and cunning;
if all is fine, honest and upright as preachers.
Befriend robust defenders of the common good,
prompt in action at their tribesmen's call.

انهه عن التيهات وان تاه تِه معه　　يا تاه قل درب الرفيق مَصيب
وحذراك تْناسب عَفْنٍ من الملا　　ولا ذِكرعَفْنٍ بْتال العمر يطيب
تلقى منزله من قفو بيت خيّر　　هَيسٍ يا شاف الضيوف يشيب
لا داعيٍ رجلٍ برفّة بيته　　وسريعٍ لمدعوّ الفريق يجيب
يثوي بْطَرَق البيت لو كان منشط　　ومشيهٍ بدرب اللازمات دبيب
لا تامن الدنيا ولا ترتهي به　　صيّور مهزامه يصير قريب
ولا احظّ من رجل بدنياه مِنْسِتِر　　يصيرعند ملوك الاله حبيب

Steer him straight; if he strays, stray with him,
as if his doing wrong were the right way to go.
Stay clear from rotten apples in your clan:
their cravenness will never improve.
He'll hide behind a hospitable man's dwelling:
a cur that blanches at the approach of guests;
He invites no one to lounge in his tent,
but is ever first to snatch up dinner invitations.
Slouched against the side, though sound of limb,[11]
coming at a crawl in the hour of need.
Eye warily a world brimful of lurking danger,
ready to pounce and catch you unprepared.
Fortunate the man with clear conscience:
he is the darling when God's angels call.

يمدح عبد الكريم الجربا

١٠٣ عبد الكريمِ الله على الناس بدّاه   رِقى سـنام المجـد ما لُه لِطـيمِ
يمشي بثوب العز والرب مشـّاه   عَطوه من اللي راضيٍ به رحيمي
من حين حوا لآدم حـين لاقـاه   ما شـفت مثـله بالاوادم كريم
مع فعله المشهور تطول يمـناوه   مع بذل جوده بالسياسه فهيم
يدوس غِـبّات المدارك يِمَشْـناه   غوّاص غِـبّات المدارك عـديم
نِقَـل بقول خُذُه لمن هو تَنَصـّاه   عليـه من تلحـين موسى الكليم
قبـلي يقوله حـبّسهن بالمـلاقـاه   بفحـانٍ اللي بـه يعوق الجـريم

فحجان الفراوي.

اللي ذلوله مـا توَنّى مـطـاياه   فرز الوغى نقـاض فتل الخصـيم
عبد الكريم اللي جزالٍ عـطاياه   يعطى الركاب ومحصنات الرهيم
شَهَدوا له الحكام والترك بحـماه   الا ومع ذلك بخيـص وحكيم

Verses in Praise of ʿAbd al-Karīm al-Jarbā

ʿAbd al-Karīm is God's favorite among men; 3.1
at his pinnacle, he basks in matchless glory.
He strides robed in power at the Lord's behest,
gifted to him at the pleasure of the Compassionate.
From the times when Eve and Adam first met,
his likeness has not been seen in creation.
With his fabled feats comes unrivaled generosity;
his liberal hands have the magic touch in policy.
He plunges headlong into heaving seas of death
without a care, an intrepid death-defying diver.
His motto, "Take it!," puts his name above all:[12]
he is like Moses, who talked to God,
As said before me by the stalwart in battle,
Fajḥān who blocks the way of avengers,

—Fajḥān al-Farāwī.

Whose fast camel mount never tires,
king of the melee, thwarter of foes' schemes.
ʿAbd al-Karīm, whose gifts gush forth profusion,
endless streams of camels and spirited mares.
Rulers and Turks recognize his power
of protection paired with acumen and sagacity.

ويقولون ان ابو زويد سيّر على الهادي الجربا ومدحه بقصيدة مَنَه يوم يقول ٢٠٣

قال الذي قاله على الشيخ بادي   وِدّي بِشَوفك غالي يابن سرّاح
يا شيخ ياراع العلوم البعاد   يا لولب ما له من مهاميز مفتاح
يا مِنّهن حِدّيَن بْرِضّام وادي   أشقر لمريوك الملازيم نطّاح

مريوك الملازيم هي الجموع.

. . . .   وعمرك رخيص يوم جلبات الارواح

وهذا دليل على ان الجربان يركزون بالسراح.

The story goes that Abū Zwayyid called on al-Hādī al-Jarbā and recited a panegyric poem in which these verses appear:[13] 3.2

These verses were recited in the shaykh's presence:
I fondly desired to see your countenance, Ibn Sarrāḥ.[14]
Mighty chief, your renown's spread far and wide!
Indestructible shard of metal, you're invulnerable!
Over a wadi's red-hot stones, camels are spurred
by a falcon unafraid to attack fierce warriors.[15]

—He means big groups of fighters.

[. . .][16]
In the market of death, you hold dear life cheap.

—Proof the clan of Sarrāh are kin to the Jarbā.

قصايده بصطّام ابن شعلان

١٠٤ يا راكبٍ حمرا تِقِل سَلْوَعَة ذيب   حمرا ولا عمْر الحويّر غذِي به
ضافٍ سِبيبه فوق عوج العراقيب   حمرا تسوف كعوبها بيسبيبه
حمرا وتِعبى للسهال العباعيب   حمرا وتوّه في جَهَلها منيبه
حمرا تِفِجّ فخوذها للمحاقيب   عليه بعيدات الموارد قريبه
حمرا تكصّم من عياها المصاليب   ترْثع بيمناها وتطوي جنيبه
من نجد جينا فوق كوره مَراكيب   جينا لشيخ جيّته ما علي به
جينا لصطّامٍ ذعار الاجانيب   اللي ليا ناكر صحيبٍ صِحيبه
اللي ليا جا حزة المدح والطيب   فعايله على العدو ينْدِعي به
يا شوق من عَيّت على كل خِطّيب   قبلك على كل البوادي عْصي به
بنت الذي وان سولفوا بالمعازيب   ابوه مصوّت بالعَشا بالجِذيبه
مِدّمي خشوم الفُوس من شِمّخ النيب   اللي يعيشون العرب من حَليبه
ما يِستوي للبيض غيره ضواريب   والبيض خَطْو المِشْتِبه وِش تِبي بِه
صَطّام ما والله يِجِبْنه ولا جِيب   من شرقي الدنيا لغربي مِغيبه
خيله على الاِقفات عِرجٍ بِهِن عَيب   والا على الرّدّات عجلٍ هذيبه
هزّاع جاب النمر والليث والذيب   وسمّ الافاعي خالطه عظم شِيبه

His Poems on Saṭṭām ibn Shaʿlān

Rider of a red-brown camel trotting like a wolf, 4.1
reddish-brown, never having suckled a calf.[17]
A thick-haired tail lashes curved hocks,
reddish-brown, the tail reaches the heels.
Red-brown camel fit to cross endless plains,
reddish-brown, fresh, first eyeteeth showing.
Red-brown, bulging thighs stretch the girths:
speedy, she makes faraway wells an easy ride.
Red-brown, she shatters saddle's wood 5
at full gallop, stretching her flanks in and out.
We came riding from Najd on camelback
toward a shaykh—I have no care for others.
We came to Saṭṭām, terror of enemy tribes,
a friend if other friends turn against you.
If the public awards the trophy of chivalry,
his feats of arms win widest acclaim by far.
Adored by a wife who sent suitors packing:
until you came, she scorned all the Bedouin;
Daughter of a legend lionized in assemblies, 10
he sounds calls to dinner from atop a hill;[18]
His blood-smeared axes felled huge camels
without a thought for people's need of milk.
Splendid beauties dream of him, a stud:
what use do they have for a defective organ?[19]
They never gave birth, nor will they ever,
to the equal of Ṣaṭṭām in the entire world.[20]
In retreat, his horses go limping as if lame,
then turn and attack at breathtaking speed.
Hazzāʿ begot a panther, a lion, and a wolf, 15
snake venom spewed by a rabid monster.[21]

رويلات والله ما بهم شَمْط اجانيب   نِعمك من العليا ومن ينْتِخي بـه
انا الذي ما اسَيِّب القيل تسْيِيب   ولا انا بحال اللي زعل لو درِي بـه

ما هو بحال حتى ابن رشيد. والبيض عقبه ما لقِي له ضواريب ان محمد عقيم ما يجيب الضنا.

رد عليه الكويكبي وطلب الكويكبي من ابن رشيد جزا قصيدته قال ابي انا ٢،٤
وخامس خمستي ما يوكل لنا لا هامل ولا مرعي عند شمر. يقول

يا بو زويـد يا جـذَيّ المـراقيب   يا وجـــه ذيبٍ دانخٍ له رويبـه
يا بو زويـد فاطرك بـه شواذيب   جِيّـتك على حِـرٍّ تزاود هـذيبـه
قلته بابن شعلان شيبٍ ولد شيب   لى غَرّ من الصيدات ياكل قـريبـه
ما قلتهـا بالضيغـمي مَنْـقَع الطيب   مـقيـم الضحى للمِنْهـزم وش يجيـبه
وشدّوا على ذورات مثل الدواليب   كِم ليـلةٍ يَسْـري ولا يِنْسِـري بـه

وقصد ابو زويد بعد بصطّام ابن شعلان عِقب ما رجع منه قال ٣،٤

يا راكب اللي لى مشت تطوي القاع   يا ضـربوا عوص النـضا كل حـاله
عشـافـرٍ يا ضـمّها الجيش مخراع   وجـنا إلى زَمْـلَت تقـدّع بحـاله
مـلمومـةٍ من فوق والورك بوسـاع   ومشيَه تخوض وكـن بيها رِفـاله
يا لولبَن بالقَـفَـل وابْلالهن ضـاع   تلقـاه توّه سـايجـاتٍ خْبـاله
يا روّحن حفيـا وطفـيا وظِـلاع   يـزمي على قـطـع الفـيافي هْبـاله

Rwalah, the pure, without a foreign strain.
Hail to their war cry, “The Sublime!”[22]
In verses I do not ramble and flounder:
Pfui! Let some ears get mad on hearing them.

He does not care even about Ibn Rashīd, who did not impregnate any of the pretty girls. Muḥammad ibn Rashīd was sterile. He remained without offspring.

Another poet, al-Kwēkibī,[23] responded to these verses and asked Ibn Rashīd for a reward, saying, “For myself and my kinsmen to the fifth degree I ask the right to pasture our camels on the lands of Shammar without risk of getting despoiled of our animals.”[24] 4.2

Abū Zwayyid, weakling unable to climb a lookout,
wolf-faced dog, busy lapping up curdled milk.
Your camel, Abū Zwayyid, isn't free of blemishes,
A noble racer spurred on to bring you in a hurry.
You heap praise on Ibn Sha'lān, born of a rabid bitch,
feeding on his own kin, too clumsy for worthy prey.
Why not speak of al-Ḍēghamī, virtue's fountainhead:[25]
unconcerned, he lingers on in battle's wake.
His camel troops race like spinning pulley wheels,
at night through wastes where no enemy treads.

In a farewell to his host, Abū Zwayyid composed these verses on Ṣaṭṭām ibn Sha'lān: 4.3

Merciless rider urging on a gaunt, sinewy camel:
under its hooves, plains roll up like carpets.
If riders draw too close, the sturdy beast shies:
scared, it hurtles forward, running flat out.
Compact on top, haunches broadly spaced,
it throws its legs with studied nonchalance.
Camels dry out on forced desert marches—
she breaks a sweat that oils her belly girths.
Camels left in shreds, worn out and limping
from deserts crossed, she runs at a crazy pace.

ما ديـر له بيـموعـة الخف مـرقـاع   تجوز لقـطّـاع الفـــيافي زْمـاله
تلفي لابو مـمدوح لاجَتْه الاوجاع   يا عـلّنـا ما عـاد نفـقـد خيـاله

ابوممدوح هو صطّام ابن شعلان.

للمـرجلة عنده مـهاوي ومطلاع   الى قِـصـر عنهـا قــريب الدلاله
يا ضاري الهيشات يا ليث الاسباع   ياللي مِـقـانيـصه دروب الجـلاله
ناس بجـرّتهـم قَنَت جيش واقطـاع   وناس بصـيانيهـم تسـقّـم عيـاله
مـذكورٍ الدنيـا فسـاده بالاطـماع   وانا كـما عـنزٍ تحـــرِّث زواله
انا غـديت وغـدوتي ما لها اسـناع   مـير اننـا المخلوق نـذكـر فعـاله

Her battered hooves can do without patches:
she's built to traverse vast and waterless plains.
Head for Abū Mamdūḥ, may he remain safe;
my eyes miss being comforted by seeing him.

—Abū Mamdūḥ is Ṣaṭṭām ibn Shaʻlān.

Generosity's every way and byway are his:
the opposite of bumblers who lack vision.
Stalker of quarry, lion, king of the jungle!
you spurn all but the mightiest trophies.
His charge's trail teems with bounty hunters:
camels, cattle galore, trays of food handed out.
Proverbially, the world corrupts through greed.
Take me! A goat digging up its slaughter knife![26]
Dumbest thing I did was to depart from you,
yet credit is due when good deeds are done.

يخلّص مشكل خالد وطراد عيال صطّام ابن شعلان عند الضيف والجار

قصيد ابو زويد الى برقت به ما فيه بيت الا تشوف مضرابه ومطلاعه. يعني يقع ١،٠٥
بطّال بلا شي. والله انه ما يقع. بعض هالقصيد هالحين مِتّوالي وقصيد حِلو مير ما يِردْ منه الا رِبعه والا ثِلثه تَلْقى خطاة البيت وارد. وهذاك قصيد متراكب ما يِرِد على نوع بين. وهوكل قصيده يِرِد ما يقول كلمه الا له نوع مُورده عليه.

من عرض قصيده قصيدته اللي خلص به المِشكِل بين الشعلان اللي منه يوم هو ٢،٠٥
يقول

يا صار لك ضيف وخالف على جار　　عــزّ الله انك طـــــــالِعٍ من سواده

يعني قبل ما يِدرَى وش الضيف والجار لا تخانق ضيفك وجارك تبلش بهم ما تَدري تصير مع ايهم. هذي صارت قانون مَنَه وجايّ لشمر ليا حال التاريخ ليا تخانق جارك وضيفك ما تَعْتِرِضهم بتِله الا بالاصلاح تقول ادخلوا على الله ما يصير حيف مع حديهم ولا تِعِد حق حديهم تقول انت يا هذا مع حق وانت يا هذا مع باطل الا كان به مصلحه تقول جزاكم الله خير تهادي بينهم مهاداه والا ما ياجب لك تحشم لواحد على واحد.

He Solves a Dispute between Sons of Ṣaṭṭām ibn Shaʿlān Concerning a Guest and a Neighbor

If you take a closer look at the poetry of Abū Zwayyid, you find that every verse is spot on: it hits the target and pierces through its target. Is any of it faulty? No more than empty words devoid of meaning? No, absolutely not, there are no such verses! Some of today's poetry is prolix, and may sound pleasant, but perhaps no more than a quarter or a third of it has anything to do with real-life situations.[27] With the exception of a few verses, perhaps. That kind of poetry is sound as far as meter and rhyme are concerned, but it bears no discernible relation to reality as we know it. By contrast, Abū Zwayyid's poems are about matters that are very recognizable. Every word is to the point and deals with a real subject. 5.1

One of his poems deals with a dispute between members of the Shaʿlān clan. It features the verse: 5.2

> If your guest quarrels with your neighbor,
> by God, seek to escape, your reputation intact!

Before this verse, people didn't know what to do in such a situation. If a guest and a neighbor under your protection became embroiled in a dispute, you'd find yourself in a quandary. Impossible to decide whose side you were supposed to be on. In his poem, Abū Zwayyid laid down the law for such cases, which was adopted by Shammar. That is, if you find yourself responsible for a neighbor and a guest in your protective embrace and they start to fight one another, abstain from interfering by any means. The only permissible involvement is an offer of good offices to assist them in achieving reconciliation. You may say things like "Turn to God for help!" and express the hope that nothing untoward will happen to either of them. In such a situation, one should refrain from taking a position about the issue at stake or about which of the two is in the right. Do not tell one of them that he is in the right and the other that his arguments do not hold water. Only use expressions conducive to calming tempers, and use encouragements such as "May God give you recompense!" Provide them with moral guidance. It is not your task to show more respect to one or the other.

هذولا بارك الله بايامك الشعلان عيال صطّام ابن شعلان خالد وطْراد صار ٣،٥
بينهم لهم قضيّه. واحدٍ عنده له ضيف طِرقْي شراري وواحدٍ له قصير عْقَلي عقيلي صار ببيته وقام يشري اباعر يوم عقَيل تشري بالبيوت. الشراري باع له جمل على العقيلي شراوه بعشرين نيره يوم النيرايه قبل وعزب الجمل مع اباعره انت يالعقيلي. ويوم وردت البل وبغى يِحول العقيلي تحسّف الشراري قال يالَوعتي انا هذا فحل نياقي وانا ثريني اخطيت على نفسي كيف ابيعه ونياقي ما لهن فحل. يا وخَيّ يالعقيلي هاك دراهمك. الشراري يقوله. قال العقيلي ما هي بيدك انت جمل بِعْته عَلَيّ وعَزَب نصيبي ووَسَمْتُه ودراهمُه هذولي معك ولا يمكن انا شريته بحلالي ولا انطيك اياوه. وعيّ العقيلي عليه والشراري يتلوّع يا لوعتي يا ويلي جْملي. وثار قصير الشراري معه. قال يا عقيلي تنطي الشراري جملَه غصب على شاربك الشراري يبي جمله. قال هذاك معزّب العقيلي لا ما ينطيه غصبٍ عليه.

هات الليف عَدّ الليف وكبرت المشكله بينهم والشعلان كلٍّ قام مع ضيفُه. وهم ٤،٥
يتلازمون هم بينهم خالد وطراد بَغَوا يتذابحون. والكل يفزّع جماعته. واحد ثار مع الشراري والآخر ثار مع العقيلي. وقالوا لا تذابحون يالشعلان يقولونه هم الشعلان لبعضهم لا تذابحون اعْرِضوَه على عوارف العرب ويخلّصونكم ما ندري من هو له الحق ما ندري هالحين هو للقصير والا للضيف. وعجزوا العوارف يخلّصونهم. وهو يعترضهم ابو زويد ويخلّصهم قال قصيدة صلْح بينهم وتقضي به الناس إلى اليوم. خلّصهم بله قصيدة بس ببيت هو اللي خلصهم ببيت واحد والا القصيده نوّعه يم كل نوع.

It happened, may God bless your days, to the Shaʿlān family: a case that involved two sons of Saṭṭām ibn Shaʿlān, Khālid and Ṭrād. One of them hosted a guest, a traveler, a Sharārī, a member of the tribe of al-Sharārāt. The other had extended protection to a neighbor who came to stay for a certain period, an ʿGēlī trader.[28] The ʿGēlī stayed in his own tent and spent his days bargaining with Bedouin over the price of camels he had come to buy, as ʿGēlī tradesmen used to do back then. The Sharārī had sold a male camel to the ʿGēlī for twenty guineas, the currency of the time. The ʿGēlī took the animal to pasture with the other camels he had bought. When the ʿGēlī wrapped up his business and was about to depart, the Sharārī felt remorse at having sold his camel. "Oh my God," he moaned, "this is the stud I need for my she-camels. Why did I wrong myself in this manner? How could I sell it, knowing that my she-camels will lack a stud?" He said, "My dear little brother, ʿGēlī, here is your money. I hand it back to you." The ʿGēlī said, "It is no longer yours. You've sold your camel to me. It has gone to pasture already. I have branded it with my branding iron, and the money is in your pocket. Impossible! I bought it with legal tender and I am not going to return it to you." The ʿGēlī stubbornly refused to go along and the Sharārī writhed with self-loathing and regret: "Oh my, oh my, poor me! Woe to me, my stud camel!" The Sharārī's host and protector felt pity for him and took his side. He told the ʿGēlī, "You must return the camel to the Sharārī whether you like it or not! The man wants his camel back." But the patron of the ʿGēlī replied for him, "No, he is not going to give up anything against his will!" 5.3

Matters descended into futile altercations, then escalated into a tense standoff between the two sides.[29] All of the Shaʿlān rallied to their respective client's cause. A tug-of-war ensued between Khālid and Ṭrād. They threatened to come to blows and cut each other down. Then some of the Shaʿlān tried to cool tempers. "Don't take up arms and fight!" they said. "Submit the case to experts in tribal law and let them find a way and solve the problem for us! We're not in a position to decide who is in the right. We don't know if priority should be given to guest or protected neighbor." As it turned out, neither did the experts in tribal law, who failed to come up with a solution. Then Abū Zwayyid came forward and helped them find a way out of the dilemma. The poem he composed restored the peace and ever since has served as a beacon to follow. This outcome was achieved through his poem; in fact, by just one of its verses—one verse that set the standard for dealing with the issue. The poem's merit is not restricted to that particular verse, however: it touches on a variety of themes. 5.4

يقول ٥،٥

يالله يا عـالم خـفيّـات الاسـرار   عـليـم ما تخـفى عـليك الجحـاده
يا خـالقٍ جـنّـه ويا خـالقٍ نار   ويا خـالق الدنيـا وبيـدك نقـاده
يالله يا رازق رذيلات الاطيـار   بْلا قوت يا مْحيي عيـال الجراده
هن جوف دارٍ وامّهن صوب لَه دار   بمـرامي الدنيـا بعيـدٍ بلاده
ليـا التـفتّ لْشـابيٍ ثاويٍ ثار   عقب الهـزل ينسَف عليها شْداده
تاسـف لقـلبٍ دبّ الايام محـتار   ان قلت هوّد جـاه شيٍّ وازاده
قـلبي غدى لمذلّق الهَيش مِحْضار   سِـدْرٍ بِسـاتينه وطَـلْحٍ بلاده
والعـين كن بموقها سـمّ جِنْزار   كنّـه لِحَى بالعـين ساق الجـراده
خـلاف ذا يا راكبٍ فوق مِذْعـار   ما فوقـه الا قِـرْبَتـه مع شـداده
حمرا على السّنْدا عديـمٍ ومِغْوار   حمـرا شناح وغاربه به سـناده
ركّابها كنَه بظـلٍّ من الغـار   لا هي دِنون ولا بطَبْعـه شـراده
جـدعيـةٍ تـزهى المِيارك والاكوار   ولا عمـرهـا من كثـر الادلاج باده
اذْنـه تشـادي لون كِرنافـة البـار   يا صـار كارهـا الشـتا من بـراده
والعـين حمرا كنّـها جمـرة النـار   تَقْلِب كما المِقباس حَذْر السواده
عـين العـديم الى سمع صيحة الجار   عيٍّ وله عـند المـلازيـم عـاده
يا روّحت فيها زعـانيف وِسْطـار   ومن حـرّ نفسه كنّ فيها عـراده
تلفي لخـالد بلّغـه كِلّ الاخـبار   عليـه يَظْـهرْن السـرايـر وكاده

خالد ابن صطّام الشعلان.

He said: 5.5

God, You are privy to deepest secrets,
matters gainsayers hide in their hearts.[30]
You are the Creator of Paradise and Hell;
Creator of the world; holder of the end-time.
You sustain tiny birds with invisible food, God;
You breathe the breath of life into the locusts' brood,
Deep in the land, the mother in another land:
a distant place, in earth's far-flung regions.
Your gaze resurrects woeful, prostrate mounts;
first they're skin and bones, then saddled and run.
Pity a heart forever perplexed and floundering:
soothing words only make things worse.
My heart is overgrown with prickly bushes:
a garden covered in Christ's-thorn and acacia.
My eyes smart as if treated with poisonous drops;
spiny locust legs are thrust into the retina.
Enough of this, rider of a spirited camel:
loaded with no more than waterskin and saddle,
Reddish-brown, it tackles slopes with panache;
a long-backed red, shoulders steep as bluffs.
Lucky rider lounging as if in a shady cave:
it does not trudge and does not run amok:
A ball of fire saddled with leather cushions,
never worn out like a draft animal at the well;
Conical ears like the spathe of a palm
when wintery cold closes the spathes' sheaths.
Eyes roll, red as a fire's glowing embers,
like kindling flaring in pitch-black darkness;
Brave men's eyes flashing at neighbors' shouts,
fiendish and resolute fighters in close combat;
On the homeward stretch, its gait is haughty:
swollen with pride, it veers left and right.[31]
On arrival, share the news with Khālid!
He has the knack of unraveling secrets.

—Khālid ibn Saṭṭām al-Shaʿlān.

يا صار لك ضيفٍ وخالف على الجار   عـزّ الله انك مــارقٍ من سواده
اصْبِر ولا بالصَبْر لك كصْم تِعْبار   يمـا لك الدنيـا تبــيّن مِـقـاده
ان سـانَعَت دِنْيـاك والحَبْل جرّار   النـفس ما تَنْسَى طواري مــراده
ما من قلوبٍ حيـل كلّه به عشـار   تَلْقَح ولا يِـدْرَى بحَـــــزَة ولاده
تلقى لقـاحه من محاضين الاشرار   اللي بحدّ السيف ياخِـذ سـداده
تلقح رجــالٍ من رجــالٍ بالاشوار   وتْثوّر الفِتْــنات عقب امّـهاده
خَطْو الولد لقــاح قِـدْرٍ الى فـار   أو زاد قبْسونٍ قِـمَعْهـــا زناده
لولا رداة البِصَـر ما صار ما صـار   مــذكورٍ الدنيـا طِـمَعْهـا فسـاده
وان كان درب البَوق بين العرب سـار   طبـيعــةٍ ما هي للاجواد عـــاده
والصِقّ خِــــلِي باركٍ له على دار   والكِذْب سـلَف للجهـامـة وقـاده
دورٍ علينـا اليوم بايـه ومِـنْـغـار   مـع كـل فيٍّ باينٍ بـه بيـــاده
ما يامن الضيف المعزّب ولا الجـار   والنــاس ما يامن بواقـه عهـاده
الذيب لو يطـلع عليـه الطِـلي نار   وصارت عقب ذيك السباعه شراده
رِكِب شـداد الشيخ من كان قـمّار   وخِـلِّي صِليب الراي واهـل السياده
وتْسـلّطـنت ناسٍ هـله ميـّتة نار   ونيــران اجاويـدٍ يحَـرَّث سمـاده
الضـايع اللي ضَـيَّعه والى الاقـدار   ولا تَنْـفَـع الكفّ البخيـل الصمـاده
رِعِيي مع الزقَيميات في قَفْر سِنْجار   أخَيـر عـنـدي من قـعود الزهـاده

If your guest quarrels with your neighbor,
by God, seek to escape, your reputation intact!
Be patient—no one gets blamed for patience—
until time brings counsel and things work out.
Favored by fortune, nicely chugging along,
a soul keeps dreaming and hankers for more.
Virgins none, souls are forever conceiving:
birth after pregnancies of unknown length.[32]
Semen from evil's breeding grounds sparks
fierce fighters bent on settling scores, swords in hand;
Plans hatched and spread by word of mouth
trigger violent outbursts to shatter the peace.
Many boys are bred by a raging cauldron,
or a gun's hammer cocked to ignite the powder.
Calamities are brought about by faulty views:
wisdom tells us that greed breeds corruption.
Dishonesty spreads far and wide, a way of life,
running counter to good and generous nature.
Truth lies prostrate on the way, trampled
beneath falsehood's brazen march.
Fated to live these insipid, rotten times,
we watch them dissipate, fleeting shadows.
Guests and visitors cannot trust their host:
no safety from tricksters' false promises!
Wolves startle, flee at the sight of a lamb;
predators are on the run, fair game for all.
Swindlers are hoisted onto saddles of shaykhs;
stout, steadfast leaders are shunned and spurned.
Cold-hearted good-for-nothings hold sway;
noblemen's hearths gone, ashes strewn.[33]
You're lost if the Almighty so decrees;
a relentless tight-fisted grip brings no gain:
I'd pasture ugly Damascus goats in Sinjār[34]
rather than spend time in miserly company.

يرضي تركيه بنت ابن مهيد يوم تزعل
على صطام ابن شعلان

١،٦ غـرّب صطام ابن شعلان ابو ممدوح ونزل الهيل الهيل جوٍّ ما ادري وين هو. يوم نزل الهيل صطام وهي تجيك السبْعَه والجلاس وفدعان والعنزتين ومن لا تِسّمي وهي تنزل الهيل. يا ما معهم من شمر الا عجلان ابن رمال وخلف ابو زويد. عجلان عنده برّاقات نياقه وضح وابو زويد هلكان ما له الا جمل هلكان بس يطوف بلسانه.

٢،٦ قال عجلان ابو زويد والله يا خلف والله ان مِقطاني للهيل اني مْتَحرّيٍ الشر الصبح او المسا شمر بوقان ويجي شمري ياخذ له رويلي ويجون الروله وياسقونن يقولون رجل الديك تجيب الديك عسى الله يستر بس على نياقي هالقيظ. قال لا انشا الله ما عليك خلاف. قال والله يا خيّ اني زملان. يقول هُم بهالحكي ما دَرْيَو الا يوم ظهر عليهم هكالخيّال من صطام هو هذاك عَمَدْهم عَمْد. قال يابو زويد صادت هذا الخيّال هو هذا جانا اويليييي واحلالاة يانياقي والله ان يُوخَذَن يقال انْهج هات اللي عند الشمري ابن عمّك. قال ابو زويد يا مِنّ الارشية تِشابكن انت اسكِت ما هي لك الدّعوى خَلّه يمّي. جاهم رجّال صطام قال يقول الشيخ تجي يا عجلان انت وابو زويد يا الله. ارا ولد بَرْغَش وكاد هذي هي. يقوله عجلان. يوم جَوا صطام يا مْتَلَصّص قايل كذا. وهم يقعدون الشمامرة.

He Comforts Turkiyyah, Daughter of Ibn Mhēd, When She Quarreled with Ṣaṭṭām ibn Shaʿlān

Ṣaṭṭām ibn Shaʿlān, the father of Mamdūḥ, migrated in a westerly direction and set up camp in al-Hēl, a vast expanse of flat land, I don't know where exactly. As soon as he arrived, he received visitors from the Sbaʿah, Fidʿān, and both divisions of ʿAnazah: Bishr and al-Jlās. All of them flocked to see him in al-Hēl. The only visitors from Shammar were ʿAjlān ibn Rmāl and Khalaf Abū Zwayyid. ʿAjlān came with his famous herd of white camels, called Barrāgāt. Abū Zwayyid was hard up: the sum total of his possessions was one male camel. Destitute, he made a living as a conversationalist, entertaining companies with his stories and verses. 6.1

ʿAjlān said, "Abū Zwayyid! Khalaf! By God, I don't feel at ease staying here in al-Hēl. Morning and evening I spend in trepidation, expecting someone to spring a bad surprise on us at any moment. Our fellow tribesmen of Shammar are a treacherous lot. A Shammarī may strike up a friendship with a Rwēlī with the aim of despoiling and blackmailing me.[35] As they say, 'Get hold of the rooster's leg and you'll haul in the bird whole.' Please God, spare my camels for as long as we are to stay here this summer!" "Nothing untoward will happen," said Abū Zwayyid. But ʿAjlān moaned, "Dear brother, I am so afraid!" As they spoke, a horseman came riding straight at them from the direction of Ṣaṭṭām's camp. "Abū Zwayyid!" ʿAjlān cried. "You see, didn't I tell you![36] There you are, the horseman is heading for us! Oh my God, what will become of us! Oh, what is going to happen to these camels, my sweeties? Oh my God, what if they're stolen, oh no, please no! For sure that rider was told, 'Get going, bring the camels of that kinsman of yours, that Shammarī!'" Abū Zwayyid told him to calm down: "When things get knotty, best to shut up. It's none of your business. Let me deal with it."[37] Ṣaṭṭām's man reined in his horse and said, "The shaykh asks you to call on him: you, ʿAjlān, and Abū Zwayyid as well. Go quickly!" "I am the son of Barghash![38] Now it's going to happen!" ʿAjlān said. They found Ṣaṭṭām in a sour mood and preoccupied. Already, ʿAjlān saw his worst fears confirmed. The two Shammar visitors sat down. 6.2

يا صطّام حريمه ثلاث حريم صطّام وحده تركيه بنت ابن مهيد مصوّت بالعشا ٣،٦
وبنت ابن سمير والثالثه جوزا منهوبه بنتٍ للمشهور من الشعلان بنت لفهد ابن
شعلان من الشيابه. كانوا الشيابه ذابحين رجّال من الصطّام وخلف على صطّام
بنته وجوزه اياوه. أثاري تركيه طَحِت عَنُه وراحت عند عبد من عبيد الشعلان
يسمى ابو دخانين دخان الصاج ودخان القهوه. قال ابن شعلان عجلان يا خوي تركيه
أم ممدوح طَحَه (= طحت) البارحه مغتاظة عليّه وابيك تردّها يمّ وغدانها اللي امتلت
افامهم من هالرقّه. قال يا صطام والله انا الرمال مِتّمَدِشْرِينٍ بي وليا رديت المرة الا
يخليه رجلَه بي نوح الا غيره باللي انت تقول. قال الله اجل انت يابو زويد ردها. قال
اردّه. أنت عَنزيٍ خبل كبر قلبك تجمّعن هاللي مثل خيل الصحابة عندك وكبر راسك
على بنت ابن مهيد وطَرَدْتَه من بيتك هالحين حنا نحسب ان عندك ذبيحة بني نَغسِل
ايدينا وناكِل والا الى صار تركيه رِدَّه انت أو يرده صِقَر وش اردَّه لُه. يردّه اللي جابه
من ابن مهيد ساق فِرسَين وعشر رَحَلٍ به. قال عاد ابوك غادي جِداك شمري ليه
ما عَلّمتَن يوم الكلام يِمَدِينن يوم هي بالبيت. هالحين انا يالاقي خير الى جيتها ذالٍّ
تلغي عليّه وذال ازعل واطلّقها وانا اغليها ما وِدّي اطلّقها. قال بس اسكِت ثاري ما
هو على غدا ولحم هِبيّت علومك.

Ṣaṭṭām had three wives. One was Turkiyyah, daughter of Ibn Mhēd, the shaykh nicknamed "Supper Host" because he was in the habit of inviting all and sundry to partake of his dinner.[39] There was a daughter of Ibn Smēr. The third wife was Jōzā Manhūbah, daughter of a well-known kinsman of the Shaʿlān, Fahd ibn Shaʿlān of the Shiyābah branch.[40] Someone of the Shiyābah had killed a man of the Ṣaṭṭām branch and in compensation ceded his daughter Jōzā to Saṭṭām. It so happened that Turkiyyah had left Ṣaṭṭām in a fit of anger. She was furious with him and went to stay with one of the slaves of the Shaʿlān clan, a man called Abū Dakhkhānēn, "Man of Two Smokestacks": one fire for baking bread and the other for the coffeepots.[41] Ibn Shaʿlān said, "ʿAjlān, my dear, Turkiyyah, the mother of my son Mamdūḥ, became angry with me and flounced out of here yesterday, mad as hell. I want you to go over to her place and persuade her to return to her children, who are stuffing their mouths with grit." "Honest to God, Ṣaṭṭām," ʿAjlān said, "my tribe of the Rmāl regards me as a person who brings bad luck, and my own folk don't want me to take part in sensitive missions. If I were to succeed in convincing a woman to rejoin her husband, he'd be sure to leave her; then woe to me. For any other task, I am at your beck and call." Ṣaṭṭām said, "Well, then it falls to you, Abū Zwayyid, to bring her back to me." "Me return her to you? Where did you get that silly idea, you ʿAnazī? Did things go to your head? You collected this stable of pedigree fillies, like the mares of the Prophet's companions, and grew so conceited that you offended the daughter of Ibn Mhēd and made her flee your home. We came to you thinking you'd invite us to a roast. We thought no more was expected of us than washing our hands and eating. As for Turkiyyah, go and fetch her yourself. Let Hell get her! Why should I be the one to do it? That is a job for the one who brought her from Ibn Mhēd in the first place, the man who paid a bride-price of two mares and ten riding camels for her." Taken aback, Ṣaṭṭām said, "What good are you to me then, Shammarī? Why didn't you give me this advice earlier, when she was still with me and I could have put it to good use? Now, even if I find her amenable to my arguments, I'm afraid she'll give me a tongue-lashing. That being the case, I fear I'll get mad and divorce her in a fit of anger, though I truly love her and do not want to be separated from her." "You'd better keep quiet," Abū Zwayyid said. "Since you did not regale us with a roast luncheon, your reputation has been dealt a serious blow." 6.3

٤،٦ قال لعبده انهج صوّت لعنّاد خَلّه يجي عبدٍ له. يوم جا العبد قال له انهج انهج رِد عَمّتك. يقول ايتك يا عناد يقول يوم طلع يقول يا مير جالسه بنت تركي ابن مهيد لحريم السّبَعَة لابسة مِزَوِيّنْها وتحكي والحريم اكثر من الرجال جالسة عنده. قالت وشو هالخيّال. ايه معروف هذا عناد لعن الله أبوك يا ثِمَن الملح. قال يا عمّه. قالت وش ترّيد. قال شوفي. قالت اقول اِلْحَق الحق انا ما أُوحِيك. يقول وتاخِذ له رضمة وهي تصّبِحُه من هانا. يوم صبحته يا مار الدم مثل ذيل الشقرا. قال امّمّمّه وهو يصبح بالقاع. يوم جا صطام يا قولته عوذا وش علمك. هي صامِخْتك. ار العن الله اَبوك يا تركيه الله الله وش الحيله.

٥،٦ قال صوّت لعجب. -عجب صانع للرشيد اول وفارس- قال انهج يا عجب يم ّتركيه رِدّها. قال والله ما انا رادّه. قال ليه. قال كود تَعَلِّمن بالله مِطِنّيه وشو علشان اني اجيها بْعِلم وارادّه واغصّبه. قال اللي مطنيها سوالف ما اني معلّمك ابها. قال كان ما انت معلمن اجل ردها انت. قال اللي مزعلها البارحه عطيت قطنه قطنه بنت ابن سمير عطيت قطنه لي درَيهمات مْتسَلِّفهن منها ورديتهن عليها وتقول قطنه اغلى مني ليه تعطيها الدراهم وزَعَلت ونْهَجت. قال زين تعطيه دراهم عاد يا جَيّه (= جت) ترضّاه. قال ما نْخَالف. قال الا نخالف قل اي بالله وارِدّه لك. قال اعطيها. وهو يجيك عجب على الفرس. قالت ايه بعد هذا عجب لعن الله أبوك وصطام معك. وهو يلكد الفرس عليه ويَلْهَرَه بالشَلْفا قال امشي اركبي وشو هالحين اللي مِطّنيك. يا عجب يلعن الله أبوك خلّني خلّني. قال اقول تمشين وانتي ما تشوفين الجادّه وشّو اللي مطنيك. قالت البارحه عطى قطنه دراهم وانا ما عطاني. قال وانتي يعطيك بس امشي. قالت افتلهن بشاربك. قال امشي والدراهم تجيك. يوم راعى صطام والى هذولا هم جايين.

Ṣaṭṭām told his slave to call another slave: "Go and get ʿAnnād!" and ordered him: "Away at once, bring your mistress back to me! Make for her place quickly, ʿAnnād! Hurry up about it!" ʿAnnād left and found the daughter of Ibn Mhēd dressed in a body-length abaya seated and chatting with her lady friends of the Sbaʿah tribe, a circle even bigger than the men's.[42] "Who comes riding to us?" she exclaimed. "Ah, I see, it's ʿAnnād. God curse your father, you piece of dirt!"[43] "Please, mistress!" he said. "What is it you want from me?" she said. "Well, you see . . ." He hesitated. "Come here, draw closer, I can't hear you!" she said. As he spoke, she picked up a rock and smashed it on his head. Blood spurted from him like the thick tail of a sorrel mare. "Ow, ow, ow!" he cried and slumped to the ground. When Ṣaṭṭām saw him on his return, he cried, "Good grief! What happened to you? She bashed you? A curse on you, Turkiyyah! Good heavens! What will do the trick when it comes to her?" 6.4

"Call ʿAjab!" said Ṣaṭṭām. ʿAjab was a blacksmith who had worked for the Ibn Rashīd rulers and enjoyed renown as a warrior on horseback. "Go find Turkiyyah and bring her back!" he ordered ʿAjab. "No," he said, "I am not going to do that." "Why not?" "First you must tell me what made her so mad at you. I cannot force her to come back without knowing what the trouble is." "I'm not going to tell you what put her into a rage." "In that case, it's up to you. Go yourself!" "All right then. She became mad at me yesterday because I gave money to Giṭnah, the daughter of Ibn Smēr: a sum of money that I had borrowed from her and paid back. She said, 'Why do you give her money? Do you care more about Giṭnah than me?' She upset me, then walked out on me." "Right," he said. "If she does come, will you mollify her by giving her money too?" "No problem," he said. "There is a problem. Say, 'Yes, by God, I will give her money.' Only then will I go to fetch her." "I will give it to her." ʿAjab rode off on his mare. "Here we go again," she muttered. "This time it is ʿAjab. God's curse on your father and Ṣaṭṭām as well." He had his mare step up to her and poked at her with his lance. "Come on! Ride with me!" he said. "Why are you so outraged?" "Damn you, ʿAjab, leave me alone! Get away with you!" "I told you to move or else I will make you go willy-nilly, by force.[44] Why are you so cross?" She said, "Yesterday he gave money to Giṭnah and he didn't give me anything." "He will make you a present as well," he said. "Just start moving!" "Twist the promise into your mustache!" she said.[45] "Just go!" he said. "The money will come your way." 6.5

فِرِح قال عدّلوا الفراش عدلوا الفرش. ابو زويد وعجلان على مقعدهم. يوم اسْفَهَل صطام وهي حَوَّلَت ونِصَت المحرم. قال هات الدراهم. قال يا رجال امر الله من سعه باكر اعطيها وانا واياه ما نتخالف. قال لا تْقَطّع الجوادّ يا صطام عط المره الفلوس رضاوتَه. يا زْناتي هو ملعون الابو عجب وهو ينهض الشلفا على صطام قال أرْوِج (= أسرع) عَطَه رضاوِتَه والله يان ما عطيته اني هالساعه لاركّبَه وانكّسَه للمكان اللي هي جت منه. ويلتفت صطام والى ما عنده من العبيد احد. وهو يروغ ناحر الصندوق يبي يطلع الفلوس يا ضارب الصندوق انت يا عجب يا هاشمه. قال تعالي يا تركيه دُوك الدراهم. بغى يجفرني بالشلفا لعن الله ابوك يالخضيري. ٦،٦

وهو يجيك ابو زويد ويلوذ على تركيه بالبيت قال سلام عليك يا تركيه. قالت يا هلا بابو زويد. قال البيت غدى ربيع ونوّار يوم طبيتيه ويا غاب سرور ما بالبيت نور يا هلا يا هلا بهالتِيَّه يا هلا والله بام ممدوح. قالت الا وِيك مير وش بخاطرك. قال والله ما بخاطري الا شوفتك وغلاك. يقول الدراهم بِمِكْنِحْتَه. قال ابو زويد يترضاه زود ٧،٦

١
قـالوا تشير وقلت انا زاد ما اشـير　　عيبٍ على من جاب شوره ولا جاز
خيل الصحابـة ربّطن بالجواخـير　　اصـايل من حال صنديد الافـراز

الجاخور حْلاق حديد تربط به الخيل ويعلقون لهن بهن.

تَخَبَّـتْن بالطبـع واقفن مـناكير　　يضـربن من دار العوافي بالاجواز
الاوله ما جت عـلى نيـّة الخـير　　ولا صاده الوكري خذه حِرّمن باز

ما جت على نية الخير لأن فهد ذبح حدى رجاجيل صطّام وخلف عليه بالانثى.

When Ṣaṭṭām saw them approaching, he was overjoyed. "Ready the nuptial bed!" he shouted, and the servants laid out the bed neat and tidy. From where they were seated, Abū Zwayyid and ʿAjlān watched, and saw Ṣaṭṭām's euphoria as she alighted and headed for the women's quarters. "Bring the money!" ʿAjab said. "Take it easy, man!" Ṣaṭṭām replied. "In God's good time. I will give it to her tomorrow, when we once again see eye to eye on things." "Don't play such risky games, Ṣaṭṭām!" he warned.[46] "Give her the money you promised to assuage her." He was a damned tough fellow, ʿAjab. He raised his lance and let it hover over Ṣaṭṭām's head. "Give her the indemnities right away, or else I will take her back to the place I made her come from!" Ṣaṭṭām looked around and noticed that none of his slaves was present. He sauntered toward his chest of valuables to scoop up some money. But before he could do so, up came ʿAjab and with one blow of his lance shattered the strongbox. Saṭṭām called to Turkiyyah: "Come, the money is here: it is yours to take! He was about to stab me with his lance." And cursing ʿAjab, he said, "Damn your father, you lowlife!"[47] 6.6

Abū Zwayyid sidled over to Turkiyyah's quarters: "Good day. Peace on you, Turkiyyah!" "Welcome to you, Abū Zwayyid!" "Spring came to this dwelling and burst into flower when you set foot in it," he gushed. "When bliss departs, darkness comes. Welcome, welcome! Hail to this arrival! Cheers for the mother of Mamdūḥ!" "Well, the same goes for you," she replied. "Tell me, what do you have in mind?" "Nothing in particular. All I wished for is to see you, such a highly valued person." He obliquely referred to the money given to her, safely stashed away in the inside pocket of her robe. Then Abū Zwayyid gave her even greater satisfaction by reciting these verses: 6.7

They asked for counsel but I stopped counseling: *1*
 if my counsel falls flat, they'll stick it to me.
Shackled mares of the Prophet's companions,
 pedigree fillies sired by stout and noble steeds.

—*Al-jākhūr* are the irons in which the feet of horses are shackled.

Foul-tempered and reluctant, they were steered away
 at a gallop from their carefree homes.[48]
The first did not come of her own volition:
 not bagged by a misfit, she's a falcon's prey.

—She did not come of her own accord, but rather because Fahd had killed someone from Ṣaṭṭām's retinue and made up for it by ceding this girl.

والثانيه بنت الشيوخ المناعير — اللي لهم عند المظاهير مِلكاز
والثالثه يرفى خماله دميثير — ام السعود اللي مع الخيل مِعْناز
ابوَه يصوّت بالعشا بالمعاسير — نفل بتصويت العشا كلّ عنّاز
يا حل بالفرسان ضرب وتجير — صُفْرٍ على عُوده ونارٍ على قاز

قالت دونك دراهم صطام. وتكبّهن بشليله. يا قولة صطام ووه ووه وِخّذتي ٨،٦
يا حَذّره يا ملعونه. قال صوّت للعبد خله يجيب الجمل. يوم جاب الجمل قال حطّوا عليه حمل هالحنطة وهالحاف لابو زويد. قالت تركيه الى خلصت يا راع الجمل اِرْوج جاي. قالت حطّ عليه بعد هالشقاق وهالقطيفه. كل هذا شَرْطٍ لابو زويد على قصيدته. يقول يا قولة عجلان يا بعد حيي يابو زويد عَطَن لي دراهم انا والله ابي احدّر ولا اخبر الريال. قال بِع من نياقك ياخوي. قال لا يابعد حيي هالحين هالغناة اغتنيت وانت قاعد وانا يابس ريقي من الصبح. قال يا شيخ دونك عشرين هالنيرة واذِلف.

The second was born to an intrepid shaykh,
fierce defender of heavily laden camel trains.
The third mends his defects, a fabled mare:
auspicious, she anchors cavalry in combat;[49]
In times of dearth, her father's call to dinner
reaches the ears of ʿAnazah far and wide;
In the melee of thrusting and smiting knights,
his fiery panache blazes a bloody trail.[50]

6.8 "Here, Ṣaṭṭām's money is yours!" she said, and she poured the coins into the fold of the long shirt Abū Zwayyid held up to her. Ṣaṭṭām moaned, "Woe, woe to me! The caravan's treasure has been pilfered! Cursed lady!" He called a slave and told him to load a camel with wheat and bedding for Abū Zwayyid. "When you're done, come to me at once," Turkiyyah instructed the man who attended to the camel. "I want you to add these rolls of textile and small woolen carpets to the load." She did so in appreciation of Abū Zwayyid's poem. ʿAjlān, who had been an onlooker, ventured a request: "My dearest Abū Zwayyid, give me some of that money. I need to go to the markets in Iraq but I'm broke." "Why don't you sell some of your camels, brother?" Abu Zwayyid suggested. "You know you're dearer to me than I am to myself.[51] This windfall has come your way, and I did a lot of work this morning," pleaded ʿAjlān.[52] "All right," said Abū Zwayyid, "take these twenty pounds and off you go!"

يـرضي نوره بنت ابن مهـيد يوم تزعـل على فـهد ابن هذالـــ

١٠٧ صار ابو زويد عند فهد ابن هذال. سَيّر عليه هكالليله يبي يتَعَلّل عنده على مَلوَى العاده شاف ان خاطر الشيخ متكدِّر وحجاجه مِنعَقِد. هاه الامر. وش مَكدّرٍ خاطرك يا شيخ. قال والله نوره طامح – نوره زوجة الشيخ بنت ابن مهيد والى بنت شيخ الى نَهَجَت ما تَرَد الا كود ترجِع هي بكيفَه – والله من نهجَتَه ما انا طيب يابو دخيل. وهو ياخذ عصاوه ابو زويد وهو ينَحَر بيتَه. يوم اقبل عليه عرفتُه وهي تاخذ هكالشداد وهي تْقَلّطه له. قالت فت فت يا عم ارتَك تريّح على هالشداد. تقول له يا عَمّي هو كبير سِنّ وهي بنت. قال يا نوره انا والله ما انا قاعد بس انا ارَكّبت لي ذلول ووصّفته عليك وْودّي تَسْمَعِين اللي قلت قبل تفرّقنا الدنيا.

٢٠٧ قالت مير مِدّ وافْلح هات اللي عندك

راكب اللي ما بعد مثلها اركاب   طويلة الساقين مثل الزرافه
مالودةٍ عند الشرارات بِضَراب   وابوَه من التيه الوحايش حيافه
بين الرباعيه عسافه والانياب   حايل ليا ما زيّن الله عسافه
يا صوقَعن مع سهلةٍ تقل عيّاب   تاطا على مثل الشواشا خفافه
تِسْهم على الممشى كما يِسهَم الداب   نَفّت ببرطمها وبالذيل سافه

How He Obtained Satisfaction for Nūrah, Daughter of Ibn Mhēd, When She Quarreled with Fahd ibn Hadhdhāl

One night, Abū Zwayyid called on Fahd ibn Hadhdhāl for the pleasure of taking part in his circle's conversation, as was the custom.[53] He at once noticed that the shaykh was preoccupied and wore a frown. What was the matter? "What's troubling you, shaykh?" "Well, Nūrah is vexed with me and keeps her distance,"[54] meaning Nūrah, his wife, the daughter of Ibn Mhēd. If the daughter of a shaykh walks out on her husband, she doesn't return until she feels like it. She only comes of her own volition. "You know, Abū Dikhīl, from the moment she stormed out in a huff I've been out of sorts," he continued. Abū Zwayyid took his cane and walked toward her tent. She knew what his visit was about the moment she saw him approaching. She picked up a camel saddle and put it down for him to use as an armrest and invited him to enter and take a seat on the carpet. "Come, come, Uncle dear, make yourself comfortable and recline on the saddle!" She called him "Uncle dear" because he was advanced in years and she was still a girl. "Listen, Nūrah," he said, "I haven't come to sit and chat with you. I've readied a fast camel that I would like to describe to you. I thought it would be nice to let you hear what I have to say on the subject before we go our separate ways." 7.1

"Go ahead and show me what you're capable of," she said.[55] "Let me hear it." 7.2

A rider perched on a peerless camel,
towering on giraffe-like legs,
Born from a mother raised at al-Sharārāt,
A father stolen from al-Tīh—free-roaming herds.
Six years old, fully grown, trained to perfection,
spared from pregnancy, God's favored racer.
When others stagger across wastes like invalids,
her smooth, rounded hooves go at a sprightly step.[56]
She zips over the ground, winding like a snake,
lower lip curled down, and sweeping her tail.

يطماه طمي ويرخي الرجل بادّاب   مثل الطموح ليا تزاود عيافه
يا شافت السندا يجي مشيَه اوثاب   عين العديم اللي يشوف الجنافه

العديم الشجاع الجنافه الخطا.

وليا ركبها الشيخ والغزو كسّاب   وحكوا بمرواح الاهل والكيافه
كثيرهم يلفي على له تقل داب   هرجاته اقشر من وِشيش الحظافه

الحظف الداب.

الصبح لجّاته تقل ذيب وكلاب   والذيب منهم خاطفٍ له خطافه
يا جابت السايه تِقِل مشي دولاب   حسّه طويل ولا تهاب القنافه

السايه النميمه. القنافه العيب.

ساقه طويل ومَنكبه تقل مِصْلاب   طويلة النسنوس بيها انهدافه
والشيخ يلفي عند ويضاح الانياب   بنت الشيوخ اللي تَلاعج رهافه
شيخ الشيوخ اللي خوالهُ لُه انساب   عَطُوه نوره من صخاهم مَرافه

المهيد خوال ابن هذال.

يا شِبه وضحا به دباديب وجْناب   اللي يُحَطّ بها الجرس والكتافه
عمّال وِبرته كن به ورس وخضاب   يَتْلِنّها حيلٍ تِطرّق شعافه
ريميّةٍ يَتْلِنّها خِضّع الارقاب   عنود ممشاها بروس الشرافه
زولَه كما غُصْنٍ رِجوحٍ ليا ساب   اللي يجّل بالهبوب انتسافه
ما شِفْت نوره عند قومٍ ولا اصحاب   ولا قيل لي رجلٍ مع الناس شافه

Wary of violent surges, the rider scarcely brushes his foot,[57]
like a man eager not to provoke his seething wife.
Uphill stretches serve to make her run faster still,
eyes fiery like a hero's, rushing to right a wrong.

—*Al-ʿadīm* is a hero and *al-jnāfah* is a wrong.

If a shaykh's raiding group celebrates a rich haul,
rave on about the adulation awaiting them at home,
Welcome for some is a wife like a hissing snake:
fangs awash in venom, portent of doom;

—*Al-ḥaẓf* means snake.

Into a mad ruckus of wolves and dogs at first light,
wolves ruthlessly maneuvering to catch a prey.
Like a waterwheel her tongue spews evil gossip;
unashamed, she yells and shouts with abandon;

—*Al-sāyah* is evil gossip and *al-gnāfah* means a shameful act.

Legs long and spindly, bony shoulders like hangers,
a hollow back tapering to scrawny haunches.
Sweet smiles of a dazzling beauty await the chief,
the pearly, chiseled teeth of a shaykh's daughter:
Shaykh of shaykhs, from the mother's side,
given Nūrah in marriage—a friendly gesture.

—Al-Mhēd is the family of Ibn Hadhdhāl's father-in-law.

A white camel caparisoned with colorful ribbons;
neck and shoulders graced by bell and tasseled rug.[58]
Insouciant, she strides in scented fur dyed yellow;
breezes stir the longhaired humps of her cortege:
Gazelles of the sands with their supple-necked retinue,[59]
leading doe, watchful eye trained on distant rims;
She's a fresh stalk, slightly bent, with juicy moisture,
when swayed by playful puffs of wind.
Never did I see Nūrah's like among kin or friends,
or ever hear of her equal from anyone.[60]

وهو يدنّق على راسَه قال انا طالبك يا بنت ابن مهيد يوم جَلَبْت جاهي ووجاهي ٣٠٧
عليك اليوم انك تَنَكِسين لابن هذّال. قالت والله يابو دخيل لو تقول طَبّجي بنار لاطَبّح به لكن بس اصبر شوين ابرّسِل هالعبد لهم وهالحين اجيك. وصّي العبد قالت رح للشيخ ابن هذال قولةٍ كان تبي نوره ترجع لك فهي تبي الفرس الفلانية والذلول زمّالته تُحمّل قماش وكِسْوه وارزاق وتنوّخ عند بيت ابو زويد وتعطيه زود عليهن بيت وقطيفه. ابن هذال يوم جاوه العبد قال لو تبي عشر من الخيل وزمالتهن لكن قولةٍ له بس تجي لبيتَه حنا ما ندري وشّي تبي تحمّل على الذلول. وهي تجي تِبارى هي ابو زويد وصَلحَوا. عاد يقول ابو زويد

يا ناشـد عـني بخـير وعوافي   متكيّف ومشروب لعبة على سيل

لعبة نويقة له.

بَنَت لنـا بيتٍ كبـيرٍ يشـافي   وقطـيفةٍ من بنت ريف المراميل

By way of rounding off his recitation, he planted a kiss on top of her head: "May I ask you for a favor, daughter of Ibn Mhēd, now that I've put my good name on the line with my presence here in the hope that you'll be persuaded to return to Ibn Hadhdhāl." "I swear by God, Abū Dikhīl," she said, "that even if you asked me to jump into a fire I'd do so without a second's hesitation. Just bear with me a little until I have sent this slave to them. I'll come back to you straightaway." She instructed the slave: "Go to Shaykh Ibn Hadhdhāl and tell him that if he wants Nūrah to return to him, he should give her the mare named such and such, accompanied by a riding camel carrying textiles, clothing, and provisions, and have the camel kneel at the tent of Abū Zwayyid. On top of that, give him a tent and bed covering." After hearing out the slave, Ibn Hadhdhāl said, "No matter! I'd agree even if she demanded ten horses with their complement of pack camels. But have her come home. We don't know which goods she wants to load on the camel." So she came, with Abū Zwayyid in tow, and they made up. Abū Zwayyid rejoiced and sang: 7.3

If you're wondering, my camel mount and I are fine,
Liʿbah and I: smug, sated, quenched.

—Liʿbah is a camel of his.

She built us a big and imposing house,
carpeted by one who provides for the penniless.

ابن مشهور يرجع ذلول ابو زويـد
عليه يوم ياخـذه ابن مُعَبْهل

خلف ابو زويد اخذ ذلوله ابن معبهل من الروله وعيّ بَه و رجّعه له واحد من المشهور ١٠٨
عاد يقول

يا راكبٍ حـمرا طفوحٍ من النـضا   عوصـا هميمٍ كالظليم الهـاربـه
لا يلحقـه المطـلب الى روّحت بـه   حمـرا صهـاة اللون مرفوع غـاربـه
ما عليـه الا قِـرْبَتـه مع زَهـابـه   واربع ظَـلافٍ في حـباله كاربـه
عليه غـلامٍ ما يكِـلّ من السَـرى   دِليـل عَيراتٍ مع رهاره سـاربـه
كم عِـقْـلةٍ دَوّج عليها ودوّجـه   وكم بِلّ قوم لافهـا من مـعـازبـه
لى واذلولي حـايـلٍ حيّـلوا بَـه   عند ابن معَبْهل مجنّف الحقّ عاتبـه
راجيك كما رَجـاي عودٍ للصـبا   الله يلومـه عـدّ رملٍ يهـال بـه
عيّ عليها واذلق السـيف دونهـا   لى وابي الا مـا حسيبي جـايبـه
خـطو الولد ثبّور بارد هـــقوه   طليب الردى والصدا فوق شاربـه
الله يلوم لحيـتي مـا زِبنَت غيـره   اللي الى صـار الجنف يستلاذ بـه
مثل اخو ربـدا راعي الجود والظفـر   اخو ربـــدا هو ذرا من اتقى بـه

اخو ربدا ابن مشهور.

صغير سن ولا هو صغيرٍ الى عدى   كبيرٍ الى جت بالامور المـتواربـه

Abū Zwayyid's Camel, Stolen by Ibn Mʿabhal, Is Returned to Him by Ibn Mashhūr

Abū Zwayyid's camel was forcibly taken by Ibn Mʿabhal of the Rwalah tribe, who stubbornly refused to return it. In the end, he recovered his animal through the intercession of a member of the Ibn Mashhūr branch of the same tribe. In gratitude, Abū Zwayyid composed these verses:[61] 8.1

Hey, rider of a red-hued thoroughbred camel:
hardy, swift as an ostrich racing for escape,
She outstrips pursuers when romping home—
Her fur light reddish-brown, tall in the shoulders,
Loaded with a waterskin and a provisions bag, nothing more,
the wood saddle's crosspiece ropes tied taut.
A tough youngster spurs her on, all night long,
inured to brutal rides through simmering plains.
A regular at hidden waterholes,
he snatches enemy camels from distant pastures.
I weep for my mount, poached through trickery
by Ibn Mʿabhal—a grave breach of the honor code.
Just as graybeards crave for youth, I entreated in vain:
"God's censures on him as often as the sands cave in!"
Obstinate in refusal, he drew his sword on me:
woe to me! And yet, I submit to God's decree.
One cannot pin one's hopes on a callous lout,
face smeared with soot from his evildoings.
Shame on me for not seeking help from others,[62]
saviors of poor devils cast about by villainy:
A courageous gentleman such as Rabdā's brother:
Rabdā's brother shields seekers of his protection.

—The brother of Rabdā is Ibn Mashhūr.

Young, yet a formidable and seasoned fighter,
most redoubtable when circumstances dictate.

قصايده بخناقة جماعته النبهان بينهم

١،٩ ابو زويد يسعى بالزين بين ربعه قبيلة النبهان. يوم كان عند الشعلان جاوه هكالواحد طِرقي قال ما عيّنت عربانا وشلونهم. قال والله ربعك طيبين ان سلموا من لهم سويلفه ان سلموا من شرٍّ يصير بينهم فهم مربّعين. تشاقّوا حصل خلاف بين آل رخيص وآل ضَوّ تغابشوا على لهم ناقه وتواصلوا الاقصى عليه. ابن رخيص عنده جار من اهل الجزيره حرَيري سميرّ السمدان الحريري من شمر هل الجزيره. جا الجار هذا وغزى مع الغزو وتغابشوا هو وحدى آل ضو لهم ناقه يوم غْباشة البدو بينهم يتغابشون البل وتغابش هو وايا الضوّيّ عْبيْد على ناقة رويليه جت من الروله. كل واحد يقول للثاني انا طقّيت الناقة قبلك. الجار يقول هذي ناقة لي انا كسبته والضوّيّ يقول لا ناقةٍ لي انا انا اللي كسبته. تشاكَلَوا عليه. يوم الفَوا قالوا ما لكم الا تِطالِبون انحروا شمر تطالبوا عليه. ويتوَلّجه الذرفي ابن شنينان على هكالفرس واَصِلَقه ادِخَلَه عن الرخيص. وتطالبوا وافلجه انت يالضوي فلج سمير الحريري.

٢،٩ قال ابن رخيص الجار ما يْطالَب ياخذ ناقته بلا طَلابه. هذا مكفوف يد قصير وناقة قصيري ما امشي به الحق. قالوا اذكر الله يابن رخيص الطلابة قانون بين العرب. قال

His Poems on a Dispute among Members of His Tribal Group of the Nabhān

Abū Zwayyid always strove to foster harmony among his fellow tribesmen of al-Nabhān. When he was a guest of the Shaʿlān, a traveler arrived and he questioned him: "Did you see my people? How are they doing?" "To be honest, your kinsmen are fine as long as nothing untoward happens and as long as they don't fall out with one another while on the spring pastures." They had become embroiled in bickering and trouble had erupted between Āl Rakhīṣ and Āl Ḍaww.[63] They quarreled over a she-camel and the dispute threatened to spiral out of control. Ibn Rakhīṣ had a neighbor under his protection, a Ḥrērī tribesman from Mesopotamia, Smayyir al-Simdān al-Ḥrērī of the Shammar confederation's tribesmen in Mesopotamia. This neighbor joined a raiding party and had a run-in with a fellow raider of Āl Ḍaww about a she-camel both claimed as booty. At that time, it was not uncommon for Bedouin to fight over spoils. He and the Ḍawwī picked a fight about a she-camel robbed from a tribesman of the Rwalah. Each of them claimed to have been first to tap the camel with his riding stick. "This is my she-camel, and I take possession of her!" said the neighbor. "No way," said the Ḍawwī. "This camel is mine and I will not let anyone else lay hands on her!" They had a heated argument over the animal. On their return, they were told to submit to arbitration. They were advised to seek out an arbiter from among the Shammar tribes and make their case to him. Ibn Shnīnān, a horseman of the Dhirfān clan of Shammar's Zmēl branch, trotted behind the she-camel, keeping a watchful eye on her as he drove her swiftly in the desired direction. He made sure to give Ibn Rakhīṣ a wide berth. The claimants submitted the dispute to a competent interpreter of tribal law. The Ḍawwī won and was awarded the camel, and Smayyir al-Ḥrērī lost. 9.1

Ibn Rakhīṣ said, "There is no need for him to litigate his claim. The camel is his whatever the case, without litigation. As our protected neighbor, he doesn't have to prove anything.[64] Our customary law does not apply to my neighbor." 9.2

"In God's name, Ibn Rakhīṣ! Litigation is the way people settle disputes!" they exclaimed.

قانون بين الرفاقة بينهم اما الجار ما يطالب بتّلِه لِله انه يطالب. قالوا وش بزعمك. قال بزعمي ياخذ ناقته بلا طلابه. وتزاودوا بينهم النبهان هل الجراف الضو والرخيص. قالوا الضو ما تحصل الناقه. قال زاد ما تحصل الوعد باكر. ورحل الصبح يبي ينزل على الضو بسبة ناقة قصيره. واشالوا الضو وزبنوا على لهم عرب غيرهم ودْخَلَوا عليهم. قالوا حنا داخلين بكم عن ابن رخيص ابن رخيص يبينا نتذابح على كيس ناقه. قالوا العرب وش المشكل. قال المشكل هالناقه. قالوا العرب حنا يا صار ابن رخيص ثايرٍ بالجار الجار حقُّه عند الرجال ما ودّنا نخرّبُه حنا يالعرب ولا نِدْخِل اللي متعرّضٍ الجار حنا ما ندخلكم الا تسوقون الناقة تِنْكسونَه لابن رخيص. العرب عنده شهاميّة ان الجار انه له قيمه. هم يبون يدخلون بناقة الجار وعَيّوا العرب لا يدخلونهم الا تنكسون الناقة لابن رخيص. وانكسوا الناقة لابن رخيص وخذاه ابن رخيص. وزانوا وهانت دعواهم.

ابو زويد عند ابن شعلان وجاوه الخبر انهم متناوخين ولا يدري وش صار عليهم ٣،٩
وتقل لايمٍ قاسم امير الرخيص يقول ليه يصول على ربعه يخلّي ربعُه يتذابحون على كيس ناقه ولايمُه. وِمِتهِم مِشْوَرٍ لُه يقول اغدي بهم مَقَرّد بهم قِراده هذي ما هي مَنُه هذي من مشاوره المقرّد. وارسل له هالقصيدة يسأل وش صار عليهم. يقول عاد ابو زويد الله يعفي عنا وعنه واموات المسلمين.

Ibn Rakhīṣ stood his ground: "Our customary law only applies to the settlement of claims among ourselves, in our own group. Claims against a protected neighbor are absolutely unacceptable. Those are matters for God to decide."

"So, what do you suggest?"

"As I see it, he should be allowed to take possession of his she-camel without any need for litigation."

From that point on, matters escalated between the Nabhān, the folk of al-Jrāf, and their branches of al-Ḍaww and al-Rakhīṣ.[65] Al-Ḍaww said, "He won't get the camel." And Ibn Rakhīṣ said, "For sure, you won't get it. Very well then, we'll meet tomorrow when I come to take it."

In the morning, he set out for the camp of al-Ḍaww to seize the camel of his neighbor, come what may. Al-Ḍaww quickly decamped to put themselves under the protection of another tribal group, telling them, "We seek asylum with you from Ibn Rakhīṣ. He is chasing after us, spoiling for a fight, just for the sake of one she-camel."

"What's the problem?" the others asked.

"Just that she-camel," they said.

They begged to differ: "If Ibn Rakhīṣ was roused to act in defense of his neighbor, we also consider that a neighbor enjoys inalienable rights among people like us. We will not condone it if anyone acts in contravention of those rights. We cannot accept responsibility for those who harass a neighbor. We grant asylum only on condition that you return the she-camel.[66] Bring the animal back to Ibn Rakhīṣ!"

They complied and were forced to eat humble pie.

News of their quarrel reached Abū Zwayyid while he was staying with Ibn 9.3
Shaʿlān. He was not familiar with the details of the case. It seemed that he held Ǵāsim, the shaykh of the Rakhīṣ, responsible. He might have wondered why the shaykh would assault his own folk. Why on earth would he, on his watch as a chief, let his kinsmen come to blows because of a mere she-camel? He held one of the chief's counselors responsible for misguiding him. He speculated that a scoundrel had insinuated himself into his inner circle. "Would it be some miscreant who sows dissension? It is not in his character to act this way. It must be some villain's evil whisperings." He therefore composed the following poem, in which he questions what happened among his kinsmen and asks God to grant forgiveness to all Muslims, living and deceased.

راكـبٍ اللي ما يعوزه تواصـيف   حمـرا تورّد بك إلى سـرّب اللالـــــ
قبّـا الضـلوع ودِقّهـا بالاطـاريف   شقرا شَعَر به من تحت تقل سِرْوالـــــ
يا زلّ جفـلَه للخلاوي على الكيف   عاقـل يِحظ المِزهَبه لين تشـتالـــــ
منوة غـريبٍ دون حَيّـه مـياهيف   اللي من الثِـنْتين يامن بـه الذالـــــ

الثنتين الخوف والعطش. يِحظ المزهبه الناقة الاصيل المودّبه تجدع مزاهبه وتطلقه تخلّيه بلا قياد ولا عقال وتستدير عليك تاكل مع ايسرك ومع ايمنك بس تِستِدير عليك تِقل انت ولدٍ له. راكبَه هذا هاللي يسوي غداوه بس تستدير عليه لين ما يقضي ويجيبَه ويعلق عليَه ويشيل ويركبَه.

يا روّحت مع سـهلةٍ ذِلّ ومْخيف   ركّابهـا عِـدّه عن الجيش خيّالـــــ
ركّـابها عِدّه ببعض الشواحيف   يا دَشّ له موج بعيـدٍ من الجـالـــــ
تلفي لربعي نازلين الاطــــــاريف   ربعي هل الطولات ماضين الافعالـــــ
يهـدّون ممـرورٍ براسـه زعـانيف   نـزّالة الخـرم المطَـرِّف ليا سـالـــــ
بتفـرّق الشوفات ياحيف ياحيف   عوذا لحَـد ما طاح بالفِكر رجـالـــــ
الفكر ساس الحَظّ والفعل بالسيف   والعِـزّ بيـلام الرفـاقـة والافعالـــــ
بير العيا من طاح به هَفّ ما شيف   هَـيّج ولا عمره ظهر منه ميّالـــــ
يا تِهْت بَـرِّق بالرجـال العواريف   الله خلق لمدوّر العرف الاسيالـــــ
شـاوِر على القـالات ربع عواريف   يجي بـراع العرف مطلع ومدخالـــــ
لا تشاور الا من هو يخاف ويخيف   يِبُوه عقل مشاور البـايه الضـالـــــ

Rider of a mount ravishing beyond description:
reddish-brown, she whisks you through mirages;
Ribs bulging, legs and frame elegantly formed;
a skirt of strawberry-red hair flutters below.
In calm mood, she comforts the lonely rider:
on a break, she minds unloaded travel bags.
Dream of desert crossers far from home,
savior of the terror-stricken from the two.

—By "the two" he means "fear and thirst." A purebred, well-trained she-camel watches the provision bag. If you unload the bags and let the camel walk free, unfettered, not hobbled, she circles you, browsing on herbage to your left and right, while keeping close to you as if you were her child. She sticks to her rider as he prepares and eats his luncheon until he is done, fetches her, fastens the bundles, loads her, and rides off.

Hurtling down daunting, featureless plains,
her rider fancies leading a cavalry charge;
Bobbing quickly up and down, like a ship
lifted and tossed by waves far from shore.
Head for my kin, unflinching in the face of danger,
daredevils renowned for chivalrous feats.
They cool the fury of hotheaded strutters
And camp in risky borderlands after heavy rains.[67]
Woe, if discord takes hold and insults fly—woe!
God is my refuge, let's not even think of it!
Sound opinion and martial feats bring results:
pride and might are born from acting in unison;
Tumble into the well of impotence, that's the end:
a fetid, brackish pool—no one clambers out of it.
If you're lost, ask judges steeped in tribal lore
for answers: sages keeping God's wisdom in trust.
If peril looms, thoughtful men of experience
probe customary law for mending solutions.
Seek counsel from humble men who inspire awe;
avoid fumbling advisers who embroil you in a mess.

ولا تطيع مقرودٍ يطبّق مع الهيف   الى سرى بك قِبْلةٍ تصبح شمـالـ
ياناس بِقـنا الله بكثر المحـاليف   وهو الذي عنده ميازين الاعمـالـ
صيّور ما القـالات تاتي مـناكيف   وتصير كسبات الحسايف لمن عالـ
امكن تراها ما تفيد التحاسيف   شي يفوتك عد له قطعة احوالـ

Keep clear of a wretch who plunges you into disaster:
if he leads you south, you'll end up north.
Folks, we've duped God with a flood of oaths,
though the scales to weigh our deeds are His.
Surely, such actions will redound to you:
your only gain from trespassing is regret.
Hurry! What use are mere lamentations?
Its moment gone, everything becomes a thing of the past.

يرجع من مجلاوه عند عنزه وينحر ابن رشيد

١،١٠ خلف ابو زويد ياكل بلسانه قصّاد ويتلي هالشيخان ويعطونه. صار عند صطام ابن شعلان وبعدين نهج من عند ابن شعلان ونحر ابن هذال. وايتك يا صطام مَسَيِّرٍ على ابن هذال وابو زويد عنده. تسالموا. قال ابن هذال يا خلف ابو زويد وش وَقْع صطام يوم انت عنده. وش وقعه لك. قال صطام ابن شعلان مثل الرغوه هكاللي هي فوقي اللبن مير انه لا تعشّي ولا تغذّي. قال ما تِنْبغي لك هالكلمه يابو زويد تسبّني وانا ما جيت على درب مِسَبّه مير الله كريم. قال الله كريم بْليّاك وش توعّدن به. هالحين عند اخوات بتلا قلوب الغرانيق ويا مني نهجت يمّ شمر احطّ بيني وبينك الضيدان شّلقوا جنب جَدّك بالعماير. طاب خاطره ابو زويد بغى ربعه. ابن رشيد زعل عليه عقب قصيدته بصطام ابن شعلان وناذر ان قضبت ابو زويد لاذبحه وبفاطر زعل ابن رشيد على قولة ابو زويد صطام ما والله يجبنه ولا جيب. وتوعّدُه ان شافه انه يذبحه ونِذَر عليه جِزور. قام ابو زويد ووَصّ لصالح ابن رخيص رجال قالط عند ابن رشيد ومشورٍ له انه يتوجه له عند محمد.

٢،١٠ ويغزي ابن رشيد من هانا ويضرب على الشعلان هو هكالوقت مِصِحِبٍ الروله انت يابن رشيد ويغزون معه. اكان على الفواعر رَعِيّةٍ هي هذي على الشطّ. يوم جابوا الكسب شمر ويقوم لك ابن رشيد يسرب كسبهم الفود يَسْرِب سَرْب يِحط الزِقِرت صفّين هاللون ويسرب مع وسطهم. يمر الحلال والكسب بين الصفين

He Returns from His Asylum with ʿAnazah and Heads for Ibn Rashīd

Khalaf Abū Zwayyid made a living from his tongue. He composed poems as he followed the trail of shaykhs who gave him presents, moving from Ṣaṭṭām ibn Shaʿlān to Ibn Hadhdhāl. While he was with the latter, Ibn Shaʿlān came for a visit. After the greetings, Ibn Hadhdhāl asked, "Now, Abū Zwayyid, tell me, how was your stay with Ṣaṭṭām, your impressions? How did he strike you as a person?" He said, "Ṣaṭṭām ibn Shaʿlān is like foam on camel milk—nice, but it will not serve you as supper or lunch." "Don't use improper language, Abū Zwayyid," Ṣaṭṭām said. "You insult me for no reason. I didn't say anything bad about you. God is generous." "God is generous without you. What is this tone of menace? Here I am with the brothers of Batlā, the Impeccable Hearts.[68] And if I decide to go on my way to Shammar, between you and me are the Ḍīdān, who split off from your ancestors' line among the tribal groups; they will protect me against you."[69] Abū Zwayyid enjoyed himself thoroughly, pleased as punch with his performance. But he longed to rejoin his fellow tribesmen. The obstacle was that Ibn Rashīd had been incensed by his poem in praise of Ṣaṭṭām ibn Shaʿlān. Ibn Rashīd had sworn that he would kill him as soon as he laid hands on him and slaughter a fat camel in celebration. The line that kindled his wrath was: "They never gave birth, nor will they ever, to the equal of Ṣaṭṭām in the entire world." Abū Zwayyid broached the subject of his return with Ṣāliḥ ibn Rakhīṣ, a close confidant and adviser of Ibn Rashīd, and asked him to put in a word on his behalf with Ibn Rashīd. 10.1

Ibn Rashīd set out on a raiding expedition and first headed for Ibn Shaʿlān, who was going to accompany him. At that time, he was on friendly terms with the Rwalah tribe. Jointly, they launched an assault on al-Fawāʿir for their herds on the Shaṭṭ River in Iraq. Once the Shammar tribesmen had rounded up the captured herds, Ibn Rashīd ordered a review of the booty. He made his cameleers stand in two opposite lines and ordered the captured animals to be driven from one end to the other, between the two rows of his men, while he inspected the parade of spoils from where he was seated, reclining on an 10.2

والامير جالس متراكيٍ على المَرْكَى مع خِدّامه واللي يدخل نَظِرُه من هالكسب ياخذُه ياخذ اللي هو يبي. إصْطِغُوا هذي إصْطِغُوا هذيك يا مير انت ياهالغَزّاي عندك ثنتين نياق كاسبْهن السرب ياخذون منك ناقه حديهن عندي انا ثلاث ياخذون حديهن السرب هاللون. والي مير ابن شعلان اللي يمدحه ابو زويد مع السرب اسربوهم اسربوا الشعلان وياخِذ عليهم العَقْبِه انت يا محمد. والى مير ابو زويد يقول هالحين انا وابن شعلان ابن رشيد ياخذ ناقتنا يقول انا ما ذلّيت مثل هكااليوم. قلت هالحين يَذْبَحَن. بعدين طلب ابو زويد من صالح ابن رخيص رجّالٍ قالط عند ابن رشيد وشويرٍ له انه يتوجّه له عند ابن رشيد.

٣،١٠ وجا ابو زويد يَمّ مجلس ابن رشيد متقلّدٍ كِفْنُه يقود هَباطِتُه تَيس. داري ان ابن رشيد ناذرٍ عليه جزور. تقلّد كِفْنه واقطع من جليسة على جليسه يم الامير بين الصفين جالسين على الزبور. وايته يزحف. يوم شافه ابن رشيد قال من هو هذا. قالوا هذا ابو زويد. قال والله واللعنه صطام ما جابَنه البيض ولا جيب - يقوله ابن رشيد - من شرقي الدنيا لغربي مغيبه. قال نعم يطول عمرك انا اقول صطام ما جابنه البيض ولا جيب، الا الامير الضيغمي ما نجيبه. قال وشّو يقول يا حمود. قال انا طالبك نقطة دم هالشمري يا طويل العمر. قال رح لعن الله ابو عين هالجراده. حَوَل هو ابو زويد حول الله يرحمه. قال يا طويل العمر والله مير ما حظّي حظك يا محفوظ يوم ابوي يَنحاش بابوك هَلَكِتَن امي وقامت ترضعك ديدَه وتقلّبت

armrest, surrounded by his security detail.[70] Any animal that caught his attention was reserved for him. He took possession of whatever struck his fancy: "Set that one aside, and that one too, here, to the side!" For instance, a raider who captured two she-camels as his booty would have to give up one of them in the course of the parade, or perhaps one out of every three pilfered she-camels. That's how the spoils pageant operates. Ibn Shaʿlān, whom Abū Zwayyid praised in his ode, was present at the review. "Orders were given for Ibn Shaʿlān's booty to be driven through the lines to be mustered!" In addition, Muḥammad ibn Rashīd reserved for himself the right to send his men to the owners of the plunder if he suspected there were animals of value that had been overlooked during the parade.[71] These he would also claim and seize. Abū Zwayyid feared that Ibn Rashīd would lay his hands on his camel as well, together with those of Ibn Shaʿlān. He confided to someone: "I was never so scared as on that day. I said to myself, 'Your last hour has come; he's going to kill you.'" At that point, Abū Zwayyid turned to Ṣāliḥ ibn Rakhīṣ, one of Ibn Rashīd's intimates and a close advisor. He asked him to intercede for him with Ibn Rashīd.

One day, Abū Zwayyid made his appearance at the assembly of Ibn Rashīd 10.3
with a shroud draped over his shoulders.[72] He led a billy goat, the animal slaughtered at one's interment.[73] He did so knowing that Ibn Rashīd had sworn to slaughter an animal on the occasion of his death. He put on his shroud and wended his way through the rows of men in the assembly toward where the prince was seated at the head of two lines. The visitors used to sit on earthen benches that lined the walls of the courtyard. He was moving at a snail's pace. When Ibn Rashīd caught sight of him, he muttered, "Who on earth could that be?" "Abū Zwayyid!" those around him replied. "By God, that cursed creature. 'Splendid women never gave birth, nor will they ever, to Ṣaṭṭām's equal from the world's east to where the sun sets.'" Abū Zwayyid said, "Yes, may you live long! What I actually said was, 'Splendid women never gave birth to Ṣaṭṭām's like, except for the peerless prince of Āl Ḍēgham.'"[74] Ibn Rashīd turned to his cousin. "What do you think, Ḥmūd?" Ḥmūd growled, "Sir, allow me to taste the blood when it drips from this Shammarī."[75] Instead, Ibn Rashīd ordered, "Get out of here, you accursed wretch, you and your locust eyes!"[76] (Abū Zwayyid was walleyed, God show him mercy.) Abū Zwayyid said, "May you live long, Your Highness. It's just that I am not as fortunate as you are, God preserve you! When my father made his escape, in the company of your father, I was neglected by my mother. When she became your wet nurse, she felt too proud

عيوني من العطش أمي بَدّتك عليّ ترضعك وانا تقول عني هذا فخّام مير لو يموت بكيفه انا ابسَقِّم شيخ شمر. وصارَن عيونك مثل الفناجيل وانا تقلّبت عيوني من العطش. واذبح الجزور يا محمد وقِصّ يالخادم من قِذْلته خِصْلة واعتِقه.

٤،١٠ عاد قال ابو زويد

راكب اللي كنّ فخـذَه من الجيـم   ماسومها الكفّه على السـاق وهلالـــ

فخذه متروز مثل حرف الجيم

ابوَه وضيحـان من ضـراب سلهيـم   وجَدّه فَحَل شَعْلان من زَمْل شوالـــ

كلهم اللحاويه سلهيم وشوال شرارية هي الذلول.

عـليـه حـلايا وصـف قوادة الريـم   شقرا وَبَرتها غاشيَه مثل الاشعالـــ
لا هي قمـر لا ريح لا شـين لا غيـم   لا هي قـطـاةٍ حـاديَه واهج اللالـــ
فيحا ومَشْيَه بالعـصا دوب تيميـم   ركّابها عِـدّه عن الجيش خيّالـــ
عليـه دليـلٍ ما بمشيه تعـاويـم   قِـطـاوي أوي والله مِـرسـالـــ
مـدّت من الخـابور من قبل تقديـم   وبالبَدّ الايمن علّق الجدي بشمالـــ
حِطّ الغـراب ايمن منك صوب توقيـم   ووادى المياه ايسر منك هو وما سالـــ
يا جيت فـرع صوّاب خـلّه دراهيـم   خـله تروّح بك مع العصر ذومالـــ
خـله تسهّـم بك مع الخِـر تسهيـم   والخـامسه تشرب من الحزل زلالـــ
ومن الصليب لخشم ربدا لابا دهيـم   يمـا تطـالع من قهـاميز الازوالـــ

to pay attention to me. While she was breastfeeding you, my eyes turned in different directions in hunger. My mother suckled you first, and whatever milk was left she fed to me. She'd say, 'This ugly mutt is just a charcoal burner.[77] If he dies, nothing is lost. I have been chosen to breastfeed the prince of Shammar!' From then on, my eyes popped out like porcelain coffee cups and each eye rolled aside—because as a baby I was kept hungry all the time."[78] Muḥammad ibn Rashīd ordered an animal to be slaughtered. A servant was instructed to cut off a lock of Abū Zwayyid's hair and set him free.[79]

On that occasion, Abū Zwayyid recited these verses: 10.4

Rider of a camel with thighs full as the letter *jīm*,
with a *kaffah* brand on its leg and a crescent;[80]

—Her thigh looks like the letter *jīm*, with its full belly.

Sired by white Wuḍayḥān, a stallion of Silhēm,
her grandfather a Shaʿlān stud in Shawwāl's herd.

—Silhēm and Shawwāl belong to the Lḥāwī branch of the Sharārāt.

She's like the leading doe of a herd of sand gazelle:
a fawn she-camel, of a flaming reddish-brown color.
She outstrips the moon, wind, clouds, all of them,
faster than sandgrouse driven by hot desert blasts.
Point the stick and she goes, the epitome of grace,
outpacing the pack, running like a cavalry horse.[81]
Her rider a desert pilot known for not losing his way:
like sandgrouse, he cleaves to the course, unbeatable!
Early morning, she set out from the River al-Khābūr,
Polestar fixed on the saddle pillow's right.
Leave al-Ghurāb's outcrop not far to your right,
Wādī al-Miyāh, famed for torrents, to the left.
On reaching Farʿ Ṣwāb, let her trot as she likes;
in late afternoon, she lengthens her stride for speed.
She whisks you at a smooth cadence to al-Khirr,
there to quaff al-Ḥazl's sweet and limpid water on day five.
From al-Ṣlēb to the spur of Rabdā to Abā Dhēm,
do not startle at sightings of frightening shapes!

على الحماطية رباعٍ مقاويم اهل كتار ونار وبهار ودلال
ربعي على ذود المعادي محاريم كم فقريٍ باسبابهم صار وبّال
خلّه تِمِرّ مولّم الزاد توليم عدّه على البايح هجورٍ وفنجال
والعصر عند مذبّحين المراديم على صحونه بس تقطيع وارسال
عند الشيوخ تقسّم الفعل تقسيم هم كنهم جيشٍ وهو تقل خيّال
شيوخٍ وحكامٍ وحصنٍ نواهيم ضياغمٍ يا شافوا الزود زِعّال
ياما عَطَت يمناه من طَرْش وغْنِيم وياما عطت يمناه معهن من المال
اللي عطاه الفين بيتٍ بتميم وانا عطان مثولثٍ كنّه الجال
لا قلتها دروا ولا زاحمن ضيم ولا خايفٍ منهم ولا انا بعد ذال

At al-Ḥamāṭiyyah, tribesmen have settled down,
known for their delicious roasts and rich coffee brews.
My kinsmen, indefatigable captors of enemy herds:
they brought untold riches to paupers in rags.
Provided with fresh supplies, now hit the road anew:
alight at al-Bāyiḥ for a midday bite and coffee,
And arrive in the afternoon at fat camels' butchers:
trains of food-laden trays, ceaseless cutting of meat:[82]
Shaykhs come in different shapes and sizes:
horsemen who outshine camel riders.
Shaykhs and rulers, like steeds chafing at the bit;
Ḍayāghim, unforgiving if heads are raised in pride.
Camels and small cattle they gift with open hand;
untold fortunes are distributed among supporters:
Some receive no less than a thousand tents;
my share is a three-poled, towering house of hair.
I don't say so to stay on his good side,
or out of fear for them, or with trembling knees.[83]

مع محمد ابن رشيد

١،١١ صار مِزاكِر على لوقه وارسل محمد العبد الله الرشيد مريزيق يبيه يرحّل سنجاره عن لوقه وينزّل بَه عبده. ابن رشيد هكالوقت يبي محمد الدماني عنده يبيه ينزل يمه بحايل. وهذا هو يبيه يبي لوقه. وصار مزاعل وزعّ له مريزيق ابن رشيد قال رحّلوه وينزل جاي. يوم انهم وّمروا عليه بالرحيل زعل وهو يعلق على الذلول ويشلع من لوقه وطبّق على الغربيه. وِتِجض معه سنجارة ليا ما نزل الغربيه ويحبسونه الدوله. ويزع خطوط ابن رشيد انكم احبسوه وحِبسته الدوله وساقوا عليه ثمانمية وضحا سنجاره وطلع على كيس لوقه. ورجع يم لوقه وتطالبوا وصارت له لوقه. يوم رجع تطالب على لوقه هو وابن جبرين عند عقوب ابن سويط وصار لسنجاره الحزل.

٢،١١ يوم ابو زويد يقصد. ابو زويد لَوّذ على ابن رشيد قال وين ربعك يابو زويد. قال يفطّن محمد ان الرخيض هم اللي زَنّبوا ابوه يوم يضيمونه آل علي

١ كبدي من الرِهَوِند يِخْلَط عشاها   والقلب معلوقه يقرّض به الفار
العين عيّي يصمد الموق ماها   يا كن يضربها مع الموق مسمار
من اللابة اللي فرّق الله شظاها   نِذْرِك بهم حقٍّ ونَذري بهم جار
تِفرَّقوا رَبْعي بحزّة شتاها   وِتْقَطَّعَت عنهم رواميس الاذكار

With Muḥammad ibn Rashīd

The well of Lōgah became the subject of tribal disputes. Muḥammad al-ʿAbdallāh al-Rashīd sent one of his enforcers, Mrēzīǵ, to eject the Sinjārah from Lōgah and allow the ʿAbdah to settle there. It was his intention to have Muḥammad al-Dimānī close to him and to let him set up quarters in Ḥāyil. But al-Dimānī was resolved to keep Lōgah and stay. When the wrangling continued, he sent Mrēzīǵ and instructed him: "Send him on his way and have him come here!" Al-Dimānī was indignant at being strong-armed into traveling. He saddled his riding camel, pulled out of Lōgah, and sped away in a westerly direction. Aggravated, his fellow tribesmen of Sinjārah joined him where he had set up camp in the west. There the forces of the state detained him.[84] Ibn Rashīd had sent written messages to request his detention. Thus, it happened. After the Sinjārah paid a ransom of eight hundred white she-camels, he was released. All because of Lōgah. On his return to Lōgah, he and Ibn Jibrīn submitted their dispute over the possession of Lōgah to tribal arbitration. They chose ʿGūb ibn Swēṭ to preside as a judge over the litigation of their claims in accordance with customary law. The Sinjārah ended up with the possession of the wells of al-Ḥazl, including Lōgah. 11.1

At the time of this poem, Abū Zwayyid had put himself under the protection of Ibn Rashīd. "Where are your kinsmen staying now, Abū Zwayyid?" Muḥammad asked. Replying in verse, Abū Zwayyid subtly reminded him that clansmen of al-Rakhīṣ had offered refuge to his father as he fled the oppression of Āl ʿAlī.[85] 11.2

A brew of poisonous leaves burns my entrails;[86] *1*
mice are gnawing away at my heart's arteries.
My eyes have surrendered to a flood of tears,
red hot as if a nail were driven into the pupils—
Because God decreed to scatter tribesmen,
justice enforcers, shields for seekers of protection.
My clan dispersed at the onset of winter;
They vanished, leaving me without the faintest news,

راحوا كما دَلْوٍ تمَصَّع رشاها   عِقْب العَمار مبيّده بعض الابيار
خَرْبَت ومن عقب العراقي رِماها   ودَلْو الروا ما يِنْصِخي به للاعيار
تنصّوا اللي جارهم ما شكاها   وساع الطعون مدَلِّهَة واله الجار

الشعلان.

يا امير ياللي ما تصافي عداها   نَفْسك كما مِلْح الشفا بَسّ الابكار
حنا رْبوعك يوم هي ما وراها   يوم الجرادي مِلْهِبٍ به سَنا النار
يوم ان ابن علي يدوّر عماها   ندوّر لك التبجير نرْكِض بالاصخار
بيوتٍ لعبد الله من اوّل بناها   ولا ظنّتي تجزا عَميلك الانكار
وان كان عندك واقفٍ مِنْتَهاها   الله لمكسور الجناحين جبّار

Like well buckets torn to bits and pieces,
ruined by some well shafts after having thrived;
Bucket broken, wooden crosspieces strewn:
who'd part with a water bucket, even as a loan?[87]
They ran to men who pamper their neighbors,
and maul the enemy—let refugees forget about home.

—They sought refuge with the Shaʿlān.

My prince! You spurn kissing an enemy's hand:
you are like purest homemade gunpowder.
When you are in dire straits, we're at your command!
Remember when al-Jarādī lit the fires of war?[88]
Ibn ʿAlī planned to poke his fingers in your eyes,
and we undergirded your views and strength.[89]
Thus ʿAbdallah's House rose from its foundations;
surely, you can't mean to snub such faithful aides.
If, despite all we did, you've lost patience with me,
God, healer of broken wings, is our last recourse.

يمدح سعود ابو خشم

يقول ابو زويد يمدح سعود ابو خشم ١،١٢

خلاف ذا ياراكبٍ عدمليه   رمـلا ولا ذاق الحويـر مسـايله
تِقْنَى لتقـطيع الفـيافي زْمـاله   وعن مسرب الدِيّان ما هي مسايله
لى طَبّقوا بالقَيض خِمْسٍ لعِقْله   لى رادها ناسٍ تْجَذِّب عـدايله
وهن بالضحى هَجَّن لمـانٍ لفى مـنه   ليا بَرِّكَن يورده الما هضـايله
مـني وملفـاها سعود ابن ضيغم   ملفاه ابن ضيغـم وجنّب بخايله
سعود ولد عبد العـزيز ابن متعب   الله عطـاه العـز مِنْشي مخايله
حرٍ فِدَع بالصـيد من غير علمه   والمـرجله حـاش اوله مع توايله
زيـزوم صفوات القـبايـل شـمر   ركضـاتهم يشكى المعـادي ملايله
جازوا من الخلفـات ربعي وكسبهن   يومٍ بـه الفـرسـان ربعي تخـايله
وردوا عليهم شمـر ساقـها الطـنا   وكلّت سـعـايـر شـمر من اوايله
واهل حايل وان قِلّط الجمع سَبَّلوا   على حيـاض الموت والروح غـايله
فداويـة البـيرق ليا حيـل زحـمه   يشكى الهضايم ضدهم من فشايله
ليا من مـزن الموت حقت مخايله   نعمٍ بضـرب ايمانهم من شمـايله
خوالك اهـل البيت الرفيع بشـمر   لى رَمّت الشيمـات هزلى حمـايله
لى رمّت الشيمـات هزلى حمـايل   الى زاملٍ خالك عن الدار شـايله

In Praise of Saʿūd Abū Khashm

Hey, rider of a fast, rugged desert crosser[90] 12.1
That's spared from procreation, not suckling young:
Rarest of prizes, she traverses endless wastes,
smoothly plunging into mirages and reemerging.
If they travel waterless for five days in scorching heat
to a well crammed with camel mothers drinking,[91]
They turn about, back to a well from which they came,
for a rest, waiting to slake their thirst with dregs.[92]
From my abode she sets out for Saʿūd son of Ḍēgham:
head straight for Ibn Ḍēgham, give wide berth to misers;[93]
Your destination: Saʿūd ibn ʿAbd al-ʿAzīz ibn Mitʿib;
God of life-bringing clouds, shower him with glory!
Streaking from the sky, he wreaks havoc on his prey;
a noble falcon, he usurps all chivalry.
A rampart who shields the purest tribes of Shammar:
thundering cavalry charges plunge enemies into grief.
My fellows spurn taking milch camels as booty:
doggedly determined to smite their adversaries.[94]
He led Shammar from the front, swollen with fury,[95]
rekindled Shammar's fire, sputtering sickly and wan.
Called to arms, Ḥāyil's men girded and marched
into pools of death, a grim reaper at their throats,
Sacrificing life, as the banner's last defense,[96]
until the enemy ran, thwarted in his quest;
Doom rained down from clouds of death:
cheers for the single-minded smiting and felling.
Your in-laws are of Shammar's prime lineages,
noblemen amid moral decay and tribal rot.
In these times of decadence and fading tribes,
father-in-law Zāmil stands as virtue's epitome.[97]

يثني على الشيمه ويطعن وينتخي   بالفعل عدّلها وهي قبل مايله
جزى الله من يثني على شيمة العرب   بخيرٍ من المعبود جزوى جمايله
واقفت مع الشيخان كل قبيله   وملزومٍ الشيخان تِحكّى فعايله
ما شفت بالشيخان شيخ مثله   شيخ معانى الطيب يجمع مخايله
ما يصافي الا كل شيخٍ خيّر   اللي بفعله مِدْرِكٍ كل طايله
صِدوق هرج الراس ما هو سِمَلّق   ما قال من هرجاةٍ إلا صمايله
هرجه من الجوهر على واضح النقا   لى من اكثر الشيخان باقت عمايله
هديّ بحال وعنيدٍ بحال   عنيد الى جا الخيل كثّر دبايله
على عندل ترفى ثلاثٍ بخطوه   على حصانٍ شوّلت ثم حايله
ما يحتاج مدحٍ عامرٍ له مضافه   في مضيفه تشبع النقاضا هزايله

He bolsters virtue with stabs and battle cries,
restores dimming values to their rightful place.
Esteeming his defense of Arab noble values,
may God reward him with bounty plentiful.
I have attended assemblies of chiefs galore:
the deeds of shaykhs make for conversation.
No doubt, he outclasses any shaykhs around,
makes all traits comprising goodness his own.
His rule scorns shaykhs of dubious repute,
favors the valiant known for proven mettle.
A straight talker who doesn't seek to please,
not beating about the bush, he tells plain truth.
Honest to a fault, he tells you exactly as it is,
unlike most shaykhs, whose deeds belie their words.
He is affable and serene or headstrong and truculent,
standfast when cavalry sows death and destruction.
His white mare kicks off with three legs aloft:[98]
since foaling once, her womb was kept barren.
Paeans are superfluous: his reception room is teeming
with starving, haggard guests eating until they burst.

يغزى مع قنيطِير ابن رخيص

١،١٣ غـزوا مع قنيطير ابن رخيص معهم ابو زويد. غزوا يَمّ الروله وعَطْشَوا ولا حصّلوا اباعر وجوك مِناكيف وقيّلوا بهالحماد. قالوا حنا متى ناصل الجوف. قال جفران المعَكّلي ناصلُه عقب باكِر صلاة الصبح. قال قنيطير قيّلوا برِّدوا خفوفهن قيّلوا. وهم يقيّلون. يوم روّحوا يا تحتُه سعَيدا ذلوله ذلول قنيطير وهو يدْغَفه بالمحْجان وهي تصقلُه ويدْغَفه من عند ابطه وتخبط وهم يزعجونهن. معهم ابو زويد. وشْعَبوهن وهجّن بهم وخذَن وهِن هاجّاتٍ بهم جميع. يوم اجتمعن قال وش تقول بهن يابو زويد وش كِنهن. يوم عَصَبهن.

٢،١٣ قال والله ما ادري يِبّاسٍ انتم واياهن تقل ثِنْكِ مْهَشّم يِبّاس انتم وماخوذاتكم من العطش

يارَبّ ياعايد من المزن بالسيل عايد على روض المحَل عقب الاصداد
يالله طَلَبْتك يا منَشّي الهماليل تفْرِج لمن قلبه به الغِلّ مِزْداد
يا رب يا جلاّي هَمّ المِباحيل ياللي على من عاقْدَه فيك عوّاد
يا مسَيِّر المحتار مِنّك التواصيل يارب يا حلاّل عسْرات الاعقاد
ياكَيل من لا جامع الناس له كَيل يا مِهْلِكٍ ناسٍ يجي كيله اتلاد
خطو الرجل يمشي الضحى تقل بالليل يشدي لسرّايٍ بليلٍ بالانفاد

Raiding with Gnēṭīr ibn Rakhīṣ

Abū Zwayyid joined a raiding party led by Gnēṭīr ibn Rakhīṣ.[99] They headed for the Rwalah, but ran out of water and failed to capture any camels. At midday, they took a rest while crossing a barren gravel plain. "When will we finally make it to al-Jawf?" they wondered. "Tomorrow after prayers at daybreak," Jifrān al-Maʿaklī said. "Get a good rest!" Gnēṭīr said. "Let our camel mounts cool their hooves—you rest well, and them too!" They resumed their journey, and at once Gnēṭīr sensed his mount's happy mood. He hit her with his riding stick and she kicked. He poked her in the armpit with the stick and she stamped. Together with Abū Zwayyid, they played with the animals and excited them. They prodded them into a wild stampede and kept up their mad dash for quite a while. When they had calmed enough to once again ride in a close group, Gnēṭīr said, "What do you think about these mounts, Abū Zwayyid? How are they?" 13.1

When they rode as a group again, he said, "Really, I don't know what to say. 13.2
You went flat out and drove yourselves and them to exhaustion. Dry and shriveled like crumpled, castaway bags. You are bone dry and these damned camels are desperate with thirst."[100]

Lord, your water-laden clouds bring succor
  to drought-stricken gardens pining for relief.
I pray, God, that you send us plentiful showers
  to soften the bitter crust choking our hearts.
Lord, You brighten sorrow-clouded minds,
  You are the Savior of those who put their trust in You.
You guide lost souls casting about, bewildered;
  Lord, You loosen knots if people feel strangled.
Humanity lies in Your cupped hand:
  You destroy people puffed up with ancient pride.
Some men walk by day as if groping in the dark,
  like travelers at night, bone-weary, distraught;

كيف الرجل لو هو يشوف الازاويل   كنه عمى عيٍّ عن الدرب ويقاد
دور تشيّخ به رجالٍ سماليل   ويأكل به الحِصْني ضراغيم الاساد
يالله تكفينا شرور الغرابيل   القلب من كثر الهواجيس مِزداد
واشفّ بالي في قرا ضمّرٍ حِيل   ان صِرْت مع شِهْب الرهاريه مَدّاد
يا راكبٍ من فوق حيلٍ مراميل   حَشْو الاشِدّه والشحم دِحْو الابداد
حيل يشادن مِمْرسات المَحاحيل   مِثْل النَعام اللي مع القاع شِرّاد
لى قيل ها وش ذا يشَهّلِن تشهيل   ليا قيل بادَن هاض مكنونه زاد

يا قيل وش هالزول ونَوَوا يشردون يشَحّلن يصيبهن سَطر عنقه وذنبه وذيله وتثافِر مثل الجمل تِشوش.

ليا عَطَن عِقب السرا والمحاويل   لى قيل من قطع الرَهاريه بيّاد
تلقى بجِرّتهن قطاع المخاليل   تدويج يتمانٍ على كَرْمَة اجواد
وان نوّخوهن العيال المِشاكيل   على طرف قومٍ يحوفون الاذواد
يشدن تِحلّفز رِجّعٍ تالي الليل   جاهن خبر عِرْسٍ وهن قبل رِقاد
كلامٍ احلى من هيوض الشخاليل   لى صرت عطشانٍ من اللال وِرّاد

How come some people, sharp of sight,
stray from the road as if blind, and yet are guided?
This era has saddled us with woeful leaders:
measly foxes feast on lions' dinners.[101]
Spare us, God, from trials and adversity:
beset by anxious thought, my heart boils over.
Mount of my dreams, lean and sinewy,
Barren-wombed, fit to tear into blazing plains.[102]
Hey you, rider of rugged, unflagging she-camels,
perched on a hump that stretches the saddle cushion:
Legs aflutter like ropes slipped off a pulley;
panic-stricken ostriches race down empty tracts.
Scolded, they speed up with peeved arrogance:
you think they're finished? They rally and surge!

—If the camels are scolded—"What kind of running is this?"—and the riders aim to go at speed, they adopt an arrogant gait. They indulge in a bout of peevish arrogance: the way they hold neck and tail, strut like a rutting stud camel, or walk like a conceited, spoiled star.

At night, in empty vastness, they give it their all,
already worn out by waterless desert crossings,
Leaving behind camel calves scampering about
like orphans in search of food from kindly folk.
The mounts, kneeled by fearless young raiders
near an enemy camp to snatch away the herds,
Fidget like excited divorcées in the evening,
hearing of a proposal before bedding down.[103]
Such verse is sweeter than a cool cascade of water
on arrival at a well, thirsting from the shimmering heat.

يغـزي مع روضـان ابن فروان

١،١٤ غـزوا مع روضان ابن فروان. يوم جا من باكر يا لاحقُه جِفْران شايبٍ قاضبه الوجه وبريان. يامار حار جفران تقل ما هو على لونه قبل وروضان تَوّه مِلْفي كاسب اخذ له طِرْقيّه. يوم هاللي يذكر يقول الخراب خراب عبد الكريم. يقول ابوي يوم اضحينا لحقنا قال روضان نَوِّخ يا جفران. قال يا ولد سعد انت اتلى الجِرّه وانا حكاتي والله انه. قال ياخوي كان من بركة تبي تْغَشانا كلنا. عيّ الشايب امير حَوّل ياروضان واقضب رْسَنَه ونوّخ بُه. وهم يداورون بِزْمَل العليا وهكالديار وهذا وايتوك مناكيف.

٢،١٤ والى مير شُوَرْدي ابن فروان له اخو اسمه رِدن يم بني صخر وجاب له رْكَيب يبي يْتَنَطّل هاللي يم شمر الاجناب. يوم جا الوادي يا هذا اثر الجِرْذان يعرفهم. قال انتم ياخوياي مير بكيفكم انا الحق هالغزو. يوم بْرزوا من الجوف يا هو عليهم. قال العن الله ابو حَيّكم جاي الذيدان يتمرّحن بهالدِيان اباعر السِرحان. يقول والله اني انخاهم مثل نخوى الرجال على الرجال. أولاد الغفل لعن ابوكم والله اباعرٍ هَمَل. ابوي مِرْدَفٍ شايش الصَّلّج على رحول له. يا مار ابو زويد اخوٍ للصلج اخو سِرّه. امير خذ مزودته

On a Raid with Rōḍān ibn Farwān

They left on a raiding expedition led by Rōḍān ibn Farwān. The next day, Jifrān came riding hard to catch up with them, an old fellow who had suffered paralysis of one half of his face but had recovered from the attack. He had once been energetic and hot-blooded, but did not look like his former self. Rōḍān was a greenhorn who started his raiding career by robbing some travelers. Jifrān, on the other hand, was a heavy hitter, terrifying, the dictatorial terror of ʿAbd al-Karīm.[104] "Here I am," he said. "I started out this morning and caught up with you." "Kneel your mount. It is an honor, Jifrān!" Rōḍān exulted. "Easy, son of Saʿd," the other said. "You are the up-and-coming one, and my story . . . well, you know." "Dear brother, your presence comes as a blessing to all of us!"[105] Seeing that the old fellow was adamant, Rōḍān slid down from the back of his mount, took the reins in his hand, and made Jifrān's camel kneel. They set out with the intention of capturing camels from the al-ʿAlyā herds in the area of the Rwalah tribe or thereabouts, but returned empty-handed. 14.1

It so happened that Shuwardī ibn Jifrān had a brother, named Ridn, who lived in the vicinity of the Banū Ṣakhr tribe. Together with a few others, he rode from there aiming to pilfer camels, heading in the direction of the Shammar tribe, looking for the camels of another tribe. When they came to Wādī Sirḥān, Shuwardī hit upon the tracks of the Jirdhān, his fellow tribesmen. He recognized the traces left by their riding camels. Excited, he told his companions, "Dear friends, it's your call; as for me, I'm going to follow and catch up with these raiders." As Rōḍān and his raiders were about to leave al-Jawf behind, Shuwardī came hurrying to them and joyously cried, "God's curse on your damned tribe. Hurray! Follow me quickly! Herds of camels right there, idling in those flatlands, for the taking! The camels of the Sirḥān!" He interlaced his words with shouted encouragements, battle cries, exhorting them to join him in his enterprise: "Come on, sons of al-Ghafal, a curse on your father, camels are roaming there freely, unguarded!" My father rode with Shāyish al-Ṣalj, who sat behind the saddle on his camel's back.[106] Abū Zwayyid was a half brother of al-Ṣalj: they were born of the same mother. Shāyish dismounted, took his bag, and fastened it to Abū Zwayyid's camel, preferring to 14.2

علقه مع ابو زويد. وهي تنكف سنجاره. وهم ينخونهم الشيبان وهم يعَفْصونهن ما من كثره.

يقول يوم نجي مناكيف الاضارع لو تعَقّل الرجّال يِشْبع كراث. يقول وحنا نلْمِس على الاضارع. يقول يوم جيناوه وحنا نعكص عكايص. يا جانا راعى الذلول أو الذلولين نْنَزّله عكايص. اتْلَى ما لحقنا غصن السعدي معه اهل خمس ونْنَزِّله عكايص. يقول وحنا يامرنا الله يوم جينا مع العصر وتدَرْهم هكالمِطايا اللي تلاوح هو معلّمْهم الولد انه بسّ رِعيانَه قال خَلّوَه تجتمع يما تجتمع مع العشا. اركبوا جيشهم وهم يدهجونه بوجهَه. يوم اقاموا المناكيف اليوم معهم ابو زويد جا باكر يا هم يصبحون عليهم. اباعر الهويري من خلقة الدنيا ما جا مثله. الهويري من السرحان. ٣،١٤

ابو زويد مع المناكيف بس اقاموا امس. قال ٤،١٤

واافاطري والكبد به تِقِل قـالي غـبايِنٍ حَطّن على القلب تشليح

يقول ليه انكِف مِنْغِبن.

غبـايِنٍ من كاسـبين المـتالي يا مِـنكِسَة تالي ربيع المصـاليح
ذيابـةٍ يتـلون ذيب المفـالي ربعٍ عوايدهـم على هبّـة الريح
ضَرَبْت انا دَرْب العفانة لحـالي ولا ظنتي ينفع مكيـل المـرابيح

ride with him. The tribesmen of Sinjārah would not be swayed, and continued on their way home. The others protested and appealed to their honor, the old fellows, but in vain, and they hit their camels hard to make them turn in the opposite direction. They were a small group.

He continued his story: On our way back we came to al-Uḍāriʿ.[107] There the edible *kurrāth* grass grew so thick that if you'd leave a man alone, his hands tied behind his back, he'd find enough to satisfy his appetite: he'd only have to open his mouth and eat.[108] We skirted al-Uḍāriʿ. When we landed amid this plenty, we folded the *kurrāth* grass into bundles, like sandwiches. Whenever one or two camel riders passed by, we made them dismount to feast them on these wraps of edible grass. The last passersby whom we urged to dismount and be treated to these wraps of edible *kurrāth* grass were Ghuṣn al-Sʿadī and his group of five riders. As God would have it, while we were there, in the afternoon the other group was trotting energetically, their mounts swaying from side to side as they came rushing in at a blistering pace. A boy had informed them that the herds were unguarded, except for a few shepherds. Jifrān told them to wait until the camels had been collected at the end of the day. As soon as the animals had flocked together, they hurtled forward and stampeded the herd in the desired direction. Abū Zwayyid had followed the group that chose to continue on its way back home. They took a day of rest amid bountiful grasses. The next morning, all of a sudden, a great mass of animals appeared out of thin air and came running straight at them. The stolen camels of al-Hwērī. Nothing like it had been seen since the world was created. Al-Hwērī was a tribesman of the Sirḥān. 14.3

Abū Zwayyid went with the group of losers who had stayed put the day before and said: 14.4

Alas, patient camel, I feel my insides boiling,
a heart sliced by remorse and frustration.

—He is saying, "Why did I return empty-handed?"

Losing bets, robbed of my share of camel mothers:
well-fed ones, swept up from lush pastures of spring
By steppe wolves led by a cunning master,[109]
a lucky pack always smiled upon by fortune.
I wronged myself by being such a lazy coward:
methinks there is no profit in seeking easy gain.

قالت عاد الذلول ٥،١٤

لى يا خلف ما زود عذّبت حالي   واسْوَيتني مع دايـرين التِـماديح
سـتين ليـله وانت نومك توالي   . . . .
لى يا خـلف وافْهق علينا ليـالي   يا مِـنّـنا ناخـذ من الرَبح ونـريح

سبحان الله عِلْم الجِرذان بالشَرّ يوم جَتهم اباعر الهويري وهم يجمّون جَمّة قِليب. سبحان الله ابـدا.

His female riding camel replied: 14.5

Khalaf, if only you knew how you hurt me
  by smearing my name in decent society.
Sixty nights in a row you slept at my side.
  [. . .]
Khalaf, bear with me! Give me nights' rest!
  Let me grow a towering hump of fat and relax.

Praise God. The capture of al-Hwērī's camels spelled the end of bad luck and hard times for the Jirdhān clan.[110] The spoils came their way like water gushing from a plentiful well.

مع خويه الرويلي عند ابن رشيد

١٥،١ هم غَزَو مع ابن رشيد ومعهم رويلي الحساوي من الدغمي خُبَرتُه جَنْب خبرة ابو زويد يعني خَوِي جَنْب. ويْسَيّرون الخَبَر على بعض. الرويلي قاصدٍ له قِصيده ومِرْكب له ذِلول. ويسَيِّر الرويلي مع ابو زويد على خبرة الامير محمد. قال ابو زويد انا داخل عليك يالامير عن مضرِّب اللقَحَه يعني مثل الحاشي اللي يتحَشّم اللقحه يعني الرجّال اللي ما يميَّز. قال ابن رشيد لابو زويد من هو خَصيمك. قال رِفيقي الرويلي هذا نادعٍ ذلولي لقيت ذِلولٍ لي عنده وانا ركابي مَقطّع بهن الطّلايب. قال ابن رشيد. علّمونَن به.

١٥،٢ قال الحساوي الدغِمي

يا راكب اللي ما وِطت جيل بالسوق	حمرا ولا بْدرب المعاضب تجاب
حمرا تشوق العين يطْرب لها الموق	مثل الطِموح اللي زَهت بالثياب
حمرا ليا يبْسَت على القَفل وِعْروق	ودَلّى يتقَطّع بالحَماد السراب
حمرا سِبِرْتِيّه مع الدَرْب دانوق	مع غايط والشمس حَدّ الغياب
تفزيز ربدا شافت الزَول من فوق	بهَزّة غَلْبها وارتِكَبْنَ الكِعاب
تلفي مداهيل المنازل هل النوق	يرْعَون بالعفرا مِكَبّ السحاب

١٥،٣ قال يا راع العَلْيا هي له خَوات والا بسّ هي فِردانيه. قال لا بالله فِردانيه. قال انهج بُه يا راع العَزل - اللي يعزَل الكسب - انهج به خَلّه يتخَيَّر من الكَسْب الناقة اللي هو

With a Companion of the Rwalah at Ibn Rashīd's Court

They joined a plundering expedition of Ibn Rashīd. One of the participants was a Rwēlī, al-Ḥisāwī of the Dghimī branch.[111] His fellow raiders camped next to the group of Abū Zwayyid. Their groups were encamped as neighbors who visited one another. The Rwēlī dispatched a qasida with a fleet riding camel. While camped together, the Rwēlī and Abū Zwayyid went to pay their respects to Prince Muḥammad ibn Rashīd. Abū Zwayyid said to him, "Prince, I seek your protection against a stud that insists on mounting a pregnant she-camel"—he meant, like a young male that harasses a pregnant she-camel, a metaphor for a boorish man lacking in discernment. Ibn Rashīd asked Abū Zwayyid, "Who is your opponent?" He said, "This friend of mine, the Rwēlī who appropriated one of my camels. I found one of my riding camels with him, though none of my camels ever fell into the hands of those who falsely claimed their ownership." Ibn Rashīd said, "Let's have it, then!" 15.1

Al-Ḥisāwī al-Dghimī said: 15.2

Rider of a well-rested, regal she-camel,
light brown, not for drawing water;[112]
A delight for the eye is the shine of her fur,
as she struts like a flirter flaunting a dress.[113]
Strong and sinewy, her frame slimmed down,
she cuts through the quivering desert air,
Reddish of hue, fast-paced, neck stretched low,
across empty flats, as the sun goes down—
Panicky like an ostrich spotting human shapes,
plumage aquiver and tendons stretched tight —
Toward the hospitable tents of Bedouin
and white camel herds on rain-fed pastures.

Ibn Rashīd said, "Well, you Rwēlī of the ʿAlyā camels, does this she-camel have any sisters or is she all by herself?"[114] "No, none at all," he said. "This is the only one, all by herself." "Take him with you," Ibn Rashīd instructed the 15.3

يِشتِهي عن ذلول ابو زويد. شاف له بَكْرَةٍ عَويرا ما هي كبيره حول اللقيّه تَعَرِش له عظم ومِنْدَلْقةٍ سِرّته وله زور هاللون. عرف الرويلي ان هذي بعدين تظهر ذلول فارق ويتخيّره. قالوا يا شين خِذ اطّيَب منه يوم الله فتق لك. قال ابد ما آخذ الا هالعويرا. وعَسفَه وتطلع ذلول طيّبه ما له لِطيم من الجيش.

٤،١٥ قال الحساوي الدغمي

١ يا راكبٍ من فوق زين التواصيف   قبّ الضلوع مرفّعات المتون
يا روّحَن مع سهلةٍ من ورا جويف   حيلٍ يشادن مثل افام البدون
يا صوّتوا عقب التراويح بخلَيف   يا تقل ينْهَش من قِفاهم جنون
يحفلن من قشع الحماد المشاريف   يجفلن من ظِلّ العَصا والغصون
٥ راع الرِديّه والقعود المجيليف   صبح ارْبَعٍ مِن دِمْنِهِن يُوقدون

custodian of the spoils, camels captured on his raids. "Take him, and let him choose a she-camel from our booty, whichever he likes best, in compensation for the camel he owes Abū Zwayyid." The Rwēlī's eye fell on a young, half-blind she-camel that was gnawing on a bone, its umbilical cord dangling from the belly, and with an outsized callus on its breastbone. The Rwēlī knew that this inauspicious-looking camel, once grown up, would make an exceptional mount and he confirmed his choice. "What a missed opportunity," the attendants said. "Why don't you take a better one now that this stroke of good fortune has come your way?" "Absolutely not," he said. "I've made up my mind to take this one-eyed camel." He trained the camel and she turned out to be fast and tough, a mount that stood out among all desert-crossing camels.

Then al-Ḥisāwi al-Dghimī composed these verses: 15.4

Hey, rider of that well-shaped mount
with bulging ribs and tall in the back:
Beyond Jwēf, on the plain's home stretch,
the strong camels speed like mountain goats;
On their last reserves, their pace goes mad,
as if jinn are tearing at their behinds.
Outlines of vague shapes make them startle:
bushes on high plains, a stick or branch.
Four days later, the riders of slower mounts
cook breakfast on a fire of their dry dung.[115]

مع دبيّ ابن فالح

١،١٦ قيّظ ابو زويد حَدى هالسنين على تربِه ولُه عشيرٍ من الشِلْقان دَبّي ابن فالح مقيّظٍ على الخَريزه. وجاهم لهم سِنةٍ دَهَرَجا وقتٍ شين على العرب وعلى اهل هالديار هذي وموّت الحلال ذهب حلالهم ولا بِقِيَ الا عَواصي البل. وابو زويد ما بقي له شين ابد ولا بعير كل رحايله هَفَن ولا بقي عنده ما يِشِدّ عليه ويرحل. يوم جا الصِفري اجْلِدَوا وغْدانه ما عنده ما يزمّلهم. وتِفَطّن للرجال وهو على تربه. تفطّن للرجال ويتذكر عشيرهُ دبّي ابن فالح عنده له اباعر تجي له رِعِيّتين. دبي رجلٍ طيب وعشير له باول الزمان. ويْتحَزم ويَنْهج يمّه يَنْحَرُه على الخريزه رِجْلي مع هالنفود.

٢،١٦ يوم جاوه ألْفى على دبي كيف انت الله يسلّمك وِشْلونك كيف الحال. قال والله الحال الحَلّي واليد الشلا ياخو عليا العربان رْحَلَت وعْيالي ما عندهم زمايل واجلِدوا على تربه ما عندهم الا الذيابه كل زمايلي ماتت البعارين ما بقي ولا واحد منهن وجِيت ادوّر عندك الزمايل. قال دبي ابشر مير بْسَعَدْك الفَنا بِهن والبِقا براسك يوم صارت بالحلال الدَعْوَى سَهّله وانا بعد ترى نياقي هكاللي تْخَبر ماتن ولا بقي منهن إلا عواصي البل عشرين ناقه ما سِلِم لي الا عشرين جِليلةٍ من عواصي البل وهالحين كنا حنا نبي نِصير اخْوةٍ نْتَقاسم فِهن قاسماتٍ روحِهن عشرٍ لك وعشرٍ لي وان كان حنا تبينا نصير اخوةٍ خَشَرا نتخاشر وحالنا وحده فانت دونك هالزوامل رِح ارْكَب هَلَك جِبْهم

With Dabbī ibn Fāliḥ

One year, Abū Zwayyid spent the hot season of midsummer at the well of Tribah while a friend of his from the Shilgān, Dabbī ibn Fāliḥ, encamped at the well of al-Khrēzah. It was a time of severe drought, a terrible period for the Bedouin and other people of that area. The drought killed cattle; all their wherewithal was wiped out. Only the most tenacious camels hung on. Abū Zwayyid lost all he had and became completely destitute. No camels—all his riding camels had perished. Not even one mount was left for riding and travel. When the great heat began to abate in early fall, his children were sitting around listlessly. There was no camel to carry them. While he was at Tribah, it occurred to him to whom he should go. He remembered his friend Dabbī ibn Fāliḥ, who owned quite a number of camels: two sizable herds. Dabbī was a good man. They had been close friends in earlier days. Abū Zwayyid girded up and went looking for him, traveling on foot across the sand dunes toward al-Khrēzah. 16.1

When he got there, he headed for Dabbī, who welcomed him: "How are you? May God look after you. How are you feeling? How are things with you?" "Miserable, as you see; my hands are paralyzed, brother of ʿAlyā. The Bedouin are gone and I have no transportation for my children, who are just sitting around and waiting at Tribah. Jackals are all they have for company. My pack camels died. Not a single camel of mine survived. I came to ask if you could spare any pack camels." "Chin up," he said. "I will help you. Your camels have perished, but you are hanging on. If it is merely a matter of animals, solutions are easy to come by. Here things are not very different. My camels, the ones you saw before, have died. Only the toughest, hardiest ones made it through. Just twenty of them. The twenty mighty, rugged camels with the greatest stamina. If you like, we become as brothers and we divide them: ten for you and ten for me. Or, if you'd rather become my partner, we can share the twenty. We'll be equal partners in one and the same enterprise. Take these pack camels and transport your family on them. Fetch them and bring them here and have them stay with us. Get your family and let's be partners in these twenty camels until God brings us relief." Abū Zwayyid felt it would be improper to take him up on the offer of 16.2

جاي نَزِّلهم عندنا هات هلك ونتخاشر بهالعشرين يَما الله يفرجه. استحى لا يقاسمه نياقه. رِكْب الركاب وجاب هلُه ونِزل عليه ابو زويد نزل عند دبي.

٣،١٦ يا هابٍّ الصِفري والبراد. يوم ابرد الوقت وِنْبَّه دبي بالمغزى قال تَرُونا غَزُو اللي يبي يترزّق الله. دبي عقيد. ويركَب حدى الزمِل اللي عندُه ويركب ابو زويد الاخرى ويغزي معه. وهي تعلّقه سنجاره اللي حاضينه سنجاره. يوم جَوا الوديان جوا حِزْوَة البل وقرّبوا للقوم وهم يِكْمنون بهكالْهَبط وهو يزعِج ابو زويد وواحد معه يَسِبْرون لهم البل. قال انت يابو زويد انهج دوّر لنا البل انت وهالثّنين معك عن تزويل الجهامه وظْلَعانَه وهذا دوّروا لنا البل وحنا تَرْنا اليوم والليلة وحنا بهالتَّلْعه. السبور يَدَوّرون مَحاري البل ويراعون للمعَدى هو البل عنده جَنَب والا ما معه الا الرِعيان والى جا قَسْم الكسب يَنفّلهم العقيد يَنَفِّل السبور ويزيد لهم كل واحدٍ ناقه. دبي ارسل ابو زويد مع السبور مِبرَّةٍ له مصافيطٍ له من شان يرجَح نصيبه من الكَسْب. هذا مصْفوطٍ لابو زويد لان اللي يشوف البل له ناقه بارُه مِبرّه له رِداعةٍ اللي يشوف البل.

٤،١٦ وهم ينَهَجُون ويوم نْهَجوا قال حَديكم ما حَدّنا نزيّن غِدْيانا حديكم يصير بهالمِرْقاب. يوم ارقب الرِقيه ما امْدَاوه يِرْقِب يوم طَبّ على الجيش بالتلعة ودَلّى يطلّقه ويجيبه. قال يا عيّال دفّقوا غِدْيانكم دفّقوا طِياسكم وعَطونا الجيش. دِري ان الرقيبة شاف البل. يوم جا الرقيه العِلم. قال العِلم اربع رِعْايانٍ هِن هذولي يِبِن يطْلِعِن علينا متبَطّحينٍ رعْيانهِن على قِعَدهن ويبِن يطْلِعِن علينا ولا معهِن الا الرعيان ما من جَنَب ولا

accepting ownership of half his camels. He did as the other suggested. He took the pack camels and brought his family to stay with Dabbī.

As soon as the weather cooled somewhat in early fall, Dabbī announced his intention of launching a raiding expedition. He said, "Hey, let's go raiding. Join me if you'd like to try your luck in stocking up on God-given booty!" Dabbī was an experienced raid leader. He mounted one of the pack camels, and Abū Zwayyid, who had decided to join, mounted the other. Other tribesmen of Sinjārah who were staying nearby followed his example. When they reached the area of al-Wudyān, they reckoned they had come within striking distance of enemy tribes and their herds. They hid in a dip in the terrain where they would be invisible and sent Abū Zwayyid and someone else ahead to reconnoiter the whereabouts of the camels. Dabbī said, "You, Abū Zwayyid, set off and find out about these camels. These two will come with you. Scout and look around in the distance for the dark blot of a big herd of camels. You search for the camels and we will wait for you here, hidden in this gully, all of today and tonight." The scouts left on their mission to spy out the whereabouts of the herds and enemy forces. Were the camels accompanied by an escort of armed guards or merely by a few shepherd boys? In a successful outcome, when the spoils were divided among the raiders, the raid leader would allot the scouts a bonus over and above what the other men would receive—an additional she-camel was added to their share of the spoils. Dabbī picked Abū Zwayyid for the scouting job as a kindly gesture—doing him a favor to make sure he would get more than a regular share of the booty. He gave him a wink, as it were: a signal that he'd get an extra camel in accordance with the rules. He did him a good turn, because the one who spies the camels is entitled to more than the others.[116] 16.3

When they had left, Dabbī said, "While our lunch is being prepared, why doesn't one of you climb that lookout?" The man who volunteered had not even made his way to the top when Dabbī ran to their mounts in the gully, unfettered them, and drove them toward his comrades. "Listen, fellows!" he called. "Forget about your lunch, empty your cups. Mount your camels!" He had noticed that the man climbing the lookout had seen camel herds. "And?" they asked the man on his return. "The payoff is this: four big herds moving in our direction.[117] The shepherds are lazing, stretched out on the back of their young male camels. Any moment now they may surface, right there in front of you. Just shepherds. No armed guards or anything!" They hurried down, and as soon as they emerged from the gully, they found themselves face to face 16.4

شي لله. يوم طَلعوا الغزو يا هذي البل. وهم لك يركبون وهم يغيرون عَلَيه ويَجْعَفونه يَصِفْقون رِعيّةٍ على رعيه ويتلَقّون به مغيب الشمس على قِبالة الليل ويَغْدون به. ها الحين ذولا كُسبوا خَذوا اربع رعايا وروّحوا. خلّوا ابو زويد وخوياوه. ابو زويد والسبور اللي معه راحَوا بوجْهَهُم يَدَوّرون البل.

٥،١٦ يوم جَوا شَنَق الوديان طالعوا البل ونْسِفوا يبون خَوَياهم واثاريهم تَخالِفوا واجْنِبَوا الوعَد والغزو بْتَلَوا على وجههم. يوم جا ابو زويد بالليل والى ما حْذى مكانهم. اصبح وِقضب الجِرِية والى والله هذا درب الوسيق وجاك مع اثرهم. الغزو بْوَجْهه هكاليوم مع اثر الوسيق ما ناموا. يوم جا من باكر العصر وطالعوا يا مير هذا اثر خوياهم البارح مِنهَزْمين باوّل الليل. وهم لك ينامون على اثرهم. يوم قْطَعَوا الجَرّة وطبّوا مع العثعث وذْخَشَوا خبّ سَحّا واشيقر وهالمحاري – اهلهم بهالنفود ما هم بعيد – يا مار هم يلحقونهم.

٦،١٦ لحَقوهم بشمالي هالنفود يا والله هم قاسمين وخالصين عازلينِ البل وكلٍّ عارفٍ حقّه ومشَطّرينٍ حق خوياهم. قالوا يابو زويد شف هذولي هذولي مَقْسَمكم وسَهَمْكم خِذْهِن. والى والله هكالناقة مَهوَى ناقةٍ مَهوَى به عقال دبي العقيد العقيد له ناقةٍ خيار العقيد دبي حاطّ عقالُه بلُه وضحا مُوطِي باوّل الولاد تبي تِلد ورقبته تقل ناعور باوّل البل ولا تمشي الا هي الاوّله قِدّام البل وتحته له دَيدٍ اسود هذا كِبر دحاليله. واثاريه شافَه ابو زويد مع اول البل قال هذي اللي تِروي عيالي. وهو يحوّل عليه

with the herds. Spurring their mounts, they raced toward their quarry. They yanked the herds away from the line of their movement, and drove one herd into another, sowing confusion and panic among the animals, until by sunset they had rounded up all of the camels. In the gathering darkness, they made away with their plunder. They had achieved all they wanted and more—four big herds—and were able to make their escape with these considerable spoils. They did not spare a thought for the fate of Abū Zwayyid and his mates.

Meanwhile, Abū Zwayyid and the other scouts rode a long way until they 16.5
reached the edge of al-Wudyān and espied the camels they were looking for. They swung around and hurried back to inform their comrades. But they failed to meet up with them; they missed their assignation. The raiders had ridden strenuously, all night long. By evening, when Abū Zwayyid reached the place from which they, the scouts, had set out, there was no one there. The next morning, he started to follow their tracks. By God, he thought, this is the path beaten by the stolen herds as they were being goaded forward. The raiders were driving the camels through the night without rest while the scouts were sleeping. The next day the scouts continued to follow the tracks the raiders had beaten the night before as they fled at high speed. They then crossed the stony plains of al-Ḥjarah, rushed down the bottom of al-ʿAthʿath, and burst into Khabb al-Saḥḥā and Ushayǵir, the approximate area where their people were staying in the sands of al-Nafūd, where they finally caught up with them.

They reached them just north of al-Nafūd while they were busy divvying 16.6
up the looted herds. They had finished dividing the spoils among themselves. Every one of them had a portion of the camels set aside for himself and each knew exactly his share and what had been allotted to others. They had set aside a number of camels for their absent companions, the stragglers. "Hey, Abū Zwayyid," they said, "those are yours. That's your share, the portion you're entitled to. Take them, those are your prize!" All well and good, but one she-camel in particular struck his fancy. And it so happened that it was marked with a ribbon of Dabbī, the raid leader. It was the raid leader's prerogative to select any camel for himself, the camel he liked best. Dabbī, as the commander, had tied his camel rope to this pure-white beauty that was about to give birth to her first young; she was close to delivery. Her graceful neck was as tall as the poles planted at the sides of a well. A self-assured female, she made it her privilege to walk at the front of the camels, the first lady, with a huge black udder hanging below her, the four parts crowned with a teat bursting with

ابو زويد وهو ياخذ عْقال دبي وهو يمِدّه لُه وهو ياخذ عقالُه هو وهو يعقدُه برقبته. ايقن دبي انه يبيه. قال ابشر بَه تستاهلَه يابو دِخيل تراه لك تستاهله يابو دخيل خْذَه واهزَعَه مع مَسْهَمَك.

هي اللي سبب هالقصيده ٧،١٦

راكب اللي للفيافي تموطِ   سِرْبال دَوٍّ ما تْلَيّش بْنَوبه
حمرا حَقَبْها للملوّح ينوط   يجوز لمسطور النشاما ركوبه
تلفي لاخو عليا عديمٍ شموط   عقيد عيراتٍ الى ضيّقوا به

اخو عليا دبي ابن فالح الشلاقي.

يا صاحبي طِيبِك فلا به غْلوط   من ماكرٍ كل المراجل غْدوا به
ياما لخطوات العجاجه تِسُوط   تسوق عمرك للنشاما جِلوبه
ليا كاد يومٍ به تِضيق القْلوط   يومٍ يشيب الراس من حرّ شَوبه
صِفت حياض الموت مثل الشطوط   وضاقت على ممهون الاريا دروبه
لى يا بعد خَطْو الشناص القِنوط   يَظْنَى الى جا قِشْدِتُه طير ذَوبه
يا شوق بيضٍ هافيات الوسوط   خواند ما سايلن عن دبوبه
ابو قرونٍ عذّبن المشوط   شقرٍ ذوايبهن تخطّف عقوبه
ابو ثمانٍ مثل دِرّ البِسوط   بِكرٍ وضيرَه فاطرٍ جمّعوا به

البسوط الناقة الحلوبه.

milk. Abū Zwayyid looked at her, spellbound, marveling at how she strode at the herd's front. "This she-camel will feed my children," he told himself. He dismounted at her side, took off Dabbī's ribbon, handed it to him, and tied his own rope to its neck. Dabbī understood that Abū Zwayyid had set his sights on her. "Don't you worry. Be of good cheer!" he said. "That's the one you deserve, Abū Dikhīl. Sure, you can have her; you are worthy of her, Abū Dikhīl. Take her and add her to your share of the booty!"

That is the story at the origin of this poem: **16.7**

Hey, rider of camel trotting through bleak wastes:
tireless, at an unflagging pace she barrels ahead.
Red-brown, too tall to be vaulted upon,
beast fit for recklessly brave youngsters.
Steer her to ʿAlyā's brother, the grizzled warrior,
who leads rugged lean camels on risky raids:

—ʿAlyā's brother is Dabbī ibn Fāliḥ al-Shlāgī.

My friend, your goodness is free of impurities,
scion of a nest that breeds the noblest strains:
Fearless, you plunge into battle's dusty whirl;
you resolutely put your life at risk without a care
When hardened fighters' hearts freeze in terror,
hair whitened from gunpowder hovering in a melee,
Pools of death swell, sparkling like mighty rivers,
men humbled and lost, as dimwits stumble about.
We want you! Not a mean-spirited, grasping miser,
one who erupts if a moth lands in his clotted cream.[118]
Wasp-waisted, lily-white beauties dream of you:
hip-swaying princesses who despise uncouth louts;
Combs struggle, stuck in their thick tresses,
light-brown curls cascading down onto firm behinds;
Front teeth gleaming, white as sweet camel milk:
like a young lady suckling a devoted camel mother;

—*Al-bisūṭ* is a suckling camel.

ابو خـدَيـــدٍ زاهي بـه نُقوط   مـعورَجٍ بيه ازرق الوشم دوبـه
نِشـداتهن عن طـايلين الخـطوط   تفتِق لهم عن مَقْرَن الجيب ثوبـه
مـتى السلوقي روس الاقدام يوطي   ومتى يذَعْـذَع له ذواري هَـبوبـه
ومـتى يجـين بوقت الاولاد مُوطي   يا عاد انا سـبرَه ليا ما غـدوا بـه

موطي اللي تبي تِلد.

لو عـقّـدوا بارقـابهن الخيوط   خـَزِيزتي تمشي وَحـَد ما شقوا بـه

يعني ناقتي مطلِّعَه مطلّعه ابن فالح. الخيوط العقل والغداف يعقدونه الغزو بارقاب الكسب البـل.

Rosy cheeks adorned with blue tattoo designs,
a light touch of dark stains etched by needles.
They ask for men whose strides are long and bold:
for them they unhook their dress to show a breast.
When saluki hunting dogs rise, stretch, go at a trot;
when breezes of good fortune stir and begin to blow;
When the she-camel is about to give birth to her calf:
am I not her scout, even if others took hold of her?

—*Mūṭī* is a she-camel ready to deliver her calf.

Never mind that they tied their ribbons to her neck!
She's mine, an exquisite favor not begrudged.

He means to say: she is my camel, presented to me as a special distinction by Ibn Fāliḥ. Ribbons, lengths of camel rope, and headdresses are tied to camels' necks by raiders who capture them.

مع خرزنة الفضيل

١٠١٧ ابو زويد تَغابَش هو وايّا له عبدي عند ناقه. البدو اوّل يتغابِشون مثل اباعرٍ نهيبيه ايام المغازي. تغابشوا لهم ناقة وَورَدَوا الحقّ. وانهَجَوا يتطالبون عند لهم عارفه. العارفه والله ناسٍ يقولون ابن شريم وناسٍ يقول ابن جبرين ولا عاد ادري من هو والا الوكاد انُه عبدي لكن ناسٍ يقولون ابن شريم اللي هم تطالبوا عنده وناسٍ يقولون ابن جبرين. لكن الوكاد انه عبدي خصيم ابو زويد. والى مير العارفه يعرف العبدي خصيم ابو زويد من عَربهم بس ما يعَرف ابو زويد. قال نبيك تخلّصنا. قال وين خصيمك يالعبدي. قال هكالرجّال. قال هذاك. قال لا. قال هذاك. قال لا. قال هذاك. قال لا. يغطّ على هالرجاجيل الكبار المتبيّنين. قال وين هو خصيمك. قال هذاك. يا مير ابو زويد عَوَرٍ اقشَرٍ وجهه. بحَّر بالديوان يوم راعى يا مير هكالخِلْقه هكالوجه الشيّفه اللي ما عمره شافه والديوان يعرفهم ربعه. قال هذا. قال هذا. قال أوه ثاريه هالوجه السميح هالوجه السِفر. هذا فليح وبليح.

٢٠١٧ وهو ينطّ بخَلقُه ابو زويد قال يا حلالي والله انا ما انا جايّك ابيك تحلّى خدّي كان تبي زين الخدّ انحَر خَرْنَة الفضيل بنت ابن رمال اللي يتخانق الحمار والبياض بوجنته والا انا ابو زويد وجه الذيب مخيّب الطِليب أجرب بعِنّة مجدور أنا جايٍّ ابي حق الله اللي بيني وبين خصيمي. قال هو انت ابو زويد. قال انا ابو زويد. قال تدري يا عبدي

With Khaznah al-Fiḍīl

Abū Zwayyid quarreled with a man of the ʿAbdah division of Shammar about ownership of a she-camel. In the olden days, Bedouin raiders often fought over camels they had captured from other tribes. In this case, they agreed to seek expert advice on how to resolve their dispute. They went to see a tribal judge knowledgeable in matters of customary law. I don't know who it was. Some say they sought out Ibn Shrēm; according to others, they went to see Ibn Jibrīn. I have no idea. But I do know for sure that the judge was from the ʿAbdah division of Shammar. And I know for certain that Abū Zwayyid's opponent was also from the ʿAbdah. The judge knew the other ʿAbdī litigant. They belonged to the same tribal group. But the judge had never met Abū Zwayyid before. The other man said, "We have come to ask your assistance in settling our dispute." "Where is your opponent, ʿAbdī?" the judge asked. "Is it that man?" The judge gestured. "Or this one?" he asked. "No." "Is it him?" "No." "This one then?" The judge kept pointing to important-looking men, those who stood out from the crowd. "Well, tell me who your opponent is." "Here, this fellow here." There he was, Abū Zwayyid, one-eyed, a man with a repulsive, inauspicious mien. The judge had been looking around the assembly to determine to whom the man of ʿAbdah was referring. Naturally, he had passed over the man with loathsome, ghostly features such as he had never encountered before. The other faces in the assembly were familiar to him: they were his fellow tribesmen. "Really, this one?" "Indeed," the other said. "Ah, this kind and generous face, this bright-eyed man! This sparkling mind and vivid presence!" 17.1

Angrily, Abū Zwayyid jumped at him. "Listen, deary!" he said. "Must I tell you that I didn't come to have you gaze in admiration at my face! If you're looking for a pretty face, you're better off heading for Khaznah al-Fiḍīl, the daughter of Ibn Rmāl, on whose cheeks the colors red and white vie for preeminence. I am Abū Zwayyid: the wolf-faced bane of his pursuers, a mangy camel in a pen made of thorny bushes where those infected with smallpox are quarantined.[119] I am here with my opponent to seek justice, my rightful share." "Are you Abū Zwayyid?" he exclaimed. "Yes, I am Abū Zwayyid." "You know 17.2

ترما لك حق عندي تراك مفلوج وانت الفالج يابو زويد بليّا طلابه. والله ما احسبه انت اسمَع بك واحسب انك ما هذا لونك هالحين يوم صِرت ابو زويد وشّو عليه تطالبون. قال علي بعير. قال ابشر بالبعير ان بغيت فالج والا مفلوج كان انت مفلوج انا انطيك بعير كان انت فالج ما تبي لاحد كرامه.

٣،١٧ دَرَت خزنة الفضيل بنت ابن رمال وْوَصّت له انّهُ لازم يجي ابي اواجهه. خزنه بنت فضيل ابو هِجْهوج من الجارد أختٍ لفهد وجارد جارد التالي ما هو جارد الاول. خزنه وصّت هكالرجّال رايح من جماعته لعرب ابو زويد. قالت يا جيت خلف ابو زويد سَلِّم لي عليه عدد ما بيني وبينه من الاشجار والاحجار. قال طيب مَنْقَلَه خفيف. بلّغُه الرساله. وابو زويد لو هو رجّال مسِيس ما هو نَظِر وحاقِرٍ روحُه يعني ان هالبنت المزيونه بنت الشيوخ تبي تَعَشّقُه. بِحِل ما يدري وش رايَه ولا بينهم اتصال وهي بنت شيوخ وْتَقْصِر هقوتُه دونَه. جا عِقِب ذلك ولَف له قصيدة بخزنة ونحر الفضيل سيّر عليهم.

٤،١٧ وهي تثور خزنة – يوم بنات البدو قبل ما يْتَغَمْغِمن هالتِّغِمْغِم وتنهج مع هالرجاجيل تْخاويهم اما وِرْد وامّا حَدْرِه كأنهم اخوانَه كأنهم اخوانه. المذاهب طيّبه ما تْهولِس واهله ما يهولسون. هالحين لو تشوف لك رجّالٍ يحاكي مِرة قالوا اوه هذا به ما لا به شف. – خزنة الفضيل مزيونه وتزيّنت وتْنَحَّر ابو زويد مثل حايل المغاتير تهَنْفَل.

what, you 'Abdī," the judge said to his opponent, "I cannot help you with your case. You have lost, and you, Abū Zwayyid, are hereby declared the winner, even without pleading. Honestly, I did not have the faintest notion that you were Abū Zwayyid. I have heard about you, but I had no idea what you looked like. Now that I know that you are Abū Zwayyid, what is it that you are litigating?" "Well, it's about a camel that I claim." "Don't you worry," the judge said. "You'll get your camel, no matter what. It wouldn't make a difference whether you were ruled the winner or loser in the case. If the verdict goes against you, I'll give you the camel. And if the outcome is in your favor, well then, you owe favors to no one."

The story came to the ears of Khaznah al-Fiḍīl, the daughter of Ibn Rmāl. 17.3
She expressed a wish to have the poet visit her and meet. Khaznah, the daughter of Fiḍīl Abū Hijhūj of the Jārid branch, the sister of Fahd and Jārid—the later Jārid, not the earlier ancestor. She passed the message through a man of her clan who was going to see people who belonged to Abū Zwayyid's group. She said, "If you happen to run into Abū Zwayyid, give him my greetings, as many as there are bushes and stones on your way between me and him." "Very well," he said. "That's an easy errand." He did as he was told: he delivered her message to Abū Zwayyid. While it is true that Abū Zwayyid was a man of good sense and smart, he was also aware of his ghastly and shabby looks. Now this famous beauty, daughter of a shaykh, was making advances at him. He looked bemused, not knowing what to think or say. They had never been in touch: as the daughter of a family of shaykhs, she was in another class, beyond his social rank. Nevertheless, he composed a poem in honor of Khaznah and he set out toward al-Fiḍīl with the aim of paying her a visit.

Khaznah seized the opportunity: This was in the olden days, before Bed- 17.4
ouin girls began to cover up and act bashfully, when they still consorted freely with men and spent time in their company, for instance on their way to water the herds or when traveling with the pack camels to stock up at distant markets, just as if they were brothers and sisters. The nice olden ways, free of whispers and base gossip. Those folk would not spread malicious talk. Unlike these days: when a man is seen speaking to a woman, people cast all kinds of unfounded aspersions. See now! Khaznah al-Fiḍīl was an acclaimed beauty, widely admired for her grace. She put on her most attractive attire and headed for Abū Zwayyid, flaunting herself like a pure-white, virgin she-camel, in her most coquettish gait. She said, "Welcome, my dearest Khalaf!

قالت يا بعد حَيِّ يا خلف جابك اللّٰه يابو زويد أنت تمدّحن عند عبده دونك طوقي – الطوق مثل الرشرش يعني بدال الرشرش وهو ذهب مبرم به سناسل – قال فهد اخوه ما انت لابسٍ طوق خزنة انت رجل مير اغَدين اشريه بجْمَلَه . وهو يشريه بجملَه الاوضح جمل الظلّه . وهو ياخذُه قال هدو خزنه مقبول . شْمِتوا به شمر . قالوا يابو زويد ما لك حَظّ كيف جمل خزنه تاخذه جمل الظله . قال ما عليه قِلّ زوامل يجيب ابوَه له جمل مثلُه من اباعر القوم ولكن انا ما متهيٍّ لي الا هالجمل هذا والا غيره ما تهيّا لي منه شين

٥،١٧ القلب يِبْرِم بالهواجيس ويدير   من جادلٍ جَتْنا طوارف طروشه

ما هي مِرْسِلةٍ لُه هي خَزْنه تقول سَلّموا لي على ابو زويد وقولوا له يسَيِّر علينا .

قام الفهيم يصَخّر القيل تصخير   طرايفٍ ما هِن قَرايض دحوشه
ابو نهودٍ شاحياتٍ مِزابير   الا ولا لِهْس الوِغد يخموشه
وِشْنيّوات التَرف غِرٍّ مغاتير   من ذاقهن يسقم بليّا معوشه
خَدّه من الموت الحَمَر به دواوير   كِنّ الصعيوي دَورجَن في نقوشه

دق الوشم دقاق مثل مواطي الصعو دقاقه .

احمر عَفَر وِمْذَكِّر دوب تَذْكير   لميع مصقولٍ بضَولات هَوشه
والعين عين اللي بروس العناقير   نجلٍ سواد عيونها مع رموشه
الرِدف يَشْدى نابيات الحَمارير   عقب السوافي كاربَتها رشوشه

God brought you here, Abū Zwayyid. You said nice things about me when you were with ʿAbdah. Here, take my necklace!" The kind of necklace that hangs down like a pendant, made of twisted strings of gold. Fahd, his brother, said to him, "You can't do that. As a man, you can't wear Khaznah's necklace! But perhaps she will let you have her camel instead, the huge white stud camel that carries the lady's litter." And he followed this advice. He said, "I am not going to refuse a present given by Khaznah." Shammar tribesmen poked fun at him. They said, "How about it, Abū Zwayyid? You seem to have run out of luck. How could you accept the camel of Khaznah, the camel that carries the lady's litter?" He said, "She has no shortage of pack camels. Her father will easily replace it with a camel he plunders from the enemy. As for myself, the only thing that will do for me is this camel, the one she gave me. Anything else would not suit me."

My heart is beset by worries, driven berserk, 17.5
since being told about a fair, curly-haired maiden.

—Didn't Khaznah say, "Give my greetings to Abū Zwayyid and tell him to pay me a visit?"

She stirred the artist in me to craft verses:
exquisite lines, not the rhymes of a dabbling hack.
Her breasts are broad and prominent,
never scratched by the nails of a suckling infant.
Small, finely chiseled teeth with a dewy gleam
sate a hungry man's craving if tasted and licked.
Her cheeks: daubed in colors of red-hot death,
dotted with tattoos like traces left by tiny birds;

—The marks of the tattoos are delicate, like the imprints left on soft ground by little birds.

Cheeks tainted red with the slightest touch of white.
Nose: glint of a sword wielded in close combat.[120]
Eyes agleam, a falcon's gaze on a rocky perch;
large and wide, shaded by lashes thick and long.
Buttocks bulging like knolls of reddish sand,
smoothed by breezes, firmed by scattered rain,

أو زاد شطّ حَوَيّرٍ له على ضـير   أمّـه جِـضور وراعِـيَه ما يِنوشـه
وقرون شقـرٍ فوق متـنه دعـاثيـر   شقـرٍ ومـريوك الخضيرا رشوشـه
سيقـان من تحت الرَّكَب كالجاميـر   ومحـاصرٍ يَشْـدِن مِـباني كبوشـه

الكبوش الزبر اللي يجلسون عليه الحكام.

لا من القصار ولا الطوال الطماريـر   ولا من العراض ولا الدقاق النشوشـه
ومْـصَوّرٍ منـبوز الارداف تصويـر   سبحان عـزّال الذهب من قروشـه
سِـرْجوف حمرا روّحت مع معاييـر   سـحوق حمـرا نايشاتـه عطوشـه
والله يالولا باقي النـــاس لاشيـر   اخـــاف من ناسٍ تَنَشّر قشوشـه

فلان يركض يبيه وفلان يركض يبيَه.

لاقول عِجُّوا بالبـنيّ الغـــناديـر   واجـرح من له عِشـقـةٍ ما يحوشـه
هِيف الوسوط ونابيات المحـاصيـر   حَوشـاتِهن تِغـري قِلـيل الدبوشـه
اِنْهَب من الدنيـا وخَلّ التـدابيـر   مـا تعـلم الدنيـا بغـايب دخوشـه

نهج ابو زويد مع الحَذَرِه. يقول يومٍ جا هكالمسرا والى والله مْتَحَيْزِمٍ قال اقعدوا ٦،١٧
اقعدوا. قالوا العِلْم. قال والله حلمت خزنة الفضيل جِتَن والله ان كل الحمول اشيلهن
هالحين يقوله ابو زويد. يقول وهم لك يقومون يشيلون. يقول يِرْكي على هِجْهوج

Or humps of calves fed by devoted foster camels;
prickly mothers, not bothered by their owners.[121]
Her tresses tumble down the back in profusion:
bright chestnut, sprinkled with delicious scents.
Her juicy calves, a palm core's immaculate white;
haunches broad like benches under palace walls.

—*Al-kbūsh* are the raised benches of clay that run the length of the rulers' palace courtyard.

She's not plump and short or spindly and gangly;
not fat and sagging or so frail as not to be touched.
With bold strokes her bulging behind was drawn
by the Lord who separates gold from baser coinage.
Belly lean and taut like a raider's reddish camel,
a long-backed animal, thirsty from desert crossings.[122]
By God, I'd counsel, were it not for some people—
my fear of scatterbrained folks spilling the beans—

—One comes running for her, then another, all eager to have her.

I'd say, "Be quick! Hasten to the pick of magnificent girls!"
Ah, wounded by unrequited love, what searing pain!
Wasp-waisted and wide-hipped girls are tantalizing,
beyond the means of poor devils lacking camel herds.
Seize the day, waste no time weighing pros and cons:
you can't foretell what future the world has in store.

Abū Zwayyid joined a caravan of pack camels that traveled eastward in 17.6
order to stock up at the markets. When the caravan rested during its nightly march, he girded himself, ready for action. "Get up, get up!" he yelled. "What's the matter?" they asked. "By God, Khaznah al-Fiḍīl appeared to me in a dream and told me to carry all of the caravan's loads without further delay." The others understood the message: they rose and loaded their chattel on the pack camels in order to continue on their journey. On this occasion, he composed some lines, addressing them to Khaznah's father, Hijhūj, the shaykh of the Rmāl tribe.

يا راكب اللي ما يـداني الحَسـاسِ　　مرعوب يشدى مصايح عقب الامراس
يلفي ذراي ظـلال بالقيـظ راسي　　نِلوذ بـه يا حـلّ تقـطيع الانفـاس
يامـير ياحـامى النضـا بالهـداسِ　　ياما كسبت بتـالي الهجن نوماس
البـارحـة وانا بغـرقـة نعـاسي　　عِـدّي مع الموتى بقِـلْبـان الادقـاس
ما انا على ما شـفت بالحلم ناسي　　كنّـه بقـلبي كـاتبينه بِقـرْطـاس
هـلَه بحَر قـالوا وَعـر مـا يقـاس　　مـا تاتي القـالات منهم بالايّاس
يا قيـل مـفْـلَى عِـقْـلةٍ مـا ينـاسِ　　دونـه من الديّان واللال والنـاس
أنت الذي يا ميـر للراي داسِ　　نبّـه على راعى الرديّـة من الراس
كم من غـلامٍ عند عمّـه يشـاكي　　يقول لذّات الغـنى عقب الاياس
وعمّـه يقول عن الظـما والشـماس　　اِرْكَب على اللي جـالسٍ خمْسَة اجـلاس

الغلام يوم يشكي على عمه يقول ابغزي يحسبه يبي يقول له الخير واجد يا ولَيدي لا تعَرّض روحك للمَهالك وعمه يقول اِرْكَب على اللي جالس خمسة اجلاس اركب على الذلول الطيبة وطِسّ لا تقعد.

ما هو من اللي منـزله بالمِسـاسِ　　راعي شـياهٍ زايـداتٍ على الراس

المساس المرا الارض الطيّبه اللي به رِبيع. هذا عند العرب اول يقول راوَسْت شياهك وِشْلَون راوَسْت شِياهك. يراوسوهن بالمرا أيام الرِبيع. الى صارن سِت شياه ياخذون منهن سَبع اصواع دِهن زايدتٍ صاع على عدد روسهن. كل نعجه يوخذ منه صاع دهن ياخذونه اهلهن حَيصولهن نتاجهن. تاخذ سبع اصواع من ست شياه لأن الارض مِرِيّه ومرَبّعه.

Rider of a skittish camel that hates getting hit,
easily scared, alert and fresh after grueling runs:
Head for the man who shades me in brutal heat,
my refuge when I feel choked, my breath cut off:
You are a chief who shields camels in a tussle,
who gains glory by fending off the enemy at the rear.
Yesterday, immersed in the depths of slumber,
tumbling head over heels down shafts of death,
In my dreams appeared a specter, not a human shape,
to inscribe dictates on my heart, as if on scrolls of paper.
Her folk, it's said, are a deep sea, hard to fathom.
Don't despair, in peril they rush to your rescue:
Herds robbed from pasture at distant lonely wells,
beyond huge plains, shimmering mirage, enemies.
You, dear Chief, thrash out matters, cut the knot—
unfailingly you spot and unmask feckless wiseasses.
A youngster who pours out his heart to an elder,
his desire to capture riches, to escape penury,
Braced for warnings of danger, thirst, glaring heat,
is told, "Go! Ride a mature mount, tried and tested!"[123]

—A young man tells his guardian how much he'd love to set out on a raiding expedition, in the belief that the elder will urge caution, telling him, "There is plenty of everything you need where we are, my boy. Don't venture out and expose yourself to dangers and risk your life!" Contrary to expectation, his guardian urges him to do so, saying, "Take a she-camel that has given birth five times, a hardy mount, and ride! Don't hang around here, go!"

Not for him long sojourns on rich pasture,
fattening his sheep and churning butter.

—He speaks about excellent rain-fed grazing covered with lush grasses and plants.[124] Such experts at fattening sheep vie with one another in making profits and keep asking their fellows, "How are your sheep doing?" From six sheep they'd take more than forty pounds of fat, more than six pounds per head of sheep, from each ewe. They'd do so because they pasture sheep on prime pasture grounds soaked by fresh rains.

مـتحـيزمٍ ويثوّر البـقـل جـاسي   شـيمـاص تلق وِذيتـه تثْـلِم الفـاس

البِقَل اللبن يطَبّخونه والى جِمَد على النار ويبَقّر بايديه بْقَر بكار تثلم الفاس ما يعرف الا معزاوه وبقله.

. . . .   ويـداوي المِخْـخَض الى صـار محْـتاس

Girded up, he boils bubbling milk into dried cheese:
the miser's rock-hard chunks dent an axe's blade.[125]

—To make dried cheese, *bigal*, he boils milk until it thickens over the fire. Then he cuts the cheesy mass into pieces like patties, big chunks so hard they would dent the blade of an axe. The only thing he knows and cares about are his goats and the cheese.

[...]
Out of sorts, dizzy, he rocks the milk skin forever.[126]

مع مكيده بنت جمعان الغيثي

١،١٨ شاعت قصيدة ابو زويد بخزنة الفضيل يا هكالبنت بنتٍ يقال له مَكيده بنت لجمعان الغيثِي مَزْيونه تَسمع عن ابو زويد وقصيده وتمنّى شوفِتُه قالت نَذْرٍ على رِقْبَتي ان شافت عيني عين ابو زويد اني لاسلّم عليه على هالكلام المليح. يقول قالت هالكلمة ما تِحَسب انه تصدف بُه كلمةٍ يطير بَه الهوا. يقول يوم جا بعض المرّات بالصيف وهي تصافق شمر وتَشرّع على خبرا اللميما بالصِليب صليب عقارب القاع ضاربها لَه رشاشٍ البارح وكاربةٍ القاع وذاريَته الذوراي وغادية الطعاميس وش تقول. غاية المطلوب.

٢،١٨ جاك ابو زويد مورّدٍ غنَيماتُه على الخبرا من عرض خلق الله. يقول ياقولة هكالواحد يا مكيده انتِ تشوفين راعى المواعزهذاك هذاك هكاللي على جال الخبرا واقفٍ على عصاوه تَرِي هذاك ابو زويد هكاللي ندرتي انك لازم تسَلّمين عليه ان شفتيه. قالت ادخل على الله ياشين. قال والله ان هذاك ابو زويد. يقول وهي تجيك تمشي يمّه مع وسط الما تِخِضّ الما تلبس ثوَيبات الفِضيحه وتِرَخي لثامه عن حنجرّته وتفتش عن سيقانَه لما طلعت صابونة الركبه مثل بياض الرِبّه وهي تِدِشّ الخبرا يمّه ناحرتُه دالعٍ مثل البَكرة الوضحا.

٣،١٨ يقول امْشَي امْشَي حتى انه وَصَلته. قالت ياولد هو انت ابو زويد. قال على الخير والشَرّ. قالت قل والله انّي انا ابو زويد. قال والله لو اموت فلا تشوفين ابو زويد.

With Mkīdah, Daughter of Jam'ān al-Ghēthī

Abū Zwayyid's poem on Khaznah al-Fiḍīl created a stir. When it came to the ears of Mkīdah, the beautiful daughter of Jam'ān al-Ghēthī, she decided that she too wanted to meet Abū Zwayyid.[127] She said, "I swear a sincere oath on my life that when I come face to face with Abū Zwayyid I will greet him warmly on account of the beautiful words he spoke." She said this without thinking it would ever happen: just things people say without giving much thought to it, words carried away by the wind. Sometimes in late spring, these tribal divisions of Shammar would pick up their goods and chattels and march toward the pools of water left by rains at al-Lmēmā in the area of Ṣlēb al-'Agārib. The flat plain had received a sprinkling of rain, a few light showers, the day before. The moisture and a cool breeze had rippled and firmed the sandy bottom up to where the sand dunes rose in waving curves. A marvelous sight, the most delightful scene imaginable. 18.1

It so happened that of all people it was Abū Zwayyid who drove his small herd of goats to drink from the large pool of water left by the rains. Someone said to Mkīdah, "Do you see that goatherd standing there at the rim of the pool, leaning on his cane? Well, that's Abū Zwayyid. You remember the sincere oath you swore—that you would greet him if you happened to see him?" "Aren't you ashamed of yourself, rascal?" she said. "No," he said, "the Lord is my witness, that's him, none other than Abū Zwayyid." No sooner had he finished his sentence than Mkīdah waded into the pool, heading straight for Abū Zwayyid at the other side. She was dressed rather flimsily. Her clothes left little to the imagination. The veil covering her mouth had come untied and dangled from her neck. Pulling up her skirt to keep the hem out of the water, she revealed her lower legs and knees, the color of a pure white flower, as she moved toward him. She headed straight for him, prancing like a playful young she-camel. 18.2

"Go, go!" he encouraged her. When she reached him, she said, "My boy, are you Abū Zwayyid?" "True enough, for better or for worse," he said. "Make yourself clear: say, 'By God, I am Abū Zwayyid.'" "Well, if I died right now, 18.3

قالت يادلالي يابعد الحيّ والميت وش علمك يادافع البلا ما ندري وراك ساهجنا وسامجنا والكلب اللي ينبح عليك ذابحينُه تراي انا ياخيّي اجدّع النذور على شوفتك وهالحين الله جابك. هو شوفه ضباعي عمشٍ رِدِيٍّ شوفه يوم بحرّ وليا هكالبنت اللي رافعة ثوبَه عن الما وليا مير سيقانه بوسط الما يوضِن مثل اللمبات. قالت ياخَيّ انت تقصد بهالجيش وتقصد بافعال الرجال وحنا ياهالبنات ما عمرك قصدت بنا. وهي تمشي عليه وهي تسلّم عليه. قالت قوّ خلف قوّ خلف قوّ خلف ثلاث تسليمات ياهلا ياهلا. وهي ترخي اللثام وهي تَعَقّب يدها من وراوه وهي تنشّه وتقمعه مع الرِمّه بثلاث حبّات يما انقطع نفسه لما غورقت عيونه طاح عصاوه من يده. قالت اللّهم ان هذا سلام وهذا وفاة لنَذْري وهذا الوداع ثلاث مرات.

ويطلعون من الخبرا وتقوم هي تحاكيه وهم يتبارون على لهم حنَيْزِيز عريقيب ذاريه الهوى وكاربه رشاش البارح. وتقوم تبْرَى لُه والى مِشَتّ قامت تَدْحَمَه بمَنْكَبَه والخاصره من هانا ويشوف ردوفها تَهتَزّ هاللون. قالت بارك الله بهالزوامل اللي خَلّتَن مير اشوفك انا لاحقتهن ابرِدّهن ويوم الله جابك اليوم بغيت اتونّس انا واياك. مير يابعد حَيّ شياهك شربن الهوا عَطَن خشومهن للهوى لا يَوَلّن يقطِعنّ من تعِلّتك الْحق الغنم ريّضَه وانا ابفْهق هكالزوامل عليك اتونّس انا واياك. ما من زَمِل. يوم اقفى يبي يرِدّ غنيماته وهي تحترف وتلوذ عنُه وتطبّ مع العريقيب وتقفي وتخلّيه. هم العَصَير تبي تغيب الشمس. ٤،١٨

you wouldn't get to see Abū Zwayyid." "Ah, honey!" she said. "My darling, my sweet![128] How are you? What are you up to, my savior from misery? Why did you forget us? What made you pay no attention to us? When we'd make short work of any dog that dared bark at you! Do you know, my dear, I made solemn vows that I must come face to face with you at any cost. And now, see! God has fulfilled my wishes!" His looks were ugly: the snout of a hyena and watery eyes that made for poor vision. He stood there squinting and straining to have a good look at that girl as she came hurrying toward him, her skirt lifted from the surface of the water and her shiny legs like lamps illuminated from below. "Little brother dear," she said, "why do you compose verses about speedy camel mounts and daring feats without ever paying attention to us, the girls, in your songs?" As she spoke, she drew closer to him and kept uttering greetings. "Strength, Khalaf![129] Strength, from strength to strength!" She repeated it three times: "Welcome, welcome!" She lowered the veil from her mouth, put her hand behind his neck and pulled him toward her, dipped her nose below his ear and inhaled deeply, then planted three firm kisses on his mouth, cutting off his breath, until his eyes almost sank into his skull, and he let his cane drop. "By God Almighty," she exclaimed, "one by way of a greeting, the second to absolve me from my oath, and the last as a farewell."

They moved away from the pond, chatting all the while as they kept walking over the crest of an elongated elevation of hard stone, its base covered with windblown sands that had been firmed by light sprinkles of rain the day before. They walked side by side, so close that now and then she would bump into him with her shoulder and hips. He could not help noticing her buttocks quivering—like this—with her every movement.[130] "God bless those pack camels that allowed me a chance to see you! I came to collect them and bring them home, but when it was my good fortune to see you, I wanted to have the pleasure of talking with you and getting to know you. But, my dearest, your sheep have started drifting away; they have turned their heads against the wind and are going where they please. Don't let them move off too far: they'll deprive me of our conversation. Fetch your sheep and goats. And I will steer my camels to you, I enjoy chatting with you so much. Do not fret!" He went to fetch his sheep and goats; she likewise turned back and then walked away, disappearing over the top of the low ridge. She had gone, leaving him all by himself. It was late afternoon and the sun was about to set. 18.4

٥،١٨ ابو زويد نِكَس ما لقاه يا مير انهَبَل وطار قلبُه. هو شيفه اصْوَر وجهه اقْشَر لكنه طيّب شاعر وطيب ذراع ومن حَموله من الرخيص. هو مِحف فقْرِيٍ ما عمره ذاق الشي هذا هالشيٍ اللي جاوه مثل لخ الكنديش بالحرّ هو راعي غنم وهي مع البل. راحت البل وخلّته. يوم جا هلُه يا مير هالشرّ معُه. دلّى يركّض وكل رجّالٍ يكهمُه يبي ينشدُه عن هالبنت يستحي مْنُه. يْنَشّد ما عينّتوا فريق رْواة بَدْوٍ اهل اباعر. قالوا والله ما عينّا الناس كله مجتمعة. يوم جا الصبح وهو يشد ذلوله وهو يحيك دوّار مثل ما تدوّر الذاهبة. يقول وهكاليوم كله. يوم بغت تغيب الشمس يامير افمه يابس وغادي لك ابد خربان.

٦،١٨ يوم طلع على هكالبل يا راعي هكالبعير مِنْبِطح على بعيره دوّار. قال يابناخي تَرَن حَرْجان كان معك مانٍ تسقينَن. قال وش اسقيك جل ما هوانت اللي احبّتك امس مكيدة بنت خلف الجمعان. وش قلت بمكيدة وش انت قلت به يوم حَبّتّك. هو ما يدري وين هي. قال هه وش تقول. اكبر وانا كبير البخت. يا مير يوم انه نِشع. قال وين هي مكيده. قال تشوف البيت هذاك. هذولاك هَلَه. قال يابناخي قَرّب قَرّب عطني عِلْمتَك احبّه تري عدّك اليوم مسقينَن وحاجٍّ بي.

٧،١٨ يا خلف الجمعان رفيقٍ له يسيّر عليه وراعي قهوة بْصَفُّه. عرف انه بنتُه ويفوت يمّ بيت جمعان. وهو ينصاهم ويجيب مطيتُه بْصَفّ البيت صيفِة خاطر وينوّخ

On his way back, he hoped to see her again but didn't. He had fallen head over heels in love with her, hopelessly love drunk. He could think only of her. But he had not much to recommend himself. His looks were awful. His eyes were turned to the side, like a locust's. His face was repulsive. But he was a good, decent man. He made a living from his own work and came from a respectable lineage, the Rakhīṣ clan. He was always hard up, poverty-stricken. A thing such as he had tasted just now had never before come his way. It felt like a blast of refreshing cool from an air conditioner at a time of great heat. All he owned were small cattle. Her folks were prestigious camel nomads. The camels moved away with their big strides and left him behind. He rejoined his relatives, carrying his heartsickness with him. He kept running around, looking for people to accost and question, though he felt shy asking about her. He pressed them urgently: "Have you come across a group of Bedouin on their way to water their camels?" "No, we haven't," they said. "Everyone has gathered in one place." Next morning, he set out, riding here and there, making the rounds on his camel, the way someone looks for a runaway camel. He spent all day searching. When the sun began to sink toward the horizon, he was overcome by fatigue and his throat was parched. 18.5

At that moment, he ran into a shepherd who was dozing, belly forward, stretched out on his mount as it circled a herd of camels. "Hey, little brother!" he called to him. "I am in a bit of trouble. Could you spare some water for me to drink?" "Who am I to offer you a draft of water? Weren't you the one whom Mkīdah, the daughter of Khalaf al-Jamʿān, was seen kissing yesterday? What did you say about Mkīdah when she was kissing you? And then you pretend not to know her whereabouts! What did you say? Huh? 'God is great and I am the most fortunate man on earth.' So mightily pleased were you." "Now tell me," Abū Zwayyid said. "Where is the tent of Mkīdah?" "Do you see that tent over there? That's where her folk are staying." "Brother of mine, come here, let me kiss your nose! You have quenched my thirst and taken me on the pilgrimage![131] Such a huge favor you did me." 18.6

The tent owner was Khalaf al-Jamʿān, a friend on whom he used to call and someone who served coffee to visitors outside his tent. He knew that she was his daughter and he headed for Jamʿān's tent. He approached them, leading his mount close to where they were seated, next to the tent, as if he were a casual visitor. But as he dismounted, he was at once recognized as Abū Zwayyid: a charming raconteur, without a malicious streak or vile intent; 18.7

يا الرجّال يعرفون ابو زويد له سوالف مليحة ولا هو رِدِي طيّب هو بسّ انه ضعيفٍ حَواله هذا شي من الله. يقول وهو يجيك ويوم ظهر على الرجّال يا مير يوم عَرْفوه وهم ينوضون. تَعَدّ تَعَدّ يابو زويد. ويجَلّسونه على المرَكّى بهكالمحلّ الحِلو. يوم قعد وسلّم وقعد عند الدلال سولفوا قالوا وش جابك يابو زويد. قال دوّار ادوّر ذاهبه. هم ظَنّوا انه اما ناقه اما نجه. قالوا تعرفَه. هي ماسومه. قال لا والله غِفِل لكن انه بَيِّنه. قالوا وشلون.

٨،١٨ قال

راكب اللي تِقِـل تـَذْرا من ايده   حمـرا على السَّنْدا ضِروم بِشوع
حـمرا تـْدَنّى للديار البـعيـده   حمـرا طواه القَفِل عقب الفِزوع
ياراكبه وَصّـِل سـلامي مْكيـده   حِبّـه مخَـلٍّ بالضمـايـر مْـزوع
والبطن ياذِرْعـة حـريرٍجِـديـده   ضامر ولا صيد اريش العين جوع

ما هي من اللي عِقْدَة سِرّه مثل دِمْنة الخلّه.

والراس ذيـل اللي تِلُوج بحـديـده   شقـرا ترادي من هواهـا الفزوع
هَـنّيتكم ياهـل القـلوب البِليـده   ما ولَّعَنّـه زاهـــيات الردوع
كلّ نهـار العيـد عـايد وديـده   وانا نهـار العيـد عيـدي دموعي
جوّ جمع من كل سمّوا بِـديـده   وجـان البـلا من ذيهبـان النجوع

ذيهبان النجوع النجوع المتفرقه شِذّان النجوع.

a good and likable fellow. It is just that he was disadvantaged by his straitened circumstances, as God had decreed. As soon as he appeared, they knew who he was and jumped to their feet. "Over here! Come over here, Abū Zwayyid!" They made him sit down in a prominent place of their circle and pulled over a carpeted camel saddle as an elbow rest for him to recline on and be comfortable. He sat down and they exchanged greetings. Coffeepots were readied and the conversation began. "What has brought you here, Abū Zwayyid?" they asked. "I am on a search," he said, "searching for one that has gone missing." They thought he meant a runaway she-camel or a ewe. "What animal? What shape are its brand marks?" "No, honest to God," he said, "she is without tribal marks, but even so it is clear who she is—she's known to all." "How is that?" they asked.

He answered in verse: **18.8**

Your camel glides, barely touching the ground; *1*
uphill the ruddy beast surges, resolute and fierce:
A fiery flame to whisk you to faraway lands,
its red-hued body wasted after grueling treks.
Hey, rider, quickly carry my greetings to Mkīdah:
Love of her is like a peg hammered into my heart.
Her smooth belly shines like a cubit of fresh silk,
flat and straight, but not for lack of food.

—She's not the kind of girl whose belly button has grown to the size of a camel dropping cluttered with sand on the caravan road.

Tresses: tail of a mare chafing at its shackles, *5*
restless sorrel horse, impatient to run and chase.
Lucky are those whose hearts are impervious
to fatal spells cast by tattoo-cheeked damsels.
All celebrate a feast by kissing the one they love;
my company are tears streaming down my cheeks.
Around the wells, joyous crowds mingle and meet:
I am haunted by the Bedouin who came and went.

—*Dhīhabān* are the various dispersed migrating groups.

٩،١٨ يقول امير يوم لاذت عليه هي من قَفْوا الذَرا وهو قاعدٍ عند ابوَه قالت يابو زويد والله ما عندي لك جزا كان ابوي راضي جيزة ثلاث ليال وتخلّينَن. قال ابوَه والله جِدَعْتِينَن بافم هالهامّه لا بالله الا راضي كان انتي راضية انا راضي. قال ابوَه والله يابو زويد بيني وبينك شرط ان قِبِلْتُه قدّام هالرجال فانا ابجيبه لك وان ما قبلته فلا لك عندي شين. قال اشرط وكل شروطك قابلهن. قال ابملّك لك عليَه واجَجر لك انت وايّاه بخيمه ثلاث ليال وتروح والله ما انا غاصبٍ بنتي عليك وان مَرِتَك ظَلَعت حامل نوصّي لك وتروح به وان كان هي ما طلعت حامل تخلّيه. قال وانا رضيت يا دلال عيني. واججروا لهم وعقب ثلاث ليال يَنْهَج من عندهم ولا قام له شهرين الا هم كازّنٍ له يقولون ترى مَرِتك حامل تعال خِذه. وتجيب دِخيل والعيال هذولا وتصيرهي ام عـياله.

From behind the tent's separation wall, she had overheard the words he spoke in her father's circle. She raised her voice: "Listen, Abū Zwayyid, I am not in a position to give you a reward for your verses. But if my father agrees, I might sleep with you three nights: after that, leave me alone." "By God," her father said, "you've thrown me into the maw of this monster. But honestly, I have no objection. As long as it is your wish to do so, it is fine with me." And he continued: "As long as you accept my condition, with these men here as our witnesses, I will allow you to have her; otherwise not." "Stipulate whatever you like, I'll accept any and all of your conditions." "After I have given her in marriage to you, the two of you will spend three nights in a wedding tent. Then you depart. Really, I do not want to force my daughter on you. If it turns out that she is pregnant, we will send you a message and you stay together. If not, you go your separate ways." "I am only too happy with that, my dearest friend!" They were confined to their marriage tent and after three nights he departed. Two months later they sent a messenger to inform him that his wife was expecting and that he should come to fetch her. She gave birth to his son Dikhīl and other children. She became the mother of his offspring. 18.9

مع ترفه بنت فلاح ابن فالح الشلاقي

١٫١٩ ابو زويد طِرَقي وجاك يبي الشلقان على طويّة هذي عِقب نَزلة الناس على الجِيّان والعربان هكالحين والبوادي. يوم طلع يا مير البيوت سبع مْثولِثايه (= مثولثات) الى مير الشلقان مع فلاح ابن فالح عَمّ لعَبَكْلي والى عنده ترفة الفلاح ما هي بجزيرة العرب كله يعني عند شمر مفهومه يوم بنات الطيّبين لهن قدر.

٢٫١٩ جا هو على ذلوله والسيف سلاحه سيف على وْروكه وِقِرْبَتُه يابسه يا مير يفرحون به الرجال هو بوقتُه هو وجنسُه وابن عنقا والهربيد اهل السوالف والقصيد والامثال. جا يوم جا والى هذولي المغاتير يوم مدّت العصر انذلِقت على المشرَع مشرع طَويّه الدِبَش يشرب هالحَزّه على المشرَع. وهو يورّد ذلوله معهن عليَه حشيّشه وعليَه قِربتُه دْغَرت الذلول مع البل وحوّل اخذ البشت وحَوّل وسلّم على الرجال آل فالح يوم انه شرّعت والى مير يوم صوّت لُه هكالواحد قال خَلّ المَجعوفة إلحق تِقَهُو ابى انَشّدك. وهو يحوّل وهو يخلّي الذلول حشيشَه عليَه وقربتُه والبل تعارف. وهو يِنْسِبت يمّهم وهو عينه للذلول.

٣٫١٩ البنت وصط الما وِتطِقّ النياق حت حت. اخوتَه صْغار هكالحين عيال فلاح صغار هي اكبرهم تَرْفِه. يقولون سيقانه مثل الجمّار بالما رافعةٍ ثِيابه وِتطِق النياق. يقول

His Story with Tarfah, Daughter of Falāḥ ibn Fāliḥ al-Shlāgī

Traveling alone, Abū Zwayyid alighted at Ṭwayyah, a well of the Shilgān, at the approach of the hot season when people, the Bedouin tribes, take up their lodgings around water wells. They had put up seven large tents, each on three tent poles. They were the clan of Falāḥ ibn Fāliḥ of the Shilgān, the uncle of ʿAbaklī. His daughter Tarfah—you wouldn't find such a girl in all of the Arabian Peninsula. She enjoyed legendary fame among all Shammar tribes. At that time, fine girls acquired a name for themselves and were highly valued. 19.1

He arrived on his riding camel. His sword—he was armed with a sword—dangled from the mount's haunches. The only other thing he carried was a shriveled water bag. In spite of his unappealing looks, people warmly welcomed him wherever he showed up. That held true for all bards of his ilk: poets like Ibn ʿAngā and al-Hirbīd, who regaled their audience with stories, poems, and wise sayings. At the time of his arrival, the later part of the afternoon, the herds of white camels hurried toward the watering place, Ṭwayyah. At that time of day, masses of camels were on the move and congregated around the pool of the watering place. He brought his riding camel to drink with the other animals. The fodder he had cut for her and his waterskin were on her back when he maneuvered her into the throng of other camels and dismounted. He grabbed his cloak, slid down from her back, and shouted greetings to the men who were seated there, the clansmen of Āl Fāliḥ. While he was busy securing a place for his mount among the other camels, one of the men called to him: "Leave the darned beast! Come over here and have some coffee. I want you to talk to us!" He did as he was told. He dismounted and turned away from his mount, leaving the fodder and the skin on her back. But camels know one another. As he hurried toward the men, he kept throwing anxious glances over his shoulder to his mount. 19.2

The girl, Tarfah, had taken her position in the middle where the camels were drinking, beating back the camels and calling, "Stop! Stop!" At that time her brothers, the sons of Falāḥ, were still little kids; Tarfah was their older sister. As she stood in the pool of water, her legs shone white like the heart of a palm 19.3

يا ميرِ طْلَعَت عليه يا مير يوم نقّزت القربة والحشيش وحطّته هناك البنت ونْسِفت مزوِيّه على الحشيش. يا مير يوم خَذَت الرِسَن من غزالة الشداد وزْوِتُه على رقبة الذلول ومدّت يده على القربة اللي على الذلول وشْلِعْتَه لا تَقِصْمَه البل وحطّته بالقَرُو تدري ان هذا ضيفٍ لهم. شربت الذلول وعْطَنَت البل وهي تدفع الرحول يم المراح. وهي تاخذ القربه على ظْهَرَه والحشيش تحظنُه وهي تجيك. يوم طبت البل المراح وهي تعقبهن عن البل وهي تجيب الرحول وتنوّخه وتكِبّ له الحشيش.

٤،١٩ ابو زويد بس يراعيه. يوم جلس عند الرجال قالوا قوه قوه لَمّ عتيق شابّ. حي الله خلف كيف انت يا خلف حي الله ابو دخيل. ويقضب يدُه فلاح وهم يسيّرون على عتيق شابٍّ عمّه عتيق ابن فالح هي بنت فلاح. وهو يقعد يوم قعد قْبالُه الذلول والبنت رَوّت القربه يوم ابْتَلّت وعلّقتَه بغزال الشداد وذفعت الرحول عند بيت هله ونوّخت الذلول حطّت قراميشَه وغَطّتْهِن. قال من هي يا عتيق مْعَزّبتي هذي. قال بنت هالرجل بنت فلاح اخوي ترفة الفلاح.

٥،١٩ قال

يا راكب اللي كن مشيه تِضِـدِّ   عليه سـنامٍ شـاتيٍ عقب تقيـيض
حمـرا على السـندا عـديمٍ تْهَـدي   مَحَـاقْبَه من سَوجـهن للحقب بيض
سجوم يوم انك لكورَه تِشِـد   يا مِسّ حبـله له تِهِـنوِص وتجويض
ميـلاف عنـد المِـزهَـبه ما تْـرَدّ   ولا عذّبت بك بالرغـا والتـفاضيض
هي مِـنوة اللي فوق كوره يِمِـدّ   عشـافرٍ مـنوة مقضّى الاغـاريض

tree. She lifted her skirt to keep it from getting wet and hit the camels with a stick to drive them back. Seeing his mount, she took hold of it, lifted waterskin and fodder from its back, put them in a safe place, and threw her cloak over the fodder. Then she took the reins from the saddle knob and folded them around the camel's neck. She reached for the waterskin, removed it from the mount's back so that it would not be crushed by the camels, and put it down near the water trough. She knew that these were the belongings of a guest. The mount drank and the camels lay down after being watered. She pushed his mount to its resting place for the night. She tied the waterskin to its back and carried the fodder in a fold of her robe. When the other camels were ready to lie down, she made sure to put the guest's luggage at a safe distance from them. Then she brought his mount, couched it, and let the fodder drop from her lap in front of the camel: its dinner.

Abū Zwayyid had followed her movements attentively. When he sat down with the men, they said, "No, not here. Let's go to ʿAtīǵ, who is preparing coffee. Wonderful to see you, Khalaf. Welcome! How are you, Khalaf? We are glad you joined us, Abū Dikhīl!" And at that, Falāḥ took him by the hand and led him to ʿAtīǵ, the coffee host—ʿAtīǵ ibn Fāliḥ, Fāliḥ the uncle of Falāḥ's daughter. As he took his seat, he saw his camel mount right in front of him. He watched the girl driving his mount toward the tent, the refilled waterskin attached to the saddle knob. There she kneeled it, and unloaded and covered the gear. "Who is she, Atīǵ?" he asked. "Is she the lady of the house?" "She is the daughter of this man, Falāḥ, my brother. Tarfah al-Falāḥ." 19.4

Abū Zwayyid composed these verses: 19.5

Hey, rider of a proudly prancing camel mount,
fully humped from winter and summer grazing;
Reddish brown, it dashes uphill with raw panache;
rubbed by saddle ropes, haunches' hair turned gray.
Couched, she tenses up when the saddle's fastened;
tug at the rope: she fidgets, gurgling and bleating.[132]
She leaves your food bag alone if you take a rest,
she doesn't vex you with wayward roars and bolts.[133]
Sweet-tempered, she's made for long desert treks,
a sturdy mount, bound to bring you where you wish.

نِصّه عتيقٍ وان نِصَيته يسد قَرْمٍ يبيع الروح بارْدَى المعاريض
من ماكرٍ طِلْعه حرارٍ تهَد ربعٍ لهم عند اللوازم مراكيض
لا يابعد عمي وخالي وجدي وباللي غدى يالقرم فيك المعاويض
باغٍ عليك اظهر خفيّات سدّي يالقرم يا زين النِبا والتقاريض
عتيق واجَرّحي بِري واستَرِد من غرغريٍّ نقّض الجرح تنقيض
عينه كما الساعه لوقتٍ تِعِد أو عنز ريمٍ سَوّهجت عقب تربيض
نهده لجيب الثوب خَطّرٍ يِقِد كن الحمام بجيب ثوبه مبايض
زملوق وسمٍ ناعمٍ له بِخَد سيله من الرقّاد ياتي تفايض
يا شفتها لوانت مقفي تِرِد لوانت عجلٍ تقصر الرِجل وِتْريض
شوفه بليا شب نار يغدي يا صار قلبك دالهٍ مع هوى البيض
ابو ثليلٍ فوق ردفه يُعَدّي وِشْلَون لوهي فزّعت عقب تقضيض
الردف شط حوَيّرٍ ما يْرَدّ غاذيه سكتي كثير التخاضيض

سكتي شاوي راعي غنم.

بنت الذي عينه لربعه تْقَدّي يوم الفريج تْلَفّض الملح تلفيض

٦،١٩ قال ار اخو عَلْيا روّح روّح قِم يم المِلّيك والا والله عيال عمه الفالح سبعه اللي محيِّرينه مجيرٍ فوق مجير مير كلهم طيبين. يوم دري ابن عمّه عتيق ابن فالح اللي هو حيّيره قال ابشر به يابو زويد. يا مير ابو زويد ما هو خِبل. قال اصْبِر اصبر يابن

Steer her to ʿAtīǵ! He'll fulfill your every purpose:
he lays down his life in the line of chivalrous duty.
A falcon born on high ledges of soaring ambition;
bands of tight-knit clansmen girded for battle.
You're dearer than all my uncles and ancestors:
for my lost ones, you are glorious recompense.
I do not hesitate to bare my heart's secrets to you,
gentle hero of great renown, sung in many odes.
My wound, ʿAtīǵ, almost healed, was torn open
by a bouncing girl ripping into the tender scar.
Large eyes shine like a glass clockface,[134]
gaze of a doe sauntering from her place of rest;
Firm breasts almost burst through her robe,
like eggs of a dove pushing out from the slit.
Ah, smooth stalk in cool meadows, rain-sprinkled
by nightly clouds, sprouted in a soaked basin.
A glimpse of her stops you in your tracks;
though you're in a hurry, you turn and linger.
Snatching a look satisfies admirers' appetites:
devotees, seasoned watchers of female charms.
A thick tumble of hair cascades onto her behind:
fancy seeing her comb the loosened tresses!
Her rump: the hump of a camel calf free to drink,
fed by a sheepherder always churning milk.

—*Siktī* is a *shāwī*, the owner of sheep and goats.

Daughter of a chief who leads his men in battle,
into crackle of firearms and clouds of powder.

"On my life, as true as I am the brother of ʿAlyā, go, go, hasten to seal the 19.6
marriage!" he called. One should know that her uncle, al-Fāliḥ, had no less than seven sons and that each of them had put forward a claim to her. One after the other had taken an oath that she was going to be his prize.[135] But they were good-natured fellows all. When ʿAtīǵ ibn Fāliḥ, her uncle's son, one of those who claimed her, heard this, he said, "Be of good cheer, Abū Zwayyid, she'll be yours." Not being a fool, Abū Zwayyid said, "Not so fast. Wait a little, son of

فالح ياخلف ابوي انا معي زِبْد المناجي شمر يسمونَه زبد المناجي مِرَةٍ لُه حلوه ترفة ما هي مجاضعتَن لكن انا لي شبيه. قال وشو شبيهك ياخو ميثا. قال شبيهي الراعي يْدلّل الحايل وهو شرُطه لقاحـه.

Fāliḥ—you're as dear to me as my own father. Don't forget that I am married to Zibd al-Mnājī, Cream of Bosom Friends, as the tribesmen of Shammar call her, a sweet woman. Tarfah will not become my bedfellow. But I can tell you in whose position I am now." "To whom do you compare yourself, brother of Mēthā?" he asked.[136] "I am like a shepherd who pampers a she-camel that is not impregnated to save her strength, though he was hired with the promise of receiving her newborn calf as his wages."

خطبته عقب ما كبر

١،٢٠ يوم كبر ابو زويد خطب له بنت من اهله وعيَّت عليه. يوم لزّم عليه طلبت منُه مهر لها ذلوله يعني سَنع تجيز تبيه اغديه يهوّن. لكنه خدعها واعرس عليها ليله وحده وطلّقها يوم هو عاد يقول

يا فاطري يازينة الفخذ والساق　　ما اسوق شقراي بحَلي الوصوفِ
أريد اعفيها لتطريد الارزاق　　لايام يوم ان النشاما تحوف
يا علّقوا من فوقهن كل مِعْلاق　　بايام يرمن القطا بالرفوف
انا وياها بالرسن هَوش وخناق　　ولا عاد تمغث خاطري باللحوف
والعلم يابنت الاجاويد ينذاق　　طِسّي ولا بالنفس يمّك حسوف

A Marriage Proposal Made in His Old Age

In his old age, Abū Zwayyid proposed to a young woman, one of his relatives, but she turned down the offer. Undeterred, he kept pressing her and at long last she agreed, on condition that he give her his riding camel as a dower. She thought that such a disabling condition would put him off. But he tricked her. Having spent just one night in marriage, he sent her on her way, a divorced woman. These are some verses he composed on that occasion: 20.1

My camel, her gracious legs tried and tested,
    a blonde I won't barter for a ravishing dame.
She's mine, kept and kempt to make my living,
    when stalwarts ride out in search of plunder,
Sling on their backs travel's bare necessities,
    in such heat that sandgrouse lose their eggs.
We fight over the reins in playful tug of war:
    not one to weary me by running off course.
Lady proud and highborn, kindly understand:
    Clear off! You're dismissed without regrets.

غـزليـه

عيـني قِـزَت عن نومها ياخو شـمَا ضـاقت عليها يوم كـثرت هموـمَه ١،٢١
أسـباب سهـر العـين والقلب دمّا مشـتاق والمشـتاق ما احدٍ يلومـه
عيـني على زين الوصـايف مُقمّا والكبـد عن زين الطعـام محرومـه
على الذي عيـنه تقـل عين جـمّا أو عين شِيهان البحر عقب حومـه
يفِـزّ قلبي لى سـمعـته تسـمّى فـزّة ربيـطٍ جـاه عفو الحكومـه
وحـياة من نـزّل تبـارك وعـمّا ما انساه كود الناس تنسى سلومـه

Love Poetry

Eyes stinging, robbed of sleep, brother of Shammā! 21.1
Worries besiege me in swelling numbers.
As I lie awake, my heart bleeds for a reason:
what use blaming lovers inflamed by passion?
Spellbound, eyes fixed on her gracious shape,
mere thought of food makes my insides revolt,
Because of a velvety glow in her doe-like gaze,
fierce glint of a sea eagle's eye after flight.
Hearing her name makes my heartbeat go wild,
as a prisoner leaps up at news of a ruler's pardon.
By God, who sent us the surahs Kingdom and Tidings:[137]
as hallowed custom is revered, so I can't forget.

يـرثي مويضي اللي غرقت بالشـط

يا حيف يالمجمول مدقوق الالعاس   غـدَى به الجـاري بيوم شـنيعِ ١،٢٢
اقْفَت مع الجاري تقل لون هوّاس   بيسـاعـةٍ منها يشـيب الرضيع
لوهو بهَوش جـابها كل مِـذْباس   وصـاح المصـيحّ وافلسوا الفِـزيع
من ضَـيّع الله ما يِفكّونـه النـاس   انا اشهد ان من ضـيع الله يضيع

Dirge on Mwēḍī, Who Drowned in the Shaṭṭ River

Woe for our tattoo-lipped beauty queen, 22.1
carried off by river currents on that evil day.
She was swept along like a ship in full sail,
a horror to turn gray the hair of a breastfed infant.
In battle, stalwarts vie to rescue her from harm:
cries of alarm ring out; assailants are put to flight.
Humans are powerless if God wills their perdition;
I affirm: you're done for if God wills your demise.

قصايده بالجيش

ابو زويد له قصيد واجد بالجيش من عَرَضه يقول ١٠٢٣

انا هوى بالي خطاة السِجِلّه هذي هوى بالي وغاية مرادي
عريضة الفَرشات طوله بجلّه حمرا ودَمْثٍ غاربه للشداد
حمرا ومِذنب عينها تقل حَلّه تَقّلب كما المِقْباس حَذر السواد
يا جلّلوا دُهْم القرَب بالاجِلّه والما بعيدٍ حال دونه حمَاد
يا ورّدوهن عِقلةٍ ما تدِلّه تتلي عقيدٍ ضاريٍ للمعادي
يا بَرّكن عوص النضا بالاظله بالقايله دَلّى قِرينه يداد
يا غاب عنها كافره واسْفَهَلّه يا تِقل له رَبّ المِقادير هادي
مع سَهلةٍ بالقيظ يِبحِل مدِلّه فيها رِديّ الخال ما له جلاد
تشدى تَخَنْطَل خَفرةٍ جاه خِلّه مِتْجَنّبٍ عقب البطا جاه بادي

His Camel Poems

Abū Zwayyid has many camel poems to his name. The following are some examples. 23.1

My passion is riding a mighty desert cruiser;
she's what I like best, pinnacle of my desire.
Haunches broad, tall, and of massive bulk;
reddish of hue, soft shoulders cushion the saddle;
Reddish beast, in her eyes lurks a red-hot stove,
under black surface, flickering like burning coal.
Dark waterskins wrapped in cloth for protection,
nearest desert well fearsome gravel plains away:
They're led to a remote water hole, known to few,
by a raiders' captain, fortified by battling foes.
Lean, hardy mounts kneeled in shade for rest;
hot noon, whipped by a devil, frenzied, they run.[138]
Once the fiend lets go, she settles into calmer pace,
as if the good Lord intervened, granting her respite.
In midsummer's baked plains where guides are lost,
beyond the endurance of weaklings from a rotten nest,
She struts about with a damsel's coquettish gait:
she loves best riding home from distant journeys.

ويقول ابو زويد بالجيش ٢،٢٣

ياراكبٍ حمـرا جِليـله من القُود   هـذيك لا دَنّى ولا هيب رَغبـه
حمـرا تقول مجـلّله جوخ مـاهود   وصايفـه تقـل ابن ريّا صنع بـه
يا قِلت بادت دَكّ به جـدّها العَود   دلوٍ رْشـاه مْصـدّرٍ وانقطـع بـه
ولا حطّ به مع حروة العقب لاكود   ولا عقّب المجان من كِثر شعبـه

ويقول ابو زويد بالجيش ٣،٢٣

ياراكب اللي كِهّـلٍ بالجـلوسِ   حيـلٍ مواحيلٍ شحمهن محيلِ
كم حـايلٍ جِضيض العـروس   وهم غاصبينه ما تريـد الحليل
مع سهلةٍ به كل ذيخٍ فـروس   مثل الدجاجه بس يتلى الدليل

الدجاجه يعني العقيد بس يتبع الدليل مثل الدجاجه.

ويقول ابو زويد بالجيش ٤،٢٣

الله من قـلبٍ تقـــل بيـه له نار   ياخـذ به القـلب المشـقّى له انواع
دَلّى يـديـرن من هواليسـه ذْيار   لو قلت له خـلّ الهواليس ما طاع
اظْماوه طامي مُوحِش القِدْر يا فار   غـادٍ كما ذيب الخَلا كان هوجـاع
تَرْعَى ذلولي بالخَطـايط والاقْفار   يما نْقِضَت للجَزْو من عِقْب مِرباع
ابي عـليهـا هَومـةٍ ناصيٍ دار   مِـيهافـةٍ ما يَقْـطَعَـه كِلّ مخْـراع
ما يَقْـطَعونه كود صَلْـبين الاشوار   ربعٍ الى ركـبوا طويلات الابواع
إن ورّدَن عِـدٍّ نِصَن ذاك عِـبار   اخْضاع ربْدٍ مع لهن جَرْهَدي قاع

And about camels: 23.2

Rider of a red-brown camel with a mighty stride,
not given to sauntering or easily frightened;
Fur aglow with a reddish hue as if silk-coated,
like a turnout rug woven in Ibn Rayyā's atelier.
If she flags, at once her father's temper shows:
running like snapping ropes, like plummeting buckets.
No need to kick her flanks with your heels
or reach backward, hitting with a riding prod.

And this: 23.3

Rider of a camel fresh from ages on the pasture:[139]
years spent piling up layers of fat and strength;
Left bare of womb, they agitate like reluctant brides,
kicking and crying in a husband's forced embrace,
On crossing vast lonesome plains where hyenas roam,
blindly confident behind a guide like a string of chickens.

—He means the raid leader: they follow the raid leader like chickens.

And Abū Zwayyid composed these verses on camels: 23.4

God help me, my heart has been set on fire:
beset by manifold torments, it suffers badly.
Anxiety spins the heart around at dizzying speed:
sternly told, "Stop worrying!" it pays no heed;
Burned by splashes from a pot's furious boil,
it goes berserk, a frantic, starving desert wolf.
My camel thrived on the herbage of virgin meadows[140]
all spring, till plants shriveled in scorching heat.
My ardent desire is for a jaunt to faraway lands
across desert wastes shunned by the faint of heart:
A privilege solely of indomitable braves,
forever mounted on camels pacing at long stride:[141]
Speedy, inured to thirst, they leave some wells aside,[142]
scorching across plains, necks held low, like an ostrich.

عِلْطٍ واماليطٍ قَراميش واكوار   العَصْر بَدَّلْن التهنْفل بزَوماع

ما عليهن دَلال.

قِعسٍ نواسعهن تِقِل صَنْع بَيطار   اخضاع ربدٍ مع لهم جرهدٍ زاع

نواسعهن ارقابهن وغواربهن مرتفعه تقل صنع نَجّار بالقِدّوم.

عرايض الفَرْشات وِرّاد الازوار   بعيد مَلْوَى الزَوْرعن نُوش الاكْواع

الفرشات وروكهن.

يشدن تِحفّز رِجّع جاهن اخبار   سَمْعَن خبر عِرْسٍ وهن قبل هِجّاع

Short-haired, loaded light with gear and saddle, nothing more;
in late afternoon they shift from trot to higher speed.

—The mounts are not caparisoned.

Angular bones protrude, as if sculpted by an artisan,
from gaunt frames tearing along hard, empty tracks:

—Protruding, *nuwāsiʿ*, their necks and shoulders tower up as if chiseled by a carpenter.

Haunches broad, calluses on the breastbones
prominent without hindering their forelegs' elbows,

—*Al-farshāt* are their haunches.

Agitated and twitchy as divorced women
roused from sleep by a wedding announcement.

يفتخر

يقول ابو زويد ١،٢٤

ياوَيل والله واحد ننطوي له   بِجَوفٍ حَدّه وِريع ومسموم
ان كان ما هِيلَت عليه النِثيله   ترى عَلَيّ مْقَنَّد البِنّ محروم
ما اخْبَلَك ياراقد بحِضن الحَليله   وانا عيوني حاربت لَذّة النوم
والله لولا حِبنّا للقبيله   ونَبْغي دربنا من بِعيدٍ على القوم
لاجْعَل على بعض القِبايل دِبيله   وان اتناشد بالعدم دايم الدوم

ويقول ابو زويد ٢،٢٤

يامَلّ قَلْبٍ فيه عَذْلٍ ومايل   لكنّ به غِلّ وغاشيه سلال
لى ضاق صدري قِمْت انا ابْدع مِثايل   مثايلٍ ما هِن تَخابيص وِهْبال
ما اعِير هَرْجي تايهين الدلايل   ولا نيب دِبٍّ بسّ شَرّاب واكّال
اعير انا هرجي عِيال الحَمايل   اللي يِمانيهم ينَقّدن الاموال
اللي يشِبّون الجْهَم والقُوايل   تاتي مِسابيرٍ لهم مثل الارسال
اللي سِريب دلالهم كالنِثايل   يَفْنون بِنّ في مَحاميس وِذْلال
اشْقَر كما دَمٍّ من الظبي سايل   من تالي المعلوق دمٍّ الى سال
واصْفَر تِمَدّ والتِتن غادٍ قلايل   بيسراك غَلْون وِيِمْناك فْنجال

Boastful Poems

Abū Zwayyid said: 24.1

Woe to one for whom we harbor evil:
    trenchant swords and poisoned blades.
Bury him under the dust of a dug-out grave
    or let me drink spiced coffee no more!
Idiot, snuggled up in his love's embrace
    as my sleep-deprived eyes burn hot.
By God, I am driven by love for my clan,
    desiring to strike at enemies from afar,
To inflict crushing defeats on tribes:
    I am sought after to tell of heroic deeds.

And Abū Zwayyid said: 24.2

My heart feels heavy; there's something wrong;
    seething with rage, worn out by churning sorrow.
Weighed down by worries, I reach for my lyrics:
    verse creations, not abstruse or silly rhymes,
Unfit for an audience of floundering dimwits:
    I am no lout who only cares for food and drink.
My words are for tribal sons, well-born, well-bred,
    generous men who spend everything to earn praise;
Whose fires, burning before dawn and at noon,
    bring guests flocking to their hearths in droves;
Coffee dregs heaped high like mounds of ashes;
    they burn through beans in roasting pans and pots,
Brew coffee tender brown, blood of a gazelle
    cut from below, gushing from the heart's arteries.
Tobacco gone up in smoke, yellow leaves will do:
    hubble-bubble in one hand, cup of coffee in the other.[143]

صِبّه لكسّاب الفخر والنِفايل ... اللي فعايلهم جديدات واسمال
ولى صار كَون وقِيل وِخذَوا شلايل ... وان جوهم الرعيان قالوا هل المال
تَخَيَّروا رَبْعي على كِلّ حايل ... رَكْبوا طَلَب من فوق عَجْلات الازوال
على بَنات العَود رمْلٍ واصايل ... الصِبْح من لوقه ويَزْهَنّ الاجلال
نَهوهُم الذلّان قالوا قلايل ... ما يطْلِبون الْفٍ ثلاثين رجّال
قالوا كبار الربع هَرْج صِمايل ... عند العَشاير يَرْخِص العُمْر بريال
مير انكِسوا ياهل القلوب الذلايل ... ما فَكْ شِمّاخ الذرا كِلّ ذلال
تبَشّرَت حُمْر الشِفا بالحلايل ... بالفَك والنِيّات يِكْتِبْن الافْعال
يوم اصْبحوا قالوا علينا فشايل ... كيف الْف ما تَنْطَح ثلاثين رجّال
وِش عِذْرنا من ناقضات الجِدايل ... اللي يروِكن الخضْر وسْط الاقذال
الكثير يِغْوي تايهين الدلايل ... والصبح بَيرقهم على رَبْعنا مال
رَقْطا لها شَوبٍ سوات الملايل ... لو شاف شوبه راصِن العقْل يهتال
الشكر للمعبود راعى الجزايل ... ما عمر باللقوات ميزاننا مال
راحوا هل القروا وربْعي شَخايل ... مع سَهْلةٍ ما بينهم كل عذّال
تمت وصلوا عِدّ وَبْل المَخايل ... على النبي الهاشمي صفوة الآل

Pour coffee for men proud of their mighty deeds,
achievers of outstanding feats since ancient times.
If herds of camels are robbed in frenzied turmoil,
shepherds raise alarm: "Owners, your camels!"
My kinsmen rally, pick the strongest mounts,
dash off in hot pursuit, sleek fleeting silhouettes:
Purebred she-camels sired by a pedigree stud,
decked out in colors, an early morning run from Lōgah,
Undeterred by craven naysayers' cautions:
"How can a band of thirty defeat a thousand?"
Elders of the clan stepped in to voice the solid truth:
"Tribesmen hold life cheap; they sell it for one riyal.
You sissies, clear off!" Tails between their legs, they went:
cowards don't recapture stolen high-humped herds.
Red-lipped damsels look to heroes for relief:
our camels' retrieval was by dint of power and resolve.
At dawn, the shamefaced enemies lick their wounds:
how did a mere thirty see off an army a thousand strong?
Taken to account by long-haired beauties: what else
appeases damsels with scented, plaited tresses?
Dim-witted men, beguiled by strength in numbers,
shocked to see their battle flags teeter, toppled.
A motley mass, bristling with arms, spewing flames;[144]
the sight alone drives men of sound mind berserk.
We praise the Lord in gratitude for His munificence:
in war the scales did not tip against us even once.
Enemies crushed, generous hosts all relaxed:
no reproaches while riding home in scattered parties.
In conclusion, prayers as plentiful as pouring rains
for the Prophet of Hāshimi descent, the noblest House.[145]

قصيده بالدنيا واختلاف الوقت

يقول ابو زويد ١،٢٥

قِمْ سَوّ ياراع المعاميل فِنْجال　　فنجال يا جا الراس يِغْدي عماسه
قالوا تْسَيِّرْ قِلْت ما من فضا بال　　دَورٍ على الاجواد ما به وناسه
هذات دورٍ من قوافيه انا ذال　　دَورٍ به الحِصْني يدوِّر الفراسه
راعى الجحش يَشْرَه على جَذْع خيّال　　مْتحَيْزِمٍ من فوق دِرْعٍ وطاسه
وقامت بصاع المنكر الناس تِكْتال　　وقامت تباع الجوهره بالنَّحاسه
ياحيف يالبّاسة الجوخ والشال　　قامت تغوّلهم عيال البِساسه
ولا يِنْتِعَدّل شَيل بَقْعا الى مال　　ومن اين ما عَدّلتها ما تواسه
اصبر وعند الله تصاريف الاحوال　　والناس مَرْجعها على بِنْي ساسه

ويقول ابو زويد ٢،٢٥

يامِلّ قلبٍ به هواليس وِهْموم　　همٍّ لِجا بالقلب من كِثْر ما رَيت
عيني ندوّشها ولا تقْبل النوم　　نومه تقل عنها بصوبٍ ورا هيت
يالله يا خالق سماوات ونجوم　　يا مِثْبت الدنيا بالاجبال تثْبيت
يا خيرٍ تَقْوَى على جَبْر مقصوم　　وتِعِزّ مَضْيومٍ وتِهْفي نِماريت
كم واحدٍ ماله كثيرٍ ومحروم　　عن الحساني من حساب العفاريت

His Poems on the World's Vicissitudes and Contretemps

Abū Zwayyid said: 25.1

Do me a favor, coffee maker, hand me a cup:
make it strong, to lift the haze and clear my mind.
I was told: "Go for a stroll, make a call!" but "No!
Fine men thwarted at every turn—where has all the fun gone?"
I stand in fear of what these times will bring,
a time when sneaky foxes swagger lionlike;
Donkey riders aim to fell knights on chargers,
bandoliered, clad in coats of mail and helmeted;
In the market of values, villainy is scooped up in heaps,
jewelry and precious stones are sold for copper coins.[146]
Atrocious! Heroes in patterned breeches and scarves
are being played with, like toys by scrawny kittens.
Once the world is out of joint it can't be righted:
no amount of tugging and pulling will straighten it.
Bear it with patience, all is in the hands of God;
human affairs depend on the strength of their foundations.

Abū Zwayyid said: 25.2

Poor heart assailed by troubles and worries
nestled deep inside, born of my trials.
Sleepless, eyes burning, dizzy from vertigo;
slumber eluded me, sped away beyond Hīt.
O God, Creator of heavens and stars,
You anchored earth with mountain moorings;
O Benefactor who heals broken bones,
You lift up the oppressed, topple tyrants.
Many amass great wealth only to fall miserably short
in goodness and charity: a rotten breed of devils!

اصبر الى ناشك بدنياك مزحوم رزقك على اللي يِحْيي الناس ويْميت
اللي كِتَب لك والي الرزق مَقْسوم اللي كُتِب ياتيك من غير تصويت
العَدْل في لَوحٍ من الذِكْر مَنْظوم ارْشَدْت ياللي تتبع العَدْل وِهْديت
حكي القِفا والزور والسوّ مذموم وزَود الهبال وبايه الكِذْب تَقْويت
وَقْتٍ دخلنا به هل البيت به قَوم مِتْخالِفاتٍ به دَلايل هل البيت
باب الحيا عن سِتْر الاجواد مقصوم والحق مجحودٍ علينا تقل مَيت
مرحوم ياللي مات بالحق مرحوم الميت ما يسمع كثير التصاويت
وقتٍ به الشيمات بِذِّلَت باللوم وِرْشاه جِرْد وباينٍ به تِباتيت
حكّاي بالمعروف غادي ومنجوم يِصْبح بمَظْماة السهال السِباريت
اليوم ما شِبّيَ من الحِصْن منهوم ليا هِدّ حصنٍ ما لِقي لاصلهن بيت
بيعَن حويزات العَجَم بابْخس السَوم صار الغلا للانكري والمِشاليت
كيف النداوي باه واسْتَفْرَس البُوم ياذيب عن فِرْسٍ باياديك عِدّيت
صاعٍ من العَنبَر بصاعٍ من الثَوم رِخص به الماهود وغِلي به الكيت
رَبْعي كما حِصْنٍ بهن كل ناهوم ضُواريٍ مثل السباع المِصانيت
هل الفعول مْزَنِّنة كلّ مَضْيوم غير الفعايل ما تبيّن لهم صِيت
يحكون بالعربي ويحكون بالروم بمكارب الارشاه حصن عتاعيت
لى صار مثلي نايشه غَلْب وِهْموم كيف الحَوَل وان زاد لي واسْتِهَمّيت
وِشْلَون همّ اللي ضعيفٍ ومضيوم ورَبْعه عفونٍ بايهينٍ مهاييت

Endure in patience if hard-pressed by the world:
none but your Provider decides on life and death;
Your fate and subsistence are foreordained,
written in heavenly script, indelibly yours;
On a tablet, codes of justice have been dictated:
divine guidance for seekers of moral propriety.
Refuse backbiting, falsehood, wicked practices,
foolish escapades, feeding minds with vile lies.
The times have lodged enemies inside the house,
pitted folks against one another in vicious strife,[147]
Unhinged modesty's doors, shaming the virtuous;
trampled upon honesty, deprived truth of life.
Rest in peace, God's mercy on you, martyr of truth:
dead and buried, you are spared this sound and fury.
The times' depravity has unseated noble virtue,
left its ropes tattered, threadbare, ready to snap.
Charity's spokesmen, dazed and baffled, wander
adrift among wild animals in waterless wastes.
Horses sired today fall short of better strains:
studs are led to mares lacking in pedigree.
See, costly Persian carpets are sold dirt cheap,
puffed-up nobodies and misfits are on their game.
Shockingly, falcons fumble, owls become raptors:
prey snatched from the claws of perplexed wolves,
Loads of ambergris bartered for sacks of garlic,
silk sold cheap; cotton bought for princely sums.
My tribesmen are my pride, dashing steeds all,
hardy fighters, lions crouched for the leap;
Forever on the prowl, ramparts for the needy,
with nothing to their name but chivalrous feats;
Eloquent in Arabic and proficient in Turkish,
stubborn, immovable during tussles at tangled wells.
If the likes of me, gripped by fear and foreboding,
sunk in despair, cast about to find a way out,
How does a penniless, downtrodden pauper fare
whose fellows, insipid idlers, don't care a hoot?

خَطّه من الحيّين مَسْحي ومَظْحوم   هذاك لو هو حيٍّ اضْعَف من الميت
خَمْس الفَرايض صَلّ والحجّ والصوم   حَقٍّ تشهّد كلّ ما اصْبَحْت وامْسَيت
والعبد ما سَوّى بدنياه مَظْموم   بيومٍ يلمّ الناس من عِقْب تَشْتيت

ويقول ابو زويد ٣،٢٥

يا راكبٍ حمرا جِليله من القُود   وَجْنا عَثافر من مِزابير الاوراك
تَضْرِم ليا من الرِسَن صار مَشْدود   وتَسْحَق ليا حَثّيت رِجْلك بمَمْشاك
تِلْفي لربعي مَنْقَع الطِيب والجُود   رَبْعي من اوّل طِيبهم ما به اشْكاك
من اولٍ حِنّا مثل دِرْع داود   نِفكّ من يضرب طواريق الادراك
قَبْلٍ تِزَبّن كل من جاك مطرود   كنه براس عويرض كان هو جاك
واليوم لو بالحَكْي يالربع منقود   أشوف ما حِنّا للاحوال فِكّاك
تَرْك اللَوازم عند الاجواد مَنْقود   كِلٍّ ليا خَلّيت عانيك خلّاك
تبيّضت ناسٍ تَغَزّز لها السود   ياصاحبي دنياك هذي به افلاك
يارب ياللي للمطيعين مَعْبود   انّك تكافينا غرابيل دنياك
تَقْوى تحِطّ من البَخت فوق مَقْرود   وتَقْوى تحِطّ من القَراده على ذاك
اليوم اشوف الخَيش انا صار ماهود   وثَوب القماش ليا تِسَلّطت عَرّاك
والجوهر الريّان بالسوق مردود   وخام الحديد الى تِكَلّمت ذَكّاك
ان كان تَبْغى الطِيب فاصْبِر على الكُود   وازْعَب على مَحالة الضِدّ بارشاك
الذِلّ ما رَدّ الذي كِنْت ماعود   ما راد قسّام المقادير لك جاك

His traces effaced, a ghost among the living,
still breathing, he is worse off than the dead.
Perform the daily prayers, the pilgrimage, the fast,
repeat the profession of faith morning and evening:
Your records in this world are kept in ledgers
for final reckoning on the Day of Gathering.

Abū Zwayyid said: **25.3**

Rider of an outstanding red-brown camel mount,
a mighty beast, mild-tempered, haunches bulging.
She feels fired up as soon as reins are pulled:
A mere toe touch and she dashes off at lightning speed.
Head for clansmen, good and generous to a fault:
my fellows whose mettle is stainless beyond doubt.
We are a coat of mail, closely woven metal rings:
if anyone's in harm's way, we rush to his rescue.
Since olden days, we've shielded refugees from pursuers
in our redoubt, safe as if ringed by mountain cliffs.
My fellows! Rude reproaches sent flying today
weaken us when unity is most needed.
Generous men detest falling short in social duty.
Turn away help-seekers? You'll be shunned!
If names marked in black bask in adulation,[148]
my friend, thank a world capricious with its favors.
O Lord, your servants bow for You in adoration:
be kind and spare us from the world's afflictions!
You shower good fortune on a loser—that is Your choice;
Or bring misery on a lucky head, as You wish.
See how sackcloth has eclipsed silken ware!
Sheer folly! Threadbare textile leaves you naked!
In markets, lustrous jewelry is spurned by traders;
iron is king: blunt, but it's enough to cut your throat.
Living a good life means to endure in patience:
pull hard at the well rope slung over your shoulder!
Cowardice provides no escape from destined Fate:
your lot is apportioned as the Almighty wills.

عساك ياصابر وهو زاحمك زود　　تعطى البَلا . . . .
لا تودع القـــالات باديان وِعْهود　　الا الى كَلّت عن الفِعْل يِمنـاك

ويقول ابو زويد　　٤،٢٥

قـال الذي شطر بتصخير الابيات　　بِطار شَطْرٍ في مَلاوي حروفه
ياقلب هات من التماثيل قِمْ هات　　قِمْ هات صَوغاتٍ لمن جا يحُوفه
ياذيب لو ترْزَع طويلات الاصوات　　لازم تِوَطّاك الغَنَم بيظلوفه
صار الحَظِيظ اللي على مِلّة الخات　　واهْل البخوت مْن اوّلٍ بـه حْفوفه
وناسٍ من اوّل كود يِرّت لها ارّات　　اليوم صـارت ما تْلَجّم سيوفه
هذا الدهَر ما هو على كِل الاوْقات　　اشوف دَلّى الذيب يَذرى خروفه
نَفْع العَباة لشيخهم بسّ الاشمات　　الشيخ ما يِسْوى من الغَزْل صوفه
هذي عقوبة ياهل العَقْل ما فات　　وكِلّ براسه من هل البيت شَوفه
ولا يِنْلِحِق شيٍّ ورا البارحه فات　　أخس ما تطرى الرجال الحسوفه

ويقول ابو زويد　　٥،٢٥

ياالله ياللي للخَفيّات عـلّام　　يا مدبّر الدنيا نهار اهْتزازه
ياخـالقٍ شيعه وكفار واسلام　　وكلٍّ على عَجْل المرُوّة وجازه
العِرْف لاهل العِرْف ما عاد يِنْسام　　مير الدعارِم ما تعرْف الميازه
ما يِنْلِبس ثوبٍ جديدٍ من الخام　　كود ببدن وردون وِلْهن ركازه
تَرى الغنم جِلّه تروّج بالاسوام　　وتَلْقَى قَراقيره لنا فيه عـازه

If you suffer in silence at being pushed around,
you deserve a painful blow, smack in the eye.[149]
Oaths and promises with no deeds to match are nothing,
until you've wearied your hands with maximum toil.

Abū Zwayyid said: 25.4

These verses were molded in the skillful hands
of a past master of poetry's turns and twists.
Come, my heart, bring out nuggets of wisdom,
cleverly crafted to satisfy its seekers' demands!
A wolf stretches its neck to release its howls,
only to be crushed by the hooves of sheep and goats.
Lucky is a person who dies in the true faith,
fondest desire of those on whom fortune smiles.
Now herdsmen calling "*arr*" to sheep and goats
are seen strutting with unsheathed swords.
Caught up in evil days without precedent,
wolves look at sheep with trepidation.
Common folk regard shaykhs with malice:
tribal chiefs count for less than a tuft of wool.
One understands: past sins come to roost
if all and sundry act by their own lights.
What's gone is gone, beyond retrieval and repair:
Goodness! Real men don't waste time on such regrets.

Abū Zwayyid said:[150] 25.5

God, You have perfect knowledge of the hidden;
You steer the world through the Last Day's convulsions;
Creator of the Shiʿah, of Unbelievers and Islam,[151]
all equally desirous of noble conduct's rewards.
People with good sense cleave to proper ways;
riffraff can't be trusted to perceive distinctions.
How to dress in cubits of untailored cloth
without bodice, sleeves, or the correct fit?
Big, full-grown sheep and goats are in demand,
yet the small and skinny are of use as well:

ويصير به سَمْن وبها بَقْل وايدام   وصُوفٍ تعَمِّر بيتكم من جـزازه
من هو يجوز لغير غـاليك الاكرام   اللي لعـــازاتك تحِطّه لْهـازه
اللي بعـازاتك تقـل مَشْي خـدّام   يمْشِي عن الحِقْران لك بالعـزازه
وان خصّ مَسْهم غاليٍ عند الاسهام   يصـير به عقب المـعـزّه لزازه
وانا ليا ركب الرشا فوق الالزام   مـا انا هـــدانيٍّ سواة الجنازه
والله فلا يَسْهـر رفِـيقي وانا انام   يمـــا نلزَّه له على مِـلْتِـزازه
يا صـار ما تَنْفَـع بعـازات الايام   الآخِـرة ما به مَنـافيع عـازه

ويقول ابو زويد ٦،٢٥

أوصِـــــيك يامن للنوامـيس دَوّار   وصِـيّةٍ من ضَيّع الصَوب تِقْــداه
ان صـار لك حَقٍّ غـدوا فيه الاشـرار   وضامك خصيمك يَفْهـم الصوب مار تاه
شـاوِر على القـالات صَلْبين الاشوار   ومن شـاوَر البـايـه على قـالتـه باه
يـرْمِيك في دربٍ مـهاليك وجْفـار   حـقـه يضيع وناقـلٍ داه بِـرْداه
وان ضـاع حَقّك واصْبَح الراي خسّار   تَـرى الرجِل يا ضِـيم يَفْعَـل بيِـمناه
وازْبِن على حِصْنٍ لهـم باللِقـا كـار   رْجـال تْهـدّي صـاحب الحقّ يا تاه
قـلتـه وانا من لابـةٍ تاخِـذ الثـار   واللي يحـاربنـا نحِـدّه على اقـصـاه
تـر قِـدْرنا يِنجِـض بواخُـه الى فـار   ويُورد رشـانا يوم يَقْصِـرْن الارشـاه
ورفيـقنـا يَسْكِـن شَنـاخيب الاوكار   نَـرْفَى خَـماله ونحْمِّل خـطـاياه
ورفيـقنـا لو كـان ياطـا على النـار   مـا كان ياطـا جـارنا كـود ناطـاه

Producing fat, dried cheese, clarified butter;
    from their wool you weave nice houses of hair.
Next to loved ones, hold in highest esteem
    men cushioning your shoulders' heavy burden;
Hawk-eyed, they look after your needs, like a servant:
    they keep you sure-footed, not held in disregard;
By allotting precious shares at spoils' division,
    he adds affectionate esteem to lofty standing.
When ropes run over pulleys, I'm ready to hoist,
    unlike impassive slackers, mere corpses on a bier.
I swear, I stay awake with my sleepless friend,
    providing comfort, heartening him as much as I can:[152]
Remember, if you are no good in your life,
    no one needs you in the hereafter.

Abū Zwayyid said: 25.6

Hear my advice if you have aspirations,
    guidance when you've lost your bearings:
Rascals made off with what's yours by right;
    you're wronged by a claimant of erring ways.
In grave affairs, seek counselors with solid views:
    fickle advisors compound confusion, lead you
Up the garden path where ruin's shifting sands
    swallow rights lost through one's own doings.
Rights squashed? Claims thrown out of court?
    Someone worth his salt takes his matters in hand:
Seek shelter with brave warriors, steeled in battle;
    they comfort a man aggrieved and flustered.
I say so as someone from a clan resolute on revenge—
    we push our foes to the brink as hard as we can:[153]
Our cauldron's steam is as hot as its furious fire;
    other well ropes fall short, ours reach the water.
Our companion is ensconced among the steepest crags;
    we make up for his defects, overlook his missteps;
He's our companion: if he walks on red-hot embers,
    duty-bound, we suffer with the protected neighbor.

ويقول ابو زويد ٧،٢٥

ما اهـرّج الاجواد هـَرْج بايـه   ولا نيب دِبٍّ للهــروج احُوس
اهــرِّج الاجواد بما يـِرْضِي النّبي   وهـَرْجي لاصحاب العقول فلوس
ولا انا جـبّايٍ الى صـار قـاله   ولا انا بغـِرّات الرجــال بلوس
ياما جِدَعْنا حالنا مع رفيقنا   ما هو تِـزَيِّن بيـلبوس عـروس
يا جـاك رجّالٍ عنيدٍ جـانِي   يبي بِغبـّـات العـلوم يقوس
أداوي التـايه بسيفٍ مشـذَّر   في كَفّ شِغْمومٍ يـدُوس النحوس
حَذْراك والمسْرى بليـلٍ غـيهب   المِقـلاع طِبٍّ لقـلْع الضـروس
وحَكْي الرَجِل يا جا على غير معنى   مِثْل تَفريض الكَبْـد بحَدّ مُوس
ثلاث معـاني هن شيمات العـرب   ان ضاع ضاع الحقّ ولا به هجوس
حق الجــار والضيف والخوي   عنـد عــــلّام النفوس

ويقول ابو زويد ٨،٢٥

الادمي ما بـه لنفسه تسـانيع   يا غَرّ من تسنيع والى الحسانِ
يالله ياللي منك درب المـنافيع   تَفْرِق علي منك النِظر بالعَيانِ
إرْثع ونفّض مِصْبَط الفقْر ترثيع   ارثع وخَلّ الفَقِر عـند الهـداني

المصبط اللي قبل نيم.

اما ذلول الحـظّ تاتيك وتطيع   والا عليك الذيب زَجّ الغَواني
مَرٍّ يشلّعن اشهب الفقر تشليع   ومَرٍّ يـدَرْبِنك بحَوض الوهاني

Abū Zwayyid said: **25.7**

Adopt a proper tone toward gentlemen;
  avoid the bombastic blather served up by louts;
In addressing them I observe the Prophet's qualities,
  speech valued by the sagacious no less than money.
I do not shy away if called upon for burdensome duty,
  nor do I put store in looking for others' failings.
Our habit is to throw in our lot with friends,
  not to doll ourselves up, swanky, sitting pretty.
Peppered with questions by impertinent visitors
  aiming to ferret out secrets of our private affairs,
I face the erring fools brandishing a sharp blade,
  as wielded by a fighter, undaunted by carnage.
Beware of traveling on pitch-dark, moonless nights;
  pincers are used as a tool to extract aching molars.[154]
If I hear foolish babble, meaningless claptrap,
  it feels like a razor-sharp knife slicing my liver.
Three cardinal principles are the pride of the Arabs—
  if these are lost, all truth is lost irredeemably:
The rights of neighbors, of guests, and of travel companions
  are held sacred by those of true knowledge.

Abū Zwayyid said: **25.8**

Humans are prone to err and stray off course
  without guidance from the Beneficent Lord.
God, the road to prosperity begins with You:
  turn Your gaze, let it look with favor on me!
Do so at a gallop, lift up poverty's begrimed torpor;
  quickly, drop my poverty on a good-for-nothing!

—*Al-muṣbiṭ*, "torpor," is slumber, just short of sleep.

Either fortune's camel comes to you willingly
  or wolves erupt in song on seeing you prostrate;
One day poverty's ashen gloom is dispelled,
  the next you are forced into bogs of impotence.

حيـلٍ عليهن دايرين المطـاميع　عـيرات بالدّيّان والا السواني

اما تغزي عليه والا سانية تاكل من فلاحته.

ويقول ابو زويد ٩،٢٥

تـنـابح الدنيـا بوسْطه كـلابه　تاكل ولا يَلْحَق طعـامه شدوقـه
ان سـانعت يزين لك فـتح بابه　ويجوز للعـبد المشـقّى وفوقـه
وعن ماكْتِب لك ما تِفكّ الحزابه　والى وَعَـد وِعيـدةٍ مـا يوقـه

ويقول ابو زويد ١٠،٢٥

قـال الذي يبني حليات الامثال　هـَرْجي كما النيرات ما به رْباعـه
الفـين رَجْلٍ ما يشادون رجّال　والفٍ برجلٍ ما يشادون ساعـه
يِبْجِل عيا رجّـالك التايه الظال　وبيـر العيا ما له الى قيس قاعـه

ويقول ابو زويد ١١،٢٥

لا تَصْـقِـر الا بيفـروخ الحـرارِ　اللي مَخـالِبهن يْشـرِّحن تشـريح
اللي ليـا هـدّيتـهن بالحـباري　ما ضَربهن لك بابرق الريش تصفيح
تـرى هْـبِلْتَن صَقْرتي بالوكـارِ　يا اوحتّهن قـامن يْخَمّرن بالشيح

ويقول ابو زويد ١٢،٢٥

لا تعرّض القـالات لاديان وِشْهود　الا الى كَلّت من الفِـعْـل يمـناك
عساك من تِصَبّر على الغِبن والزود　تِعَطى البَلا من مامِنك فوق بِشْواك

Camels: strong mounts for you to go raiding,
to cross waterless deserts, to irrigate your palms.

—Either you ride her on raids or you use her to draw water to irrigate the fields that provide your food.

Abū Zwayyid said: 25.9

The world is filled with dogs, barking loudly;
morsels are devoured without touching the teeth:
If things go well, you gladly open Fortune's door;
a long-suffering person may yet strike gold.
You can't loosen Fate's hold, it is decreed:
good or bad, ineluctably it comes your way.

Abū Zwayyid said: 25.10

Listen to the charming verses I composed,
words measured in gold bullion, not in dimes.
Two thousand don't measure up to just one real man;
of cowards he'd soon dispatch a thousand and one.
A man, perplexed and weak, astray and lost,
tumbles into a bottomless well of infirmity.

Abū Zwayyid said: 25.11

For hunting choose young peregrines:
they strike, claws tear prey to pieces.
Let them fly to swoop down on bustards,
striking them as a fatal bolt from the sky.
Falconry with weaker birds drove me crazy:
if I call, they evade me, hiding in sagebrush.[155]

Abū Zwayyid said: 25.12

Do not submit grave affairs to oaths and witnesses[156]
until you've exhausted your own forces all!
If you feel put upon and decide to give in,
may a hit pierce your underbelly at the bladder.

كون الجميما

١٠٢٦ عقب كون الجميما جا ابو زويد الصبح يمّ الشيوخ يا مير الوليد سعود ابو خشم بِمْضَرَّبٍ على نومته. مَلّكوا لُه على فَهَدة تقول انه يلعب على كبدي وينام. يوم وَعى غسّلوا عليه العبيد وجاك وقَعَد يامير ابو زويد بالمجلس يقول له ياعمّي. قال صبحك الله بالخير ياعمّي. قال

هلا هلا لا واهلا بك وترحيب	الفٍ باثره الفٍ والوفٍ تقوده
يا شوق من حطّ الشِمَطري على الجيب	تجوز للبيض العذارى هدوده
المَرْجِلة عيّت على كلّ خِطّيب	واشوفها لسعود شَدَّت قعوده
لى واهني من نادى الاموات وتجيب	لو هو يقوم محمّدٍ من لحوده
وعبد العزيز يشوف حصن الاطاليب	ويشوف قوم سعود وِش لون فوده
حشوه يجيبه محملٍ له عراقيب	ومن ذاق ضربه ما لك الله يعوده

Battle of al-Jmēmā

The morning after the battle of al-Jmēmā, Abū Zwayyid visited the shaykhs. On 26.1
arrival, it was clear that the young prince, Sʿūd Abū Khashm, had been sleeping with his wife: they had married him to Fahdah. She used to say that he liked to play around on her belly and then fall asleep. When he woke up, the slaves gave him a washing. Then he came and sat down with them. Abū Zwayyid was present in the majlis. The young prince called him "my uncle." He would say, "Good morning, my uncle!" The poet said:

Hello, hello, hello to you, a hearty welcome,
  a thousand, another thousand, and thousands more!
Sweetheart of a girl with civet-scented breasts:
  how fresh creamy beauties love your raw rutting!
Manly virtue looked down its nose at all suitors,
  then expeditiously sent its camel running to Sʿūd.
How I wish one could summon the dead;
  if only Muḥammad would rise from his tomb;
ʿAbd al-ʿAzīz! See the fast horse of hot pursuit!
  Marvel at the tons of booty captured by Sʿūd!
Young camels fringe a long caravan of spoils:[157]
  by God, one struck by him is out of combat.

١٫٢٧ ابو زويـد يطلبه عبدٍ من اهل حايل من عبيد الرشيد يقال له محمد الصالح يطلبه فْلوس يطلبه ست وعشرين نيره. وابلش بُه يقول اوفَن يابو زويد وابو زويد يقطّع الخيوط بايديه يقول بْرخا ويقول ما ادري كيف. يقولون يابو زويد ليه ما توفي هالعبد. ربعُه يقولونه. هالعبد اللي ابلش بك عَطُه دراهمُه. قال انا يالربع ما معي شين اوفي ولا عمري اوفيت الديّان اتّحَرّى هالقطامي باكر يِدْلي بْروض واحِطّ بُه لُه ابيات ويوفي عني.

٢٫٢٧ عاد يوم صار كون الجوف جا ابو زويد لسعود وقال يا طويل العمر مبارَكٍ هالفود. قال الله يبارك بك. قال والله طال عمرك انا استسمحك معي لي بوَيتاتٍ ابقولهن بك لاجل انك تستاهلهن. قال لا باس هاتهن. ويا مار يْخَبّر دينة العبد يبيه يوفي عنه العبد وشكر فعلُه عاد اللي هو شكر. قال مبدا كلامه يمدح ابن رشيد وانه يستاهل وانه اخذ اهل الشمال خذى نوّاف ابن شعلان جاب كل هل الشمال يحوشَه والسعدين ما يْتَراكِبَن وخذاوه واستجب ابو زويد ويمدح ابن رشيد ويبيه يوفي عنه.

٣٫٢٧ يوم قْصِدَه عليه قال وش يطلبك العبد. قال يطلبن ست وعشرين نيره. قال هاتوا بارود لابو زويد من البواريد اللي ما ثِوَّر بهن بواريد ابن ليلي. قال يا دلالي هي

War of al-Jawf, Poem in Praise of Abū Khashm

Abū Zwayyid owed money to a slave named Muḥammad ibn Ṣāliḥ, who lived in Ḥāyil and was one of the slaves in the service of Ibn Rashīd. He owed him twenty-six guineas. He kept urging him to pay back the money and settle the debt, but Abū Zwayyid was hard up and penniless. He asked his creditor to wait until things eased up for him, and other similar pleas. People, his own folk, would prod him gently: "Abū Zwayyid, why don't you pay back what you owe the slave? The slave who keeps bothering you, give him his money!" But he replied, "My dear fellows, I don't even have a penny to show him. And I have never paid off my debts my whole life long. Let me wait patiently and see. Who knows, tomorrow this fierce falcon may strike riches in bountiful orchards.[158] Then I will compose some verses to laud his feats of arms, and as a consequence he will settle my debts." 27.1

As fate would have it, the battle of al-Jawf was fought soon after. Abū Zwayyid called on Sʿūd and said, "May your life be long, my congratulations on these blessed spoils!" "God bless you." "By God, may you live long, I humbly ask your permission to recite some simple verses that I composed because you are truly deserving of them." "No problem," he said. "Go ahead." Sʿud Abū Khashm was aware of the debt problem. He knew that the poet hoped he would settle his debt to the slave. And he did so, a generous deed for which Abū Zwayyid gave him proper thanks. He opens the poem with praise for Ibn Rashīd and stresses how deserving he is, and how he routed the people of the north. He stripped Nawwāf ibn Shaʿlān of his possessions and looted all the people of the north. Two good fortunes do not go together: you either win or lose.[159] Abū Zwayyid, awed by the quantity of booty, sang Ibn Rashīd's praises and asked him to pay off his debts. 27.2

When he had finished declaiming, Ibn Rashīd asked him, "What is the amount you owe the slave?" He said, "He wants me to pay him twenty-six guineas." Ibn Rashīd called his servants: "Bring a rifle for Abū Zwayyid!" He meant one of the new rifles, the ones provided by Ibn Laylā that were never used for shooting. "Dearest," asked Abū Zwayyid, "are those for me or for ʿĀmish?"[160] 27.3

لي أو لعامش. قال لا الا لك وهاتوا لعامش مثلَه. قال هاتوا لابو زويد ذلول من من المنقية من الركاب الطيّبات اللي يخصّن الشيوخ. قال يا دلالي هي لي أو لعامش. قال لا الا لك وهاتوا لعامش مثله. جابوا ذلولين وبارودين وهو ينطيه لُه ورقة يكتبه لُه قال هذي حطّه بمخباك يما يجيك العبد والى جاك العبد مِدَّه لُه وترى وفاوه علينا ما هو عليك.

٤،٢٧ وطلع مع ذلولين وبارودين جزانٍ للقصيده وست وعشرين نيرة وفا للعبد. ابن ليلى رجّال الدولة رجّال العصملي ابن ليلى من اهل لبده. زعجوه الله يسلمك لابن رشيد بالف بارود اللي يقال لهن امهات خمس وحطّهن ابن رشيد عنده بحايل وفرّقهن على رجاجيله وعلى شمر من جاوه من شمر انطاوه. ألف بارود هِن سمّوهن بواريد ابن ليلى والا هِن جَن من الترك أمهات خمس.

٥،٢٧ يقول ابو زويد

أنا اذكر الله عِدّ رمل الحمادِ   وعد النفود وعد مزبور الاطعاس
يا ربّ يا خالق جميع العبّادِ   يا منزّلٍ علمك بحبرٍ وِقرطاس
تعزّ ابو مِشْعَل بِعِيد المعادي   اطلب عسى ما فوق راسه يجي راس

ابو مشعل سعود ابو خشم.

طبّق على دينٍ لنا قبل غادي   اللي يقول عبيد يحكم عبّاس

عبيد يذكر يقول الجوبة خليناه علشان عباس من الدوله يوم هو يقول يادار خليتك على شان عباس، والا لابن شعلان ما ني مخليك.

جابه بضرب مصقّلات الهنادي   لو هو وفى من صاحب الدين لا باس

"These are surely for you," he said, and he called for the same to be brought for ʿĀmish. "And bring Abū Zwayyid one of the best riding camels, from the selection!"—that is, the first-class mounts owned by shaykhs. "My dear, is she for me or for ʿĀmish?" "No, for you. And bring a similar camel for ʿĀmish!"

They brought two riding camels and two rifles. And Ibn Rashīd gave him 27.4
a piece of paper in his own hand, saying, "Put this in your pocket and give it to the slave when he comes to you. I will take care of the money you owe him. I'll pay your debt; it's not your affair anymore." Thus, he departed with two riding camels and two rifles in recognition of the poem he had composed, and the debt of twenty-six guineas he owed to the slave settled. Ibn Laylā was a man who served the state, the man of the ʿUṣmalī rifles, from the Lubdah quarter in Ḥāyil.[161] The Ottoman Turks sent him to Ibn Rashīd with a thousand rifles, called "Mother of Five (bullets)." Ibn Rashīd stored them in Ḥāyil and distributed them among his henchmen, bodyguards, and Shammar tribesmen. Shammaris who came to visit and pay their respects were given a rifle. The thousand firearms used to be called "rifles of Ibn Laylā," but in reality they came from the Turks, the "Mothers of Five."

Abū Zwayyid said: 27.5

As sand grains are abundant, that often I repeat God's name,
grains of the golden dunes, towering hills of sand.
Lord, You are the Creator of humanity;
You sent down your message in ink on paper.
Glory to father of Mishʿal, who raids far and wide!
My prayer for him: "Let no head be over his head!"

—Abū Mishʿal is Sʿūd Abū Khashm.

Our ancient debts from time immemorial he settled,
accounts from the rule of ʿAbbās, said ʿUbayd.

—ʿUbayd (ibn Rashīd) said that in earlier days we abandoned al-Jawbah because of ʿAbbās, ceding it to the Ottoman State, in his verse: "O land, we left you alone because of ʿAbbās; for Ibn Shaʿlān's sake we'd have not left it."

He conquered, gleaming Indian swords in hand;
a campaign that settled all unpaid debts as well.

حِرٍّ شـلـع من خشم اجا ثـم صـاد   يِدْهِش وهو ما جدّع الريش قرناس
ما ياكل الا صـاخنات القـنـاد   صـاد ابو تايـه والشرارات وجـلاس
ويوم ان نوّافٍ نــــزل بالبـلاد   جا صايلٍ من كل بِدٍّ معه ناس
نوّاف هـايجٌ صـايجٍ جا يْقـادي   حطيت بـه شـابور وهْجار وزكاس
نوّاف من الصولات ويش استـفـاد   غير التشمّت والدعاوي والافلاس
جا صايلٍ وجموعهم له حوادي   ويـزيّن الدحّـة لهم كا هوّاس
يبي يصـيد ولا يحسبه يصـــاد   يما فـراوه اللي على الصيد لهّـاس
افعال ابو مشعل صحيحٍ وكاد   وافعــال نوّافٍ تواقَعَن بالسـاس
سـرى وخلى الفـرش هن والوسـاد   وعقب الهدير افثى وبدّل بالاضراس
وخــلّوا غوالي قشّهم والسواد   وهَجّوا على ظهور الحـراذين يبّـاس
أيسـر هجيجه سـنّدوا بطن وادي   وايمن هجيجه بين نـدفا والامحاص
جـريـرةٍ منها يشيب السواد   افقـرت به ناس واغنيت بـه ناس
كِثر بربعه من يدور الميادي   ومن غاب عنكم كسبه الغبن واليـاس
فوق الحمول يوسّطون الفــراد   كل بنى له بيتٍ اطناب وامراس
محمد وعبدالله لسيفك جْناد   تحيزموا لك بالرشا حين الامراس

محمد وعبدالله الطلال.

حـامُوا مـعك بالدين حقٍّ وكاد   جَوا صولةٍ تْحَمَى بَه العام والخاص
يوم ان عبدالله رِكِب بالشداد   خـلّى السراد وجاب لك ذربة الناس

A falcon soaring up from Ajā's crest for the hunt,
stunning, not one ruffled feather, pure peregrine!
His fare the bleeding flesh of a prey's breast:
he bagged Abū Ṭāyih, al-Sharārāt, and ʿAnazah.
War started with Nawwāf marching into town;
lusting for a brawl, ragtag troops came prowling,
Led by Nawwāf, rutting stud foaming at the mouth:
you tied his legs, crippled him, ringed his nose.
Nawwāf, what's your gain from reckless charges
but malicious gloats, empty claims, and bitter failure?
He charged, goading his troops with rousing chants;
beguiled, the dazzled fools swung in a *daḥḥah* dance.
Aiming to hunt, he didn't think he'd be hunted:
how our grizzled huntsmen tore him to pieces!
Abū Mishʿal's feats of arms are certainly true;[162]
Nawwāf's exploits have tumbled into the gutter.
He ran off by night, pillow and bedcover left behind;
quiet after earsplitting roars, he gnashed his teeth.
They abandoned precious luggage and black tents,
fled riding bareback on their mounts.
Veering left, they galloped up the wadi bottom;
veering right, they raced between Nadfā and al-Amḥāṣ.
Heads of black hair turn white at seeing such a rout:
some plunged into poverty, others wealthy in the blink of an eye.
Shaken, his demoralized troops flagged and wavered;
they absconded with the prize of failure and frustration.
Pack camels carried passengers, seated among loads,[163]
installed up there as if with ropes and tent pegs.
Muḥammad and ʿAbdallah are your sword's scabbards,
girded up for you at the well with rope and bucket.

—That is, Muḥammad and ʿAbdallah al-Ṭalāl.

Every inch as eager as you are to collect old debts,
their ardor for battle cheered each and every fighter.
ʿAbdallah mounted his camel and marched
with the pick of men, not the chickenhearted,

عبدالله ابن طلال اللي عاد عقبٍ ذبح الامير هو اللي فزّع شمّر وضاري ابن طواله.

يوم أَرْتَعَوا هـزلى الرجـال السـراد   المـرتعـة مثـل الحصـاني والابسـاس

المرتعه اللي يسوقون الرتاعه يسوقون للاجناب من شان يرعون معهم بديرتهم.

المـرتعـة يسـتاهــلون السواد   اسود من الظلما الى حـلّ الادمـاس
جـاك اخو صلفـة فوق قبّـا سـناد   من مـاكر تِبعـه على الخيل مِـذْباس

أخو صلفه ضاري ابن طواله.

يا صـاح عن حِسّـه تِقَفّى العـياد   والشحص بالفِرْسان ياخَذَن مِرْواس
وِفهْـران ابن هيشـان للخـيل قـاد   يسـري وخيله ضِمّـرٍ مثـل الاقواس

فهران الصديد جاك من الجزيره تقطّعن الزمالات وخلاهن.

ولحقت بمـطني مثل حِرّ الهـداد   هـلّوا بـزيـنين المحـازم والالبـاس

مطني ابن شريم.

بالليـل يسـرون العـيال العوادي   يلفون بالذخـرة شيخ الاشخـاص
وخوالك اللي ما بعـرقك فســـاد   بافعـالهم ردّوا حـمَوا تالي النـاس
اخوات موضي يوم عضّ النجـــاد   اخوات موضي لى هبى كل نسـناس
ونعـمٍ باهل حايـل الى جـا المنـادي   اهـل مـراكيضٍ على الفـعـل لِهـّاس
أفـعـال زيـنين المحـازم بعـــاد   يـردون حوض الموت والرمي مِحْتاس

—Yet ʿAbdallah ibn Ṭalāl was the one who later murdered the prince. On this occasion, he mobilized the men of Shammar, together with Ḍārī ibn Ṭwālah.

Weaklings who cravenly pay for grazing rights,[164]
submissive appeasers like foxes and scrawny cats.

—As the price for permission to pasture their animals on another tribe's land, they give the owners one of their sheep.

To pay for grazing rights is a shameful deed,
blacker than impenetrable dark of night.
On a broad-chested steed came Ṣalfah's brother:
his nest's feeblest falcon ravages enemy riders.

—The brother of Ṣalfah is Ḍārī ibn Ṭwālah.

At his battle cry, seasoned horses shrink back;
diffident, they gallop off, unrestrained by their riders.
Fihrān ibn Hēshān leads the cavalry charge;
all-night marches left his horses lean like bows.

—Fihrān ibn Hēshān of al-Ṣdēd of Shammar rushed to the assistance from the Jazīrah area. The pack camels accompanying the horses were so exhausted that they had to be abandoned.

They linked up with Miṭnī, falcon set upon prey,
a violent rush of bandoliers and colorful jackets.

—Miṭnī ibn Shrēm.

Horsemen launching the assault came at night
with arms for the shaykh of shaykhs:
Maternal uncles did not harm your breed:[165]
their chivalrous feats paved the way for offspring;
Brothers of Mūḍī, when teeth are clenched;
brothers of Mūḍī, when wimps are useless.[166]
Plaudits for Ḥāyil's folks, who live up to the call,
who without dismay always gallop into the fray.
Girded with ornate belts, they stop at nothing;
shots ringing, they drink from the pool of death.

عبيدك اللي مثل زمل الهداد   ارداهم اللي للمناعير مِذباس
وربعي على الشطّات بيهم سِداد   اللي محامينٍ على الحكم من راس
ما ليلة ما جاك منّا منادي   حنا بحلق اللي يعاديك لولاس
يا البيض عرّضن الشياب الزباد   يوم ان ابو مشعل لفى عقب الايّاس
اللي الى منه حدى الخيل حادي   ينطح ويضرب ما يسنّد لها راس
لو تنظرنّه يوم عجّ الطراد   يشعّ نوره يوم الارياق يبّاس
يا مير ما لك بالقبايل ملادي   لا بالعرب لمّا ولا من بني ياس
ولا جابن الخفرات مثلك ولاد   ولا زهملن مثلك على الديد لَسّاس
أفعال ابا زيد لفعلك تشادي   اللي ولى دار الزناتي وقباس
يوم ان كل دِنيّت له جوادِ   ترخص بعمرك كان شحّوا بالانفاس
ويوم ان نشت بك موضيٍ فيك عاد   أطلب عسى ما لَه من النار مسّاس
زبن الرفيق ان حسّ بيه الشداد   شيلي ثقيلٍ يا بو مشعل علي حاس
يا مير شرّي دينة من عباد   عبدٍ عديم ولا عن الدين ينفاص
وانا بغيرك ما يسرّي زنادي   أبي منّك عن دينة العبد لي باص
لى دكّ بك سيل الندى تقل وادي   يا مير طرخات النواميس بالراس
نيّات خيرك بالسما له منادي   يصير للحسنات كايل وقوّاس

Your slaves advance like rutting stallions;[167]
the least of them lays waste to the enemy's champions.
In a crunch, my fellows fulfill the needs of the hour,
resolute in protecting the princely house.
Each night we sent a herald to your aid:
we're at your assailant's throat like a cord.
Beauties of ours! Sprinkle your cloth with civet!
You waited anxiously for sign of Abū Mishʿal:
He sings ditties urging on his horses and men,
storms forward, striking out at all on his path.
See him dueling on horseback in whirling dust,
resplendent, while others choke on dried spittle!
Among tribes, your equal is nowhere to be found,
not among the mass of Arabs nor the Banū Yās.
Maidens did not bring forth a boy like you,
never suckled such an infant at their breast.
You, intrepid warrior, the equal of Abū Zayd,
victorious over lands of al-Zanātī and Qabbās.[168]
When warhorses are led to every fighter,
others hold back—you hold dear life cheap.
Once Mūḍī swoons in your sweet embrace,
pray that she will never burn in Hell's fire.
Your friend's back is racked by a wooden saddle;
I writhe under a heavy load, Abū Mishʿal, my refuge!
O Prince, I am bedeviled by debt owed to a slave;
an intrepid warrior slave does not easily relent.
Without you, my fire steel cannot strike sparks:
I beg you, free me from the debt the slave has levied![169]
You are like a valley flooded by torrents of generosity,
Prince, your stores of fame and glory are almost bursting.
Your noble aspirations will be proclaimed in Heaven,
when charitable deeds are weighed and measured.

خضير الصعيليك

يرد على قصيدة خلف ابو زويد بسطام ابن شعلان ١٠٢٨

يا راكبٍ نابى القرى كنّه الذيب   عليه من رِعْيِ الخطر كالزباره
سِهْواج ما مِسّت عليه المِصاليب   يَشْدى ظليمٍ جافلٍ من مغاره
لا تيل لا بابور عجل التواثيب   والا السهم من بندقٍ يوم ثاره
لابو زويد تِدّي الهرج وتجيب   بيّنت كِذبك للمخاليق شاره
يابو زويد كِبّ عنك التكاذيب   اهْفيت حَظّك بالمرا والقماره
ما خِفْت ربٍّ يعلم السِرّ والغَيب   هو ما يغِيب ولا لمغيبه غياره
اما الشجاع محمّد ما بعد جيب   وْلا ذِكر مولودٍ يلادي اختباره
من حدري الخُرْمه الى جاري السِيب   للشام لاسطنبول لى قندهاره
تاتيه مطوّعة الشِفايا المِصاعيب   من كثر ما يَجْزَى عدُوّه بغاره
الكايد القاسي لمن به تَحانيب   الهيّن الليّن لمن به خياره
لصديقه احْلى من قَراح اللهابيب   لعدوه اقْطَع من شلاهيب ناره
سِكّر عَسَل حِلوٍ عَذِيّ المِشاريب   حَنْظل عَقِد شَرْيٍ قطوع المراره
وابْهَى من عقب من لِفوا له معازيب   يا جَنّبَتْ دَلْو الثريا بذاره
يا جَوا يحثّون النِضا بالعراقيب   وانْوَن هجاهيج النضا للخطاره

Riposte of Khḍēr al-Ṣʿēlīć to Abū Zwayyid's Poem in Praise of Ibn Shaʿlān

He made a poem in reply to Abū Zwayyid's poem on Saṭṭām ibn Shaʿlān: 28.1

Rider of a big-humped camel, tough as a wolf,
layered with fat from grazing on pristine enemy land;
Pampered, not grated by a wooden saddle,
speedy as a male ostrich racing at full tilt;
At staccato pace—no telegraph or steam engine—
as guns fire deafening salvos.
Make for Abū Zwayyid! Take his verse in reply!
I made your lies apparent to all the world.
Abū Zwayyid, leave off the spreading of falsehoods!
Do not forfeit honor by swagger and reckless games.
Fear the Lord, privy to secrets and the unknown,
Never absent—for Him there is no substitute.
No knight as shining as Muḥammad was ever born,
nor can any creature claim to be his peer.
From south of al-Khurmah to Shaṭṭ al-ʿArab River,
from Syria to Istanbul, all the way to Kandahar,[170]
Subduers of defiant strongmen flock to him,
in awe of his vengeful punishment of enemies:
Ruthless and severe with arrogant recalcitrants,[171]
good-natured and gentle with loyal supporters;
For friends sweeter than rainwater in shaded rocks;
to enemies crueler than flames of blazing fire:
Wholesome drafts made of purest sugar honey;
or stinging colocynth, bitter apple of biting taste.
Happy are his guests, made masters of the house,
when seeds are forsaken by the Pleiades rains;[172]
Visitors hasten, spurring camels with their heels
to run at a frantic pace to the welcoming host.

يا جَن نجوم الليل مثل المِشاهيب وصَكّوا على حَبّ القرايا تجاره
يْحَنّي خشوم الفوس من شمَّخ النيب اللي يعيشون العرب من فِقاره
ربعٍ براي الله هم مِسْهَم الطِيب اخْلَت لهم كِلّ القِبايل ذْياره
اخوه ابو ماجد حصان الاطاليب من دَور عبد الله تقَطّع شراره
بمْصَقّل الهندي مِضَى له تجاريب عَوق العديم وعوق من به نماره
محمدٍ هو الفحل للرعابيب اللي مع البِدْوان واللي بداره
صلاة ربّي عِدّ رَمْل العراقيب على الرسول اللي تِلَقّى البشاره

As stars start to twinkle, sparkling like torches,
misers shut doors, loath to share their coffee,
His axe blades are smeared with camel blood,
though people make a living from their backs.
Clansmen favored by God, cream of the crop,
they forced all tribes to concede their lands.[173]
His brother, father of Mājid, rescuers' steed:
Ever since ʿAbdallah's rule his sparks fly.
His routine is wielding polished Indian swords:
nemesis of enemies, scourge of baleful rogues.
Muḥammad is the stud of bell-shaped beauties,
stylish Bedouin girls and village stunners.[174]
Prayers of the Lord, abundant as the dunes' sand grains,
for the Prophet, receiver of His revelations.

راضي ابن فاران

١،٢٩ وهـذا راضي ابن فاران قديم مات ما لِحقت عليه انا. هو من اهل جبّه بس بتالي عمره انتزح يمّ الجوف. يقصد يردّ على قصيدة خلف ابو زويد بسطّام ابن شعلان. يقول

يا راكب اللي سِـنّدَت بالبواكـير   ما عِمِـر سوّاق السواني سـناهـا
ولا استلحقت لابنـه ليالى المِصـاغير   ولا شـدّها المِذْهِب ليالي عفاهـا
تشـدى ظِليـمٍ جافـلٍ من حـداديـر   ما تلحقـه صِـمّ الرمك مع قـفاهـا
ليا استلحقت قَفْو اليـدين المواخـير   تمسي بـدار ودار تصبح وراهـا
تلفي خلف بيوسط عوج الدواويـر   نسي الرضـاع وديده اللي غذاهـا
ما جـاك في ماضي زمـانك تنـاكير   دونك ينـاحن الضواري عـداهـا
بيوت الشـرايع وافـيات التشـابير   سور الدبايـل يا تعـاقب قَـناهـا
بيضرّ اخو متعب خَصاب الخطاطير   ومن آدم مـا زهـملتّـه نسـاهـا
لا شـاخ مثله لا وزيـر ولا امـير   لا باول الدنيـا ولا اللي تلاهـا
حصـان يقـلّط للمهـار العـنابير   وِتفْـهَق عنـه كل العلاوي وراهـا
اللي ولى نجـدٍ لحَـد المـعـابير   بسـيوف يِسّقِن العـدو من طناهـا
من فوق قِبٍّ مثـل روس الخواوير   والموت يلقى عنـد صوتٍ وراهـا
وزولٍ بوجـهه ما عبى للمـصـادير   وقبـيلةٍ شوف العـدو من مـناهـا

Riposte of Rāḍī ibn Fārān to Abū Zwayyid's Poem in Praise of Ibn Sha'lān

Rāḍī ibn Fārān died a long time ago. Before my time—I never saw him. He was 29.1
from Jubbah, but toward the end of his life he moved to al-Jawf. In these verses, he gives a riposte to Abū Zwayyid's poem on Saṭṭām ibn Sha'lān, saying:

Hey, rider flogging a camel with a crop,
not a beast to toil drawing irrigation water,
Nor brought up to suckle her newborn calf
or harried to carry a needy man's loads.
Like a startled male ostrich, she hurtles down:
hard-hooved horses can't catch up with her.
Forefeet and legs behind move in rapid sync:
one desert abode at night, another in the morning.
Find Khalaf among the camp's slanting tents.
Did he forget who nursed him at her breast?
Never did you meet with their disrespect:
they kept you safe from marauding predators.
Liberal-minded, most hospitable of hosts,
with spears flying, a rampart from disaster,
He is Mit'ib's mighty brother, fattener of guests:
no woman suckled his like since Adam's days.[175]
No shaykh, minister, or prince has his stature,
from the world's beginnings until its very end;
A champion stud led to thoroughbred mares
to sire, without peer among noblest stallions,
He reigns from Najd to the Iraqi river crossings,
He quenches grim swords' thirst with enemy blood;
On horses with heads massive as camels', sounds
his raucous battle cry, sowing death and doom:
His orders have no words for "turning back":
facing the enemy is his tribe's pride and joy.

يا اللهْ يا خــــالق مـزونٍ مـزابير   يا باسـط الدنيـا ورافـع سمـاهـا
تاقى محـــــمد عن دروب العواثير   بحجابك اللي مـا يقصّـر غطـاهـا
خـليفـةٍ حـطّـه اله المـقـادير   سورٍ يلوذ الشمّـــري بيـذراهـا

God, Creator of layered rain clouds,
You spread out the earth and raised the sky:
Keep Muḥammad from stumbling on the road;
spread over him Your infallible protective veil.
As decreed by God, he is His viceroy on earth,
A walled bulwark to shelter his Shammar tribe.

عدوان ابن راشد الهربيد

ʿAdwān ibn Rāshid al-Hirbīd

حياته

١٫٣٠ عدوان الهربيد على دور محمد ابن رشيد لُه سوالف وله قصيد ونَهَج كلامُه مع الناس بس الناس اشْتَهَرَت ذْلان عندهم الشيخه من قصيدُه والا هو قصيدُه كثير. ديرته الغوطه وموقَق والامرار ولا هو راعي فْرَج. لُه نْخَلاتٍ بحيَه باجا ويصيرّ على الخِنْفة الزريب ويربّع.

٢٫٣٠ وهو عند آخر عمره لفّت بُه الدنيا كفانا الله شرَّه ولا بقي الا هو وْحَدى عيال اخوتُه وْغيدٍ صغيرِ ورِع اللي هو جريس يِشِيله ينقّله مثل ما تَزمِّل الحُرمَة وِرْعَه والحوَال ارْدى من ذلك. اخوته سبعه هو عيال راشد سبعه ابوه راشد واخوته سبعه كلهم صقاقير وكلهم بخدمته وكافينه هو اكبرهم. يقولون بيتهم مسَوّبع بُه سبع قْطوب وكل عَميرةٍ بَه رمح. وحيا حياةٍ زينه هو واخوانه معهم حريم واخوته مع ايمنُه وايسرُه وعندهم خيل وزمل وحلال واذواد بِلّ تروح وتجي عليهم ورعيّة غنم.

٣٫٣٠ راح هو يدوِّر مرازق الله. نَهَج من عند اخوته بالربيع وهم باحلى ما همب به ونهج يدوّر المصالح. يوم انه اخذ الى الحول عانِقُه لُه واحْدٍ يعرفه قال وش لون فلان. ينشد عن اخوه. قال يطلبك الحل. قال وفلان. قال لا تنشّد العرب اللي انت تخبرطْحَنَتهم هالدنيا الله يكفينا شره ولا اجلد (= بقي) الا جريس ولد اخوك وامه والا كِلّه راحت عِقْب جريس وامه ما اجلد من هالكناس اللي تخْبَر احد.

His Life

ʿAdwān al-Hirbīd was a contemporary of Muḥammad ibn Rashīd. He was known for his stories and poems. People eagerly followed his sayings and doings. He was a prolific bard, but during his lifetime he became especially famous for a poem called al-Shēkhah. He hailed from the area of al-Ghūṭah, Mōgag, and al-Amrār, but often traveled deep into the desert. He owned gardens of date palms at Ḥayyah in the Ajā Mountain. Following the late-spring rains, he used to stay in a booth made of palm leaves at al-Khinfah al-Zrēb, where he pastured his animals.[176] 30.1

Later in life, he faced much adversity—may God spare us from the world's tribulations—and as his family's sole survivor he had the care of a little boy, Jrēs, the child of one of his brothers. He used to carry the infant around as women do. But his circumstances were much worse. He was one of seven brothers, sons of Rāshid, skilled falconers all. Because he was the elder brother, the others vied to be at his beck and call, eager to impress him favorably by doing odd jobs for him. He was the firstborn. I was told that they lived in a tent with seven main poles.[177] In each of the seven compartments there was a lance. He and his brothers were married men who lived a contented family life. His brothers' quarters were to his right and left. They owned fast riding horses, pack camels, various properties, herds of milk-producing camels that pastured nearby, and large flocks of sheep and goats. 30.2

One day, he went on a journey to attend to some business. He left the camp where he and his brothers were staying. It was spring, and the desert had bloomed magnificently, but he had to travel to look after his interests. When he had been away for about one year, he ran into someone he had known from before. He asked him how so-and-so was doing, one of his brothers. The other said, "He asks your forgiveness; he is no longer with us."[178] "And so-and-so?" "Ask no more," the other said. "Cruel fate has crushed all your dear ones, may God protect us from its evil. The only ones left are Jrēs, your brother's son, and his mother. The others perished. Except for Jrēs and his mother, not a single one of your close kinfolk have survived." In ʿAdwān's absence, the Shaʿlān of the Rwalah tribe had sprung a surprise attack, killing everyone in the camp 30.3

أثاريهم أغاروا عليهم الشعلان الروله وعدوان غايب وذبحوهم واخذوا حلالهم. قال فود عوجان.

٤،٣٠ وهو لك يجيك يشري لُه مطيّة بالقرِيشات اللي معُه قال اغدين امكن الولد غدي الله ما يَقْطَعنا. يوم جا المراح اللي هم بُه والى والله بس نوّار العِشب يِغيف واثَر المطر والهوادي ما يِطِبُّه من الخوف احد هكالحين ولا بُه لا والي ولا قاني ما على الدار ديّار. يا والله هَذَا مَحَلّ الحلال وهذا مَحَلّ الهوادي وهذا مَحَلّ البيت. واقعد بُه وتذكّرهم وتذكر عِزّهم يوم هم جميع هو واخوانه واليوم اخذتهم الدنيا اخوته واجلد بس هو لحاله.

٥،٣٠ واقعد وِابْك وتَخَلّف الله وهو يتمثل

يادار يادارٍ نزلنا بك العام   بين الجلَد يادار واشراف ضاحي
وَبل السماك اسقاك غضبان الارزام   جَضْرٍ دِفَق ديهوم صافي القراح
يادار ما بك من هلِك جِرّة اقدام   والمال ما لُه جِرّةٍ بالمراح
ما خَذَى الثلاث اللي تِقِل روس خِدّام   وارضٍ تِصَفّق بَه نشيط الرياح
وين الرجال اللي تَخَطّى بك العام   أقْفَوا كما بَرقٍ بالامطار لاح
راحَوا كما حلمٍ تحزّاوه حلام   أو برق صيفٍ باوّل الليل لاح
كلّنهم سود الليالي والاوهام   وانا كما المحروج تحت السلاح
ياجريس يامشكاي واطيرنا حام   واخون لذّات الليال اللقاح
حطّن بنا هَجْرٍ عواقيد وخْزام   واسقتّنا ياجريس مر الملاح
حَظّ رِبض لو قامت السمر ما قام   وبابٍ عصانا بْقِلّة الانفتاح

and making off with their possessions. "ʿŌjān's gain," he said, meaning that such a criminally wanton and bloody raid merely brought dishonor.

With the little money he had, he bought a camel and rode back, saying to 30.4
himself, "Perhaps the boy will grow up and be good. Perhaps God will allow us to perpetuate our family's existence and not cut off our lineage." On arrival, he found their former settlement empty. He gazed at blossoming herbage and thick growth, pools of rainwater that had not yet dried up, slabs of stone from which the cooking pots had been suspended over the fire. No one had dared to set foot in the place since the catastrophe. No one at all. No human being had the courage to come close to it for any purpose. "My God, here is where the animals used to stay, here the cooking pots, here the tent." He sat down, overwhelmed by memories of his loved ones. He thought of their happy days together, their self-assurance and confidence in the future. And now evil fate had carried off his brothers. There he was, all alone by himself.

He sank to his knees and wept, praying to God for help. These verses welled 30.5
up in him:

A year ago was my last view of our desert abode,
  between hard plains and soft sands of Ashrāf Ḍāḥī.
May rumbling clouds shower you with the rains of Arcturus,
  shaking with anger, and drench you in limpid water.
Abode! Where are your inhabitants' footprints?
  Where the traces herds leave at resting places?
Three stones for cooking pots, like servants' heads;[179]
  a bowl of dust, stirred up by gusty winds—that's all.
Where are the men who sauntered here last year?
  Gone from view! Ephemeral as lightning's flicker.
They went, like a dream in a soothsayer's tale,
  thunderlights seen in an early summer evening,
Vanished into a dark maw of night and plague,[180]
  leaving me mortally wounded, felled by a weapon.
Jrēs, my soulmate, over us hover birds of death:
  treacherous are delights of doom-laden nights!
Held by a nose ring, fettered and shackled,
  Jrēs, we're made to swallow horrid brine.
Even if mountains fly, our luck remains prostrate:[181]
  Do not fancy that good fortune's gates are still ajar!

واقَدّ قلبي قدّهم لازرق الخام   أوقدّ غَرْبٍ من شِفا البير طاح

٦،٣٠ وبعد مدّه مَرّ مراحٍ لهم وليا مير اخوته موّتوا. مرّ من الدايرة يا مير هذي مِرِحَهُم. والى والله بس الهبايب والهوادي باقية به. ويتذكّرهم يا هذي منازلهم العام بلهم لهم ارضٍ العشب والقطعان عندهم. ويوم مرهالسنة يا مير تدفّق هالهماليل على قاعٍ بيضانٍ ما بَه الوالي. وليا بس الهوادي شريدة هكالعِربان والحلال والبيت بس الهوادي الثلاث.

٧،٣٠ يقول

راكبٍ من فوق مسطورة العين   قطّاعة الدَوّ الخلاوي بالاهذال
مثل القطاة اللي تِشوح الجناحين   كِدْريةٍ حدّه قطوع اشهب اللال
عَمَلت انا ياجريس لي وَقْم بيتين   اوَيّ بيطارٍ للاشعار عمّال
شَغَلْتهن شغل الفرنج الملاعين   وخلّيتهن يمشن مع الدرب جَودال
قِطْمٍ كما النَيرات بالقالَم الزين   ما قيل بيتٍ عن سَنَع دَرْبهن عال
ياجريس يامشكاي بالله تشاكين   افهم جواب اللي على النِضو مِرْسال
شِف دار اهلنا ما بها من يحاكين   ما خَذى الثلاث السود والمِرح الاسمال
عقب المخومس والنشاما الحبيبين   اليوم لا طربه ولا حِلْو مِنْزال
اقْفَوا كما غَيمٍ نِشا باول الحين   تقفّته غَرْبيّة العصر وانجال
دلّيت انوح من الجروح الكوانين   عِدّي خَلوج طاولَه خِلْج الاعوال
راح الطرب والكيف والمقعد الزين   وعقب الجواضع رَصَّن الله على الجال

الجواضِع يعني لِين المواسد والفَرش من اين ما بغى يميل يرتكي.

My heart is torn to shreds like cheap blue cloth,
a bucket rent by a well casing's jutting stones.

Some time later he passed their former camp. His brothers had died. 30.6
These were the herds' resting places. An eerie silence reigned, broken only by breezes whistling around the cooking pots' stone slabs. He delved into his memories. Yes, here stood their tents only a year ago. They had space, herbage, and herds in abundance. He looked at the place. Plentiful rains had drenched the flat desert bottom, devoid of any sign of human life. The stones that held the cooking pots were the only mementos of a time when the place bustled with people, cattle, and tents. Only those three slabs of stone, nothing more.

Then he said: 30.7

Rider of a she-camel with blazing eyes,
eager to cross wastes at an impetuous pace,
Vying with sandgrouse swift on the wing,
thirst-driven to plunge into shimmering heat.
Jrēs, I roused myself to craft my verse for you;
like a deft artisan I mold my rhymes;
Trimmed with an accursed Frank's finesse,
they're released, and hit the road in single file.
Gold coins, rounded like pads of camels' feet;[182]
Never am I told: "Your verses stray off course!"
Jrēs, listen to my complaint, feel for me,
heed my message, delivered by a hardy mount!
Behold our folk's abode, the mutes don't speak,
hearthstones, resting places blown about by dust:[183]
Where are the five-poled tents, my cheerful fellows,
on a grim day, stripped of the dwellings' sweet gaiety?
Swept away like an early-morning deck of clouds,
dispersed in the afternoon by heady western winds.
I groan, a warrior clasping at his grievous wounds,
a camel mother gone insane after losing her calf.
Life is bleak, tasteless without human contact:
from my pillowed bed, God smashed me against the rocks.

—*Jawāḍiʿ* are soft pillows and coverings that give into whatever direction you lean on them.

مع جريس

١،٣١ عدوان الهريد فَجّ بس على بناخيه بس يَكْفَى على بناخيه جريس. جريس ولدٍ لاخوه سحيمان من اللي ذِبحوا وَغيد. قام لك ينقّله ويجي أم الوليد اسمَه بقَيشه قال والله انا ما انا هاوي عليك وانتي ما انتي حرمةٍ لي ابي آخذك لاجل هاليتيم. وخِذ ام جريس تزوج امّه. وقم لك ينقله على ظَهَره. ويجمعون لُه السويد منايح وزمايل وابنوا لهم بويت وصيروا عرب. هكالحين الصيد ماجود مار الظبا عِدّه غنم. وجريس ياطويل العمر دلّى عدوان يَعَمَل بُه عمل طير يِعلِفُه اعلاف طير. من الحول الى الحول سنة كامله وهو حاطُّه بالطويل بَراف رافي لُه بَلُه غضايَه (= غضاة) عِشّ يتيم وعاشٍّ لُه. ويطِبّ للنفود معُه لُه فِتيل ويقنص. ومن الحول الى الحول وهو يقنص ويوكّلُه لحم. ليا منه صاد هالقَحَم وتعشّت هالناس اخذ لُه كِسر وحطُّه فوق البيت ويوم يقعد الوليد نصف الليل ولد اخوه ينطيه اياوه بالليل مِبرّه. يعني يحطّ لُه لحيمةٍ يَفْهَقَه ليل الشتا طويل وليا منه جا ليل الشتا هُمّين بكى الليد (= الوليد) عطاوه ايّاه وسِكَت.

٢،٣١ وجريس ما هو شرواكم طلع ما هو بالحيل يشرّيه ويَقْصِد بُه ويمدّحُه ويقول بُه ويخاوه على الطيب يا مير ماش رجليه بالارض جريس انكَم. هكالحين بالزمان الاول هذاك

With Jrēs

Al-Hirbīd always kept a watchful eye on his young relative Jrēs. He made sure that he did not lack for anything. Jrēs was the son of his brother Sḥēmān, who was among those killed. When Jrēs was a little boy, ʿAdwān used to carry him around. He went to see Jrēs's mother, Bgēshah, and said to her, "Know that I do not feel in the least attracted to you. You are not the wife I'd have chosen for myself. Yet I will marry you for the sake of this orphan boy." And so it happened. He took the mother as his wife and carried her little boy on his back. His fellow tribesmen of al-Swēd joined forces to collect sheep and goats for their use and camels for transportation. At the place where the tribe gathered in early summer, they put up shacks for him and his dependents. In those days, game was still plentiful: in fact, gazelles may have outnumbered the goats and sheep. ʿAdwān, may your life be long, pampered Jrēs as a bird looks after its chicks, year after year. While Jrēs was a child, he always put him in the first and highest place, as if on top of Mount Rāf, as if he built a feathered nest for him in a euphorbia shrub. He felt deeply for the orphan and cuddled him. He'd go to the sands, carrying a rifle, and hunt for game. Year after year, he went hunting and fed the boy on game. If he had shot an ibex ram and people were done eating from it, he would take a chunk of the roast and put it on top of their dwelling. If the boy, his brother's son, woke up at night, he'd reach for it and give it to him, because of his tender feelings toward him: a piece of roast meat set apart for the little one to sustain him in the long nights of winter. He'd give it to him to chew on if he cried. Then he'd be quiet again. 31.1

But Jrēs was not the kind of person you are.[184] Something was missing as he grew up. ʿAdwān tried to steer him in the desired direction, urging him to be on good behavior. He did so in verses composed to advise and encourage him by applauding whatever he did well. He did what he could to stimulate him and fan a flicker of ambition. All to no avail. Jrēs's feet were planted on the ground. He wouldn't soar. He was self-absorbed, not the outgoing type. In the olden days, someone might give you a sheep for your personal use. You'd 31.2

الرجّال يعطيك لك شاة منيحه بس تِحْلب لبنه وترجّعه عليه جِمالِه. عدوان جامعينٍ لُه ربعُه شْويهات يِحَلِبْهن ودايع. قال لجريس رح رح بهالشياه هذولي وانا عمّك مِدّ بِهِن. والله جريس يوم صار آه جذع وسرح بعض السرحات والله يوم انه فِطِن يا مير فوتة اباعر السويد هالقطعان. قال يا عمي ترما انا سارح. ليه يا وليدي. قال كان تبين اسرح حِط لي نياق. ما انا سارح بالغنم ودايعٍ جايبهن لي ما انا سارح كان تبين اسرح حط لي نياق. مْثَبّتٍ ان الغنم ما هن لهم.

٣،٣١ قال والله ياوليدي النياق ما هن رِضَم نجيبهن من البَرّ وحنا هذولي بْلنا نعمةٍ هالشياه متعبّرينٍ بهن والا حلال الرجال ودايعٍ هذولي لكن صوفتهن تْعَمل مْنَه امك لنا بيت يظللنا بالقيض ويدفّينا بالشتا ونْتذرّى بُه عن المطر وفذّة لبنهن تبقله وفذّة دِهْنِهن بالنِّحْوْ ومتعبّرين بهن عِبِر دنيا. قال ما هي علومك انا ما اسمع هالسوالف امَا عَطِن نياق والا ما انا سارح. والاوه حارجٍ عليه ياوليدي ياوليدي. ما حصل. قال انا عقب الِحسْنى كيف يتيم وادّبه عقب ما جرى غدي صديقٍ يحكي عليه او امُّه او هه. ويسرح الشايب. سرح لُه كم يوم ما حصل شين.

٤،٣١ قال

milk it for your household and at a later date you'd return it to the owner. It is given by the owner for a certain period of time, as a charitable deed. ʿAdwān's fellow tribesmen joined hands to provide him with four such sheep for his personal consumption, as a loan in his safekeeping. ʿAdwān told Jrēs, "Come now, listen to your uncle, take these sheep to find some grazing." One day, when Jrēs was old enough to be sent on such errands, a young adolescent already, and had taken the sheep to pasture a couple of times, he ran into a herd of camels that belonged to men of the Swēd, and he started to mull over his situation. On his return, he said, "Uncle mine, I am not going to take the sheep to graze anymore." "What now? Why is that, my boy?" He said, "If you want me to be a sheepherder, give me some camels as well. It will not do for me to be stuck out there with just a few sheep. They're not even our own. I am through with playing shepherd. You want me to take them to the field? Very well, give me some camels!" And again, he made the point that the sheep were not theirs.

Taken aback, ʿAdwān said, "What do we have here, my boy? Camels are 31.3
not like pieces of rock, something you pick up from the desert floor. We have reason to be grateful for the comfort we draw from sheep. Thanks to them, we provide for ourselves. True, the owner is someone else; they have been given us on loan. Still, your mother uses their wool to furnish the dwelling that shades us in summer, that keeps us warm in winter, and that protects us from getting soaked by rain. Surplus milk is turned into dried cheese and the fat is stored in skins. This is how we make ends meet." But the boy was adamant. He said, "From now on, things will not go the way you were used to. Say whatever you want, but I am not going to listen. Give me camels or else I won't take the sheep to graze!" ʿAdwān had devoted himself wholeheartedly to the boy's upbringing. "Oh my boy, my boy!" He had nothing to show for his efforts. He was at his wits' end. He said to himself, "Is this what I get in return for the love I bestowed on him? How could I discipline this orphan child after having raised him with tender care? Perhaps someone will talk sense to him, a friend, the boy's mother, or anyone." The old man was left with no choice but to take the sheep to the pasture himself. He did so for days on end. His endeavors had met with complete failure.

He said: 31.4

اعدّل الابيات وانا ابو خزيّم   مثل ما قال ابن مِرْداس شايع

خزيم ولد له ميت.

شايع يقول بلابةٍ شوشليّه   وانا اقول بجريسٍ خبيث الطبايع
ياجريس ما لك الله اصْدَق من شِياهنا   حبيباتنا ياجريس لو هن ودايع
أخير عندي من تْحِرّي رفاقتي   كثيرين زَلْق الحكي والبَطْن جايع
قِريبين بالعَصَبه حليّين بالنبا   بعيدين بالعازات يوم النفايع
الله يلومك ياالبناخي ملامه   ملامةٍ عرضه وطوله شنايع
تاصل الى مصرٍ على شِمّخ الذرى   وتِشَنّى بدار مدرّعين الوشايع

يم اليمن.

حطّيت بعيني ياالبناخي عبره   سريع جيبه للدموع السرايع
قلبي كما ياجريس غربٍ مْعلّق   على عضود مطيّحات الشرايع
ياما هوى الجمّة على شِمّخ الذرى   وياما يِشحّنه عوج الارقاب رايع
من الوِرد واقْفاة الصدير اذهبنّه   يما جْدِع من روس الارشات مايع
نقلتك بجود العزم يوم انت غِيّه   يوم ان مثلك هزل الايتام سايع
واليوم ما بالحق تَجْزان عبره   كَوَتْني بحلبه للدموع السرايع
أخاف من خطو الموالي يجرّنا   على مثل حسك الشوك والبصر ضايع

٥،٣١ ويْتَشَلّبُه عدوان يتشلّب جريس وجريس والله انه المِعْجور ما نِفَع طَلَع عْفين ما هو موافقٍ العمّ والا العم هامّه صيّاد وبواردي. تِصَنّت عدوان يوم والى مير جريس ينهج

I straighten my verses: I am the father of Khzayyim!
Proud moniker, as Ibn Mirdās's cry: "I am Shāyiʿ!"

—Khzayyim was a son who died in infancy.

Shāyiʿ speaks of his well-intentioned fellows;
let me tell you about my foul-tempered Jrēs.
Jrēs, may God forsake you, our sheep are the best:
lovely animals even though given on loan.
Much better than begging friends for favors
and getting sweet words foisted on empty stomachs:
Your relatives, well versed in smooth talk,
nowhere to be found in your hour of need.
Shame, nephew! You deserve God's reproach,
vicious, spiked tongue-lashings left and right,
All the way to Egypt, chained on camelback,
to be dumped in the tattoo-tappers' land.

—To Yemen.

My nephew, for you I bathe in floods of tears;
you made my eyes gush in swiftly flowing rivulets.
My heart, Jrēs, is jolted like a bucket pulled hard
by powerful camels, emptied into a basin,
Plunging down again to the bottom of the well,
heavy with water hoisted up by the sturdy beasts,
Up and down, worn thin and fraying at the ends,
its mouth's wrinkled leather torn from the ropes.
I carried you, innocent child, with my strength:
often skinny orphans like you are abandoned.
Is this my recompense, that you make me cry,
searing drops burning open the sluices of my eyes?
No greater fear is there than being dragged by dependents,
hauled, helpless and blind, over beds of thorns.

ʿAdwān had taken him by the arm to help him. But Jrēs, by God, was a good-for-nothing, useless. He grew up to become a disagreeable, selfish person. They had nothing in common. His uncle was a forceful, enterprising character: 31.5

يم لُه عِشْران كِبُرُه والى هم اللي يشيرون عليه يقولون كان تبيه يسرّحك يحط لك نياق والا خلّه هو يتكوكع باثر غِنمه. والى بعض العشران يرصّك اما يزَنْدك اما ينفعك بدين او دنيا اما بالمراجل والا يسولف عليك بالرِّدَى وتِنْثِر. على ما قال العدو يرحم والجاهل ما يرحم نفسه. والا حارج عليه شايبٍ عمه. والى مشبّهٍ العشران مثل عيبة الصلبي هكاللي ما لقيت حطيتُه بَهً هكاللي تلقى بُه قصمة مِبْرد تعمله زناد تشِبّ نارك وبعضهم تِنكَةٍ ما يصلح الا صِنّارة مِغزل.

٦،٣١ قال

ياجريس يامشكاي شاكي واشاكيك — وتــرّك حكايا كل عيبة مِـباقـه
ياما تطـلّق من ورا حـلقي ايـديك — وياما عقـدت ايديك مثل العـلاقـه

يعني يزمُّه يشيله على ظهره يوم هو صغير.

ياجريس اخذت امك على شان تاليك — وجبناه من عِرق الرحـامة غْشاقـه
ياجريس خلّيـتَن وانا ما اقوى اخلّيك — وانكِس كما تَنْكِس على الولد ناقـه
ياما بْعـدْلات المـناظـر اعشّـيك — يوم العشا ياجـريس عندك شفـاقـه
ياما على كْسور السـميـنات اهوّيك — واحط لك فوق الخـزيزة لحـاقـه
واليوم عِفـتَن يوم غـلّظن عـتاريك — وجمـعت مع خبث الطـبايع نـزاقـه
اللي نِبَت بـــدقون ربعك نبت بيك — مـير ان تنـفـيل اللحى بافـتراقـه

a hunter, a gunman.[185] When he became the boy's guardian, ʿAdwān overheard a conversation between Jrēs and other youngsters of his age, who were telling Jrēs how to handle it: "If he wants you to go and graze the sheep, have him give you some camels. If not, let him stumble after those sheep himself!" Some friends put you in a tight spot. Others give you strength: they are of benefit in this world and the hereafter; they do not shy away from difficult tasks. Others speak ill of you and plot your downfall. As the saying goes: "An enemy shows mercy, but a fool is merciless to himself." Jrēs's old uncle had stayed at his side as a devoted father. At this, ʿAdwān compared the boy's friends to the large bag carried by itinerant blacksmiths: the kind of sack you fill with whatever objects you come across that one day may prove useful, like a junkyard where you'd find a metal piece broken off from a hand plane, and that might be turned into a hammer which sparks the powder of a matchlock gun; or scraps from a vessel made of metal sheet for the transport of dates that may come in handy for the manufacture of simple objects like the large needle of a spindle.

He said: 31.6

Jrēs, hear the cry from my heart—I hear yours:
let's leave aside shameful and dishonest talk.
How often I felt your hands hold my neck—
your little fingers gripping me in tight embrace!

—That is, when he was an infant he lifted him up to carry him on his back.

Jrēs, for you I took your mother as my wife:
from love of her progeny.
Jrēs, you left me in the lurch but how could I leave you?
I follow you like a camel in thrall to her calf.
Often I took aim, eyes glued to my gun's barrel,
to not leave you hungry, Jrēs, after a paltry meal.
Many times I handed you fat chunks of meat
so that, spoiled with such dainties, you'd have more.
Now you loathe me: with your muscled neck
came a churlish temper and a peevish obstinacy.
On your chin you carry the growth of your age,
but a beard's dignity depends on the wearer.

عـنزٍ يحطه والى الاقـدار بيـديك   اخير من الشـرشوح عند الرفـاقـه

العنزحتى لو ما بَه لبن ازْيَن من المِفْلِس اللي ما معُه شين.

يا حورفوا غصبٍ صـديقك يخلّيك   يا صـار ما لك مع هل النوق ناقـه
سـبع العُوَذ يا جـريس خلّن واخـلّيك   يا جـريس ما بعـيال الاخوان فـاقـه
مـا لي باقـاصـيّك ولا لي بادانيك   لَى حِـطّ فوقي مِحْـزَم من دقـاقـه
لى صـار بالدنيـا صـديقك يخلّيك   ما من ورا عوج النِصـايب صِداقـه

رد عليه عبَيد راعي بقعا ابو فهد هااللي شف الله يكفينا شر الدنيا هم كلهم صاقّين عدوان وراعي بقعا. راعي بقعا بناخيه ولد فهد اللي جده عبيد ذبح نفسه خالد. زِهِد. هم كلهم صاقّين كل بهوايتُه. ٧،٣١

يقول عبيد راعي بقعا ٨،٣١

ياليت بالدنيـا صـديقك يخـلّيك   يا كـفّ شرّه ما تبي لُه صداقـه
مـير البـلا يا جنّب الحق ناصـيك   اومـاة ركـبٍ ما عليهن عـلاقـه
بحِـبْرٍ وقرطـاسٍ يبيـعك ويشـريك   ويحـط دون الله عـلومٍ دْقـاقـه

يوم كبر جريس قام عدوان يتذكّر الطيب لازم تذكره يالرجل سوا انك تطريه بلسانك والا تذكره بقلبك. قام يذكر البِرّ اللي هو يعمل بُه يوم هو صغير اوْجَس منه الرِدَى والا عاد يبي ازْوَد يبي يحثُّه على شيٍّ مما بقلبه وجريس صغير والجهل يرمي الرجل نوب الجهل ظُلمايه. والله ما حصل جريس يستقعد غَلِطه ٩،٣١

One goat bestowed on you by the Almighty Lord
is worth more than a kinsman's small camel herd:

—Even having a goat without milk is better than having nothing at all.

If he migrates, a friend with camels forsakes you:
without camels to carry loads, you remain behind.
God is my refuge, Jrēs! Go! Leave me be!
No use expecting comfort from brothers' children.
What's my benefit from relatives, close and distant,
the day a mound of dust is shoveled over me?
Without a friend to lend a helping hand in life,
a grave's stone slabs seal your utter loneliness.

His verses received a response from ʿBēd, the chief of Bagʿā, Abū Fahd. May 31.7
God spare us from this world's evil tricks. Every word they say on this topic, both ʿAdwān and the headman of Bagʿā, is very true. The headman's relative Khālid, the son of Fahd and grandson of ʿBēd, killed himself. He had become tired of life. Both of them spoke the truth, each in his own way.

ʿBēd, the headman of Bagʿā, said: 31.8

You're better off in life without such a friend,
spared the evil ways you'd suffer in his company.
Beware if that pack of lies and deceit arrives
on worn-out riding camels swaying with fatigue:
He buys and sells you, properly, ink on paper,
without awe of God in his vicious slander.

As Jrēs reached the age of discernment, ʿAdwān took it upon himself to 31.9
instill in him principles of good conduct, as is one's duty: in speech and by fostering civilized norms in one's heart. He kept reminding him of the many good turns he had done him when he was a little kid. In spite of some unpleasantness experienced from Jrēs, he had not given up on him. He wanted to prod him, to stimulate him to do better. He had pinned his hopes on him. As a youth, Jrēs might be forgiven for committing a folly or indulging some foolish urges. Unfortunately, ʿAdwān's efforts did not bear fruit and Jrēs's character defects proved uncorrectable.

قال ١٠،٣١

ياراكب من فوق بنت العمانِ   وَقْم الرباع وتَوّما شَقّ نابه
تِضْرِم الى رَخي لَه طويل الشطان   يجوز لمندوب النشاما انسحابه
تِلْفي غلامٍ بالمدارك رماني   رَمْيَة حَصاةٍ في هَدايم خَرابه
جريسٍ عسى ما هو جريس اليماني   والا جرس وضحا تموح الجنابه

جريس اليماني من العِجْمان كريم وشجاع.

اظهرت راسك يوم ربي هداني   من الشوحة اللي يستدير الرشا به

يعني يوم انت تِغْيّةٍ لِغيّه.

ياشين ما قطّعت عنك الحَساني   ولا وِلْيتي قشرا تدور القضا به
ياجريس وابرَد التَسيعي كواني   حزَة طلوع الشمس والا غيابه
ياما لجيت بكل خضرا مثاني   بالمرتع العالي ندور الذرا به
بايام ياكلن الضرا كل واني   وبايام طرد الضيف لو به عتابه
عمّك الى منّي نِقَلت الوزان   بالبرّ والا بيمِشاني هضابه
ياما عشيتك قايدات الذهان   والقايده ياجريس نَشْلِم حسابه
اعشّيك من فرق الجزال السمان   في ليلةٍ ما كان يِرْجى العَشا به
اللهٰ يخون جريس بكَى عياني   اللهٰ يخون جريس واللي هقى به
اما كفاك من الضنا كل داني   ياجريس ما بعيال الاخوان ثابه
تركت انا ياجريس كل المعاني   كود الغنم ياجريس واللي حكى به

He said: 31.10

Rider perched on the back of an Omani camel,
six years old, its eyeteeth just broken through,
Capable of scorching speed when given full rein,
the ideal mount for undaunted emissaries:
Head for a young man bent on my destruction,
throwing me like a rock into ruin's abyss.
Jrēs, a far cry from his namesake Jrēs al-Yamānī
or Jrēs, bell of a white camel with fluttering trappings.

—Jrēs al-Yamānī of the ʿIjmān tribe, a generous and brave person.

With God's guidance, I struggled to lift your head,
just as a bucket scrapes the walls of a wide-mouthed well.

—He means, while you are a blah-blah-blah.

Thankless tasks! I never severed you from my care,
a guardianship not brutish, deserving retribution.
Jrēs, remember us frostbitten in ice-cold winter,
before sun's first peek at dawn or in early darkness?
How we'd seek cover, hide in sprawling bushes
on high pasture grounds, desperate for shelter?
When starved predators devour weak creatures,
hosts send guests packing, disreputable as it is.
Me, your uncle! Carrying a powder horn,
I stalked game in deserts, on craggy heights,
For a watchful doe, your dinner roast:
my kill flusters all of her flock of gazelle;[186]
Nourishing you with joints prodigiously fat,
at nights without supper anywhere in sight.
May God trip up Jrēs for making me cry;
waylay him for dashing my high hopes.
Surprised your friends don't give camels, Jrēs?
What delusion to expect help from relatives!
Take me, Jrēs! I've relinquished all delights
but sheep and goats, and likeminded fans,

لى استلحن عقب الحيال المغاني   وجابت قناديل الشِجَر كل ما به
واللي مغيب لديرته جاك عاني   وكلٍ تِذَكّر دار حَيٍّ ربى به
أخبّ باطرافه خَبيب الحصان   باطرافهن نحى فروس الذيابه

باطراف الغنم.

عن قولة الهربيد ياجريس جاني   وقت المنايح مثل هافي كلابه
عن قولة الطلّاب لا ما عطاني   وعن قولة المطلوب لا لا سَعى به
يا انْطِيت عَنْزٍ من كراب اليمان   انْهَج كما الكسّاب لو كان ما به

ويقول عدوان ١١،٣١

ياجريس بوقوت الصفَر لا تهاب   صَكِّ شياهك لا يقولون سعبوب
اخير عندي من تَحَرّي حَبابي   اللي ذراهم بين الاقراب مكروب
هل الشلايا مِكِرْمين الكلاب   صاروا شيوخٍ لو بهم كل عذروب
يدور بي ياجريس لو ما لقى بي   ياما شِذَب عرقوبنا كل مذهوب

يقول ايضا ١٢،٣١

يا صِرت من عمسين الاشوار تختار   من شمّرٍ تاخذ جريسٍ على الراس
عَيٍّ عَوَج ما فيه وردٍ ومصدار   وبير العيا لو قيس ما فيه قرياس
انت الذي تَجْزَى عَميلك بالانكار   وانا بعد مثل الذي يطبخ الفاس
يبي المرق ما بين قِدْرٍ وفوّار   بصطوغ فاسٍ طول الايام يبّاس

On meadows clad in green after barren spells,
lustrous with flowering bushes, plants, grasses;
The faraway hasten back to the land in droves:
everyone fondly recalls original tribe and abode.
We prance and trot like horses around the herds,
beating back circling hungry wolves into retreat,

—Around the sheep and goats.

Jrēs, since I don't want to hear: "Al-Hirbīd came,
a starving scruffy dog begging for sheep on loan,"
Nor a supplicant's mutter: "No, he didn't give,"
or an addressee's denial: "No, he never asked."
If the goat of a niggard lands in your hands,
walk away a winner, even if it gives no milk.

ʿAdwān says: 31.11

O Jrēs, do not fear early mornings!
Graze your sheep, don't be called a slouch![187]
Better to herd sheep than mooch off relatives
whose tent flaps are shut tight to keep out kin:
Sheep magnates, coddlers of herding dogs,
risen to a shaykh's status despite their faults.
They prey on me, though I did them no wrong:
countless bastards schemed to lay me low.

And he says: 31.12

If you're aiming to find the greatest fool,
among Shammar, Jrēs is first choice by far:
Tried and tested in perverse obstinacy;
bottomless, unfathomable well of ineptitude!
You're superb at letting down your partner;
as for myself, I'm a man who boils hoes
In a bubbling pot, to produce meat gravy
from his axes' thin, albeit blunted, blades.

١٣،٣١

يقول عدوان

أنشـدك انا ياجريس عن عسكرٍ سـار　　ياطا على ياجريس مثل السَنايف
لولا التِبَصّر ما اظْهَر خيامه من الدار　　لولا البكار الحيل هن والكلايف
تبصّروا به دَسْمين الشوارب هل الكار　　حاضوه خالين اليدين الضعايف

And he says: 31.13

I ask you, Jrēs, about soldiers on the march:[188]
you see them walking, Jrēs, as if on crutches.
Clever, they decamped from the land in time;
yet it took sprightly camels, hardworking men:
Delights for hosts, mustaches dripping with fat,
and gathered by paupers in their shirts' folds.

ما ظنّـتِي بارى هل القود حـمّار

١،٣٢ عـدوان راعي غنم ونازلٍ بِقبـلي جبّه وقاموا حَضِر جبه يَمْنَحونه نخل يغلونُه هم. حطّوا لُه مَحْضَرسَنَع دار يعني يِجِدّون من النخل ويحطّون بَه لُه سِقْمِةٍ لُه ولعيالُه. ومَلّوا داره تمر وعيش اهل جبه. وبالنهار من قَهْوةٍ لقهوه ومن سِفْرةٍ لسفره. وهو رجلٍ راعي سوالف وراعي رِبَابه تَخْبَر يوم الجهل يوم الناس بَه غَفْله. يوم جا من الدايرة ويتصادف هو وايا نِجَع هِجْهوج ابن رمال. الرمال كاتّين من الخنفه. قيّضوا يم الخنفه وقيّضوا يم ديار عنزه والشرارايّه (= الشرارات) الغربيّه. يوم جا من الدايره ويتنازلون هو واياهم على جبه. قيّضوا الهجهوج على جبة الله يهديك معهُ الرمال وهو عدوان يستانس معهم. هم يَخَبّرونُه من العام وهو بمكانُه قالوا من العام وانت بهذا يا عدوان. قال والله ما فارقت مراحي من العام من خبركم ياما جيتونَن.

٢،٣٢ يوم بَغَوا يرحلون ثاني نوبه يا مير رحايلُه شَوَيّايَه (= شويّات). يوم جا وقت الحولات شاروا عليه بدو الرمال إنه يحول معهم. قالوا والله ياراي معنا لك ياعدوان انّك تبارينا ولا معك الا هالشياه القَرايف ليا عِجِزت كَلّيت منهن ياخوي نِحطّهن بهالقَنَنَة معنا والا كل نجةٍ عَنه لَه ناقه يالهربيد وخلّهن. قال والله يالربع انا ابي معكم ابخاويكم ولا انا والله مِطْلِقٍ شياهي ما زول جريس يمشي معهن وانا ابي معكم والى كَلّت

A Donkey Driver Cannot Keep Pace with Camel Nomads

ʿAdwān tended to his sheep. When he put up in the southwest of Jubbah that year, the inhabitants gave him palm trees because they held him so dear. They also built him a booth of palm fronds and provided him and his family with plentiful supplies of food. The folks of Jubbah filled his shack with dates and rice. During the day, he would move among assemblies of coffee drinkers and go from one lunch invitation to the next. He entertained people with his stories and accompanied his recitations with tunes from his rebab. You know, in those days people still lived in the time of ignorance. Back then, people were innocent, lacking in awareness. On arrival from his own tribal area, he ran into Hijhūj, Ibn Rmāl. The tribesmen of al-Rmāl came hurrying down from al-Khinfah. They used to spend the hot months of summer in the area of al-Khinfah and the tribal lands of ʿAnazah and the Sharārāt, to the west. His arrival coincided with their return, and they all settled down together in Jubbah. Hijhūj stayed put to spend the rest of the summer in Jubbah, may God guide you, with the Rmāl tribesmen, and they enjoyed ʿAdwān's company. They knew him from the year before, when he had lived at that place. They said, "You're still here, ʿAdwān?" "Yes," he said. "Really, I haven't left with my animals since I last saw you, until you came back right now." 32.1

When they made up their minds to travel once again, he was there with his flock of skinny sheep. They were about to migrate, and this time the Bedouin of al-Rmāl sounded him out to see if he'd be inclined to accompany them. They fondly looked forward to having him with them. They said, "Don't you have a mind to join us, ʿAdwān? If you march along with us, all you'll have are these feeble sheep. Therefore, brother, if you cannot keep up with us and have grown tired, we'll put them in these large camel-borne baskets. We will assign one camel to each ewe. A she-camel for each of your sheep, al-Hirbīd, so you don't have to worry about them and you can have them come with us!" "Really, men," he replied, "I do want to join you on your journey. In any case, I will only allow my sheep to move from here as long as Jrēs is with me to keep an eye on them. And when I weary, by God, you must take the sheep from me 32.2

اللّٰهم انكم آخذينهن مِني والا شايفٍ لهن دِبْره. قال عجلان انا عندي لك ذلول تسلّف عَلَيْه معنا. قال جروح ابن هزيم ولد صايل أنا عندي لك جمل تشيل عليه وتركبه ام العيال. قال رحلنا يالله. عَطوه زواملٍ يشيل عليهن ومنايحٍ يشرب لبنهن. وهو يرحل معهم وَيَدْوُون يم النفود وهو الى احتاج يرجع لداره اللي بجبه ويِتزَهّب منه تمر وعيش.

٣،٣٢ العرب اول يذلّون علشان كذا جَوا لهم بنازيه وحطّوا بيتُه بيت الهربيد بالوسط وهم داير ما دار عليه. والى جا الصبح وحِلبَوا كلٍّ ارسل لُه حليب لما تمتلي صملانه وقدوره حليب وزبد وخير. يوم جا وقت الحَدْرات والمِكيل ويكتّون شمر للعراق ييكلون والى اكالوا عاد نكِسوا لديرتهم بالمكيل على شنق هالنفود. بعدين تنَسَّفت لك هالعربان عاد تبَرْزَخت كلٍّ على فاله وعلى هوى اباعره. هكالحين يِذلُون العرب ويصير وجههم واحد من شان الخوف. مِثل انت تبي تغزي تبي تدوّر البل يا صاروا اهلك بوصط العرب تقْوَى تغْزي ما يجيهم احدٍ غِرّ اللي يجي من هنا يَنطِحونه الغزو واللي يجي من هناك يَدْرون بُه الحَدْرِه. أما ليا صاروا اهلك لحالهم نوبٍ يَعقِبك عليهم لهم غزو مثلك وياخذهم وانت غزّاي.

٤،٣٢ الرمال صاروا متلوِحين فوق. قالوا حنا انقطفنا بفُوقي هالنفود. شمركَتّ للمِكيل وحنا اجلدنا تلوَحنا بهذا مير نبي نِكِتّ مع هالنفود من شان اللي يبي يكّال يكّال واللي يبي يغزي يغزي ينطلق ظَهرُه. المراد عزّموا على الرحيل. بهالحكي هذا يا هذاك

or find some way to transport them." One of the Rmāl, ʿAjlān, said, "I will put a riding camel at your disposal so that you can join us, riding at the head of the caravan." Jrūḥ ibn Hazīm, son of Ṣāyil, said, "And I have a strong male camel to carry your gear and the mother of your children." "Fine," he said. "Let's go. I'm with you." They brought pack camels for his luggage and some milk-producing camels for the use of his family. They embarked on the great desert crossing, toward the Nafūd Desert. To his mind, in case of need, there was always the option of returning to Jubbah in order to stock up on dates and rice.

In the olden days, people were always on their guard; there was no security. 32.3
Therefore, if they came to a sandy prominence and put up the tent of al-Hirbīd, they made sure to place it in the middle of their circle of tents. In the morning, the other tents would milk their animals and send pails full of milk to him, enough to fill all his skins and pots with milk, butter, and other tasty food. Inevitably, the day came when they had to send a camel train to the northeast in order to stock up on the necessary supplies. The Shammar tribesmen marched at a rapid pace to the markets of Iraq and, supplies replenished, hurried back to their camp at the edge of the Nafūd Desert. Next, the Bedouin would disperse; from then on, everyone would only look after his own interests. They followed their camels no matter which direction the animals wandered off, at their camels' whim. Back then, the Bedouin used to live in fear; the enemy was constantly on their minds. For that reason, they tended to stick together and move as one group. For instance, if you had a mind to go raiding and capture some camels, and if your folk were sheltered within a larger tribal group, you might be able to embark on your adventure without having to worry about your folk's safety; they would not be helpless when faced with a surprise attack. Those coming at them from one direction would be met by the cameleers bringing supplies, while assailants from the other direction would run into the raiders who had set out from the camp. On the other hand, folk somewhere on their own might be vulnerable to raiders in the absence of their men who went raiding. Families might be robbed while their men were away on a plundering expedition.

The Bedouin of al-Rmāl had built their camp on the highest spurs of the 32.4
sand hills. They said, "If we stay here on top of these sand hills, they can pick us off with ease. Some of our Shammar men have set out for the markets while we are in this spot like sitting ducks. We'd do much better marching as they do, along these sandy ridges. Let everyone do as he likes. If you wish to go

البرق يخيلونه على اللبّه. يوم جا بعض هالليال واحسبوا للبرق والى مير لُه خمسين ليله. قالوا البرق لُه خمسين ليلي (=ليله) هالحين يشبع بعيرك خلونا نحرُه ويا نزلنا اللبّه نبي نْغَزي ورا اباعرنا ونبي نحدِر طلوع. عَلَيه عَلَيه وهم يرحلون. يا مير ما عندهم غنم الرمال بس اباعر الا الهربيد معُه هالشويهات.

٥،٣٢ قال لْهَلُه الرمال تحاكوا بالمحدار والمغازي وحنا ما معنا الا هالشويهات نبي نحترف نتزل بينهم وبين جماعتنا بجبه والى اعتزنا ألحقنا لنا زهاب من دارنا بجبه. قالت مرتُه لا والله انت تبي تَكْفَى صبوحنا عقب القِدِر مليان لبن وزبد. قال يابنتاخي ما انا عايف مير ما نقوى نلحقهم هذولا اهل طرش وليا انووا يم وجه راحوا وخلّونا. قالت والله ما اتليك ان فَرَّقت عنهم. قال تدرين معهم. وهم يرحلون الصبح ويزوعون مع النفود مثل السيل الداوي.

٦،٣٢ الرمال كلهم بكبرهم ما معهم الا شويهاتٍ لحمدان ابن حامد يجي لهن ثمان شياه وحْمَيّرٍ وانت تَكَرَم. وهو وايّا جريس مع الغنم قَفُو. وجريس يتيمٍ غاذيه عنده ودُّه انّه ما يلحقه شِطّه. يوم جا وصط المرحال وهم يجدعون الرحايل يتحرّون جريس مع شياهه. ما جاوه من راعى اباعر منبِطٍح على رحوله وماشي ياولد ما عَيّنت جريس.

and stock up at the markets, fine. If someone feels an urge to go raiding, let him do so. No one is under any obligation to stay here." The long and short of it was that they decided to break up camp and move. As the story goes, distant flashes of lightning were observed toward al-Labbah, night after night. They calculated that this spectacle repeated itself every night for fifty days. They deliberated: "It has been fifty nights since we spied the first flashes of lightning. Now there must be enough herbage for the camels to eat their fill. Without further ado, let's move there straightaway. Once we've put up camp in al-Labbah, we are free to go raiding from wherever our camels are grazing and we may also trek to the markets from there. Let's move, the dice have been cast, off we go!" The tribespeople of al-Rmāl did not have any small cattle with them, only camels.

ʿAdwān told his family, "The Rmāl talk about stocking up in Iraq and raiding expeditions, while we are stuck here with our sheep. Let's turn back and stay between where they are going and our folk in Jubbah. When we start running low on some articles, we can fetch whatever supplies we need from our house in Jubbah." His wife said, "No, by God, never! You want to deprive us of our morning drink of milk, the joy of getting our pots filled with milk and butter?" "Listen, dear cousin," he said, "I have nothing against that. But there is no way we can keep up with them on their journey. Theirs are herds of camels: if they feel like setting course in a certain direction, off they go, without thinking twice, leaving us far behind." She remained adamant: "By God, I won't be of your company if you go your separate way." "As you wish," he conceded. "So be it." That morning, they broke camp and like a rushing torrent filed in a long stream over the sand hills. 32.5

Numerous as they were, none of the Rmāl had any small cattle, with the exception of Ḥamdān ibn Ḥāmid. He brought a few sheep, about eight of them, and a small donkey (no offence!).[189] He and Jrēs, as drivers of sheep, were the stragglers at the camel train's tail end. Jrēs, as an orphan in his care for whom ʿAdwān felt responsible, was always in his thoughts. He worried lest he should come to harm. On completion of their trek's first stage, they offloaded the camels and waited for Jrēs to arrive with the sheep. Whenever a herdsman passed by, comfortably stretched out on the saddle of his camel, or walking, they asked, "Hey boy, did you see Jrēs by any chance?" "Well, we last saw him yelling to his sheep, somewhere far behind." To any herdsman who came by: "Hey, did you see Jrēs and his sheep?" "O yeah, somewhere behind." 32.6

والله عِلمنا بُه يتّاحي لشياهه قَفُو. وكل راعى اباعر يجيه ما عينت جريس هو وشياهه. والله قفو. الثمرة ما جاوه جريس الا تالى الليل. ولا يروّحون على العرب الا تالى الليل على النيران. والليلة الاخرى ما وصلوا مِرح العرب الا مع الصبح والليلة اللي وراه يَقلّب عليه ولا يجيبه الا وجه الصبح.

وهم يرحلون من باكر وهاللون. يوم نزلوا العرب المغيرب المغيرب ويتفرّق لك السلف هذا يهِدّ طيره هنا وهذا يهد طيره هناك وهذا يدرّج حيرانه. نزلوا المغرب وهو يقلب عدوان على جريس ولا يجيبه الا الصلايه وجه الصبح. وهكاليوم ومن باكر ومن عِقبُه. حمدان وش عَمَل. نِكَس على الذلول لولدُه يوم جا الى متكرفتاتٍ الشياه لهن بجرعا قال يافهد. قال هَاه. قال اطلع جايّ خلّهن اطلع جاي اطلع اطلع اطلع. قال شياهنا يايبّه. قال خلّهن للذيب والا للمولّي اللي يولّي بهن. ثمان شياه وحمارهن والله يقول الى هالحين على وجههن. ما لَه قيمه هكالحين ما لَه قيمه. حمدان جد طَماش ابو فهد. ٧،٣٢

يوم جا عدوان هلُه وهو يقوم يدق الافكار. قال وش لون اللي هذا مراحهم البارحه يالله جيناوه مع وجه الصبح أجل وين مراحهم الليله. قال انا وش مصلحتي من هالعَمل هذا. يا دام ما اناب غازيٍ مع هاللي يبون يغزون ولا انا حادرٍ مع هاللي يبون يسفرون أنا مصلحتي وشّي. وينكس على جريس بعض النكسات يوم نِكَس عليه قال ياجريس. قال هاه. ترو جريس بالتالي يوم شاف هالشطه صار يشير على عمه ٨،٣٢

The upshot was that Jrēs did not arrive till late at night. On reaching camp, they found all had gone to sleep and the fires were embers. The next day, they did not reach the place where the Bedouin had stopped off the evening before until it was almost morning, and the day after that it was the same story: ʿAdwān would retrace his steps to find Jrēs, and would not be back at the camp with him and the sheep in tow until it was morning.

By then, the Bedouin were ready for early departure on their journey's next stage. The vanguard of the camel train, the tribe's fighting men mounted on fast riding camels, would reach that stage's campsite some time before sunset. There they'd amuse themselves by setting their hunting falcons on prey, one here, one there, while another man might busy himself putting his camel calves through their paces. A little before sunset, the camp was set up. Anxious, ʿAdwān retraced his steps to see if Jrēs was approaching. But when he arrived, it was time for morning prayers. Morning had dawned already. The same thing happened that day, the next, and the one after that. And how about Ḥamdān? He turned back on his riding camel to look for the boy. He was greeted by the sorry spectacle of sheep, miserably assembled in disorder at the foot of an oval dune. He called to him, "Hey Fahd!" "Yes? What's up?" "Get out of there! At once, now! Leave them there! Come here, right now, now, now, at once!" "But what about our sheep, Dad?" "Let them go to hell. Food for the wolves or let the devil take them." Eight sheep and a small donkey. They have been drifting about in the wilderness ever since, it is said. Under those circumstances, they did not represent any value, worthless. Good riddance. Ḥamdān was the grandfather of Ṭmāsh, the father of Fahd. 32.7

Deep in thought, ʿAdwān returned to the camp. What to do? Even with utmost exertion, they would count themselves lucky if they reached yesterday evening's camp by the next morning. God knows where they would alight the coming evening. He said, "What's our gain from this business? In any case, I am not joining those who want to set out on raiding expeditions. Nor will I be traveling with the company heading for the markets toward the northeast. So what on earth am I doing here? What interest does it serve?" A couple of times that day, he retraced his steps toward Jrēs. At last he said, "Listen, Jrēs!" "What?" he replied. He had understood the magnitude of the problem much earlier and had already given his opinion to his uncle: "Uncle dear, where are you going to take us? To somewhere far away, we don't know where. Let's go no farther. We cannot keep up with the Rmāl and their camel train. They are 32.8

يشير عليه ياعْمِيي انت وين تبي تَقْلَعْنا خلّنا بهذا ولا نْناحي الرمال وظعونهم سنة مغاريب وسنة مشاريق وين حنا واياهم.

قال وش تهق. قال الهقوة انا ما حنا حولهم. قال أجل انا توّي أطعت شورك عز ٩،٣٢
الله ولا والله طَرَت نتبعهم لكن يمينك يمينك ياجريس هاك عَنْهُم بني نِنْهَزع بحدى هالجَرَف حنا العام انهزعنا وهالسنة بني نهزع مير يامِرِه يا منُّه مشى الدِبَش أطلقي الذلول والجمل خلّيهن يتبعنُّهم وحنا نجدع على بعارينا - بعارينهم اثنين - وبني ننكس لفلاة جبه. وهم يَهَزْعون يتْيامِنون وعلى مَهَلْهُم ينزلون بينهم وبين جبه.

عاد يقّصِد عدوان يقول ١٠،٣٢

مـل قلبٍ جوف الاسـناع ضـاعِ   القلب ضاع وضيّعه عَمْس الاشوار
وِقـعت أنا بالضـيق عقب الوسـاعِ   عِدّي عن الدرب المسانع بِتحْيار
جيـنا بِجِـل الحبـص مثـل الوداع   من شافنا كد قال ياجريس خِطّار
مـا يطّـرِدن الجوع لو هن شـباع   قـرايفٍ ما بين رامي ومِـصـفـار

يعني ما يصلون الا بالليل مثل الخِطّار الضيوف. الحبص غنم أردى من الغنم النجدية صوفهن أبيض قصير. الرامي جادعة وِلدَه وغارز ما بَه لبن والمِصْفار اللي تلد وقت الصفِري والى جا الربيع والى ما بَه لبن قاضيٍ لبنَه. قرايف هزلى. ما بهن حليب النعاج اللي رامية ولده واللي جايبة ولده بالصفري.

نتـلي مـصـلّح ناقتـه والمـتاعي   ربعٍ يـدورون المـغـازي والاسفـار

يتاعون للخيل.

accustomed to it; it is their routine: one year traveling long distances to the west, the next far toward the east. We can't possibly keep up with them—our sheep are no match for their camels."

ʿAdwān asked, "Well, what do you suggest?" He said, "My idea is that we should give up trying to accompany them." "Yes," ʿAdwān said, "I've just now come to the same conclusion. You're right. God Almighty, it really wasn't my choice that we should keep at it. Now take to the right! To the right, Jrēs! Veer away from their track along the flank of this sand hill! We did so last year. This time, let's likewise go our own way at our own pace. You, woman, listen! When the sheep start moving, unfetter the riding camel and the other male camel! Have them follow the sheep while we load the two pack camels. There we go, on our way back to the plain of Jubbah." And so they did. They branched off from the track to the right, traveling at a leisurely pace to spend the night at a place somewhere between the camel nomads' whereabouts and Jubbah. 32.9

Then ʿAdwān composed this poem: 32.10

Pity a heart torn loose from its bearings,
driven off course by misguided counsel.
After life in plenitude, walls are closing in;
have I strayed, lost the path in bewilderment?
We take care of scrawny sheep in our keep,
anxious, Jrēs, like guests late for dinner.
Well-fed, the wretches' roast leaves you starved:
skinny, some miscarry, some lacking in milk.

—He means, they are like guests who also arrive toward the evening. This kind of sheep, *ḥibṣ*, is the worst of Najdī sheep. Their hair is white and short. The ones that miscarry, lose the embryo, and do not produce milk. The ones that give birth in fall, in autumn, have run out of milk by the time of spring season. It's finished. "Skinny ones" they are called, ewes without milk: those that miscarry and those that give birth in the fall.

Breathless, we pant after camels and horsemen
who raid for sport, cross deserts on mounts,

—Who call to the horses, *ytāʿūn*.

مثل القبيس ليا انتهض بارتقاع   حلالهم ياجريس حثّات الاوبار

البل وضح مثل لون القبيس الضباب.

حيرانهم تشدى حفيد الضباع   وِضْح تعاود بين مِلْحق وقهّار

مَشْي الحيران هاللون مثل حفيد الضَبْعه مَشْيَه.

مدارجه مثل دِريج الأفاعي   والا الغصون اللي مع القاع جرّار
مِطْنين راعى الضان بالانمزاع   ومِرْضين بِعْصَير النزل كِلّ صقّار
غفَيلات قِطّاع الفجوج الوساع   مرباعهم عشب الخطايط والاقفار
هل الشداد مْلَعْفِظين القطاع   كم راس حَيدٍ زوّلوا عنه الاشجار

هل الشداد يعني العقاده يسمّونه الشداد. ملَعْفِظين القطاع يعني ما همب يجون ياخذون اباعر مثل ما تقول اهل الجوبه. يتقطّع منه حلال إلى جَوا كاسبينه واللي ينقطع يخلّونُه.

يا جا العشا تسمع حَساس الدواعي   داعي ورا داعي ونارٍ ورا نار
ياجريس نستاهل ثمان الطقاع   أقصرهن اطولهن تجي تسعة اشبار
من واحْدٍ ما هو بالاطلاق واعي   قبل التّحِزّب والتنبه والافكار
يهيا لمن مثلي حْكي له واطاع   وانت البري ياجريس ما لك بهن كار
ياجريس قل عن دربهم بانهزاع   ما ظنّتي بارى هل القود حمّار

Camels phantasmic white, a mist when it lifts:
camels are their pride, Jrēs, curly-haired giants.

—Pure-white camels, the color of white mist, a cloud of white fog.

Their young shy and jog like hyena cubs;
men run to catch and check the white imps:

—Camel calves run with a sideways tilt, like hyena cubs.

Like snakes, they leave winding traces in sands;
or like the branches torrents drag over desert floors.
Dashing off at speed, they enrage sheepherders,
their camp a delight for falconers at day's end.
Tribesmen of Ghfēl, they cross vast desert tracts,
graze camels on strips of green, virgin meadows.
Raiding, they pick the cream of captured herds;
their legions flatten growth on low stony ridges.

—They are people of the camel saddle. The saddle they call *shdād.* Herds so big, more than they have use for, like food spilling from their mouths. Don't they bring robbed herds, for instance from the people of al-Jūbah? Some of the spoils, the captured animals, are left aside for any takers.

Come evening, loud dinner invitations fill the air,
calls shouted in staccato, fire after fire is lighted.
Jrēs, we deserve eight resounding belches,
short farts and flatuses singing their long song,
Fired off by a fellow unaware of his flatulence,
before straightening up, giving heed, or thinking.
Aim them at such as me, who did as he was told!
You, Jrēs, are innocent and free of blame.
Jrēs, tell them to veer off the road and turn:
camel nomads do not ride with donkey drivers.

ويقول عدوان ياصف البل ١١،٣٢

طالعت انا المجمول مردوع الاوجان   العصر قلّط للقطيع اللحون
التايه اللي صار مثلي مع الضان   ما يتبع الضينان كود العفون
البل عطايا الله مجانيس الالوان   عوج الرقاب مرفّعات المتون
ما يعلم الله ينصخي بَه للاخوان   لولاه تجزا راعيه بالغبون
عذروبها الغِيَيِّيب شَينين الالوان   اللي يقزّون الولد بالطعون
من فوق حيلٍ ضارياتٍ للاقران   بس الحبال ويابسات الشنون
البل ذبايحها عَطيبين الاطعان   لبّاسة الجوخ الحمر والزبون
قادت من المربوب والسعن مليان   والعصر حشوانه على الما عُطُون

In these verses, ʿAdwān speaks about camels: **32.11**

My eyes caught sight of a tattooed beauty,
  singing her tunes to herds in late afternoon.
To raise sheep takes dazed idiots such as me:
  sheepherding is a pastime for boorish egoists.
Camels, in colors and sorts, are a gift from God,
  necks graciously curved, their backs elevated.
Too dear, God knows, to be gifted to friends,
  though owners live in fear of instant loss:
Ruthless robbers launching surprise attacks,
  thrusting and stabbing, are the camels' scourge;
They ride hardy mounts at unflagging pace,
  carrying reins and dry waterskins, nothing more.
Camels slaughter fighters, adept target hitters,
  warriors dressed in red silk jackets and long coats.
They ride from al-Marbūb, skins filled with milk;
  In the afternoon, looted young camels rest at the well.[190]

يقْصِد بجَزْعِة اللذيذ

١،٣٣ سـنة من السنين صار عليهم وقتٍ طَوّل الشتا وليا عدوان بشمالي هالنفود من يم الخَمْس بارض الخمس. يوم جا يومٍ من الايام والى مير العرب هم هذولاك يوم نَزَلت شمال مَنُه. ويجيك مْسَيِّرٍ علَيهم وشَم هالعرب. وشَم هالعرب. يقول يا والله هذولاتي الرمال الامير هجهوج هكالوقت ابن رمال. ويجي مْسَيِّرٍ عليهم. يوم انه اقبل على العرب والى مير راعية هالزوامل هكالبنت هكاللي تِذود زوامله يوم البنات لهن دور.

٢،٣٣ يقول سلم عليَه يقول قالت وش انت ياخي ياهاللي جيتنا. من اين جيتنا يا هالرجال اللي ما عرفناك ولا نعرفك ولا انت من طارفة عربنا. يقول قال والله انا من هاللي رامي بهم الزمان وجايٍّ ابي هالعرب اسيّر عليهم. يقول قالت ياخَيّ كل ما تْسَيّر عليهم تَرَن استَفْلي بينهم وبين هَلَك. يقول قال هذي مير الساعة المباركه. ويأخذ ياطويل العمر هو واياهم ياخذون لهم مْراح. عْرِفوه الرمال والى جا هلا بالهربيد ياهلا والله بشاعر شمر. وليا منه قعد عندهم هذي قصيدة يجيبه وهذي سالفه. وليا ثار وليا هذي جَزْعة اللذيذ مع زوامْلَه هُمّين قعد عندَه مع هالزوامل الوضح وتونّس وانبسط وغدت الدنيا عنده عِدَّه مجيوبٍ هكاليوم.

٣،٣٣ يوم جا يومٍ من الايام ثاريهم مْرَوّدِينٍ هالعرب باثنا هالمتيتة هذي مْرَوّدِينٍ الهوج يم الخِنْفه. ويوم جَوا الرواويد قالوا لعن الله أبو مجناكم العِشب راكبٍ الشجر وحنا

He Sings the Praises of Jazʿah al-Lidhīdh

One winter, they suffered a long dry spell. ʿAdwān spent those days to the north of al-Nafūd near al-Khams or thereabouts. One day, a group of Bedouin put up their tents to his north. He decided to pay them a visit. "Who are they?" he wondered. "What is their tribe?" It did not take long for him to conclude that they belonged to the tribe of Rmāl. Their chief at that time was Hijhūj, Ibn Rmāl. Accordingly, he brought himself to call on them. As he approached their camp, he passed a girl whose task it was to keep an eye on the tribe's pack camels and to water them. Yes, in those days the girls had their role to play. 33.1

He greeted her, and she asked, "Who are you, little brother, visitor? Who are you, man? We haven't seen you before. We don't know you. Surely you are not one of our kinfolk." "By God," he said, "I am one of the ill-starred people cast adrift by fate. I came because I wished to pay a visit to those Bedouin." "Little brother," she said, "whenever you come to pay a visit, you'll find me here on your path, watching over the camels browsing on your way to our place." "Thank God for this blessed occasion!" he said. At that, may God prolong your life, he moved toward those Bedouin and the resting places of their animals. The Bedouin of al-Rmāl at once knew who he was, though. As he approached, they called, "Welcome, al-Hirbīd, a hearty welcome to the poet of Shammar!" As soon as he sat down, he began to regale them with his stories and poems. And whenever he rose and took his leave, he found Jazʿah al-Lidhīdh and her pack camels on his way. Before continuing, he paused for a chat, surrounded by the white camels. They enjoyed each other's company and conversation. It gladdened his heart and time flew by quickly, as if the world had been born anew. 33.2

Then one day, all of a sudden some of their Bedouin who had gone scouting came rushing in. They had gone to reconnoiter an elongated stretch of dunes, al-Hūj, toward the area of al-Khinfah. On arrival at the camp, they exclaimed, breathless with excitement, "God's curse on your fathers all! The herbage there has grown so tall and thick that it has overgrown the bushes! And here we are sitting idle, wasting our time!" The Rmāl jumped up as one man and dashed off with all their belongings. The order was given: "When the morning 33.3

قاعدينٍ بهذا نَهَج علينا الوقت. وهي تْشَلّع الرمال. قالوا الوعد طلعة النجمة الفجر لا لكم عِلْقٍ بالمراح. وهم يركبون وهم يعلّقون على زملهم.

٤،٣٣ يوم انه جا الصبح وهو يجيك عدوان على جارى العاده مْسَيّر عليهم والى والله بس المِرْح تَحاجَل بَه الغربان انا ولد ابوي. من جاهم. عليهم غاره. عليهم نذر. الى والله لا هذي ولا ذيك. قصّ اثر العرب يا العرب المظاهير هذي عراجيده مْسَنّده. وهو ما يروح هو راعي غنم انت ياعدوان. البدو راحوا وخلّوه. بالاول جالسينٍ عنده ومستانس هو وايّاهم. جت البل واشالت جيرانه وخلّته هو.

٥،٣٣ طالع الزمل يا هذا قلبُه قام يَرْجِف عرف ان الجيران راحوا. مدّوا الصبح. يا مير هو لُه شَفّ على كل ابو حال لُه ملاحيظ مع هالعرب والعرب مدّوا الصبح. إنكس يم هَلُه تَعَظّم عند هله. يوم جا من باكر ويجيه لُه طِرْقي قال الرمال تطارخ سلفانهم وتبرى لهم المظاهير يما طَبّوا على الِخنْفه.

٦،٣٣ إيه قال

١ حَلّ الفراق ودَنّوا الزمل مزعوج　　عسى يِلطّونه محاريم الاجناب

العقيد المبخوت اللي دايم يكسب يْسَمّونه مِحْرام. يدعي عليهم انه يِنْهَب ظعنهم وحلالهم من شان يعَوّدون عليه.

مَدّوا من الدار الجديده وانا الوج　　على المراح وعِدّ الاقدام عِيّاب
عِدّي قريصٍ ساقنٍ غِلَّق العوج　　نقّال عزراييل بيعكف الانياب

star appears, we do not want to see even one thread left lying on the campground!" They readied and mounted their camels, and loaded the pack camels with all their gear.

That morning, ʿAdwān came for a visit as usual. On arrival at their place, he rubbed his eyes in disbelief. The campsite was empty but for ravens hopping among the litter. "Good God, as sure as I am my father's son, what happened to them? Had they been raided and stripped bare? Did they run away on receiving a warning?" It was neither. He followed their traces. And then he caught a glimpse of the Bedouins' loaded camel train as it made its way upcountry, the tops of their ladies' litters on the backs of the strongest camels swaying like branches of palm trees laden with heavy bunches of dates. He made no effort to catch up with them. He couldn't have if he wanted to. You're a sheepherder, ʿAdwān! The Bedouin and their camels had gone, leaving him far behind, all alone. Gone were the days when they enjoyed his entertainment and he had been as pleased as punch in their company. The camels had been brought and loaded to carry off his neighbors; he had been abandoned. His gaze fixed on the disappearing camel train, his distressed heart began to tremble. It dawned on him that he had lost his neighbors. They had set off at first light. But he kept the Bedouin in his sights: he had designs on those Bedouin, regardless. 33.4

They had set out on their trek that same morning. Downcast, he returned to his folk and slumped on the ground, huddled deep inside his cloak as if he were ill and bedridden. The next morning, a passing wayfarer told him that he had seen the Rmāl's vanguard marching with mad energy, the train of pack camels straining not to fall behind, with no intention of halting or easing up their pace until they had reached al-Khinfah. 33.5

Ah, yes! Then he said: 33.6

Separation struck! News of herbage sent them packing: *1*
may their camels be robbed by champion raiders!

—The lucky raid leader who invariably returns laden with booty is called *miḥrām*. He prays that a redoubtable robber will attack their camel train and herds, which would force them to return and once again be near the poet.

They left the new abode and I'm writhing
on the camp's remains, my feet unable to move:
Curved, poisonous fangs sank into my flesh,
venomous slashes from the Angel of Death.

السم اللي بناب الحيّه هو عزرايل من قِرِصتُه ما عاش.

اقفي ظعن نابي الردايف نصا الهوج   على اوضحٍ يتلي بعيدين الاطلاب
قَفّوا وانا قفّيت وارقابنا عوج   ياللّٰه تجمع شمل عوجان الارقاب
لي صاحبٍ يتلي فراقين هجهوج   يتلي قطيعٍ ما صرخ دونه الباب
ياصاحبي خدّك من الوَرْد مدلوج   أبو ثِليلٍ فوق الامتان ينْساب
عَمْهوج يا وايًا من البيض عمهوج   كنّه بعيني لو زرى كل عتّاب
زملوق وسمٍ صبح الامطار مادوج   صبح القِبَيسي صفقه كل ذلعاب

ويقول ياصف رحيل البدو ٧،٣٣

البدو ياعايد على نجّة النور   خانة رِحيل البدو ما اعجل مِديده
فرّة طيورٍ مع شفا راس عنقور   حين الضحى جَتْهم علومٍ وِكيده
يم الزكاة محوّلينٍ بلا شور   جتهم وصاة الشيخ واول عبيده

يوم يرسل لهم ابن رشيد يجتمعون من شان يزكّيهم.

الا ودنوّا لَه من الزمل مصطور   اشقح توَصّف بُه خطاة البديده

يعني يقولون هكالعرب اللي معهم هكالجمل اللي هذا لونه.

مرٍّ يربّع بَه ثميلٍ وابا القور   ومرٍّ يجيبه من ديارٍ بعيده
ومرٍّ له الغوطه تقل لون مقهور   ناب القرا ما تَلْهز البدّ بايده

من طوله ما تطول يد الرجال الى وقف بِدّ الحداجه.

—By the poison of the snake's fangs, he means ʿIzrāʾīl, the Angel of Death, whose bite is always lethal.

A buxom beauty is carried off to al-Hūj
  by white camels taken to distant destinations.
They left; so did I, turning to catch a glimpse—
  God! Reunite lovers who throw pining glances!
My darling travels in the suite of a chief, Hijhūj,
  in desert freedom, far from villagers' creaking doors.[191]
Darling, your cheeks are daubed with rose extract,
  thick tresses flowing down your back in waves.
Tall, succulent, she outshines all creamy beauties:
  she's pinned into my vision, whatever people say.
A juicy stalk, dewy with a shower's drops at dawn,
  as balmy breezes dispel banks of morning fog.

He composed these verses on the Bedouin's departure: 33.7

ʿĀyid, at blush of breaking dawn—the Bedouin:
  Oh my! At what pace they pack and leave!
Like birds flying up from a steep peak's ledge,
  they're aflutter when true reports arrive at morning;
Rush off without a thought to bring alms taxes,
  pay obeisance to the shaykh's severe slaves:

—Given orders by Ibn Rashīd, they collect the payments of the zakat.

A male camel was arraigned, mighty and proud,
  tinted a rosy white, an emblem of tribal fame,

—If people want to refer to a certain tribe, they say, "You know, the tribe of that camel, called so-and-so."

Well fed on meadows of Thmēl and Abū l-Gūr,
  or brought home from faraway pasture lands,
Halted, penned up at al-Ghūṭah, standing tall:
  outstretched hands can't reach its saddle's lining.

—The camel towers up so high that a man's outstretched hand does not reach the saddle cushion.

يَقْصِـد بطلقـه البِهـيّانيّـه

١،٣٤ قِصَد عدوان بَعَد بُله بنتٍ عُميميّه من جماعتي عمّةٍ لي اسمه طِلْقه البهيّانيّه تِعْلِمّتُه هذي تِوُّه مْتَعلِّم القصيد وهو ما فَنْهَر يعني ما بَرع. ايه الله علم. وعْشِقه عشق العميميّه. وليا العميميه أويّا بنت ابد عَنود غزلان.

٢،٣٤ ويَقْصِد به

اوّل بِـــداة وْلا على الله بادي   طَلْبة وِليّي كل ما اسعى بالاصباح
عـدد نجوم الليـل ضـافي السواد   وعْـداد ما نادى المصلّي بالافـلاح
دَلّيت انهـّض غيـبهن من فوادي   قصـاويٍ ما يِقنْـعَن كـل ما لاح
هاضن عَلَيّ مثـل ارتكـاب الجراد   حين العصـير ليا تـدانى للامـراح
حطّيت بالمـيزان قيـمة مـرادي   ونظمتهن نظمٍ تِقِل شِغـل مِسْباح
وزعجتهن من صوب خـلّي وْكـاد   الجـادل اللي شَوطن القلب بِشْـباح
لى شـفت خـِلّي بالعـيون القوادي   اطلع طلوع الطير لى شاف شُولاح
والعـين عـين مْـبرَقـعٍ بالهـداد   القـاطـع اللي لابْـرق الريش ذبّاح
الصـايـم اللي مـا يعوق المـنادي   القـاطـع اللي لابْـرق الريش ذبّاح

موافِقه ما دونَه الا قِرية الحمد. يقول انّه على حَدّه البنت ابد مِجّوز مثل الصايم اللي

Poem on Ṭilgah al-Bihiyyāniyyah

One of ʿAdwān's poems was inspired by a girl from my tribal group, al-ʿMēm. She was a relative of mine.[192] Her name was Ṭilgah al-Bihiyyāniyyah. It was one of his first poems, composed when he was still an apprentice poet and before he had attained excellence.[193] Well, God knows best. He had fallen in love with this girl of my group. No wonder: she was a stunning beauty, without question! The finest doe of the gazelle species. 34.1

He sang her praises in these lines: 34.2

I commence by saying prayers to God,
  my Lord, as often as new days break,
Abundant as stars twinkling in dark of night,
  calls to perform daily worship resound.
Verses I stir up from my heart's recesses:
  selected with finicky care to my taste.
Inside, they rise thick as clouds of locusts
  coasting to landing grounds late in the day.
Weighed in scales for a precise amount,
  they are spun as a string of prayer beads
Sent expeditiously on its way to my love.
  Her glances bound my heart in fetters.
Ordered by my eyes to turn and gaze at her,
  I jump as a falcon at a waving piece of cloth.
She looks about, a fierce unhooded peregrine,
  merciless hooked claws to tear bustards apart;
Ravenous from fasting, at her falconer's call
  she strikes bustards like a bolt from the sky.

—The girl is suitable, old enough to be married off. It is only a matter of reciting the marriage formula. He says that the girl has grown up and is ready for marriage consummation. Like someone who is fasting, clutching a date in his hand, who brings the date to his nose to inhale the smell, ready and all set,

ماسك سَحتّه بيده يتنشّاه بخشمه والم يحتري الاذان يِذّن ياكله وابْرق الريش هو لحيته بيضا.

ذاك الوحيش اللي عن الزول نـزّاح   او زاد عـين غـزيّـلٍ بالحـماد
فِياضٍ يقَذّفن الطّفَل عقب ضحضاح   يرعى جوانب كل داروج وادي
رضـاع رَدّ السِّكّرة حين ما صاح   خـدّه شقـاقٍ باج روس النوادي

شقاق النوادي نوادي النخل شقاق الكافور النوادي القنا الطَلْع هذا يا طَلَع وانفتح مشبّهن ثوبه ان الجيب على الغِرّه وان الجِلْد الصافي الابيض هذا مشبهه على القنا الابيض. السكرة الجمارة هاللي تقول مغطوطة بسكر وهي طالعة من هالشطيب المِرّ.

زمّن كرانيـفـه شِـمّخ عنـد فـلاح   بِعَـلّوّ ليـف رَخيـمي بالبـلاد

رخيمي نوع من أجود أنواع التمر.

مِـرْزاب يُودِع زامي الغَفو ينـزاح   من ضرب سِهّر الحيـل هن والعداد

يعني السواني تسقي النخل وِتزهي عليه الما يصير اطْيَب لُه.

يَطْعَن ويَنْزَح عن مزاريق الارماح   والقـرن ذيـل مجـّـل بالطـراد
ضافى الشليل اللي تقل صدر سبّاح   اشقـر يشـبّى عسـفهن والعـياد

عريض صدرُه تقل يسبح.

يا تِقِـل مـدّادٍ على نِيّتـه راح   يا قيل ياهل الخيل نادى المنادي

نِزع الغَوج من الجوّ راح.

just waiting for the call to prayers to sound for him to set his teeth in it. By "bustards," or as we say, "the one with spotted feathers," he refers to himself.

Or is it the tender gaze of a gazelle on stony plains,
untouched wildness shying from human shapes,
Nibbling at trees on the flanks of a valley bed,
watercourses moistened by sprinkles of rain?
Cheeks creamy as hearts of palm bursting forth:
a grating sound, the crack sucks up its sugar.[194]

—*Nuwādī* are stalks of date bunches when the inflorescence, the fruit, appears. The comparison is with a woman who acts absent-mindedly but, as if inadvertently, opens the slit at the side of her robe to show the creamy white of her breast, which is here likened to the white inflorescence of the palm's flowers. The "sugar" is the *jammārah*, heart of palm, which looks as if it is coated in sugar when it rises from the bitter wood of the crack in the tree's stem.

Hidden in green crowns, the land's tastiest dates,
dense gardens of palms raising thick fronds aloft,

—The *rkhēmī* is one of the best kinds of dates.

Watered day and night by camels and drivers:
a jet of the well's spout sweeps debris aside.

—He is referring to the camels that draw water for the irrigation of date palms in such abundance that the fruits are exceptionally tasty.

Her plaits: tail of a horse with white-spotted legs,
swerving in battle, from stabbing to rapid evasion;
Gold sorrel, ready to mount mares young and old,
tail fanning out and breast wide as if swimming:

—The horse is barrel-chested and runs as if it is swimming.

If the call resounds: "Horsemen, in the saddle!"
the champion stud pulls away from the pack.

—The horse streaks away from the water holes, gone in the blink of an eye.

يَقْصِد بمنيره بنت ابن بشيّر

والله قلط عدوان وِنزل موقَق وليا موقَق هكالحين تحاش من الحَفَر حفر النفود الي بيضا نثيل كله بالزكاوات على موقَق موقَق قويّة هكالحين من اقوى قرايا الجبل. والله جاك يمشي هو وهكالربع قدّامه هم ما دَرْيوا به. الاولين يا جا بالقايله تقنّع عن الشمس متقنّعين ويمشون. قال واحدٍ يافلان. قال وش تقول. قال تِمَنّ. قال وش اتمنّى. قال تِمَنّ الرجل كود يتمَنّى. قال وش اتمَنّى. قال بس تِمَنّ. قال اتمنّى هَنيّك يابْهَنايا الدنيا يامن عقد طِنْب بيتُه بصفرا عراجد هذي ونِسي هَمّ هالسنه يَلْقَطه وتاليه يحطّه بعدوله. الارزاق قِصيفه هكالحين. قال هذاك انا هنيّك يامن عقد طنب بيته بهاللي وراه. والى الحَير ثلاثميه يقولون لُه حَير شايع. والاوه يسمعهم عدوان قال يامال المولّية ما تمنى الحير كِلّه. واسكِت. ١،٣٥

يوم صلواْ الظهر وجلسوا عند لهم غْفيلاتٍ يقال لهم المرامشة من اهل موقَق قال والله يالربع انا وقعت بلي مْغيبه والا والله ما من دفايع مير عاد تقل اني اشوى ٢،٣٥

Poem on Mnīrah, the Daughter of Bshayyir

35.1 ʿAdwān traveled to Mōgag on an errand. People from as far as Ḥafr al-Nafūd and Bēḍā al-Nithīl went to pay their alms tax in Mōgag. At that time, Mōgag was of considerable importance, one of the most vibrant settlements in the region of the mountain. In front of him walked a group of men who were not aware that he was within earshot. In the olden days, people used to cover themselves against the sun during the hottest part of the day and walk with their heads enveloped.

One of them said, "Hey, so-and-so!"

"What is it you want?"

"Make a wish!"

"What should I wish for?"

"Just make a wish! People make wishes just like that."

"But for what?"

"Make your wish now!"

He said, "Oh, how happy I'd be if my wish would be granted! I want my tent peg fixed in the ground next to these palms with yellow date bunches so that I have nothing to worry about this year—so that I can collect these dates and store them in large sacks."

In those days, people had difficulty making ends meet. There was scarcity of everything.

The other said, "Oh, how fondly I wish for my tent peg to touch the tree behind yours." The entire garden counted no less than three hundred trees: the "Garden of Shāyiʿ," it was called.

ʿAdwān had overheard their exchange of wishes. He said to himself, "May the devil take you! Why not wish for the entire garden?" But he kept the thought to himself.

35.2 After performing the noon prayers, he sat down in a circle of tribesmen of al-Ghfēlāt, a group called al-Marāmshah, inhabitants of Mōgag, and said, "On the way here, I fell in with some strangers, folk not so different from myself, yet I think I'm a little smarter than they are." "What's the story, ʿAdwān?"

شوَيّن. هاه ياعدوان. قال والله رَبْع تِمَنّوا كل تمنى لُه نخلة بلهم حير ولا هو يبي يقول هذا قَدّ جْلِبي أو هذا كثر فلوسي وانا تمنيت الحير كله الحير ثلاثميه وبس تِمَنّوا على نخله وحده وهم ما همب خاسرين دراهم مِنْوِه كل تمنى لُه نخلة وخلّوا الحير كله وانا ما من دفايع مير عاد تمنيت الحير كلّه الى صارت منوه ما انا قايل ثمني يقصر.

ويعد مسكان الفلاحة ياصف مسكان الفلاحة يقول ٣،٣٥

شـفّي مع الحِضران واسكن بْديره   ولا لي بلجّـات البهـم والمخـاليل
واشِـمّخ زرانيقـه على جـال بيـرَه   وادني عليهن قيمة اربع محـاحيل
بيـرٍ وسـيع وجمّته مسـتديـره   نِـدْني عليهن كِنْسٍ رِجّـعٍ حيل
وِدْلي غِـلْسٍ ما بهِن الصـغيـره   وساع الفروغ مقذفات الشّخـاليل

غلس كبار. الشخاليل الما الحلو البارد.

ومـناخ ما يكسب علينا معيره   تنصاوه من جوف البلاد المراميل

المراميل الركب اللي قاضيٍ زهابهم من طول المسافه جاييّنٍ من بعيد.

ومحمـاسةٍ تـرِكى على جـال كيـره   ودلال يِطْرِب شَوفهن والفناجيل
قولي حـلولا يالنخـيل الكثـيره   ما هو غلى بمكرمات الشمـاشيل
ابي اتقـرّب واتقيـرب مـنيره   الصاحب اللي وَذّر القلب توذير

مكرمكات صفرنماهن. منيره بنت زيدان ابن بشير امير موقّق.

He said, "Well, a group of men walking ahead of me started making wishes. Each of them asked for a date palm in a garden, without saying what they'd give in exchange or how much money they'd pay for it. If I made a wish, I'd ask for the entire garden of three hundred trees, whereas they asked for no more than one tree each. They're not losing any money over it. It is about making a wish. All they wished for was just one tree. It did not occur to them to ask for the entire garden. Not that I'm a much better person than they are; nevertheless, I'd want the entire garden for myself. If it is a matter of expressing a wish, I'm not going to say, 'I can't afford the price.'"

At that, ʿAdwān launched into his description of a farmer's life. He said: 35.3

I'd wish for a settled life among villagers,
far from bleating sheep and camel calves.
I'd wish for the tall pillars at a well's rim:
four pulley wheels I'd mount over the shaft;
Wide-mouthed, gushing bottom circle-shaped,
worked by draft camels, fit and well behaved.
Elongated leather buckets, no small skins,
hoisted up, their necks spouting limpid water.

—The buckets are large and the water is sweet and cool.

That'd be my travelers' haven, no mean affair,
drawing journeyers whose supplies run low;

—*Al-marāmīl* are travelers who have consumed all their supplies on a long-distance journey. They have come from far away.

At the fire's edge leans a roasting pan for beans,
coffeepots—a joyous sight—and porcelain cups.
My wishful sigh for palms in rows, gardens full,
isn't lust for bunches of dates, yellow and lush:
I'm scheming to steal up closer to Mnīrah;
the dream girl sliced my heart into slivers.

—The tree's fruit stalks are yellowish. The girl is Mnīrah, daughter of Zēdān ibn Bshayyir, the headman of Mōgag.

عـذروبـه انـه ميرتوّه صغـيره   يامـال ياغَضّ الشباب التماهيل
ياغــصن موزٍ مَـنْبتـه بِجـبيره   راسُـه على طَلٍّ وجِذْعُه على سـيل

الجبيره الارض الزينه اللي يمشي بَه الِشرك الما اللي لا هي نفود ولا هي خِجْرِه والسير سِرِيّ الما اللي يمشي الساقي.

والنهـد طلع زَبيـدِي بيحـيره   يا مَـزْنَـزّ مَقَـذّفات الشخـاليل

الى مز المطر من الارض نز فوق طلع اللي هو الكما مَقَذّفات الشخاليل السحاب.

قالت اخطيت يابواردي مير يوم تمنيت الطمع والطيب وانا تِلْحَقَن تالي هالابيات ٤،٣٥
لا قبول لهن انا القصيدة اللي ما هيب من مِشَدَّه الى تاليه كله بي لا قبول له.

She's perfect if it weren't for her pristine age—
  may freshness of budding youth last forever!
Ah, supple banana stalk planted in fertile soil,
  tips sprinkled with dew, its roots on a stream.

—*Jibīrah* is good, fertile land, not sandy as the dunes or stony, and irrigated from a small channel, *shirć*, water that flows at the roots of the palm trees. *As-sēr* is a synonym of *siriyy*, "small irrigation channel."

Breasts protrude as truffles in a marshy field,
  soaked by heavy showers, pop up their heads.

—If it sucks up the moisture from the earth, it pops up: the truffle shows its head. The "throwers of cascading water" are the clouds.

She said, "Well, gunman, you missed the mark. How could you wish for the 35.4
nice things you crave, and only at the end add me to the list? I cannot accept a poem unless it is entirely devoted to me, from the first line to the last."

يَقْصِد بنت ابن جويعد

عدوان أكرى ابن جويعد من اهل موقَق حَضِري من اهل موقَق اكراوه جَمِلٍ لُه. الهربيد أكرى الجمل ابن جويعد. يوم اكراوه الجمل وجا الوفا واثمر النخل وهو يجيك عدوان يبي الكَرْوه. يوم جا يا لُه بنتٍ اسمه نوره انت يابن جويعد مخلّيه عبيد ابن رشيد البنت مطلّقه. وتَنْذَخ البنت. قالت يابيه هذا من هو. قال هذا كِرِيّنا هاللي جَمِلُه نِسوقه يبي كَرْوتُه هذا عدوان الهربيد. قالت هذا عدوان الشاعر. قال الله الله هذا هو. ١،٣٦

والى الحريم ما لَه عْقول تبي الشاعر. والبنات يقولون الهربيد جاي ويعرّضِن يَبِن كوده يَقْصِد بهن. وهي تِصِك الحير لا يَطَبّ لا يِطِبّه احد. طرّدت الحريم. صكّت باب الحير ما يُوتَى لله. يوم جَدّوا وحطّوا الجداد ودلّوا يكِيلون الكروه ويبون عاد ياخذون الزبيل يحطّونه بِعَدولِه قالت لا اناكود احطّه ابد والله انه ما يَلْمِسُه وانكم ما تلمسونه. ٢،٣٦

ويشيلون الزبيل عَلَيه والعدول بهذاك. وتقول هاك تِكِبّ الزبيل وتْنَسّف قَرونَه. وبَه لَه سناسل وحِلِي الله حاليهن مع زينه. تقول والله ما تِنُوشهن انت انا اللي اخيّطهن وازيّن عَراهِن هي تقولُه له لعدوان. هو بس قاعد ويراعي. المراد اطلعوا قشُّه. ٣،٣٦

والله طلع وشالَوا على رحايلُه الكَرْوه قال ٤،٣٦

His Poem on the Daughter of Ibn Jwēʿid

ʿAdwān rented out a draft camel to Ibn Jwēʿīd, a sedentary man who lived in Mōgag. He gave him a male camel needed for the irrigation of his grove. On expiration of the loan, as was customary in the season of the date harvest, ʿAdwān presented himself at his place to receive payment. On entering the terrain, he saw a girl named Nūrah, the daughter of Ibn Jwēʿid. The girl had been recently divorced by ʿBēd ibn Rashīd. She flaunted herself as if she wished to show off her attractions. "Who is this man, Father?" she asked. "He gave us a camel on loan for the irrigation of our palm trees and comes to collect his wages. His name is ʿAdwān al-Hirbīd." "Is he ʿAdwān the poet?" she asked. "Yes indeed, that's him." 36.1

Now, it is a fact that women go nuts when it comes to poets. Girls would say, "Look there! Al-Hirbīd!" They would show themselves to him: "Who knows, perhaps he will sing some verses about us!" She lost no time in shutting the compound gates. She made sure that no one else came to drop in on them. She chased away all other womenfolk. The garden's gates were barred so that she'd be left alone with him. They cut off bunches of dates, put down the harvest, and started weighing what they owed him for the hired camel. They dropped the dates into a pail and emptied it into big sacks of the sort that are transported on camelback. "No, stop!" she cried. "Don't touch it—I'm the one to do this. Be warned, I am the only one allowed to do this work. Keep off it!" 36.2

The pails were carried to her and she filled the sacks. "Ha, there we go!" she said in a cheerful voice. She poured the pail's contents into the sacks, and while doing so she loosened her tresses. Her beauty was enhanced by the chains and assorted jewelry she was wearing. "Keep your hands off, you!" she scolded. "I am the one who is going to sew up the bags and make the right kind of nice knots in them." This was how she spoke to ʿAdwān, who was sitting there, watching until they had loaded his belongings and the sacks onto the camel. 36.3

He left, perched on the camel carrying the sacks of dates he had received in payment for his loan. Then he said: 36.4

نوره كما وضحا تِمَرْجَح لعنّاف   وضحا تْراوِز هَضْلة البير مِهْضالـــ

العنّاف هو اللي لُه صوت مع اول البل يشايع لَه.

عطـرا الى قـادت مع النشِر مـيلاف   ما عِوّقَت عن زوعة الصبح بعقالـــ
وقـرون كالِشرْطان سـافٍ على سـاف   شرطان نحّاسٍ سَلَبْهن للاشغالـــ
وثْنَيّواتَه كلهن بيض وزْهـاف   لا هن قْصار ولا عْراضٍ ولا طوالـــ
كالضيق من مزن تـروّح لُه ارجاف   يا جاوه من بعض الشفاشيف مِشْخالـــ

لى جاوه هوا صْفقُه.

باشفاة غِزْوٍ ما تلى المال صيّاف   مجمول مقبولٍ بالاقفا والاقبالـــ

يقول انه ما هي بدويه تتلي البل المال.

عوق الهواوي كان هو شاف واحتاف   ما بيك يامنبوز الارداف ما يْقالـــ
ما زِينٍ الا زين منـــبوز الارداف   لِميع هندٍ مع تضاويل الاضوالـــ
حس الريال اللي مَغَــــنّه بالارياف   ابو عـمود اللي على الصبع صلاّلـــ

ابو عمود الشوشي الفرانسي. هكالحين يوم ريالات الفضه الى قاموا يحسبونهن يحطّونهن رجم مثل العمود.

بنت الذي يطرد هفا كل ضَيّاف   يا قَلّ مِير السوق والسعر ما يْنالـــ
بْليّاي يخبر كل ما فيه ويشاف   ياغلّقوا حدب المفاتيح الابخالـــ

بْلياي يعني بليّاي انا ياعدوان هو معروف بكْرِمُه لو ما مدحته.

Nūrah, a white camel, flaunts herself for the leader,
anxious to be ahead, to be first to drink at the well.

—The *ʿannāf* is the man who leads a train of camels from the front by calling to them and chanting.

Rosy white, in the herd she's sweet and smooth:
in morning's push and rush her ankles aren't strapped.
Tresses curl down in plaits; strips embroidered
with copper shine like a robe's costly ornaments.
Her small teeth, pure white and finely chiseled,
are agleam, not too short, nor too broad or long,
Pure as hail pelted down by rumbling clouds,
sifted fine grains, slightly melted, frozen anew,

—That is, when the clouds are shaken by the wind.

Between the lips of a delicate lass, not a shepherdess,
a charming good-looker from behind and in front.

—He says that she is not a Bedouin girl who must accompany the camel herds.

Shielded from lovers hunting for prey and gain:
this curvaceous stunner is beyond reproach.
Fine girl, with bulging buttocks that defy description—
the blinding flash of Indian swords in a melee;[195]
Voice: clinks of riyals in brisk market trading,
tinkle of a pile of Maria Theresas gliding through the fingers.[196]

—A pile of Maria Theresa thalers, *al-shūshī*. Back then, they arranged the silver riyals in a pile, like a pillar, for the purpose of counting them.

Daughter of a stalwart who sates guests' appetites
in times of dearth and unaffordable prices.
No need to say more—all and sundry know
his wont when bulky keys lock misers' doors.

—That is: Without me: there is no need for me, ʿAdwān, to tell anyone. He is well known for his generosity, even without my praise for him.

يقْصِد بخنسا بنت الجمعي

١،٣٧ سنةٍ من السنين عشق خَنْسا بنت الجمعي من الشلقان. يوم تعاشق هو وايّاه قالوا لُه شمر وبعض الناس اللي عنده ياشين ياعدوان انت وش تبي ببنت الجمعي هذا بس يعضّض جِمْعُه يما قطّع جموعُه يعضّ جموعه بسنونُه باكر تاكل يديك وتاكل راسك ولا تِنْحَطّ هذي ولا تِنوخِذ لك هذي تاكلك ياعدوان ولا تعرّضه ولا تَقْصِد به.

٢،٣٧ نوى يرحل الجمعي من جبه يروح لجماعته. عدوان عاد يبي يشير عليه انه ما يرحل لكنه رحل. قام عاد عدوان قِصَد قال

كونٍ على الهربيد جوف العرب شاَع   كون النْجات اللي بساعٍ يشيع
على فريقٍ كَتّوا العرق نِجّاع   ترْجِرهم النكبا ليال التسيعي

ليال التسيعي هي شدّة البرد.

شفّي بخنسا لو كَلَت كل الاجماع   جِمْعي مع جموع الجماعة جميع
ولو تاكل اجماع الجماعه والاصباع   واجماع جمْعات الامير الرفيع
ياجريس يامشكاي لا جتك الاوجاع   ابيك يا منّي نخيتك تطيع
قل للحبيّب كان ترميه الاطماع   انا لتجميع المطالب سريع
واعزّل النيرات عن دِقّ الارباع   ولا ينقص الزرّاع رِبْع السبيع
خنسا فتاةٍ مع شراشيح الاقطاع   تتلى الكلاب مدلّهين القطيع

His Poem on Khansā, Daughter of al-Jimʿī

One year, he fell in love with Khansā, daughter of al-Jimʿī, a tribesman of the Shilgān. Noticing his infatuation with her, people of Shammar and some of his kinfolk told him, "Have you lost your mind, ʿAdwān? How could you possibly fancy a girl such as the daughter of al-Jimʿī? He is in the habit of biting his fists, so much so that he has cut up his own hands. He eats his fists, chewing away at them with his teeth. Next thing you know, she'll devour your hands, and your head as well. This is not the sort of girl you'd like to marry and have around in your house. She'll eat you alive, ʿAdwān, so keep a safe distance from her! Don't even think of composing verses on her!" 37.1

It came to pass that al-Jimʿī decided to travel away from Jubbah and rejoin his own group. ʿAdwān thought of asking him to think better of it, but he traveled regardless. ʿAdwān could not resist the urge to compose a poem on her: 37.2

War is declared on al-Hirbīd, joined by all, 1
 a sudden attack grown virulent from whispers,
Because of a clan hurrying down the sands,
 at night in westerly winds' freezing bite.

—The nights of *al-tsēʿī,* the most severe cold.

I long for Khansā, even if she's biting fists:
 my clenched five with our folk's fists all.
Let her binge on our tribe's fists and fingers,
 fists of the prince's sublime court thrown in.[197]
Jrēs, my consoler, stay safe from trouble: 5
 if I appeal to you, come at once and rescue me!
Tell my darling, if she's beset by lusty beasts,
 to count on me, avenger at her beck and call,
Smart at separating gold guineas from dimes:
 a farmer, what do I care for trifling sums?[198]
Khansā, my damsel, keeps herds for company,
 followers of al-Klāb, camels' loyal devotees.

ابو ثليلٍ فوق الامـتان شِـرّاع   ياجريس ما فـرْهَد عليها الرضيع
نهـدٍ على المجمول لو تَلْمِسه مـاع   يشـدى لروس محفـرات البـقيع

الطرثوث الحمر هو محفّرات البِقيع. قال بناخيه جريس واويلي ياخي ثاريك عاشق وعندك هالحلال اللي لُه راس مال وله سبيع وزرع وتعطي من ثُمرتُه وانا فاجّ علي لي عِدْلٍ مع هالقرايف الشياه.

قال عدوان على لسان جريس ٣،٣٧

ياعم ياللي من هوى البيض مِرْتاع   ياللي عـلى ما قلت كـونك فِـنيع
ياعـم راع لْسِبِّقٍ بيك نِسّـاع   بيـضٍ لهن عنـد العوارض لميع
مثل المغلّث شوفهن يِخْرَع اخراع   يودِعِن مسطور النشـاما هَكِيع
الشيب عيّب كل هنفا وشعشاع   وخـلى ذيابٍ عن مـردّه يـريع

الشعشاع الرجل اللي على اوّله بشبّتُه ونشاطه. ذياب ذياب ابن غانم.

تبي تصير بسوق شـاري وبيّاع   وانت الذي مـا عـندك اللي تبـيع
يامعـزّل النَيرات عن دِقّ الارباع   دِرْ لي عـباةٍ عن ليـالى الصـقيع
وش لك بْغِـرْوٍ توّما شدّ فـزّاع   يومي لجِهْـيل العِـيال الفِـزيع
ويلعب بنا لعب الزنانيع بالقـاع   ياما يخـلّينا حبيبك نِضيع
بالحفـرة اللي ما معـه كل مِطْلاع   وتقـفي على الساق العـزيز المنيع
الله الى منه خـلق ضـايعٍ ضـاع   وعـز الله أن مْـضيّع الله يضيع

Her flowing locks cascade down her back;
infants, Jrēs, have never suckled her nipples:
My sweetheart's breasts are silken to the touch,
imbued with a thumb plant's scarlet glow.[199]

—The red *ṭarthūth* plants are truffles. His cousin, Jrēs, said, "Dear brother of mine, what a thing to say! Your sport is dalliance. You own a capital in animals. You pay zakat from your produce of the land and surplus of dates. All the while, I have to make do with clothes sewn together from pieces of old camel sacks and I'm saddled with these wretched skinny sheep."

ʿAdwān impersonated Jrēs when he said: 37.3

Uncle mine, you're in thrall to female beauty,
while claiming you're fighting a savage war.
Uncle mine, your hair is flecked with streaks
of gray, a glistening sparkle on your temples.
Your looks of a rabid dog scare them off:
vile gray trips up the bravest gentlemen,
Mars gorgeous ladies, sprightly youngsters,
causes Dhiyāb to retreat in defeat.

—A man who is *shiʿshāʿ* is young, energetic, up-and-coming. Dhiyāb is Dhiyāb ibn Ghānim.

You want to wheel and deal, to buy and sell:
with no attractive wares on offer, how can you?
You separate gold guineas from lowly dimes:
get a cloak to shield me from the freezing cold!
Why gape at budding girls gesturing
to juveniles hot to trot to their rescue.[200]
Your love plays with us, skimming stones,
only to abscond, leaving us lost on desert flats.
Interred in a dug-out trench, enclosed, with no escape;
proud stalwarts checked out before, join them!
If God created you a lost case, lost you'll be:
God Almighty ruins whomever He leads astray.

يَقْصِد بنت الصقيري

١،٣٨ هو عدوان ما هو رجّال حِكِم ولا يشابل الحكّام يتكلم بالشي اللي يجري عليه. جا مَرّةٍ على الصقيري رفيقٍ لُه يا هي هذي بنته تسوق السواني.

٢،٣٨ قال

سيّرت انا يَمّ الصقيري شِربي   وطالَعت زولك ياغزال الشعيب
عند السواني واقرادة نصيبي   ياعين شرقٍ يِنْدَه العصر بشلاح

٣،٣٨ ردت عليه هو يتخيّل انه ترِد عليه بس هو اللي يَقْصِد قالت

صِقٍّ لِقيتَن فوق جال القليب   وفِتَقْت قْران الثوب وارخيت جيبي
واوريتك النهد العَفَر من قريب   واودعت قلبك للقرانيس مِلْواح

٤،٣٨ قال

يابنت قلبي بالزميّم خذيتيه   وانا اطلبك يازينة الوَسِر خَلّيه
ياعين ظبيٍ جافلٍ من مفاليه   ذورٍ الى شاف الازاويل يِنْزاح

٥،٣٨ قالت

قلبك ترى لو قلت ما هوب عازي   لو دوني الضِلْعان هن والنوازي
بين النهود القِعّد البيض لازي   كِيِّف وعامل له مساريح ومراح

His Verses on the Daughter of al-Ṣgērī

ʿAdwān was not a poet who hankered to be in attendance at princely courts. Consorting with the high and mighty was not his style. In his compositions, he speaks about what he came across in his life. Once, on a visit to a friend, al-Ṣgērī, he saw his daughter driving camels hoisting heavy buckets from the well for irrigation. 38.1

He said: 38.2

On my way to call on al-Ṣgērī, my mate,
    I saw your lithe figure, gazelle of the creek,
Driving draft camels, and stood transfixed:
    your falcon's gaze at the lure in late afternoon.

She riposted—that is, he made as if it was her reply, but he composed the lines himself: 38.3

Indeed, you've run into me at the well:
    I unhooked my shirt and opened the slit,
Showing you up close my milky breasts:
    your heart flutters like cloth waved at a falcon.

He said: 38.4

True, girl, by a nose ring you pulled my heart;
    I beseech you, stunner, loosen your cruel fetters!
Eyes of a gazelle, startled from its meadows:
    panicked by human shapes, she dashes away.

She said: 38.5

Your heart cannot suffer in patience, you say,
    though I'm beyond daunting heights and dunes,
Haunted by lying snug between big white breasts,
    to do as you please: morning jaunts, evening rest.

اذبَحَك بخـــدٍّ تِقِـل نَوض بارق   وانسِف على مَتْني تقل ليل مـارق
حمـرا من اللي يِسَرجَن بالمعـارق   قَبّا قحومٍ سَمْعَت الرَمي وِصَياح

With my cheek's flash of lightning I smite you,
felled in my loosened tresses' pitch-black night:
A chestnut mare saddled and ready for the ride,
barrel-chested, she's thrilled by shots and shouts.

يقْصِـد بالبنت على المـارد

١،٣٩ قِطْعـة رَبْع على ما ولا عندهم بعيرٍ يَسْنون عليه. ومعهم بنت تَزْعَب لهم. البنت طالْعٍ صدره من مِجَلّ ظلوعه فوق. طالَع عدوان يا هذيك البنت. هي تعرف ان عدوان انه شاعر وصار لَه شَفٍّ بُه. بس فيه واحْدٍ من العرب مخيّرَه ويتحرّاه على انه بعدين انّه يجي يخطبه تصير حرمةٍ له كِنَّه نِغرشوي من عدوان.

٢،٣٩ هي قاضبةٍ راس الرشا وهذاك يدْلي الدلو. وهي تلْتِفت يمّ عدوان. ذاك خِطّيبَه صَلّ الرشا وهي ما وَعَت تلْفت هناك. وهو يمسكُه وهو يِتلُّه قوّه يا طايحه. يا مار هكالتّله كنّه بضِلْع عدوان كِنَّه بُه.

٣،٣٩ قال

١ مـا تِنـْثِنِر ياراعي الدلو خَـــــلّه تَلّيت وسط صخَيّف الروح بِرْشـاك
يـاشـين عـين الجـــازِيه لا تِتِـلّه الله يكَـوّب فـرْتَك عنـد مولاك

يكوّب فزْتك مثل قولتهم فلان والله والكَوبه يعني ما بُه خير.

شِـف العـذارى كِلّهِن عينهن له خل الغَضي يسْري سرى الذيب بِشْواك
بَطِن عسيفٍ راعْـيَه مِــــرْخي له تَـتْـلي عقيدٍ ضـاربٍ درب الادراك
٥ مـع كِـنّس العـيرات ما رَيَّضَن له تمـازعوا مـعـهـم غـلاوين تِنْبـاك
يا جَن من العِـذوان مثـل الاهِـلّه نِبّـاي مـا بين المِــيارك والاوراك

His Poem on the Daughter of al-Mārid

For lack of a camel to draw water, some people at a well asked a girl to do the pulling for them. The girl's large breasts rose up from her ribcage as she heaved at the rope. ʿAdwān was watching her. She knew that ʿAdwān was a poet and she cast hopeful glances at him. However, one of the young men there had claimed her as his bride and was looking forward to the day he'd ask for her hand and she'd be his wife. It seemed that ʿAdwān's presence roused his jealousy. 39.1

She held fast to the end of the rope and he lowered the bucket into the well. She turned her face toward ʿAdwān, while her fiancé lowered the bucket's rope hand over hand into the well. She paid no attention; she was looking the other way. Then he took the rope in a strong grip and pulled so hard that she tumbled to the ground. That pull cut through ʿAdwān. It hurt him as if the rope had been fastened to his ribs—as if he himself had been pulled so violently. 39.2

He said: 39.3

Bucket man, don't mess up, leave her in peace:
a brutal pull slammed into the tenderhearted.
Aghast, seeing the doe-eyed pulled so rudely!
May the Lord not answer your prayers![201]

—*Ykawwib fazzitak,* as one says, "So-and-so, let him face failure"; that is, the person is no good.

Look, the girls are waiting to take her home.
Leave the belle alone—wolves eat your guts!
A lean young thing, freshly trained, given rein,
struggles to keep up with death-defying raiders,
Given no quarter by pitiless, hard-bitten mounts
ridden by boisterous, hookah-smoking toughs:
Racing home, bellies curved as slender crescents,
bags of skin and bones from saddle to haunches;

جايَاتٍ نكيف من الغزو ضامرات.

مـثل الطَخا الشِـرّاد عَجْـل الاظِـلّه   نَحـايفٍ يِـدِّن هــذولا هــذولاك

—On their return from a raid, the she-camels are wasted.

Fleeting shadows cast by scuds hurtling in the sky,
lean and mean, they trot to distant lands in a breeze.

غزليات أخرى

قالوا شيّبت ياعدوان وتطرد البنات. ١،٤٠

قال ٢،٤٠

قالوا تِتوب عن الهوى قلت ما اتوب   حتى مَحاري شَيبتي كان ابْتَناه
طَرّد الهوى ما بُه عْتوبٍ ولا عْيوب   سَلِمٍ لكل الناس من رَبّ الاله
بالتّرَف عذروبٍ ولا حْذاه عذروب   وضحا فتاةٍ زان دَلّه ومَمْشاه
شبّهتها الوضحا الطيوح ام دِبْدوب   تَتْلي مِكَبّ المِزْن والقَفْر مفلاه
كِنّه حلايا الشّوق تَرْجَح بجِنْدوب   راع الرَحول مْفَتّل العقل يقداه

مفتّل العقل هو الراعي على قعدة البل.

قلبي كما عشبة ربيعٍ بلاهوب   اخطى السماك وماطر الصيف ما جاه
شرّي ليا من الهَبوب الْصَق الثّوب   على ضميرٍ خاليٍ من شواياه
الراس يا ذيل الذنوب ام عرقوب   وجهٍ سميحٍ ولا حَلى من مْقَفّاه
ياعين يشبوبٍ ربى بام زنقوب   أوعين شرقٍ بام الارسان مرباه

اليشبوب الظبي والشرق الطير الحر.

عِشّه بلَهْبوبٍ ورا سبعة شطوب   وصفّق حدى الضبّان دونه وخلّاه

Other Love Poetry

People said to ʿAdwān, "You are an old man by now; how come you're still composing love songs?" 40.1

He intoned: 40.2

"Repent from passion's way!" "No!" I said.
"Not until old age stops me in my tracks."
Chasing love is neither cause for blame nor flaw:
it's people's inborn trait since Creation.
My girl is pretty, her sole defect a lack of fault:
creamy white, adorable of gait and mien;
Jaunty white camel, with bells, colorful trappings,
on lush meadows untrodden, refreshed by rain;
Beauty's paragon, her worth eclipses herds
whose diligent shepherds knit hobble ropes.

—While on his mount, the shepherd is twisting rope used for hobbling camels.

Spurned by Arcturus and late spring's rains,
my heart is lashed by poisonous hot winds.
Woe to me if breezes bare her body's curves
over a belly flat as if born without intestines.
Her hair fans out like a resolute mare's tail;
sweet in countenance, her behind is gorgeous.
Black eyes of a gazelle at home in Umm Zingūb;
gaze of a falcon, its nesting haunts at Umm al-Arsān,

—*Yishbūb* is a gazelle and *sharǵ* is a peregrine falcon.

Her aerie on a ledge beyond seven rocky crags;
al-Ḍubbān clapped hands in vain, no falcon came.

وقال عدوان الهربيد ٣،٤٠

ونّيت ونّـة من وِقع لُه بمظـماه	بالقَيض خـلّنّـه ركاب المـعـايير
تجيـه سِحْـمٍ تِـرْعِب القـلب بعواه	سِحْـم الضّـرا وانيـابهن كالسـنانير
ياونّتي وَنّـة خـــلوج مشـنّاه	مـشْنِيّـةٍ لا عنـد بوٍّ ولا ضِـير
تِحِنّ له مع وسـط الادباش هوباه	تَنْصَى الطـياح وتِنْشِـني للمقاهير
عيـنِي بكت غصبٍ على غير مجلاه	علـى الغضي ياناس ما هي تِداهير
تَـذْرِف كـما دَلْوٍ تلوَح بِمدْلاه	يا جت تلوح بالمـدالي من البـير
او المطـر من مـزنـةٍ ضيّعت ماه	خـرْفِـيّـةٍ عجْـلٍ مطـرها شخـاتير
وقـرون خـلّي مثل مفتول الارشـاه	والا الرطـيب اللي عليهن دواغـير
يا فـرّعت يوم الغـنادير زافـاه	ترقص بوسط منقّضات الدعاثير
جـديلته قـامت بالاصباع تازاه	تازاه باللي مثل وصف الجـمامـير
وان سَلْهَمَت بالعين عقب المراعاه	ما صَـيده اغضا مير عَمْله تقامـير
تـدور كـتلي هي وانا ميّت بلاه	من شَوفـتي لَه حارَبَت كبدي المـير
نَشْـميـةٍ وصف القحاوي ثـنـاياه	صَفٍّ سَوى بيضٍ رهافٍ مغـاتير
والعـين عين اللي على الصيد ماذاه	فـرخٍ عـديـمٍ علّموه الصقـاقير

راح عدوان يوم راح وجا المرّة الاخرى وجلس يا مير يوم مَرّته لُه وحدةٍ خواله ٤،٤٠
السويد ومَسَيّرةٍ عليهم. وهي تجدَع عصاه جَدْع بالعِنْيه بس عندُه قِدّام عينُه.
قالت ياعدوان طالبتك تعطين عصاي. قال خذّامك قدّامك. وهو يخَطفه بلحظه

ʿAdwān al-Hirbīd said:[202] 40.3

I moan as a man forsaken in waterless wilderness,
in midsummer, stripped bare by mounted robbers,
Scared by howls of dark predators drawing near,
flashes of grimace around hooked canine teeth.
Moans of a grieving she-camel, doubly fettered,
bereaved, not even given her dead calf's skin;
Insane with grief, she runs back and forth,
from sprightly camels ahead to stragglers behind.
Helpless, my eyes shed tears, for no good reason—
because of a pretty face, folks, not a calamity,
In streams, like water gushing from a bucket
hoisted from the bottom, turning and rocking;
Or a cloudburst pouring down rain in sheets,
in fall, curtains of steady, rushing drops.
My love's tresses resemble knotted well ropes,
bunches of early dates fed by water channels;
Svelte beauties braid cluttered hair into plaits,
ready to swing into dance, swaying their hair;
Thick messy tresses disentangled by fingers—
fingers creamy and white like heart of palm.
Glances shot from the languid gaze of dreamy eyes,
disguised as coy, spells cast through trickery;
Seek my death? Pointless: I'm already dead;
since seeing her, my insides have refused all food.
She has no peer, her chamomile-white teeth
arrayed in even rows of finely chiseled ivory.
Eyes with the fierce glint of a lethal peregrine,
born a fearless chick, taught by falconers.

On another occasion, a woman, one of his relatives on his mother's side of the Swēd tribe, came for a visit. She dropped her cane at the spot where he was sitting; she did so on purpose, right in front of him. She said, "Hey ʿAdwān, get to your feet and hand me that cane!" "Your servant is at your beck and call!" he said, and immediately reached for the cane and handed it to her. He was secretly amused that she felt at liberty to issue perfunctory orders to him and 40.4

وهو يِعطِيَه اياوه وهو مكيّف على انّه بس وَمَرت عليه. وهو يِعْطِيَه اياوه. يوم جا الليل قال والله اني ودّي بِتعْلِلّةٍ مع هالعرب اللي عندهم هالانثى لكن اني والله مستحي من هو اللي يَغَصّبن يِجْبَرَن ويتعذر عَلَيّ. قال هكالواحد انا. وهو يجيبه. قال والله ياجماعه عدوان راح من هانا يِيي يم هَلُه قلت والله ما تروح لازم نبيك عندنا تونِّسنا. سولفوا هكالليلة.

٥،٤٠ يوم راحوا تكلّم قال

مشويّـةٍ جتـنا ليـالى الربيـدِ　　تشوي مـعاليق الضـماير بلا نار

هي ابوه يقال لُه المشوي. الربيد يعني وقت المحضار وقت المرطاب.

لا هي تحت رجلي ولا هي بعيدِ　　خَطْرٍالى دِرْتَه مع النجع تِنْدار

يعني قرِبّه.

جـابن لها عِرد العيال الكبـيدي　　مجعول ما يقضب يده كل جبّار
جـَرّن عليها يـمّ نيّـة وديـدي　　جـرن عليها بين قـايد وجـرّار
عطيته البـاكور بايده من ايـدي　　مثل الخَدَم عجل المِطُوعة للاوزار

٦،٤٠ يوم جا الصفري يا هذا ابوَه جاي قال اركبي. وهو يروّح. ثاريه يناظر لَه يوم راحت. قال عدوان ابوَه هذا ابن حلال ما لي عليه سبيل لكن انا الجمل هذا ابدَعي عليه لعله يموت.

٧،٤٠ يوم اقْفَت قال

الصاحب اللي شعّب القلب ياشعيب　　يا شعيب يـمّ الشِّعب ياشعيب راح

الشَّعَب اللي من ورا الجبال.

passed the stick to her. That same evening, he said, "By God, I'd like to go over to those tents where that lady came from and have a chat. The thing is, I feel a bit shy. Anyone want to volunteer to force me, to prevail on me to go there, and to provide me with an excuse?" "Fine with me to do so," one of them said, and he took him over. When they arrived, his companion said, "Listen, men, just now ʿAdwān happened to pass by and wants to go back home. I told him, 'No. No way we'd let you go! We want you here with us! Entertain us for a while!'" He spent the evening telling stories.

On his return, he said: 40.5

Date harvest brought al-Mashwī's daughter;
  she roasts my entrails without the need for fire.[203]

—Her father is called al-Mashwī. *Al-ribīd* means the time of the harvest, when the dates are ripening on the trees.

She's not at my feet, nor is she far away:
  search for her among the nomads—you'll know.

—That is, she is close by.

Fellows bold as kestrels brought me—
  may she not be fondled by a despotic brute.
They dragged me to my sweetheart's haunts,
  one leading from behind, the other pulling.
I offered her the staff, my hand touching hers,
  a servant most eager to please his minister.

In early fall, her father let her take her seat on camelback, and off they went. 40.6
He stood there, forlorn, watching their departure. ʿAdwān said to himself, "Her father is a decent fellow; I hold nothing against him. Her male camel, on the other hand, is a different matter. Let me invoke a curse on it—perchance it will die on the way."

As soon as they had gone, he spoke: 40.7

O Shʿēb, a lady lashed my heart with two-pronged sticks,
  Shʿēb, toward al-Shiʿab it galloped off, O Shʿēb,[204]

—Al-Shiʿab, a place on the other side of the mountain.

فوق املحٍ جعله يَعَلق المِكاسيب   ياخذنه الشِهْب العرابيب طِفّاح

يبي الخيل يكسبن جَمّلَه.

شهبٍ يقلّبنه مع القاع تقليب   شهبٍ يطيّر خمرهن الصياح

الخيل نشيطه الى سمعن الصيّاح يزهم عليهن طارن تِقِل سِكارى.

والا ياعلّه بين جضعٍ وتقليب   وملحٍ يسقّى بالشِنين الضياح

يبيه اجرب.

والا ياعلّه بيدين القصاصيب   يرمون عن عالي قراوه الصفاح
اللي قَلَع سيد البنات الرعابيب   ياما ضرب صافى الثمان المناح

هو يبي لُه بنت وعارفٍ انّ ابوه ما بُه دين مَذهبُه غير قال ٨،٤٠

ياحيف يانابى الردايف يهودي   دينُه شَنَق ما دينها دين الاسلام
بنت الذي ما ذاق بِرْد الجِدودِ   عِفْريت ما يقبل صلاة ولا صيام
سميّها اللي داحرٍ بالنفود   اللي باطاريفه تقاحمن الاروام

اسمه طعيسه الطعس داحر بالنفود.

ياليت جده من نسايل جدودي   من شان نشري لَه مفاتيل وزمام

طلع العصر والى هي هذيك البنت يوم عانِقَت اخيٍّ لَه صغيرّ اسمه غيّاض وهي ٩،٤٠
تحبه. يا مير ابوَه تفّاق.

Mounted on a black male; let it be snatched by robbers
riding fleet, dust-colored steeds of pure Arabian race.

—He wants horsemen to capture her male camel.

Let them spur the camel along vast barren plains,
horses chafing at the bit, rearing up at cries of war.

—The horses are fired up. On hearing shouts and being called, they run at full speed, madly as if intoxicated.

Or let it roll and twist in agony from itching mange,
salt poured in wounds, mixed with watery milk.

—He wants the camel to be infected with mange.

Or let it land in the care of butchers to handle:
knives hacking and slicing chunks from its hump.
Serves him right, abductor of ladies' curvaceous queen,
so far away, night after night, camp after camp.

He had his eyes on a girl, knowing that her father was not of the religion: he belonged to a different faith. He said: 40.8

How unfortunate, a Jewess's curvaceous behind:
her faith is another, not our religion of Islam.
Poor daughter of less felicitous ancestry:
rascals not beholden to our prayers and fasts.
Her name is tucked away in al-Nafūd,
dunes teeming with flocks of gazelle.

—Her name is Ṭʿīsah, meaning a *ṭiʿs*, a big dune inside the Nafūd Desert.

I wish her grandfather had our ancestry:
I'd buy her golden nose rings and bangles.

He went for a walk late in the afternoon. On the way, he met a girl with her little brother, Ghayyāḍ, and saw her giving the boy a kiss. He knew that her father was a renowned marksman. 40.9

قال ١٠،٤٠

ياحيف يا غيّاض ياحيف ياحيف   ياحيـف حبـك للحبـيّب قـبالي
عـز الله انك ذايقٍ لذّة الكـيف   ذِقْتـه ولا انت مسـايلٍ عن حوالي
ياغَضّ ياغطروف زين الغطـاريف   شـبّهت زَولك يوم تمشي قـبالي
زملوق وسمٍ ذاعره ماطر الصيف   غـاذيه عقب الديـم هِذف الخيال
حاميه عن رِعي البكـار المواليف   جِـرْد السِـبايا والرجـال الدوالي
بنت الذي نقّـال زين التطـاريف   تقّـاق ياما صـاد لُه من غـزال

١١،٤٠ راح عدوان طِرَقي. يوم جا لُه ديرةٍ بارضٍ خلا بالقيض يا هذيك الانثى. يا مار ما يَخَبَر بالمَحَلّ هذا يعني احد. شَكّك ما يدري هي انثى جن والا انثى انس ارضٍ خلا ما يسكنه احد. يوم جا والى والله البنت. يابنت انتي جِنّ والا انس. قالت لا بالله انس. يا ميرهي على طريق الموت عطش. عرف انه مستهلكه واسقاه يما طاب كيفَه. وقعد عنده حتى انه وعت وهو يِرْدِفَه على بعيرُه وهو يجيك ساري. وين. قالت انا رحت من المحل الفلاني ابي المحل الفلاني.

١٢،٤٠ لحاجة هاللي مفرّته اكيد فرّار من له شي. شف عاد مع زوج ما تبيه مع اشيا ما يشبه ذلك. راح هو واياه خُوّةٍ حلوه حتى انه وصّله هَلَه. قالت هذاك البيت المحل لكن نوّخ عند البيت والجَزوا انشا الله تبي تحصّله. قال يابنت الحلال انا ما جيتك وانقذتك من على طريق الموت وانا ادور الجزوى الا من عند الله لكن روحي بس اسمحي لي ابتكلم لي كلمتين. قالت وش تبي تقول.

He said: 40.10

What a shame, Ghayyāḍ! Too bad, too bad!
What a shame! In front of me! My sweetie's kiss!
Good God! You tasted succulent delight;
you savored it without asking how I feel!
A juicy twig, suppler than any other sprig:
scanning her shapely figure calls to mind
Luscious rain-fed stalks, moist in late spring,
from seamless overcast skies' slanting showers,
On forbidden pastures, kept from intruders
by fearless hardy fighters on spirited horses;
Daughter of a marksman highly esteemed
for bagging gazelles in astounding numbers.

ʿAdwān went on a journey, traveling alone in midsummer. One day, while traversing a swath of empty desert, he ran into another person, a female. He had not expected to meet anyone there. He felt doubtful, wondering whether she was a female jinni, a desert spirit, or a human. That particular stretch of land was empty, uninhabited. He drew closer to the girl and asked her, "Hey girl, are you a jinni or a human?" "Not a jinni," she said. "By God, I am a human." She was about to die of thirst. Seeing her so exhausted, he poured water for her to drink until she was sated. He remained with her for a while until she had recovered somewhat. Then he offered her a ride, a seat behind him on the camel's back, and gave his mount the spurs. "Where shall we go?" She said, "I came from such and such a place and was heading for such and such a place." 40.11

Was she on the run? She must have had a reason to run away. Perhaps a man she did not want to marry, that sort of thing. They journeyed pleasantly enough in good companionship until he had delivered her safely back to her folk. "Our tent is there—that's the place." She pointed. "Kneel your camel for me to dismount, and receive your reward, God willing!" "Look here, my dear girl," he said, "I didn't come to rescue you from perdition in order to gain reward. I did it for the sake of God. Sweetie, allow me to recite a few verses, just a word or two." "What do you want to say?" she asked. 40.12

قال ١٣،٤٠

يابنت ياحـالي عـنود الغـزالِ   خـطيرةٍ من واهج القيـض لولاي
انا سـقـيتك من قـراحٍ زْلال   وبالله عطيـني من ثمانك ثِمن ماي
من قـربـةٍ قَبْلٍ رويتـه لحـالي   بمِقْـطي ومحّالي ودلوي ومِدْلاي
قلبي كما غَيمٍ حـداه الشـمال   يا جاه من بـرد الطويلين حـدّاي

برد الطويلين الطويلين الرجّال والبعير وقته آخر الشتا.

جاوبته قالت ١٤،٤٠

ياللي سِـقـيتَن من قـراحٍ زلال   واسِعد عينك واهنيّك بحِسْناي
لا تطـالبن لا طـالبتك الليـالي   وخَلّ الطلابه يافتى الجود لحْذاي

He said: 40.13

Gazelle, were it not for me,
fiery heat would have cut short your life.
I let you quaff from my sweet, limpid water.
By God, let sips from your lips hearten me!
I myself filled the waterskin from a well,
hoisting rope, pulley wheel, bucket.
My heart scuds like clouds in a northern gale,
lashed on by deep winter's ice-cold blasts.

—*Aṭ-ṭiwīlēn, ar-rajjāl wa-l-biʿīr,* "The two tall ones, the man and the camel," signify deep winter.

She replied: 40.14

Listen, you poured me a sweet, limpid drink.
May God quicken your eye for doing good!
Don't ask of me, keep safe from Fate's demands!
My brave, save your demands for someone else.

نقز الجربوع

يَقْصِد لُه ببنت والطَرْق هذا يسمى نقز الجربوع ١٠٤١

عَود عَود يا مريّح السلامه بالعدايم بالسعود   عِذْت عِذْت يا يومٍ دومٍ جرى بيذاك المراح
شِفْت بُه دافى الحشا غضّ النهود   شِفْته بالقمرا الزرَيق من الفريق جا وراح
والردايف بالوصايف والجعود   كالميارك فوق عجلات الرواح
ياغزال ابن الغزال امك عنود   رابيٍ بالصواير بالزباير والبياح
هاربٍ عن شِهْب الغوارب والشوارب والفهود   خالقك رب الملا ليّه ذبّاح
عُود موزٍ وين ماهَبّ الهوى ثمّ التوى دلّى ينود   من كريمٍ وهفل الديم هو شخاليل القراح
علمي به ركبت قعود   ياعيونه كالثمايل بالمسايل يوم غبّ الما طِفاح

A Jerboa's Jumping Dance[205]

This love song is composed on a beat called "dance of the jerboa," the jumping mouse. 41.1

Come back, come back, blissful dell at the happy dunes!
    Return, return, forever-lasting days at your camp!
Where I first saw a girl with budding bust, warm belly;
    at the tents I saw her moonlit silhouette walking to and fro:
Buttocks curvy beyond description, plaited locks aflutter
    like fringed leather cushions of camels on a nightly run.
Gazelle, you were born from a herd's finest doe,
    flocks roaming wide plains or among sand knolls,
In fear of rugged mounts, mustachioed riders, ferocious panthers:
    God Almighty created you His instrument of my execution.
Stalk of a banana tree softly astir on circling languid breezes,
    the beneficent Lord sent you drizzles sieved from sweetest water.
Last I saw her, she rode a camel marching in a tribal caravan—
    goodbye, eyes crystal as rock-held water in freshly flooded dales.

قصايده بالكيف

شرّابة التنباك جوزوا ما هو كيف   يامـدوّر الشكلات ما بُه شكايل ١٠٤٢
لا جالي هَمٍّ ولا مِقْري ضيف   ولا مُودِعٍ خـطّ الرديّين طـايل
اعلّمك بالكيف يادايرالكيف   الكيف دربُـه مايبي لُه دلايل
اعلمك بالكيف يادايرالكيف   رِكْب العقيليّات والدلّ مايل
اعلمك بالكيف يادايرالكيف   حطّ الكِبَن والجوخ فوق الاصايل
اعلمك بالكيف يادايرالكيف   ضـربة عـدوّك بالجموع الثقايل
اعلمك بالكيف يادايرالكيف   تدليل حد السيف بيكل عايل
اعلمك بالكيف يادايرالكيف   شيٍّ تَخَلّق من ضـروع الشوايل
اعلمك بالكيف يادايرالكيف   وضحا من الخفرات شقرا جدايل
اعلمك بالكيف يادايرالكيف   دِنين نِجْـر المـاو بين النـثايل
اعلمك بالكيف يادايرالكيف   بَنْي الرباع السود وايّا مـقـايل
بـرباعـهم بيض الدلال المهاديف   مشروبهن وقع السحاب الشخايل
فنجالهن يشدي خضاب الغطاريف   ورسٍ صِبَغ بكفوف شِقْر الجدايل
وصينيةٍ يِقْلط عليها مَراديف   وحَبّ اللقيمي فوق عِصْبان حايل
واعلمك بالكيف يادايرالكيف   ياباغي المشخول هـذا الصـمايل

المشخول الصِدْق.

Poems on Having a Good Time

Smokers, leave off! Tobacco isn't any good! 42.1
Want to be classy? Smoking has no class![206]
Smoke dispels no worry, fills no guest's belly,
lends no proud luster to ignoble trash.
Looking for good cheer? I'll teach you,
though jollity's way needs no guide.
If you're chasing good cheer, I tell you:
jolly is riding 'Gēlī camels, trappings astir.
If you're chasing good cheer, I tell you:
horse rugs, silk jackets on noble steeds.
If you're chasing good cheer, I tell you:
hitting the enemy with all your might.
If you're chasing good cheer, I tell you:
giving attackers a taste of your sword.
If you're chasing good cheer, I tell you:
foaming milk from large camel udders.
If you're chasing good cheer, I tell you:
creamy brunettes, sporting long plaits.
If you're chasing good cheer, I tell you:
The peal of the pestles pounding coffee beans.
If you're chasing good cheer, I tell you:
lounging at high noon in a black goat-hair tent.
Curved beaks of shining pots awaiting guests:
coffee's water from the sky, sieved by clouds.
Porcelain cups smudged like the hands of beauties
daubed with yellow dye matching reddish curls;
Trays carried by men staggering under their weight,
garlanded with cardamom-sprinkled entrails.
You're looking for good cheer? Listen!
Sift for the gist! That's the truth, hard as rock.

—What is sieved is the truth.

ويقول بالقهوه ٢،٤٢

ابتـمنّى مـنوة الكيـف واختـار   لو كـان يِضْحن التـماني على فوش

على فوش مثل قولة على ماش.

صفّـة بغـاديدٍ على صـالي النـار   بيـضٍ خواتٍ فوقهن كـل طـربوش
هِدف المذالِق كارِهن حَبّ الامصـار   يا حـافِهِن من نقوة الغَوش مَـدْغوش
وِبجَـرٍ غـريبٍ باللّحَن يـدْعِي الجـار   تَوّه لِقِي من دار الامـصـار شـايوش
وِمْـبَرّزٍ يِبْـعِد يميـنك عن الحـار   يشدى لِعنْق الديك والخشم مَقْـطوش

المبرّز هو المِلْقاط.

وِمحْماسةٍ تقـدم على كل مصهـار   ازرق قفـاه لْحـامي الجَمْـر مفـروش
وصينيّـةٍ سوقَـه خفـيفٍ بالاديار   علَيْـه من الذَود المَغـاتيـر قـنطوش

الذود المغاتير هِن الفناجيل

مـع قِـطْـمانٍ تبكي على كل صـبّار   تنـثر دموع وتمحش الدمـع بقـروش

القطما القهوه.

مثـل الطِموح من المنـاعير تختـار   ما تاخـذ الا مِـرْخص العِمْـر بالهَوش
وبطحـة جروسٍ من حسن كل ما صار   ما احلى سعيله مع سعيل اصفر القوش

الجروس الهيل واصفر القوش النجر.

ما احلى قِبلْهن مع مجالس هل الكار   حلوٍ قِبلهن مع نِبا كـل هشهوش
مع حـايلٍ تَنْدَى عظامه على الدار   حَبّ اللقيـمي بازرق الصَفْو مرشوش

A poem composed on the subject of coffee. 42.2

Wishing for good cheer, I'd make my choice—
though wishful thinking comes to naught—

—*ʿAlā fōsh* means "for nothing, in vain."

I'd choose pots from Baghdad on the fire,
immaculately white, with fez-shaped lids,
Beaks curving down, coffee beans from afar,
handled with skill by fine lads, the cream of youth;
Mortar pounded, proud purchase from town,
its pestle's peals sounding open invitations.[207]
Tongs to keep hands safe from flames,
like the necks of geese with trimmed beaks;

—*Al-mbarriz* is the *milgāṭ*: the fire tongs.

Shallow pan to roast coffee beans over a fire,
bottom burnt blue by the embers' radiant heat;
Platters to effortlessly serve earless porcelain cups,
upside down, like a humped white camel herd.

—The herd of white camels are the earless porcelain cups.

Round Yemeni beans, patiently roasted,
sweating tears, drying to leave gleaming copper coins,

—*Al-gaṭmā* are the coffee beans.

As an unhappy wife yearns for a better man,
a dashing hero storming resolutely into battle.
Spiced with town markets' best, pounded
peal after peal at the mortar's copper rim.

—*Al-jrūs* is the cardamom and the copper *gōsh* is the mortar.

Joyfully, gentlemen gather at the coffee hearth,
good-natured company, bright and welcoming;
A slaughtered camel, rib roasts shiny with fat,
the carved tray's borders sprinkled with grits.

صبّه لِعضمان الشوارب بالاذكار   يـرْوُون عنـد قْطِيِّهن كل مـرهوش
واثْنـه على اللي ما يْتَـغالون الاسعـار   لو عـاضبت يَشْـرونـه بْقِـرَّح البَوش
هـذي حَلاته مع طـرَف كل مِسْيار   يا صـار مـا لك يافِـتى الجُود لابوش
وِكثْـرَه وِقـلّه عـند عـلاّم الاسـرار   صـيّاد باسـباب القِـدَر كل منحوش

٣،٤٢ قضى الدِخان عن عدوان وْتسوهَج. وهو يظهر بْلَه راس مِرْقاب يا هذاك البيت. يوم جاوه يا مير مَرّان ابن هزيم واحْدٍ من الرمال رجّالٍ شيخ راعي بيت ومِكْرِم. وهو يجيك عدوان يمُّه. يا هم هكالحين يعرفون شرّاب الدخان وجهه الى انلاع. وهو يِلْتِحظ عليه مران يقول يا مير عِرَف انه قاضي عنه الدخان باينٍ وجهه. وهو يخبر انه ما عنده شي.

٤،٤٢ قال هذا يمكن انه يِحْتِري نفسه ضعيفه قِضَى عنه الدخان نفسه ضعيفه. قال ياعدوان تراي ادري ان الدخان قاضيٍ عنك وانك جيت لهالبيت ترجي لعلك تلْقى بُه دخان لكن هالبيت هذا والله انه ما هو تحته واخاف ان نفسك تَرَدَّى تحسب ان عندي شي عندي حَوض هالبن وسَحّة هالحلوه الله يحيِّك.

٥،٤٢ يقول يا مير ما هي بنَفْسُه وهو يقيف كأنه يعني انكسح. ثاري بعض الحريم نُوبٍ تشيل الشي هذا لعازتُه والرجل ما يَدْري. واثاري مَرَة مران مَدِسّةٍ عندَه بعض

Pour the coffee! For thick-mustachioed stalwarts,
thrusting cavalrymen who drench their blades.
Pour again for free-spending hosts, heedless of cost;
in famine they gladly slaughter their finest animals.
Such are the delights encountered on leisurely visits,
a chap's worry-free ramble to happy entertainment.
One is allotted, much or little, by omniscient God;
His hands hold the strings of all creatures' destiny.

42.3 Having run out of tobacco, ʿAdwān became distracted and restless. On reaching the top of a spur, he espied a tent. As he headed for it, he discovered that it was the camp of Marrān ibn Hazīm, one of the Rmāl, a true shaykh who hospitably entertained guests in a tent always open to visitors. ʿAdwān walked up to him. It was common knowledge at the time that smokers showed unmistakable signs of withdrawal when they'd exhausted their supply of tobacco. Marks of suffering and a bad mood are written all over the face of a person craving a smoke. It did not take Marrān long to notice that something was wrong. He understood right away that his visitor had run out of tobacco. ʿAdwān's face spoke volumes. He knew that he was desperate for the stuff.

42.4 He said to himself, "Perhaps he pinned his hopes on something; perhaps he smells an opportunity. He does not have himself under control: his pockets are empty of the stuff and he cannot resist the urge." He told him, "Listen, ʿAdwān, I know that you have run out of tobacco and that you came to my tent expecting or hoping to find some here. But I assure you, there is nothing of the sort under the roof of this tent. I fear that you may hold it against me and start harboring wrong ideas. You may suspect me of not being up-front with you, thinking that in fact I do have some hidden here. But the truth is, all I have and can offer you are bowls of milk and these sweet dates. You are most welcome to help yourself!"

42.5 Gentle though his tone was, his words did not go down well with ʿAdwān. Frustrated and deeply disappointed, he turned away from Marrān. He knew that at times womenfolk carried some of the stuff for their own use, without men's knowledge. And indeed, as it turned out, Marrān's wife had tucked away some for her own consumption! She said, "Look, Marrān, be kind! May God's bounty come your way! You depend on God for your subsistence." Hearing

الشي. قالت يامرّان عَيّن خير يمكن الله يرزقك ما تدري لو الله يرزقك. عرف عدوان ان ما من ورا مران لون كان هنا من شينٍ فهو عند راعية البيت.

يا مار اصغر عياله واحْدٍ اسمه طامي وهو يقيف بمحَلّه وهو يحترف يمّه قال ٦،٤٢

عـز الله اني فـايع من مـنامي   مثـل الربيـط الى تِطَلّقن الافلاك

عـز الله اني عـاني لام طـامي   ابيَـه تـدوّر لي مع النجـع تنبـاك

اصفـر كما الجـرجير يغـدى الهيام   عسى تَهَبّى ياصفر اللون ما احلاك

نصيت بنت مقطّعين المظـامي   سِقْم المعـادي فوق نِبَاي الاوراك

that, ʿAdwān understood that Marrān had spoken the truth when he said that he had nothing of the sort. If there was any tobacco in the house, it was to be found with the mistress.

Their youngest child was called Ṭāmī. ʿAdwān lingered and, turning to the boy, said: 42.6

Almighty God, I was startled from sleep,
  jumping as a prisoner freed from shackles.
I beg Almighty God, beseech Ṭāmī's mother
  to ferret out for me some tobacco in the camp:
Yellow leaves like salad, the stuff of my undoing—[208]
  damn you, yellow poison, how dearly I love you!
I turned to a daughter of hardy desert crossers,
  foes' scourge, lofty astride a high camel back.

يتأمل في خلق الله

١،٤٣ مـرة عدوان رمى لُه خبارى يبي ياكله. شَلَق الحبارى شَقّ بطنه ويلقى بُه حبينانيّه ويقدّ بطن الحبينانيه ويلقى بُه طحيحي ويشلق الطحيحي ويلقى بُه عنقبوت ويَشِلْقَه ويلقى بَه نمله يا مير اربع انفس ببطن الخامس وهو السادس يبي ياكل الحبارى. يعني كل واحدٍ اكل الثاني هو السادس يبي ياكل الحبارى. قال عجيب ثاري شي من شي يعني مطاعم هالانفس معاوشه من بعض. تهوّل وقعد يتأمل في خلق الله سبحانه وتعالى.

٢،٤٣ جاب هالقصيده

يالله ياللي مـا بْخَـلقك مِـعيـــره   خـلاّق يامِحْصي عـدد كل خـلاق
تسعـين مِيّـة رنق وانتـه دبيـره   تـرجيك ياباني جحـر كل شوهـاق
شيٍّ طـلوع الشـمس حـزّة نشيره   وشيٍّ غياب الشمس فَكّـه للارياق
اشـداق تـرعى من ثمـر كل ديـره   واشداق تُوجِد لَه مَعُوشه من اشداق
واشـداق دِقٍّ مـا يميِّـز نِشـيـره   واشداق ما يِعْرَف مذوقه ولا تـذاق
تـرزق كبـيره مع دوابي صغـيره   المِنْفِـهِق واللي على الرزق مِـطّفـاق
رزّاق فتّـاح الافــــام الكثيـره   ومِـرْضِي جميع رْنوق خَلْقك بالارزاق
شيٍّ تـزيله بالمـــنايا المـريـره   وشي تخـلقـه توّ من كـل الارناق
دنيـــاك يامولاي وانتـه دبيـره   مـرٍّ ربيـع ومـرّ يـذْون الاوراق
ومـر دجى والعـين يِظْـلَم نظيـره   ومـر نهـار وكـل دنياك مشراق

In Contemplation of God's Creation

One day, ʿAdwān al-Hirbīd shot a bustard for food. He slit the bird's stomach and in it found a lizard. He cut the lizard and, in its belly, there was a smaller lizard that in its turn had swallowed a spider. Inside the spider was an ant. He discovered that the bustard carried four other species in its belly and that he, ʿAdwān, was about to become the sixth species through his consumption of the bustard. Each species had devoured the other and he would be eating the bustard. Amazing, he thought, how one thing leads to the next. These beings were meant to serve as food, the one for the other. Awestruck, he sat down to reflect on God's Creation, praise the Exalted Lord. 43.1

Then he composed these verses: 43.2

God, Your Creation shows no flaws;
You keep a ledger of all Your creatures.
You steer one hundred and ninety species,
at Your mercy, Builder of soaring peaks.
Some venture out at first ray of daylight;
others wait till sunset before eating breakfast.
Some jaws munch on fruits found in nature;
some jaws chew what other jaws have eaten.
Yet other jaws are too small even to be seen;
some aren't eaten: what they eat is unknown.
Big animals, tiny insects, all in Your care;
shy recluses as well as resolute chargers.
You feed all living beings' hungry mouths;
all of Your creatures' subsistence allotted.
You let bitter Fate remove some beings;
You bring forth fresh ones of all kinds.
Your world, my Lord, is at Your command:
one day it's springtime, the next leaves are wilting.
One moment darkness reigns, blinding the eyes;
The next day arrives and bathes Your world in light.

دنياك تاتي ما تقلّط نذيره ومن فَظّ عن لوذة منايا ينعاق
تبعث محيلٍ حال دونه جبيره وتعوق طيرٍ بالجناحين خفّاق
انا دخيلك يوم يِشْتَبّ كيره بالنار لا تصخى لحالي بالاحراق
تشفق لعبدٍ جاعلك لُه ذخيره عبدٍ الى منّه نوى بيك ما باق

Your world comes and goes, no warning given.
    How futile to seek escape from ordained Fate!
You revive a cripple, make him run again;
    a bird is downed mid-flight, as You decide.
I seek Your refuge from the pit of Hell:
    Do not roast my flesh in those roaring flames!
Be kind to a servant who put his trust in You:
    never has Your loyal slave meant to cheat You.

مع الرشيد

على دور حكم بندر المتعب جا محمد العبدالله الرشيد من الدوله من هنا ويَوَصّي لشمر ١،٤٤
يوم طب العراق يَبْيَه تصير مِعُه جمهور يبيَه تطلع لُه حملةٍ معُه تجتمع عنُده يا معهم
عدوان الهربيد يا عدوان نصيبه رِدِي والا راعي ذْراع وراعي فِعِل كِلّهن. قال
صَوّتوا لعدوان - هم سراة بالليل - صوتوا لعدوان نبيه يونّسنا. صوتوا صوتوا صوتوا
صوتوا. قالوا السويدات ياعدوان ياشين انهج ابن رشيد يزهمك. قال والله ما انا ناهج
أول بِداة هوما هو حاكم وثاني بِداة ذالٍّ بَعَد بندر يْواتْبَن (= يؤدّبني) يزعل علي. هالحكي
هذا على شيخة بندر المتعب. ويجي التبيناني لابن رشيد ويعلّمُه على ان عدوان يسمعك
لكن ما بغى يجي. وبالتالي يوم حكم محمد صار يا منّه سيّر عدوان عليه عطاوه لُه آه شٍ
سَهِل طِفِسه. ما لقّاوه وجه محمد يوم توَمّر بْسِبّة هذي آه ياخَيّ الخيل ما ترَفّع من
راب دَمُّه واللي بُه مخّ ما يبي نَخّ.

ومَرّةٍ من المرار قالوا السويد لعدوان ياعدوان انت فاهم وقصّاد وانت هالحين ما ٢،٤٤
نِفَعْتنا بشين - الرشيد اول بهم ظلم وياخذون الذلول الزينه والفرس الطيّبه - قالوا
لُه جماعته انت هالحين ما نفعتنا بشين خَلّنا نحط رْكابنا ودِبَشْنا عندك وكل ذلولٍ
نْطيك عليَه ريال - هكالحين الريال يسوى لُه الف - وانت يا منّهم جَوا مْزَكِّيَة ابن
رشيد غديهم يجَنّبونك لأنك قصّاد. وهو ضِعيف انت ياعدوان.

With Ibn Rashīd

During the rule of Bandar al-Mitʿib, Muḥammad al-ʿAbdallah al-Rashīd returned from Ottoman territory. He issued orders for a sizable body of Shammar fighters to join him in Iraq. He needed their assistance for the transport of the goods he had amassed. One of them was ʿAdwān al-Hirbīd, but his enlistment turned out to be ill-starred, respected though he was as an energetic and determined person, a man of action. Ibn Rashīd said, "Call ʿAdwān!" They were traveling by night. "Call ʿAdwān. Let him come—we need his company and entertainment!" They went around shouting his name as they put themselves out to find him. His fellow tribesmen of al-Swēd spurred him on: "ʿAdwān, you scoundrel! Go over there to Ibn Rashīd! He has given orders to summon you. He wants to enjoy your company!" But the poet stubbornly clung to his refusal: "By God, I'm not going. First of all, he is not the ruler. Second, I am afraid that Bandar will hold a grudge against me if I do and punish me. If he catches wind of it, he'll be angry with me." This episode occurred at the time of Bandar al-Mitʿib's rule as chief of the House of Ibn Rashīd. The poet al-Tbēnānī approached Ibn Rashīd and informed him that, yes, ʿAdwān did receive his message, but chose not to answer the call. As a consequence, when Muḥammad became ruler and ʿAdwān paid a visit to his court, he was fobbed off with a trifling gift. From the day of his accession to power, Muḥammad never deigned to receive the poet in person. Yes, brother, riding a horse doesn't help if you're scared. If you're smart, you need no prodding. 44.1

One day, his al-Swēd kinfolk told ʿAdwān: "Hey ʿAdwān, as a poet you're supposed to be smart. But so far, we have not benefited in any way from having you in our midst." In those days, the al-Rashīd rulers behaved despotically. They'd seize whatever struck their fancy: a nice riding camel, a good horse. His kinfolk said to him, "Until this moment you haven't been any use to us. Therefore, allow us to bring our riding camels and herds, and let them be penned up safely at your place. You'll be paid one riyal for each animal." (At that time, a riyal was worth a thousand riyals of today.) "When Ibn Rashīd's servants come to collect the zakat from us, who knows, they might leave you alone because you are a poet."[209] ʿAdwān was a poor man, devoid of means. 44.2

وايتك الله يسلمك وقل لُه بيتين ٣،٤٤

قـال الذي يبـدع بيوتٍ غـريبـات   محـمدٍ وِحْمود مِكْدين الاجنـاب
حَكَمَوا بحـدّ السيف ما بَه مـراوات   واللي جِـزع يـرضى على غـير ما طـاب
ربعٍ يـذورون العـــدا فوق ذروات   الكِنْس الجبْرات نِسّـاع الارقـاب
رَفْـضـات بالتـنويخ بالمشي عجّـلات   يشدَن دعيق السيل مع ضك الاسراب
باطـرافهن شمـــر يـزجّون الاصوات   وبنحورهن مـال العـدا مثل الاجـلاب
انا دخـيلك عن جميـع الزكـاوات   وخـطٍّ يلالي والقـلم بيـد كـتّاب
عن قولة الخِـدّام يالتِـرس قِمْ هـات   اقوم عجـل وشـاربي بيْـد قـضّـاب
ذرفـين ولمـينٍ والاقـــلام ولمـات   ولا يْقـلّطون الا يِسِـــدّون الانواب

يا هذا سبهان المزكّي. قال من اين لك هالجيش يالهريد. من اين لك هالجيش ٤،٤٤ يا صار ما لك الا جمل املح. قال كان هو الفضل منك ما لك جماله وان كان هو من اخو نوره طِسّ باللي ما يحفظك. وهو يفوت. وكلٍّ ينطيه ريال وينهج بذلوله. فك ركاب ربعه.

On that occasion, he said: 44.3

As a creator of exquisite art, I herewith state:
Muḥammad and Ḥmūd scatter tribes like chaff.
Unflinching, they rule by dint of mighty swords;
like it or not, there is no choice but to submit.
On high-humped, long-necked, sturdy mounts,
they come swooping down on terrified enemies.
Calm when kneeled, strong-paced on the march:
torrents crashing through a narrow riverbed;
Shammar warriors chanting victory songs
goad the booty calmly, like herds driven to market.
By your honor, dispense me from paying taxes,
shiny paper and ink, quill pens wielded by clerks;
From servants barking, "Hey lout, get up, fetch!"
pulling me up, my mustache in their iron grip.
Diligent and expeditious, pens held at the ready:
sent on a mission, count on them to perform.

Sibhān, the tax collector, said, "How is this possible, al-Hirbīd? How did you acquire such a large number of riding camels? How did you come by this collection of fine mounts, whereas before you owned no more than one black male camel?" The poet replied, "If they became mine as a result of your kindness, the favor granted me was not yours.[210] And if it was kindness shown to me by the brother of Nūrah: beat it in the name of God, may he not protect you!" And the other left without a further word. His fellows paid ʿAdwān a riyal for each animal and he left riding his camel. He had saved the day for his fellow clansmen. 44.4

يـرد على بركه ابن عوجـا

هـنا واحْدٍ يقولون لُه بركه ابن عوجا الغيثي عند ابن عريعر وقايلٍ لُه بيتين يقول ١،٤٥

شِبْنـا وتِقـطّـع عـصـبنا كمـا يْقطّعْن الظلاف الوسايق
ياما سـديتـه والقـرانيس خِنّـع على حوضهـا مثل الحنيش المَوايق

يعني سديت الفتيلة اللي يضربون به الحوض وتقبس البارود وفتيلته العلِقه تِدَلّى مثل الحنيش.

انا صـادرٍ علّقت حوضي بمنكبي وهـنّيتكم ياهل العْداد الجـدايد

عدوان الهربيد يذبح الصيد. يومْ كِبر وشاب ليا البدون لِهن مِقاطِع مع الضلعان. وهو يجيهن مع المقطع وهن يَسِبقِنّه. يا مير يومْ الْعَجَز ركبه تثّنت ركبه وصار ما يقوى يْجَي للصيد. قال ايه هذا اللي ذكر ابن عوجا الكِبَر. ٢،٤٥

قال ٣،٤٥

قـال الذي وان حَلّ بالصيد هَرْجـه مثل ما قال ابن عوجا بحرف القصايد ١
تقطّـع عَصَبنـا من رْقِي كل عَلْطا تـرْمْـلَة باد الشّـذب كـل كايد
يامـا عَطـنّن كيـد ويامـا عـطيتهن مْعطّشات البكور بْصافيات الحدايد

الفتل.

خشـمَه يِشـمّ الريح واذنه سِميعـه وعيـنَه للغَشـرات مثـل الوقـايد

He Replies to Brikah ibn ʿŌjā

A poet, Brikah ibn ʿŌjā al-Ghyithī, while at the court of Ibn ʿRēʿir, composed a few verses, saying: 45.1

We've grown old, our strength was broken,
  just as a wooden saddle cuts into camels' backs.
I lowered the serpentine's smoldering fuse,
  bent over flashpan like a viper coiled to strike.

—That is, I lowered the slow-burning cord used to ignite the powder in the flashpan. The slow fuse attached to the lock coiled downward like a snake.

I'm done; the bucket is slung over my shoulder.
  Dear fellows with new gear, good luck to you!

ʿAdwān was a hunter before his hair turned gray with age. He used to hunt ibexes in the granite mountains, stalking them as they bounded ahead along steep trails. Then one day, he felt a sudden stab of sharp pain and his knee buckled. From that time on, he was no longer able to crawl lying on his stomach so as to go unnoticed within shooting range of game. Ibn ʿŌjā's lines on the subject of old age came to his mind. 45.2

He said: 45.3

Hunting for prey, if that is my verse's game, *1*
  I take my cue from poetry recited by Ibn ʿŌjā.
Climbing steep heights, our strength was broken
  on slippery granite rocks too daunting for most.
Cunning ibexes dodged me and I'd blast them
  with thirsty bullets from my matchlock's barrel.

—He is speaking about matchlock firearms.

Nose in the wind, sniffing, sharp ears pricked up,
  glowing eyes on high alert for sudden threats:

تقطّع بين الامـرّة مع كل هـيفـا تقود الخـــماسي والصخـال الولايد
اقفـيت وخـلّيت للاولاد طـردهن جـديدين المذاخِر والسبَت والجنايد
من لا يصـيد الصـيد بايام شبّتـه مـا هوب عقب ما شـاب صـايد
يامـل شوف مع قـرا كل هـيفـا مثـل سراب الصيف مع كل ذايد
انا شـــــايب والا بايام شبّتي ياما جبت من جبرات الرقاب الجوايد
انا صـادر وعلّقت حوضي بمـنكبي وهـنيتكم ياهـل العـداد الجـدايد

A prima donna leads the ibex to bitter mountain wells,
adults with five annular rings, kids in tow.
I turned back, and left hunting to young devotees—
bright-eyed, belt-strapped, sporting dagger and powder horn.
If you're not taught how to hunt in your youth,
forget about becoming a good shot in old age.
On high ridges, my eyes strain for clear vision:
hazy mirages in distant deserts, wrapped in fog.
A graybeard now, but in halcyon days of old
I garnered uncounted stout-necked trophies.
I'm done; the bucket is slung over my shoulder.
You, fellows with new gear! Good luck to you!

مـردّه على ولدُه يوم طلّق امـه
واخـذه اذان الذيــب

طلّق مرته واخَذَه اذان الذيب من الغَيثِه يسمّونُه اذان الذيب. وبكى ولدهُ علي قال ابي ١،٤٦
امي قال وين امك مع لَه واحْدٍ من الدغيرات.

بيبَطْـنها ذيبٍ وبيظهـرهـا ذيب   ياعــلي حـالَوا الدغـيرات دونـه
حـالوا عليها مِتِـعبين المصـاييب   اللي يجيـهـم ياعــلي يـذبحونـه
تسعين مع تسعين مع طلعة الشيب   وتسعـين ما نبْت الشعر بيدقونـه

Reply to His Son When He Had Divorced His Mother and She Married Adhān al-Dhīb

His divorced wife remarried Adhān al-Dhīb of the Ghyithah tribe. The man's nickname was Adhān al-Dhīb, "Wolf-eared." ʿAdwān's son ʿAlī was in tears and kept crying, "I want my mother back!" "Where is your mother?" he said. "She is with a man of the Dghērāt." 46.1

One wolf in the belly, one on the back:
ʿAlī, she's with the Dghērāt, unreachable!
With men forever pouring lead for bullets:
ruthless avengers, ʿAlī, not to be trifled with.
Ninety, another ninety grizzled fighters,
ninety youngsters sprouting facial hair.[211]

يمدح اهل جبه

١٠٤٧ له قصيدة ما اعَرْفَه يمدح بَه جبه واهَلَه منها

عساه تنفض عسكره فوق نايف   وابن عبيكه يمّه السيل يستن
عساه تنشي طايفٍ فوق طايف   . . . .

Praise for the People of Jubbah

He composed a poem in praise of Jubbah and its people. These are the only lines I know: **47.1**

Let a steady drum of rain come visit Nāyif,
  winding torrents race toward Ibn ʿBēkah:[212]
Let massive clouds tower, layer on layer.
  [. . .]

نخَلَه بمْتَالِع

١،٤٨ عـدوان الهـريد لُه نخلات بحيّه باجا بمْتالِع بالجبل المتالعيّات غرسٍ لابوه راشد. يا مير هو عدوان مِسّمِيهِن الشيخات مثل مجلس هالوجيه الفليحة يعني شيخات تقول بناتٍ حفّالات. هالحين كل شَيٍّ خِرب حتى النخل اذقَل. ويمنّى لهن السيل

وِدّك الى جَت مـزنـةٍ مِـذْلهـمّه   مَلْكٍ يِـدَرْهِش لَه ومـلك يسوقه
غـرّا غـياب الشـمس وايّا عجيـبه   تَسْمِك كما ارقاب القَلَع من وسوقه
غـرا تغصـّص بالرعـد هيثميـه   وتلقى الثعـالب تنهـزم عن حَقُوقه
تمـطـر على هـدلا وهـدبا ونوره   والعـاذر اللي سايحاتٍ عـذوقه
نوِيّر كما عيني الى نِيشْت اهملت   وانا الذي ما اصبر الى نيش موقه
. . . .   دلاخـيمِ صفـرا من خواويـر نوقه

٢،٤٨ تعرّض لُه راجي ابن طوعان. قال

ودّك الى جت مـزنـةٍ مِـذلهـمّه   مـلكٍ يشـايع لَه ومـلكٍ يسوقه
تِمطر على حيّة وعلى العين والظهر   على جوّنا اللي سايحـاتٍ عـذوقه
اهـل عشاشٍ ما بيّدوا من بتيره   ومن هَبشةٍ بس العـرابي بـروقه
شـلقٍ لاهـلنا يوم هي جـاهليـه   كسبٍ لعـليٍ يوم علي يبوقَه

His Date Palms at Mtāliʿ

ʿAdwān al-Hirbīd owned a garden of date palms at Ḥayyah in the Ajā Mountain, at a place called Mtāliʿ. He inherited the grove, al-Mtāliʿiyyāt, planted in hollows surrounded by rocky mountain slopes, from his father, Rāshid. ʿAdwān named the stately palms al-Shēkhāt, comparing them to an assembly of high dignitaries. "Lady shaykhs," you might say, girls dressed in festive attire. Now the garden lies in ruins. The palms have shriveled. He wished they'd be irrigated and revived by a torrent following heavy rains: 48.1

I wish for pitch-black rainclouds to visit you,
    one angel goading the rear, one leading in front,[213]
White-blazed crests illuminated at sundown:
    thickset as mountain shoulders raised aloft.
White-blazed, choking on its rumbles, exuberant:
    barrages of rain send foxes scurrying away.
Let it fall on Hadlā and Hadbā, and Nūrah too,
    swirling roots of sagebrush in the undergrowth;
Like my eyes, Nwayyir cries when she's hurt;
    I go berserk if someone pokes her in the eye.
[...]
    creamy camel udders overflowing with milk.

As these lines came to his ears, Rājī ibn Ṭōʿān threw down the gauntlet to him: 48.2

You wish for pitch-black clouds to visit you,
    an angel goading the rear, one leading in front,
For rain on Ḥayyah's eyes and hinder parts—
    our vale of dense growth and swirling roots;
Cabins of clansmen who extirpate their foes,
    serve guests grits drenched in melted butter—
Our inheritance from days immemorial,
    captured by ʿAlī through deeds of cunning:

ياوَيّ كسبة شايبٍ ما خِسِر به   بْعَقٍّ ولا توّ العوارف حـــقوقه
خذها بصنع البنت يا حفّدوا لهن   اللي ليـا ثارت قِليـلٍ غـَـتوقْه

صنع البنت الفتيل.

والا ديرتك مـاكرحنيشٍ مصـدّع   ما يسمع القاري شطوبٍ شدوقه
الله يهيّي لهن النيصة الحضرميه   النيصـة اللي كـل ضبٍّ تذوقه
نيـصٍ ورا نيـصٍ ونيـصٍ وراهن   ونيـصٍ يباحث لَه ونيـصٍ يحوقه
ويـبْـرَى لُه اللي مثل مبْسم مشاري   ما تِصـبح الا مشَيِّنن لك وفوقه

٣،٤٨ مشاري شايبٍ لُه سنون طوال. آه يهتّلهن راجي. قولته شَلَقٍ لاهلنا يوم هي جاهليه راجي من الدغيرات من عبده هذا علي ابو الدغيرات ولد يحي كان اول بحايل. يوم ضاموهم ربعهم دَغَرهو علي مع وغيدانه باجا يابِرنخل عند ابن بقّار وصار اسمهم الدغيرات.

٤،٤٨ يوم جَوّا البعيّر مع ابن بقار والى هذي بنته بنت علي سلمى هاللي ينتخون به الغيثه. قال هكالواحد من السلف اوي والله بنت لولاك بنت ابّار. وبكت عند ابوه. قال والله وانا ابوك انهم ما يحضرونَه. وهو يركب زملُه يوم مشوا من عنده وينهج للشفا ويجيب ملح من الشفا اللي مع ايمن خيبر هنا ما ادري وين مِلح. ويركب زمله ويجيب

What marvelous loot! The old man's smartest act!
By shooting, not by pleading in tribal courts;
By volleys of bullets fired from a trench he dug,
hit after hit, hardly an enemy escaped unhurt.

—*Ṣanʿ al-bint* means the matchlock.

Your hideout: snakes coiled up inside fissures:
Qur'an recital does not countervail dented jaws.
May God unleash against them Hadhrami porcupines
with a taste for munching on the palms' young shoots,[214]
Porcupine after porcupine, and yet another porcupine,
a porcupine digging the base, a porcupine from the side.
Flanked by a male with the monstrous grin of Mshārī,
gruesome hooked incisors inflict grievous wounds.

Mshārī was an old man with long teeth. Yes, Rājī ridicules ʿAdwān's date palms. What did he mean by "Our inheritance from days immemorial?" Rājī was a member of the Dghērāt, a tribe of the ʿAbdah division of Shammar. Rājī refers to the ancestor of the Dghērāt, the son of Yaḥyā. At first, he lived in Ḥāyil. Resentful of indignities he suffered at the hands of his fellow tribesmen, he, ʿAlī, "forcibly entered," *daghar*. Hence the name of the clan, al-Dghērāt: ʿAlī and his children moved to an area in Ajā Mountain. He started out as a laborer whose job it was to fertilize palm trees for the owner of the garden, Ibn Baggār. From that time on, they were known as the Dghērāt. 48.3

They came to al-Bʿayyir with Ibn Baggār. One of them was the daughter of ʿAlī, Salmā, the name that became the battle cry of the Ghyithah. One of the men in those olden days said, "What a gorgeous girl! Such a pity she is the daughter of a worker who fertilizes palm trees." She went to her father, crying. He said, "By God, as true as I am your father, they are going to rue it; they will not live to see the next harvest." When the others had left, he took his pack camel and headed for the highlands of al-Shifā in search of saltpeter, which he found not far from Khaybar, to the right side, I don't know exactly where, and he used it to make gunpowder.[215] He rode back, fetched a quantity of lead from Medina, and melted and cast it to produce bullets. He kept adding to his stock of ammunition until the others returned. He was lying in ambush for 48.4

رصّاص من المدينه ويصبّ من رَحْلَتهم ليا ما جَوا. يوم جَوا وهو يقعد لهم بالحَجا وهو يذبحهم وياخذ نخلهم على مُوجِب هالكلمه.

٥،٤٨ هاه رد عليه عدوان

انا ذوَى العـايـل وانا ابو خـريـّم   مثل الحـَريشا تـذبح اللي يـذوقـه
ياخـيّوني ويش اسوّي بـراجي   وجـه العجوز اللي تـروّك نِشوقه
يـدعي لهن بالنيصـة الحضرميه   ادناة غـصنٍ بالتـبصـّر يعوقه
الله يهـيي لملكك قبسةٍ من جهنم   تضـفي على روس النوابي شروقه
لى صـار ما بُه للنشـا ما عريشـه   ودايم خَفـافٍ بالمـبادي عَذوقه

٦،٤٨ واستعرعْنيق نخل راجي. يَخَبّرونُه هالرجال. الشيخات هذولي سنةٍ من السنين ما اطلعن عقب القصيد هذا صار بهن ظَليع رِدي. ونخْلاته اللي بحيّه مع ربُعه طيّبات. قال ياشاري تمرالشيخات هذولي ابى ابيعُه وابحَضِرمع السويد. شراوه لُه واحْدٍ بمجيدي المجيدي هكالحين لُه قيمه يعني لُه قيمه.

٧،٤٨ نَهَج راجي يم حوّاس التبيناني حوّاس اهيمس وهذاك اجْبَص انت ياراجي اجبص ويقول الصحنين ما يشبعِنُّه. هو بس سهمته هالقصيد. قال ياحوّاس شف الهربيد اللي يقول لي وجه العجوز اللي تروّك نشوقه نَخْلاتُه اللي هو يمدّح كل قبالتهن باعه بريال مير نبي نَقْصِد بُه وابيك تعاوَن ياحوّاس.

٨،٤٨ قال زين. قال

them, and when they had drawn close enough, he opened fire from behind a protective wall, killing them to a man. Thereupon he took possession of their gardens of date palms. This story explains how they acquired their tribal name, "Those who enter by force."

ʿAdwān did not take it lying down and replied: 48.5

I am Abū Ḥzayyim, any aggressor's cure:
mustard oil poison, fatal to the consumer.
Little brother mine, what shall I do with Rājī,
with his wizened face of a granny mixing snorting powders.
He prays for their ruin by a Hadhrami porcupine,
ruthless destroyer of palms' every root and branch.
God strike you with a thunderbolt from Hell,
its flash illuminating sand dunes far and wide.
At his booth, he treats visitors carelessly;
in season, his gifts of dates are laughable.

ʿNēg caught fire and burned down the palm trees of Rājī, as everyone here knows. One year al-Shēkhāt did not carry a lot of fruit and the harvest turned out bad. That happened after these poems had spread. The trees produced a small harvest of unappetizing fruit, while al-Hirbīd's trees at the settlement of his clan, Ḥayyah, were doing well. He invited buyers to come forward: he wanted to sell off the fruit in advance, so that he could return to the company of his fellow tribesmen of al-Swēd. He sold the coming harvest for one *majīdī*. At that time it was a valuable currency, not a trifling sum of money. 48.6

Rājī went to see Ḥawwās al-Tbēnānī. Ḥawwās had suffered the loss of his eyelashes and Rājī had rheumy eyes, messy with white discharge. It is said that he was capable of wolfing down two trays of food and still have appetite for more. He sought help from al-Tbēnānī, a poet who specialized in this kind of verse, saying, "Ḥawwās, did you hear how al-Hirbīd compared my face to that of a wizened granny who busies herself with mixing snorting powders? This is our chance, now that he has sold for one riyal the harvest of those palm trees that he praised so effusively. We should compose some verses about it, and to do so I need your help, Ḥawwās!" 48.7

"Fine," the other said, and recited these verses: 48.8

ياراكبٍ حمرا من الفِطّرَ الفيح عند اللحاوي له سِمَر جِدٍّ او خال
تلفي لعـدوانٍ خـيار الذوايح عوق البدون الى اعرضن كبر الاجمال
قِصَمت وجه الغيد ياخامد الريح بعت القبالة كلها بس بريال

دري عدوان ان التبيناني مساعده. قال ٩،٤٨

ياراكبٍ حمرا تبوج الصحاصيح قطّاعة البيدا غَرَض كل مرسال
تنزيز جمّا لفعت خشمَها الريح او رَبْدانٍ شافت دعاثير الازوال

الريح ريح البارود.

تلفي لراجي يشرخَن بالتماديح لكن ما سوّى سواياك رجّال
يابو كلامٍ مثل قرْط الصلافيح اقضب مكانك لا تعذّر بالاهزال
اجيك باللي مثل نظم المسابيح دومٍ الى احضرت القلم جنك ارسال
من غاويٍ مركاوه بين النحانيح ما قيل بيتٍ عن سنَع حرفهن عال
من شالهن ينقّل على الفطر الفيح مع واحدٍ يَثْنى مقابيل الاجيال

وين هو عدوان هالحين نَقْصِد كلامه.

انا ذْواي مرتّنات الذرانيح وصاعٍ من المطحون حلاب الابلال
اطلاك كبٍّ هم جضعٍ وتنقيح لما يجيك من اشهب النِفر شلال
عند العذارا يسهجنّك سواميح طربيل ما قالن لك البيض خيّال
ولا قيل يرعى بيذراك الشراشيح يا حلّ بين البدو راحل ونزّال
لا عاد صقّارٍ تِذِبّ الشلاويح ولا راميٍ فِرق الظبا عقب مجفال

Rider of a swift, reddish-brown desert crosser,
al-Lḥāwī's stock on father's and mother's side.
Head for ʿAdwān, pick of prodigious butchers,
marksman, nemesis of ibexes bulky as camels.
You've dishonored your trees and cut their faces,
you oaf, selling off their harvest for one riyal![216]

ʿAdwān understood that al-Tbēnānī had lent Rājī a hand. He said in reply: 48.9

Rider of a red-hued camel cleaving sandy vastness:
it burns the miles, dream of messengers in a hurry,
Swift as bounding hornless gazelles, nose in the wind;
or like ostriches startled by distant human shapes.

—The wind: he means the smell of gunpowder.

Go to Rājī, whose laudations tear me to shreds:
your doings are not a real man's comportment;
Prattle, off the mark, haphazard rock-throwing:
stay put, do not protest your indisposition!
Take it! My tight-woven verses come flocking
in well-arraigned strings of beads if I lift the pen,
Assiduous, bent over my spring's relentless gush,
checking that no verse veers off course, goes awry;
Carried by messengers riding fast desert crossers,
verses sown and waiting for future generations.

—Where is ʿAdwān now? And we are still reciting his poetry!

Take your medicine: rattling venomous bullets,
pounded saltpeter drains your insides' sap of life.[217]
Down! Smear that mangy face! Roll and writhe!
Let gray gunpowder make your limbs lame!
Laughingstock, women heap scorn on you:
impotent male, travesty of chivalrous ideals.
You've no inkling how to pasture camel herds,
how to migrate amid the Bedouin hustle and bustle;
Lure falcons by running and waving cloths,
take a marksman's aim at fleeing gazelle herds.

زحـــزيح ياويّا من الربع زحـــزيح   ذيب الصحن بالعيد يا قلّ الاكـّال
جنبّت ملكك كنهن حاجر الشيح   والا العـرايد يبّسن عقب الامحـال
ولِذنا على الشيخات مثل التفافيح   صفـرٍ عراجدهن عن الليف مـيّال
حوشٍ لفضـلي والعـيال المفـاليح   حـاشه من الجال الشمالي ليا الجال
مع وسـط ربعٍ بالمـلاقا ذوابيح   يا جيتهـم من نيّـة الخـير تهـتال
وحوّاس يذكر لي ركـابه مشاويح   نبي نخـمّه بالمخـالب على الفـال
ابو عـــــيونٍ مثـل لون الذنابيح   شـرّي على اللي مثل لونه ليا عـال
الشـايب اللي مثـل جِـردّ المفـاتيح   لا هواشـقٍ خـدِّه ولا يقني الحـال
حـنا عـراضٍ نحسـبه بالتصـافيح   واليوم ما حـالك لابو قـاعدٍ حال

جاوه حوّاس يزحف عاضٍّ بُهـُمه يقول التوبه. ١٠،٤٨

Some help you are, real asset to your kinsmen,
at the tray, gorging on food at plentiful feasts.
I skirted your palms, like a flimsy sagebrush fence,
drought-stricken, brittle as *ʿarad* acacia shrubs.
We'd rather stay among apple-colored Shēkhāt,
yellow racemes graciously curved, heavy with fruit:
Well-watered gardens of Faḍlī and his spirited kin,[218]
our treasured property from north to its other end,
Guarded by warriors, unflinching killers in battle,
amazingly generous in displays of benevolence.
Ḥawwās has the gall to vaunt his tireless mounts:
fair game to us, we'll maul them with our paws.
Watch your eyes, wormy like locust bellies:
woe betide your ilk if you spoil for a fight:
Senile graybeards, worn out like wooden keys,
cheeks colorless, vigor spent, wan, debilitated.
We're not bothered by such trifles; we take them lightly.
Be careful, Abū Ǵāʿid, you're not in great shape.

Ḥawwās paid him a visit. He came as a penitent, on his knees, biting his thumbs with regret. He said to ʿAdwān, "I am so sorry for what I did." 48.10

الخلاف مع صماعين وسعيد اللي سبب الشيخه

١،٤٩ عدوان بينُه وبين صُماعين اوّل لهم سويلفةٍ بْصِفَة المزح ولِمس عدوان هو بْلُه بيت. صماعين من العمران. السبب عدوان لُه نْخَلاتٍ يقال لهن المتالعيات هن هذولن بضلع مْتالِع ضلع هو هذا غربٍ من اجا ومسمّيهن اسامي بنايه بهن نويّر وهدبا وهدلا يعني آه من غلاهن عليه مسمّيهن اسامي بنايه. وله نْخلات اسمهن الشيخات باجا.

٢،٤٩ وتوافقن هكالسنه اطلَعن النخلات كلهن صار طِلْعِهِن جميع كلهن صارن قِبال اجا ومْتالِع يعني كلهن هكالسنه صارن قِبال صار بهن طلِع جَيّد. وهو ما لُه عيال ما عنده الا لُه اناثي ضناوه بنات ولا يقدر يفرّق روحه. قال انا ان حضرت بالمتالعيات غرّيت من الشيخات ومن وناسة السويد بالضلع باجا عند الشيخات ومحاضيرهم ومجالسهم وان حَضرت بالشيخات باجا المتالعيات يُوذَن ويوكّلن ما استفدت منهن لأنهن ما حولهن نخل بس هن بمْتالِع وانا ما استفيد منهن شي لكن انا ما لي الا اقطّع طِلْعِهِن المتالعيات من شان يخالفِن طلع اجا يصيرن هن السنة الثانية يطلعن ويصير القبول لهن يوقِّرِن. وقم على طِلْعِهِن وقطّعه وحطّه تَحَتهن يَبيهن من شان يْفاختِن النخل يِطِلْعِن داير.

His Dispute with Ṣimāʿīn and Sʿēd That Occasioned the al-Shēkhah Poem

Before these events, ʿAdwān had a dustup with Ṣimāʿīn. Initially, the two had engaged in lighthearted banter, but then one verse recited by Ṣimāʿīn rubbed ʿAdwān the wrong way. Ṣimāʿīn was a member of their tribe's ʿUmrān subdivision. Their falling out had to do with the fate that befell ʿAdwān's date palms in al-Mtāliʿiyyāt, his garden in a bottom surrounded by rocky ridges of Mtāliʿ at the western end of the Ajā mountain range. He had given his palms girls' names, such as Nwayyir, Hadbā, and Hadlā, as a token of how much he treasured them: he felt for them as if they were his daughters. He also owned palm trees called al-Shēkhāt in one of the open spaces inside the granite slopes of Ajā Mountain. 49.1

In a certain year, ʿAdwān's palm trees burst into fruit all at the same time. Both of his gardens, Ajā and Mtāliʿ, flowered and produced dates. In addition, their fruit promised to be of excellent quality. ʿAdwān had no sons, only daughters. Therefore, he faced the work alone: there was no way he could divide himself in two and be in both gardens at the same time. He argued: "In al-Mtāliʿiyyāt, I am at a far remove from al-Shēkhāt and will miss out on the good cheer and company of my fellows of the Swēd who live in Ajā, near my al-Shēkhāt palm garden. I won't be able to take part in their social gatherings and lively assemblies. On the other hand, if I take up my abode at al-Shēkhāt, the palms of al-Mtāliʿiyyāt will suffer: their fruit will go to waste and bring me no benefit. (There were no other palm gardens in that area; it was an isolated place.) What's my gain? I have no choice but to cut off the fruits, the date bunches, from the trees at al-Mtāliʿiyyāt. There is no other way to make sure that, going forward, both gardens will not bear fruit at the same time, but in alternate years. Thus, the trees of al-Mtāliʿiyyāt will carry fruit in the year that follows the harvest from al-Shēkhāt: the dates we need to regale our guests with." He matched his words with actions. He lopped off the clusters of fruit and left them lying at the bottom of the trees. It was his intention to delay the harvest until the year after, so that the palm trees would produce dates in alternate years. 49.2

٣،٤٩ يا صماعين صيّاد هكالحين يطرد الصيد ونهج يوقّف بالضلع رِقى يدوّر البدون بالضلع. يوم انه فاض على المتالعيات على نخلات عدوان وزّن بهن وليا هذا طِلعهن مقطّعٍ ومكوّمٍ تحتهن. قال هذا وَكاد انه رجّالٍ يبغض عدوان وانه فدّع بنخلاته. لكن انا ابشوف جرّتُه وشّو. وهو يَهزَع يبي راعي الجِرّه. راح يِقص الاثر الارض تِثر ارضهن بَرْقا تِثر يبين به الاثر. يوم راعى يا هذا اثر عدوان يعرفُه هم اهل نفود يعرفون الاثر. ويا هذا طلع نخلاته هاللي مكوّمٍ تحتهن. وايقن ان هذا مقصد عدوان.

٤،٤٩ وجا يوم جا تِليّة هكالنهار يم هله قالوا لُه الرجال وين الصيد يا صماعين. قال واللّٰه انا اليوم وِقعت بلي بَلْشةٍ وما ني يم الصيد. قالوا ليه. قال يوم جيت وشَعْت هالضلع رقيته والى اسمع لي صياح اناثي اناثٍ يِصِحن وهزَعت عليهن قلت هذولي اما مغيرٍ عليهن سبع والا جايهن شيٍّ مِزمِلهن. يوم طبّيت مع شعيب المتالعيات يا مير ما من اناثي ولا من شين ولا بالشعيب أحد شعيب المتالعيات. قلت هالصياح وين هو. قالن حنا اللي نصيح المتالعيات. يا هو عدوان مسمّيهن اسامي اناثي هدبا وهدلا ونويّر النخلات انت يا عدوان. قلت ليه وش عِلمِكن. قالن شف يا خي طِلْعنا هاللي تحتنا رِزقَنا اللّٰه بهالنعمة وجا قِليل هالبركة وقطّعه وخلانا بَيد لا جانا جراد ياكلنا وبس هو فدّع بنا هالمقرود. راعيت يا واللّٰه مفدّعٍ بهن يوم شفت هذي السالفة رجعت. قالوا طيب وش قلت. يا عدوان بالمجلس قاعد يسمع كلامهم فلكن مُمازح بينهم.

Ṣimāʿīn was a dedicated hunter. He spent much time roaming the Ajā Mountain in search of game. He clambered over the rocks looking for ibex. One day, as he came down toward al-Mtāliʿiyyāt, ʿAdwān's garden, and walked past the trees, he was shocked to discover the cut-off bunches of dates, stacked in heaps under the trees. He said to himself, "Such wanton destruction of the trees can only be the work of a man who harbors a deep grudge against ʿAdwān. Let me follow his traces and find out who is guilty of this dastardly deed." He veered off course and went in another direction, following the tracks that remained clearly visible on the soft ground, a mixture of rock and sand. The traces were easy to follow. But as he looked closer, lo and behold, those prints were the steps of ʿAdwān himself, no two ways about it. Men such as Ṣimāʿīn were past masters at the art of reading tracks, having grown up near the Nafūd Desert. He looked again. These were the fruits of his trees, stacked in big heaps at their feet. It dawned on him that it was the work of ʿAdwān himself, and he became convinced that he had done this on purpose. 49.3

Toward the end of that day, he returned to his folk. His kinsmen asked him, "Haven't you brought us any game, Ṣimāʿīn?" He said, "By God, this time I ran into a problem that scuttled my hunting plans." "Why?" they wanted to know. "When I ascended the ridge, during my climb, I heard screams for help. Female voices—females shouting as if in grave danger. At once, I turned sideways toward where the sound came from, thinking that they were being attacked by predators or frightened for whatever reason. When I had come down to the bottom of the narrow valley, the gully of al-Mtāliʿiyyāt, there were no females to be seen anywhere. There was no one in the gully of al-Mtāliʿiyyāt. I wondered where these anguished cries might have come from. Then I heard their tearful voices: 'It us, we are the ones crying, al-Mtāliʿiyyāt.'—Had not ʿAdwān given his palm trees female names: Hadbā, Hadlā, Nwayyir?—So I said, 'Tell me, what's the matter?' They said, 'Look there, brother, do you not see the fruits lying at our feet? God has bestowed on us these riches, but it was our bad fortune that he cut them off, leaving us denuded of any fruit. Not because the harvest was devoured by swarms of locusts. It was his wretched intention to lay us to waste; he did it on purpose.' By God, I saw it with my own eyes, how he had laid into them and brought them to ruin. As soon as I understood the story and what had happened, I decided to come back home." "Very well," the others said. "Any verses?" ʿAdwān was one of the visitors present in the majlis, listening to what so far had been jocular conversation. 49.4

قال صماعين ابن عمران ٥،٤٩

١ نَهَجت يم الضلع مِقْصادي الصيد   وضاق الحشا من زود همٍّ جرى لي
جيت النواعم شامخات العراجيد   كِلٍّ بِكت فَرْعَه من الطلع خالي
قالت نويّر ياحسايف نِمي الغيد   لِعب بنا بايّام وقت العدال
لا مَن الجراد ولا مَن الله ولا بَيد   قطّعتهن لا يا خبيث العمال

ولا هن بيد يعني انهن ما هن طِلْعِهن ردِي أوانهن ما أطلعن. إيه بعدين ما ادري وش لون يسمّيهن فلانه وفلانه وكل تشكي لُه ببيت مير قال بتالي القصيده

٥ عملت عملٍ ما عْمَلوه الاجاويد   ياحيف ما سَمْتِك سْموت الرجال

٦،٤٩ يقول يا مير يوم قام عدوان من المجلس. أول يضحك ويقول حسيبك الله ربي وربك الله. يوم انه قال هالبيت التالي يا مير يوم قام من عندهم زعلان. يوم انه نهج قالوا السويد ألين انك ياصماعين تراك ازعلت عدوان بْلِك كلمة قلته وانت ما لقّيت له بال ما فطنت لروحك. قال وشّي. قالوا يوم تقول ياحيف ما سمتك سموت الرجال وخَطْرٍ انه يَقْصِد بك لكن اما احتسب انت للقصيد والا سَنْع الرجّال.

٧،٤٩ وهو يقوم عليه يوم جا العصر وهو ينحُره وهو يزوره ويحب راسه. قال والله يابوخزيّم استسمحك انا اخطي نوبٍ جبته مزح هالكلمه والله ما فِطنت له. قال والله ما هي مشكلةٍ علي وكل القصيدة راضي بَه وواردةٍ عَلَي وانا مستحقّه على حسب

Ṣimāʿīn ibn ʿUmrān said: 49.5

While roaming the mountains on a jolly hunt, *1*
I was hit in the stomach by harrowing events:
I stumbled on tall stems, curved branches
crying, robbed of their crowns, shaved bald.
Nwayyir said, "Woe, woe, my shaded fruits!
With malice, we were ill-treated in the high season,
Not by locusts, no act of God, not plain rot:
you hacked them off, you nasty scoundrel."

—They were not laid waste by natural causes. Their fruits were not inferior, nor had they failed to come out. I don't know the poem in its entirety. He calls the trees by their names and makes each of them utter her complaint in a verse. But it is known for certain that this verse is the one that ends the poem.

"No honorable man would commit such an offense: *5*
What shame, your lack of real men's noble poise!"

49.6 No sooner had he finished his declamation than ʿAdwān stood up and left the majlis. Initially, he had put a brave face on it, grinning along with the others and making comments like "God will settle accounts with you" or "My Lord and your Lord is God!" But at the recitation of the last verse, he stood up and walked away, offended and angry. When he had gone, the other men of the Swēd said to him, "What have you done, Ṣimāʿīn? Your words have hurt and angered ʿAdwān! And in his presence at that, as if you couldn't care less about him sitting there. How could you be so insensitive and rude?" "What do you mean? What are you talking about?" he asked. "Your words 'What shame, your lack of real men's noble poise.' Now you run a serious risk of him retaliating with verses of his own. Count on getting a poem in reply or else go and placate the man!"

49.7 That same afternoon, he mustered up his courage and pushed himself to head for ʿAdwān and call on him. He kissed his head and said, "Truly, honest to God, Abū Khzayyim, I ask your forgiveness. Sometimes I go wrong and then I really act stupidly. It was meant as a joke, honestly. I didn't pay sufficient attention to what I was doing." ʿAdwān said, "It is no problem as far as I am concerned. I did not hold anything against the poem and I'd even say that it hit the mark. I deserved it, considering that I cut off the fruit of the palm trees. It is only when you said, 'No honorable man would commit such an offense:

اني قطّعت الطلع ولكن بس يوم تقول ياحيف ما سمتك سموت الرجال يوم تقول ما سمتك سموت الرجال ليه. قال انا جايّك لاوّله واتلاه يابو خزيّم - هو ينجّب بولدٍ لُه اسمه خزيم مات وهو صغير - انا جايّك لاوّله واتلاه ما ني جايّك ابيك تخزّ علَيّ. قال مسامحك جتك ولكن احْرِص لا عاد تعترضن من هذا وبعد. قال ابد ما اعودَك عقب هذي والله ما عاد اتعرّضك.

٨،٤٩ عاد اللي سببّت الشيخة طال عمرك السويد كلهم هكالوقت مع عسّاف الهربيد ابو فِرِح جِدّ خلف هذا اللي بالخبّه. كل السويد يمكن ان الذبيحه تِشْبِعهم هكالوقت ما هي كثيرةٍ الناس. ويدلّهون البل يوم البل ويوم البداوه ويوم القومان ويوم الناس بعادٍ خطاه. يوم حْضَروا وجا الصفري ووقع المطر ويصير اول الحيا على الخِنْفه يم ديرة الشراراية. هكالحين الخنفة كله قوم ما يطِبّونه كود دَحم من الخوف قومان الناس قبل هذا يَمْعَط هذا. قومٍ على الشهب. كل قبيلة تقاوم خَويّته. مير ابن سعود برّده يوم المشنّى يقول

ثَـرّيَه على جاموس والدود والسوس　　وابا الصراير شرّهـه طـير شلوى
ابن سـعود حـدّد الحصن والروس　　الطيّب اخدم والردي صار بلوى

٩،٤٩ هم بهالغوطه بالصفري شمالي موقّق هذا. ويجيهم راعي هكالذلول طرقي قال لهم من الخنفة الى جبه ليا شمالي هالعويد بُه لُه صيفية ما رِعْيَت - يحكي عليهم - والوضيحيات البقر والله انك تخيّر كل قِعْرٍ تجي بُه خمس وعشر وعشرين - يقوله

What shame, your lack of real men's noble poise!' Why should you say that?" He said, "I've come to you because you are completely in the right, Abū Khzayyim." (So named after his son Khzayyim, who died in infancy.) "I take full responsibility for what I did. But I dearly wish to avoid a situation where you'd jump me and ride my back." He said, "It's all right. I will let it pass this time, I promise. But be warned, henceforth be careful never to come across my path again and make me cross!" "Absolutely! From now on, I will refrain from touching you in any way. By God, I am not going to rub up against you a second time."

Now we come to the events that gave rise to his composition of the al-Shēkhah poem, may your life be long. At that time, the leadership of the Swēd rested with ʿAssāf al-Hirbīd, Abū Frēḥ, the grandfather of Khalaf, who currently lives in al-Khibbah. They were a small bunch back then: one sheep was sufficient to feed the entire group. People were few in number at that time. They were fond of pampering their camels; those were the days of camels, Bedouin life, tribal warfare, days when people's strides were long. They led extraordinary lives. The tribe stayed in settled country until the rains arrived in fall. The early rains came to al-Khinfah, an area on the way from here to the land of the Sharārāt tribe. At that time, al-Khinfah was known as a dangerous place, infested with enemies. One would only enter it with a show of force. Back then, tribes stood in adversarial relationships to one another. One tribe would plunder the other. Foes clashing on horseback. Each tribe against the other. Ibn Saʿūd poured cold water on those practices, as the poet al-Mshannā said: 49.8

Fortune smiled on buffaloes, maggots, and worms;
misers behind locked doors beat Shalwā falcons.[219]
Ibn Saʿūd has curbed warhorses and chiefs;
nobles became servants; bastards went on a spree.

When the fall season started, they were in al-Ghūṭah, north of Mōgag. A camel rider arrived, a wayfarer. He told them, "From al-Khinfah to Jubbah, north to al-ʿWēd, the desert pastures of late spring have remained intact and untouched. There is an abundance of wild cows as they are called, oryxes. Take my word for it, by God, in just about every hollow between the sand hills you'll find five, ten, twenty of them," or so the wayfarer claimed. "Therefore, you'd be well advised, ʿAssāf, to head straightaway for those spring meadows! There's plentiful grazing for your herds, and game meat for your children and visitors who flock to you while you're there. So much better than the long journey to 49.9

هالطرقي - وانا ابشير عليك ياعساف انك تَخْر هالصيفية هذي للحلال وصيدٍ لعوايلكم وطرقيّكم اللي يجيكم اشوى من روحتكم تِسفرون يم العراق تهجون يم العراق يوم يجي الحدّار يا مير اكْلٍ نصف حِمْلَه زهاب. هذا صيدٍ يسقّمكم واباعركم تربّع لو هي ديرة خوفٍ شوين لكن انه ربيع وزينة لكم.

١٠،٤٩ وهم لك يسنّدون السويد ويجرّهم طال عمرك من هانا ويحطّون جبة على يمناهم مع هالنفود على اقبالة الوسم. زاعوا يم الخنفة وابْعَدوا ونزلوا الطوِيل الطويل هاللي بْظَهر الجوف يمّ ديار الشرارات. وهم هذولا. يوم جَوا وسْط هالنفود يا مير على قول راعى المطيّه لقوا بُه لَه صيفيّةٍ ما فتّق نورَه ومربّعة الارض. ويضربهم المطر بَه الوسم. يقولون وِقَع عليهم مطر الاول خريف وعِقْبُه وسمي وشتوي وعِقْبُه وقع عليهم مطر السماك. ودلّى يتجَدّد العشب. ويذْعَر لك هالنصيّه ويذعر الحماط ويذعر الخَخم والارض حلوةٍ هكالحين ما وقّف بَه الحديد وحرّثَه قَفر. ويربّعون بالطويل. وكِثْر الربيع وطوّل عليهم ثلاث شهور. وابطوا وغرّقوا وتخبّر البدو وقتهم مع البل ومع طراة البل يوم البل قليلة الوالي.

١١،٤٩ وياخذون طال عمرك ثلاثة اشهر بَه وهم وناسه وطرْبات وتْعلّله. والعيشة وِشّي. لحم الصيد ولبن البل. حاطّينٍ لهم عِنّةٍ بوسط البيوت. وليا روّحت البل ركّدوا بواريدهم على العِنّه جَنْبٍ مع البل يما يصبحون هوسات ورمي يما ينهج الليل ويصبح الصبح. كل شادٍّ محزمه عند نياقه الرجال جَنْبٍ مع البل. الناس قوم هكالوقت.

Iraq. Consider this! If you send a camel train to Iraq, it will consume about half of the supplies on the way back. You're much better off trekking to those meadows: you'll feast on game meat while your camels graze to their hearts' delight. True, at times it may get a bit risky out there. On the other hand, think of the plentiful herbage and the many good things within your grasp."

Accordingly, the Swēd tribe took the route upcountry, may your life be long, keeping Jubbah to their right, along the edge of al-Nafūd. It was in the early days of late fall. They rushed toward al-Khinfah, marching all day long. They put up camp at al-Ṭiwīl, an outcrop at the outer rim of al-Jōf, on the way to the tribal lands of al-Sharārāt and so on. As soon as they came to the middle of al-Nafūd, they saw that everything was exactly as the wayfarer had described. Lush herbage of late spring everywhere. It was as if the flowers had just opened, covering the soil with a carpet of sappy green plants. No sooner had they arrived than the rains of late fall drenched the desert floor again. As we were told, they were blessed with consecutive rains, those of early and late fall. On the heels of these downpours came the winter rains, followed by the rains of Arcturus, the rains of spring. More and more growth of herbage, renewing itself all the time. A marvelous sight, this profusion of fresh green: *nuṣiy* grass, *ḥamāṭ*, *khimkhim*.[220] In those days, the land had retained its lovely original character; it had not yet become worked and plowed with iron tools. Pure virgin land. They pastured their animals at al-Ṭiwīl. The soil was in full flower, and they stayed there for three months. Engrossed in their daily activities, they were loath to depart and tarried. You know how the Bedouin love to consort with their camels and indulge in endless conversations about camels. At that time, camels were a relatively rare commodity. 49.10

They spent no less than three months at that location, enjoying one another's company, in merriment, having endless conversations and spinning yarns. And great food too: game meat and camel milk. At the center of the place where the tents were pitched, they had built a pen made of brushwood. Once the camels had safely returned at dusk, they placed their guns against the enclosure. A detachment of guardsmen was always at the ready with the camels in case of an attack by raiders. They entertained themselves deep into the night with song, dance, and festive firing of guns. Come morning, the men girded themselves up for work with the camels. They'd accompany the camels to pasture as protection against the ubiquitous enemies. They did not visit the markets of al-Jūbah, and Ḥāyil was too far away. The reason they gave for staying put was 49.11

الجوبة لا يجونه وحايل ابعدوا عنه. الكل يقول انا لو اطرش أخاف ان اهلي يوازَون عقبي أبحضر نياقي. وعِنّتهم اكثر عنتهم بقر وضيحيّات والصيد ما لُه عداد وحليب البل قدورٍ عندهم عند العنّه. وعسّاف محتزيهم بعِدْل قَهْوه وبِقيرة تِتِن دخان للفرّيس اللي الى كلٍّ منهم ملا غليونه وعَمّر لِكد على القوم.

١٢،٤٩ بالتالي طرّف الربيع وانهرس العشب. السويد ما عندهم غنم هالحين يا غرّت عن عدوان معُه لُه قطعة شياه والباقية اهل ناقه. قالوا يا صرّم العود مسرى ومصباح وحنا بِدّيارنا. يوم فِطِن عدوان لأن عدوان رجلٍ فِطِين ومَدابرِ الرجال ورجلٍ فطين يوم راعى عدوان يوم من الايام ولّيا مير هذولي النجوم يوم غابن. وليا مير الثريا ليا منّه غابيّه (= غابت) لا ترتجي صيف الا صيف داير. يوم فِطِن يا مير يوم والله غابن النجوم اللي ما بعد غيبة الثريا يا طلعت ابتدا القيض وهم بديار الاجناب. قال وش لون هالحين لو تصير علينا هالمعارك والاكوان وحنا بالشمال وديرتنا يم حايل متى نبي ناصل. هو راعي غنم. يقولون انه فِتِر لُه خِطْوَة صخل قال هذا وين يبي ياصل ديار حايل هاللي هذي خِطْوتُه وكيف يبي يتعلّق البل يا منُه زاعه (= زاعت) والنجوم هاللي غابن. يعني ذونَب الربيع والدنيا كله خوف تصطلي عليهم من يمين وشمال بين ضنا سليمان وبين الروله وبين الشرارايه وبين الحويطايه كل القبايل هكالوقت ناهب ومنهوب.

١٣،٤٩ تضايق عدوان. هو راعي غنم والوقت طرّف وشبْعوا من الربيع وودُّه لو هم يصيرّون قبل يجي وقت الحرمن شان الغنم. وايت ياعدوان قال ياعساف حنا

always the same: "Imagine if I'd leave on a journey; I wouldn't have a quiet moment for fear that my folk would come to harm in my absence. Therefore, I must stay close to my camels and their pen." Most of the space in the enclosure was reserved for hunted oryxes. Game was bountiful. There they also kept a store of large vessels filled with camel milk. ʿAssāf would entertain them from his supplies: coffee and a leather sack stuffed with tobacco. Their cavalrymen filled their pipes and hookahs at his place, lighting up to be ready at a moment's notice to vault onto their horses and charge headlong at the enemy.

Inevitably, time came when the excitement of spring began to wear off and herbage withered. The families of the Swēd did not keep small cattle at their camp; ʿAdwān's flock of sheep was the exception. The others were fast-traveling camel nomads who said, "When twigs become dry and brittle, one night's march and next morning is all we need to be back home." The first to notice the change was ʿAdwān. He was an alert and clever man whose foresight influenced the opinion of others. One day, looking up at the sky, ʿAdwān tracked the stars that were on the descent. As a rule, when the Pleiades are about to set, then that year's season of late spring, and with it the chances of rain, had come to an end. Sometime later, the stars that followed the setting of the Pleiades appeared: an unmistakable sign that the hot season had started. Now they ran the risk of getting mired in the heart of enemy country. What should we do if we are attacked and get caught up in the warfare while we are stuck here, so far north? How long will it take us to reach our tribal land near Ḥāyil? For him, a sheepherder, things looked even more ominous than for the others. He measured a lamb's stride between his outstretched thumb and index finger. How long would it take such a small animal to cover the distance from here to Ḥāyil? How could it keep pace with the hardy camels, especially in the hot season heralded by the disappearance of those stars? Spring season had come to an end. One should reckon with the possibility of attack from any direction. They were exposed to red-hot danger from the enemy on the right and on the left: surrounded by Ḍanā Slēmān, al-Rwalah, al-Sharārāt, al-Ḥwēṭāṭ. In those days, tribes had no choice but to rob or be robbed. 49.12

ʿAdwān began to feel anxious. He was a sheepherder, it was getting late in the season, the animals were well fed from grazing on the grasses of spring. He was strongly of the opinion that they should lose no time in moving to their summer quarters before the arrival of the greatest heat, on account of his sheep. He decided to make his pitch: "Hey, ʿAssāf, the weather is getting hot and you 49.13

ضَربْتنا الصخاني ورعيتوا اللي بُه بركه وحلالكم ما يمشي من الشحم كود يَلَمّ - يحزمون افامه عن الرعي - خلّوكم على ما قال مقام ورَحَلِه لما تاصلون اهلكم لا تجيكم لكم حيّةٍ رقطا تاكلكم وتوخذون وانتم بوسط هالمظمايّه وحنا هالحين جانا خير ما احتزيناوه. يشير على عساف. وسمعهم هكالواحد وقم لك لِزّ لعدوان قال له وراك ياعدوان ما تجهَلهم لهم بقصيده حتى انهم يتفطّنون غَديهم يصيرّون. وقِصَد لُه قصيدة يبي ينهّضهم من شان يصيرّون القصيدة اللي تالي اوجبت الشيخه.

١٤،٤٩ هم الله يسلّمك طَرَّفَت عليهم القهوه والقهوه هكالحين قِليله ما توجد الا عند عساف ولا يشربه من المجلس الا يمكن ثلاث شيبان اربع شيبان ما تِشْرَب هاللون أكثر ما يشربون التِتن الدخان وطرّف عليهم الدخان بعد. عساف يقولون عنده لُه بقيره شنّة جلد داحْيَه ماليَه. يا جا الليل عبّى للرجَال نوبه وقال تيزيكم عاد. يا جا الصبح عبّى لهم كل يعبّي له الشرّاب منهم ومشوا مع البل. قال عدوان ياجماعة الخير انا اليوم يالربع شفت لي لي علامةٍ انتهى الصيف والنجوم وَقَعَن واليوم يالربع دوّروا الامواه تَرُو يا منّه سَقِطن النجوم ما عندنا الا الما وهذا القيض ابا العيدان.

١٥،٤٩ يقول عدوان

١ زِعَـنا من الديـرة شمـالٍ بتغـريب   وصارت بِنا عن سوق حايل مناحي
يمـا ارْتِجَـنا بيـنحور الاجـانيب   وقِـمنا نـزوح الصيد بالارتمـاح
يمـا حـدينـا بالطعوس المـراقيب   يوم ان كـلٍّ بالامـان اسـتراح

have pastured to your heart's content. Your animals have grown so fat they can hardly walk: you'd have to strap their mouths, make it impossible for them to graze. Let it be, now! Let's travel in leisurely stages till we reach our folk back home. Be wary of attacks, of the bite of spotted vipers, of being despoiled of all possessions, stranded and helpless in the midst of this waterless desert! So far, we have remained safe and well. We've been fortunate and have raked in a plethora of good things." With such arguments, he sought to convince ʿAssāf, offering him friendly counsel. Someone overheard what he said, then sidled up to him and said, "Why don't you show them, ʿAdwān? Compose a poem on how stupid they'd be to stay here any longer. Perhaps that way you'd bring it home to them that they'd be well advised to return to their summer quarters." He accordingly composed a poem prompting them to go home. This poem set in motion the train of events that led to the al-Shēkhah poem.

May God keep you safe, their supply of coffee was running out. Back then, coffee was a rare commodity. ʿAssāf was the sole person to carry coffee beans with him and the only guests in his majlis to be served coffee were perhaps three or four senior men. It was not served regularly, not as a matter of course. Instead, they'd smoke. But tobacco was also running out. The story goes that ʿAssāf kept a tobacco sack with him: a leather bag, a skin stuffed full of tobacco. In the evening, he'd sometimes allow his visitors to fill their pipes and light up. He'd say, "Here, this amount will do for you!" Likewise in the morning. The smokers would fill their pipes and light up before setting out to pasture with their camels. ʿAdwān said, "Worthy fellows, listen! This morning I saw an unmistakable sign that late spring has come to an end. The stars have set, fellows: it's time to turn back to our water wells. Everyone knows that if the stars have disappeared there is no choice but to stay in the vicinity of water wells. This great heat we experience now heralds the end of pasture: dry twigs and withered stalks, that's all there is." 49.14

ʿAdwān said: 49.15

We surged from home, trekking to the north, *1*
many stages removed from Ḥāyil's markets.
We thrust ourselves deep into enemy lands,
set game bounding from inner desert retreats.
We sent our watchmen to the top of dunes
while others rested in peace and calm;

بايسـر مكيحيـلٍ رعيـنا لغـايبب   وفِـرسٍ تجضّـع بالسهـال السمـاح
بديرة بني يكلب وكـلاب وكليب   بين البـيات وبين خوف الصـباح
يَرعن بنا من بين حَمْقَى الاجانيب   تسعـين ليـله ما رمينا السـلاح
ربّع بنا عسّـاف درب النواهـيب   قـفْـرٍ تغـذّيـه الغشـين الرواح
ربّع بنا بـذِرّ الرجـال المـراعيب   يوم الخطـر من يم كـل النواحي
والتـتن قـل وعـذّبوه الشواريب   ورعـنا لابو عوينـان مثـل الطياحي

ابو عوينان عساف الهربيد امير العرب. يلبّقونه على ولده فريح يسمّونه عوينان يقولون مجيوب على عوينة الكلبة خبرا هي هذي بالمِسّمى. الطياح البل اللي ميلاف ما تعقل بلا عقال اللي ما تروح لو تقطّعه.

مودع عصيف الشاوري كنه السيب   وبـرَيّـةٍ ريحـه على الجمـر فـاح
ما كنـه الا العـيلمي مـدْهـَل النيب   لى نشّت الغدران هي والضحـاح
ياخو شقـا راع الاناثي مـغـاريب   زَلّ الربـيع وفـات وقت الصـلاح

اخو شقا عسّاف. الجوزا والثريا والشعرى هذولي الاناثي. إلى غابن خلص الربيع ودخل القيض.

ياميـر دون ذيارنا يتـلف الذيب   قولوا لونـدات الحـريـم الرواح
شيلوا على العتلات هن والمصاعيب   مثل الصـديـر من المقور القـراح

يوم قصَد هذي عليهم قال عساف تروه صاقّ (= صادق) عدوان - يقوله ١٦،٤٩
امير العرب - تَرُوه صاقّ عدوان هالحين خلص الربيع وخلص الصيف ما بقى الا

We pastured to the left of Mkēḥīl at Laghābīb—
  rolling plains where *firs* plants stir in the wind,
Tribal lands of Banū Yaklab and Klāb and Klēb,
  fearful of nightly assault and morning raids,
Camels surrounded by stiff-necked strangers:
  ninety nights we did not lay down our arms;
ʿAssāf led us over robbers' highways to pastures,
  virgin meadows fed by night-traveling clouds.
Let us graze on the lands of awesome fighters
  where danger lurks in every crag and crevice.
Our tobacco dwindled, went up in smoke,
  as we galloped time and again to Abū ʿWēnān:

—Abū ʿWēnān is ʿAssāf al-Hirbīd, the chief of those people, so named after his son Frēḥ, whose nickname was ʿWēnān because he was born at ʿWēnat al-Kalbah, a depression where rainwater gathers, or so it is said. *Aṭ-ṭiyāḥ* are sweet-tempered camels that do not need to be restrained by hobbling them: they won't run off even if they are treated roughly.

Puffs like misty banks or distant coastlines,
  mingled with wafts of coffee boiled on embers.
He is a gushing well, the camels' favorite haunt:
  when desert pools run dry, water is scarce.
Shigā's brother! See, the Three Females have set:[221]
  spring gone, no green plants to fatten our herds.

—The brother of Shigā is ʿAssāf. Gemini, the Pleiades, and Sirius are called "the females." When they set, spring has come to an end and the season of great heat begins.

Chief! Wolves roam along our homebound trek;
  tell our hip-swaying ladies: "Break up and pack!
Load the camels, well-trained, wayward ones;
  file out like camels watered at a rock-dug well!"

When he had come to the end of his recitation, ʿAssāf said, "ʿAdwān is right, 49.16
absolutely right. Spring is over. Even early summer has come to an end. The hot days of midsummer are upon us. And look, there we are, lingering in this

القيض وانتم بهالمضماة بالنفود. تكلم عليه سْعَيد سويدي ابن عم له سعيد الوعيلي راعي اباعر وودُّه بالصلاح يبطي وقال له قال ياشيخ اتركه هذا تَتَّانٍ قِضى عنه التتن ويبي ينهج يدوّر التتن وَلّ ياعدوان ياشين لا تزرب السويد عن تالي ربيعهم تَرْكل قصّاد بامر الله يصير زاروبه خلّنا نرعى من هالنعمة هذي ياشين لا تَزْرِبْنا عن هالفِرْس وهالضمران وهالعشب. قال ادخل على الله ياسعيد لا ما هو كل قصاد زاروبه خِص ولا تِعم.

١٧،٤٩ والى سعيد وصماعين متراكين قال وش تقول ياصماعين جَلي ما هو كل قصاد زاروبه. ياميرصماعين قصاد وذل لو قال لا ماكل قصاد زاروبه ان سعيد يقول على حسب انك انت قصاد ونسي عاد السالفة الاوله اللي بينه وبين عدوان الممازح اللي بينهم. قال بلى هو صادق سعيد اشهد بالله ان كل قصادٍ زاروبه. ترادّوا بينهم واحْدٍ شهد لواحد.

١٨،٤٩ قال هالحين الاشراف قواصيد والهلالات قواصيد وشيخان شمر وشيخان عنزه وشيخان عتيبه وشيخان مطير وما خَلِطَه من سَمّو القبايل كله شيخان فِرّس كُرما قواصيد. قال عدوان انا لي الله عن هالعرب اللي معهم أنت ياسعيد وانت ياصماعين. والى سعيد يقولون فارس قصاد بس انه بخيلٍ بخل والا فارسٍ قصاد. والله زعل عدوان. غِمِضُه انه قال كل قصاد زاروبه. عاد يوم هو طال عمرك يلقطُهم عدوان

صماعين ما سَمّتُه سموت الاجاويد   وسْعَيد ما راجوا عليه الرجـال

سرح عدوان هكاليوم ويوم جا الليل وهو يهضل يا والله يشوفون انه طَنْيان.

waterless desert of the Nafūd sands." His arguments were rebutted by Sʿēd, one of the Swēd, a relative of his. Sʿēd al-Wʿēlī was a camel nomad bent on staying there as long as possible with the aim of fattening his camels to the utmost. He said, "Listen, Shaykh, forget about him! The guy is an addict who has run out of tobacco and is angling for a way to leave in search of his stuff. Beat it, ʿAdwān, you wretch! Stop scheming to scare the Swēd away from their enjoyment of this last stage of spring! That's how it is—God has ordained that every poet should be a cowardly babbler. Leave us alone to do as we like and to pasture at leisure on these wonderful blessings. Shame on you! Do not scare us away from the *firs* and *ḍimrān* and other herbage!" "Seek refuge with God, Sʿēd!" ʿAdwān exclaimed. "No, it is not true that every poet is a poltroon. Be specific, and do not include all poets under one heading."

During that session, Sʿēd and Ṣimāʿīn shared a camel saddle, each leaning against one side of it. Turning aside, Sʿēd said, "What do you think, Ṣimāʿīn? Isn't it true that every poet is a coward?" Now, Ṣimāʿīn was also a poet. He was afraid that if he contradicted Sʿēd by denying that every poet is a coward, he'd shoot back that he would say so because he was a poet himself. He had forgotten about his earlier dustup with ʿAdwān, the teasing that degenerated into a quarrel between them. He said, "No two ways about it. Sʿēd is right; what he says is true. God is my witness: I agree with him when he says that every poet is a coward." They colluded against ʿAdwān, each of them affirming that the other spoke the truth. 49.17

"How come then," he argued, "that the Sharifs were poets; the Banū Hilāl were poets; the shaykhs of Shammar were poets; the shaykhs of ʿAnazah, ʿTēbah, Mṭēr, the remainder of the tribes. Each of those chivalrous and generous shaykhs was a poet as well." ʿAdwān concluded: "I turn toward God and away from these folks with you, Sʿēd, and you too, Ṣimāʿīn." Sʿēd was known as a brave fellow and poet, but also a niggard of the worst kind. And yet, a stalwart man and also a poet. Really, ʿAdwān was furious. It cut him to the quick to be told that every poet is a coward. But, may your life be long, he did get back at them with a stinging reply: 49.18

Ṣimāʿīn's conduct lacks a real man's poise;
Sʿēd's hearth lies fallow, shunned by visitors.

ʿAdwān walked out on the circle of men. In the evening, he came ambling back, ponderous and looking haggard. By God, everyone understood at

يا مار يوم جا بصدر المجلس ويبرك مثل بروك الجمل وهو يزحر. قال هو اللي قال هالكلمة ياويلنا ياصماعين من هالزحرة ان وراه شين.

ويجيب عدوان الشيخه ١٩،٤٩

المجلس اللي بُه صماعين وسعيد   ينعاف لو قِربه على الكبد غالي
صماعين ما سَمّتُه سموت الاجاويد   وسعيد ما راجوا عليه الرجال

بخيل ما يجونه الرجال.

غنيّ لك الضمران والفِرس ياسعيد   مجعول ما لحميض الاطعاس والي
ياسعيد حيكك بُه مْغير ومراديد   تُوقر من الحكي الرخيص الجمال
حكيٍ على اكناف العذارى مناقيد   ما يْطيّب الصبيان كود الفعال
ياسعيد لو تِضرَب على دارة الديد   بزرقا تِسِلّ الروح بالاشتعال
بديار فَطْمات البقر مِغتِر الصيد   ما عندك اللي عن حوالك يسال
انا بلاي مزهّبين البواريد   اللي لهم ياسعيد قول وفعال
اخاف من قومٍ تْسوّي براريد   ترزمي على روس النِدَف له ظلال

براريد جوّادَ.

ما بين شمطان اللحي والاواليد   نضّة عيال فوق مثل السيال
الغلمة اللي ينقلون البواريد   يِفقَد على مركاضهم كل غالي
ركضاتهم ياسعيد ما بَه تصاديد   ذباحة الطيب نهار الكتال

once that he was fuming with rage. He made his way to the head of the majlis and kneeled, coming down with a thud, the way a big male camel sinks to its knees, and he groaned, breathing heavily. Someone muttered under his breath, "This bodes ill for us, Ṣimāʿīn; these groans are a harbinger of evil things to come."

ʿAdwān launched into delivery of the al-Shēkhah poem. 49.19

A majlis attended by Ṣimāʿīn and Sʿēd
  is loathsome, though I cherish the company.
Ṣimāʿīn's conduct lacks a real man's poise;
  Sʿēd's hearth lies fallow, shunned by visitors.

—He is a miser who receives no visitors.

Growth of *ḍimrān* and *firs* enticed you, Sʿēd—
  may all salty plants of the dunes go to hell!
Attacking, Sʿēd, your words charge and turn,
  though they carry camel loads of cheap crap:
Girls hear your words: aren't you ashamed?
  Young men should impress with noble deeds.
Sʿēd, imagine you're hit right in the nipple
  by a spear: a sharp flash, your body lies lame,
In pristine land roamed by wild cows and game:
  not a soul to ask about your fate, or care.
I stand in awe of fighters with loaded firearms,
  warriors as truthful in deeds as in words, Sʿēd.
I fear prowling enemies, fresh traces left in sand,
  sudden shadows beyond the dune ridges,

—*Barārīd* are tracks left in the sand.

Grizzled veterans, swift-footed youngsters,
  pick of camel riders, sturdy as acacias;
Valiant men, guns slung on the shoulders,
  littering fields with bodies of men dearly missed,
With the irresistible surge of their charge, Sʿēd:
  fine noblemen massacred on the day of battle;

ياما ايتموا من عيّلٍ يرضع الديد   هذي عوايد مبعدين المِدالي
ذرّب جوابك يافتى الجود ياسعيد   عن قولةٍ ثاري سعيد استزال
عميت بالساية جميع القواصيد   ما قلت بالشعار طامن وعالي
عَمّيت نمر والمهادي وابا زيد   عِزّ الظعن حبس الكمين الهلالي
وعرار وعميرٍ هل الكود والكيد   مخَلين سروج الخيل وايّا دوالي
والاشمل اللي من مناه الاضاديد   ومطلق مطبّق بالغدير الزلال
وصَعَب من الصيداد سقم الاضاديد   وعبدالله المسطور فِرز العيال
وشايع مجفّل بالفلاة المفاريد   وجارد مْلَقّي بالشخيل الجلال
وحتى الشريف اللي يقولون ياسعيد   وسعودٍ ابن سعود راعى العمال
ومشعان والطيار كنعان وعبيد   وعنتر يا من مْعَدّل الشيل مال
ومغير ابن غازي ونومان ياسعيد   زبْن الحشور ليا اعتلاه الجفال
والعسكري ومْصيخ وهْدَيب ورْشَيد   وحْسَين حمّاي الركاب التوالي
وجمل وابن حثلين والفغم وفهيد   وساجر مْسوّي للهجين النعال
وجْديع خيّال السمان المِصاعيد   مُودِع مع الدِغثور مثل العزال
وحطّابٍ اللي بالصحن ينفض الغيد   وبريكٍ محَيّي بالركاب الهزال
وجْرَيسٍ اللي كرْمته كنه العيد   وحاتم بعد مِعطى العطايا الجزال
وابن دعيجا ربعته كنها الحَيد   وابن سمَير اللي بقرن الشمال
رمَيزان هو والعرْفجي ذاك ابو زيد   وبرْجَس دَلال مْعبّسات الشمال

A trail of suckling orphans left in their wake:
debris scattered by massive far-reaching blows.
You're not so bad, Sʿēd, just refine your words:
avoid speech, Sʿēd, that's bound to be your undoing.
You've poked your fingers in all poets' eyes,
indiscriminately lumping good with the bad.
You've defamed Nimr, al-Mhādī, and Abū Zayd,
the Hilālī, the caravan's pride, steadfast in ambush.
Also, ʿRār and ʿMēr, men strong and crafty,
heavy hitters whose thrusts unsaddle foes;
Al-Ashmal, who cherishes his many opponents;
Miṭlag plunging into pools freshly filled by rain;
Ṣaʿab of Shammar's Ṣdēd, the enemies' bane;
ʿAbdallah, a raging beast, a linchpin in battle.
Shāyiʿ, putting young camels through their paces;
Jārid racing on mighty spirited steeds;
Even the Sharif they rhapsodize, Sʿēd;
Saʿūd ibn Saʿūd, accomplisher of major feats.
Don't forget Mishʿān, al-Ṭayyār, and ʿBēd;
ʿAntar, who restores balance to sliding loads;
Also, Mghīr ibn Ghāzī and Nōmān, Sʿēd,
rampart of troops gripped by panic and fear;
Or al-ʿAskarī, Mṣīkh, Hdēb, and Rshēd;
Ḥsēn, whose onslaught secures the troops' rear.
Remember Jimal, Ibn Ḥithlēn, al-Fighm, Fhēd;
Sājir, patching up his camels' bleeding soles.[222]
Jdēʿ, guardian knight of fat camels in milk,
when cavalry charges cut deep into sands.
Ḥaṭṭāb, serving layers of dates on his trays;
Brēk, who revives worn, emaciated mounts;
Jrēs, his generosity extravagant like a feast;
Ḥātim, his irresistible urge to give away all;
Ibn Dʿējā, rampart as a sheer cliff of rock;
Ibn Smēr in his corner far to our north;
Rmēzān, al-ʿArfajī, and famous Abū Zayd;
Barjas, fond of camels with speckled udders.

عشرين مع عشرين لا انْقص ولا ازيد   وافين من غير القِصيد الفَعال
ثنواي انا ياسعيد دون الاجاويد   هل المناسف مِتْعِبين الدلال
اللي لهم ياسعيد صِدْرٍ وتوريد   وفَهْقٍ وتقليطٍ وقول وفعال
حتّى انت ما بك عن ربوعك مِقافيد   وانا تَرَن مثلك على قدّ حالي
حنا عباةٍ ما باباطه لواكيد   ولا زاد حنا بالدروج العوالي

Twenty and another twenty, no less, no more:
    masterful poets, noble achievers one and all.
In my admiration, Sʿēd, for fine gentlemen,
    tireless hosts of roasts, forever pouring coffee,
O Sʿēd, tough men, forever coming and going:
    men who take and give, both words and deeds.[223]
Even you aren't the worst of your kinsmen;
    like you, I'm not less than my folk either.
We are as sound as flawless woven cloaks,
    but without pretensions of higher ranks.

عجلان ابن رمال

ʿAjlān ibn Rmāl

مقاصده مع خلف الاذن

١٫٥٠ عجلان ابن برغش ابن رمال رجال راعي شَور وراعي مجلس وجليس شيوخ وقصاد وراعي بيت ومَنْصى والى منهم بَلْشَوا بالراي نحروه ياخذون رايُه. وعقادات يعني فاخرة بالحيل لا ما تعَيقد وهو ما يبيَه بْغَيان ما يبيه. قاصر خلف الاذن ابن شعلان يوم خلف نازلٍ بخشم حَذْله وجاهم الثلج. بعد مِدّه جاك عجلان يبي يرحل عن خلف يبي يستقبل يم ديرة شمر. قال خلف ابد والله ما تِشدِ والله ما تشد نبيك عندنا ونبي الشيوخ ييكلون لك ويخَرْجونك. عَنْوُه الشعلان يوم بِلش عجلان. قال لخلف اقول انهج رِدْ هالخبرا اللي شمال مناكان عليه صَلاح نبي نرعى نبي نرحل باكر يَمّه. وايتك يا خلف وانحر الخبرا رَوّاد.

٢٫٥٠ جا عجلان قال للحريم اشلن. واشِلِن وهن يكتّن ويحدّدون الفرس وعجلان قاعد ببيت خلف. يوم تَعَدّى عند راعيات العَلْيَا هكالخبز انت ياعجلان وانحر مِطَبّ هلُه يامير بس الفرس محدّده واركبه وايتك منحاش. شادّينٍ هله شَرّقوا. هم بلهُم فيضة بينهم حَزيم ولا دَرّين بهم حريم خلف يوم شدّوا. جا خلف مروّح وضرب على بيت عجلان يامير بس الغربان على المراح. وين عجلان. قالن والله ثار منا هالظهر.

His Exchange of Poems with Khalaf al-Idhn

ʿAjlān ibn Barghash ibn Rmāl was a shrewd, opinionated man, a conversationalist in the majlis, someone whom shaykhs liked to have around them, and a poet who also entertained at his own tent. If people were at a loss how to handle a certain affair, they'd ask for his opinion and advice. Leadership of spectacular raiding expeditions? No, he was not much of a fighting man, nor someone to command bands of robbers. He did not aspire to such distinctions, nor did he covet rich spoils. He had put up camp as a neighbor under the protection of Khalaf al-Idhn ibn Shaʿlān, who sojourned at Khashm Ḥadlah. The weather was freezing cold: they had snow and ice. After a while, ʿAjlān wished to depart from Khalaf's place and proceed toward the tribal lands of Shammar. "No!" said Khalaf. "No way I will let you go. You must stay with us. We'll make sure that the shaykhs take care of your household's necessities and more, including money." He meant the shaykhs of the Shaʿlān. ʿAjlān felt trapped. He said to Khalaf, "Well, how about you go to check out that large rain pool to our north, to see if it would be any good for us to graze our animals there. If it is, we can move to that place tomorrow." At his suggestion, Khalaf rode toward the rain pool to reconnoiter the terrain. 50.1

As soon as he had gone, ʿAjlān called to his womenfolk: "Hurry up! Load the pack camels as fast as you can!" At his orders, they started rushing to and fro, and brought his mare and shackled it while ʿAjlān waited and rested in Khalaf's tent. He ate a lunch of bread brought by Khalaf's female household, "Ladies of al-ʿAlyā," a female name given to the camel herds of the Shaʿlān. Then he returned to his own camp. The mare stood at the ready, shackled in iron. He jumped into the saddle and raced away. He fled. The folks of his household made off, marching to the east. Their campsite had been in a dip in the terrain—a low hill separated the two camps. The womenfolk of Khalaf's camp did not see them pulling out. On his way home, Khalaf first went to look for the tent of ʿAjlān, but all he found were crows hopping around on the deserted abode. Where was ʿAjlān? The women of his household told him that ʿAjlān had left after lunch at noon. "But I found no one at their camels' resting places," he said. Sometime 50.2

قال ما بالمراح احد. عِقبَه خلف عانق الشعلان ويرحلون وينزلون على الهزيم اللي ورا قريات الملح.

٣،٥٠ يوم نزلوا عليهن جَوا هكالركب ومَرّوا على خلف الاذن وذُكَروا له ان عشيره عجلان نازل الدهيمي. ويقومون لك يتقاصدون هو واياوه يتزاورون بالقصيد. قوموا ياهكالربع يتخانقون واحد يقول ذلول خلف اطيب وهذاك يقول قعود عجلان اسبق. آه هاللون. قال خلف الاذن تراهنوا يالروله. قالوا من يفلج لنا. قال هن يجِنكم.

٤،٥٠ يقول خلف

يا راكبٍ حمـرا عليهـا السليمي　　مِنخَـرْعَةٍ من حين طيحـة حواره

السليمي وسم بني عطيه.

. . . .　　تلقى العـتاري حاشياتٍ عَـذاره
خَطِـرٍ عليهـا داخشه له ظليـمِ　　مـير ان اهلها حافظـينٍ عَشاره
الصبح كن ظَـلالها له جريـمِ　　والعصـر كن ينَهَّشـنه سعـاره
تِمِـدّ من الثايه وِتمّسى الدهيـمي　　ويجذبك شيخ بالعشا ضوح ناره

الدهيمي نبا طويل به حجر وتحتيّه ابرق بحَدّ الدمث من الحجر.

شيخ ولد شيخ قـديمٍ فْهيـم　　أمـا يمـين الخـرّ والا يســاره

الخرّ شعيب من العراق الى النفود هاللي يقولون قِبْليّه جَمِر – شجر الغضا – وشماليّه تَمِر – بالعراق.

ولو أن رحّـالٍ رِجَـع للمـقيـم　　انطَيت ما حاشت يِميـني بْشاره

later, Khalaf rejoined the other tribesmen of al-Shaʿlān. They traveled together as one group and set up camp at al-Hzēm, beyond Grayyāt al-Milḥ.

During their sojourn there, a group of camel riders called on Khalaf al-Idhn and mentioned to him that his friend ʿAjlān was staying at al-Dhēmī. That news set off an exchange of poems. They visited one another, so to speak, by poem. His fellow tribesmen bickered among themselves: one said Khalaf's riding camel was the better mount; the other claimed it was outpaced by the male riding camel of ʿAjlān. They indulged in that kind of squabbling. Khalaf al-Idhn called to them: "Place your bets, all of you, Rwalah!" "Who will be our arbiter?" they asked. "Don't worry," he said, "they are coming to you and then you'll be able to make your own judgment." 50.3

Khalaf said: 50.4

Rider of a red-hued camel, branded al-Slēmī,
skittish ever since she gave birth to her calf;

—Al-Slēmī is the brand mark of Binī ʿAṭiyyah.

[. . .]
massive neck muscles stretch the halter's cord.
It's not far-fetched, a male ostrich might impregnate her,
but for custodians of her stud's sperm: they know.[224]
Early morning, a fight with her shadow, life or death;
in the afternoon, a mad rush as if bitten by rabid dogs,
From al-Thāyah reaching al-Dhēmī before dark,
drawn by a shaykh's welcoming fire and supper;

—Al-Dhēmī is a prominent rocky elevation, mixed with sand at its bottom, at the border of the soft, sandy terrain and the stony desert.

Shaykh, son of shaykh, high-born, sharp-witted;
perhaps to the right of al-Khirr, or else the left.

—Al-Khirr is a dry watercourse that runs from Iraq to al-Nafūd. People refer to its southern end as "glowing embers," meaning *ghaḍāh* bushes, which make excellent firewood, and to its north as "dates"; that is, the date palms of Iraq.

If, after wanderings, he'd settle down with me,
I'd give my all as reward for such glad tidings.

رَدّ عجلان على خلف ٥،٥٠

يا راكبٍ حمرا عليها الهتَيمي   حطّ القَطيمي فوق ساقه واداره
حمـرا تِضيم الدّوّ ما تِسْتضيمِ   حـمرا ودمثٍ للعقَيـلي فِقـاره
مِشّهاه من عذفا الى ام الصريم   ومـرباعـه اللّبّـه تـرمّس قراره
عليـه غـــلامٍ بالدلالة فـهيم   الصبح حِطّ رْعون كبدٍ يسـاره
مـدّت من المركوز حين الجهيم   وتَخَـمّش الثايه بتـالي نهـاره

الثايات قويراتٍ يم الحماد.

تِلفي لصيّاد الشيوخ العـديمِ   يا ضيّعت شِقّ العشـايـر حْواره
عوق العديم ولا يهاب الغـريـم   كم فـارسٍ أهفاوه ما وْخذ بثـاره
اللي قصيره كـل يومٍ حشيـم   ولا قيل ينحى زملهـم عن مـداره
وان كان جا المشتى ليالى الصريـمِ   ذبّاح نابيـة القـرا من فـقــاره
يا خَمّ باليمْنى نْصاب القـديمي   قَلّب حدق عينه غَشاها حَمـاره
الضيـف عنده يحنـان النعيـمِ   ذبّاح نابيــة القـرا من بْكـاره
منهـم نشوم لطير شلوى القديـم   اللي يقـدِّم للمـعـادي بغـاره
قبٍّ لهن بالجـــر الاول رهيـم   عليـهن اللي يـدحمون السـماره
عـيال الشيوخ منوّخين الخصيـم   يـزين طبعه عقب زايـد سطـاره

٦،٥٠ جاراهم خلف ابو زويد حمرا تبرى لهم بها القصيدة كَزّه لصطام ابن شعلان.

ʿAjlān replied to Khalaf: 50.5

Rider of a red-hued camel branded al-Htēmī,[225]
fasten a small saddle on its back, let it run,
Punishing ground, not the other way around.
Reddish brown, soft-backed and comfortable,
Grazed from ʿAdhfā to Umm al-Ṣirīm in winter,
browsing al-Labbah's luxuriant green in spring,
Mounted by a consummate young desert pilot:
come morning, to his left he skirts the bluffs of Kabd.
Departing from al-Markūz in dark before dawn,
she brushes up to al-Thāyah at the end of day,

—Al-Thāyāt are small, flat-topped elevations in the hard plains of al-Ḥamād.

To reach the intrepid hunter of shaykhs
in melees as camel mothers lose their calves;[226]
Nemesis of the fearless, dispatcher of avengers:
no vengeance was taken for knights he slayed.
He enthrones neighbors on thrones of respect:
never does a pack camel of theirs go missing.
In winter evenings bleak with severest cold,
he butchers his fattest high-humped camels.
Beware if his fingers grip his dagger's hilt,
bloodshot eyes roll in the sockets, terrifying!
His guest basks in the comforts of Paradise,
savors roasts from young she-camels' humps.
He is my pride, a famed Shalwā falcon of old,
bold in the frontline attacks on his adversaries.
On broad-chested mares, whinnying at dawn,
they plunge into darkness thick with eerie shapes;
Sons of shaykhs, who force foes into close combat;
once the raging ire subsides, they make for gentlest company.

Lured by the contest, Khalaf Abū Zwayyid joined the fray with a poem he sent to Ṣaṭṭām ibn Shaʿlān: 50.6

يا راكبٍ حمرا كثيرة لحَيمِ   كن وْبَـرَتها غـاشْيَتَهْـا شِقـاره
حصّا وِبِر مِقْدَم بِدَن عنق ريم   يَنْبي بْحَدري ساقها تقل فـاره
تِمـدّ من لَوقه وِتمّسى الهـزيمِ   وتلفي لبـيتٍ نابيٍ تِقّـل قـاره
عشـاك رِزٍّ مع كثير اللقيمي   وايدام سـمنٍ سايحٍ فوق طـاره
تِلْقى العظـام بْرِفّتـه كالهشيمِ   يعيش عنـده من يدور النقـاره
شيخٍ ولد شيخٍ قـديمٍ فهيمِ   فَـرّك لواليب البواشـا واداره

Rider of a brownish-red camel, well-fed, 1
wool covered with chestnut-colored shine,
Short-haired, high in front, gazelle-necked;
leg muscle: a mouse running up and down.[227]
Set out from Lōgah, at dusk reach al-Hzēm,
tents soaring up like a flat mountain's tops;
Supper: rice, crushed wheat heaped on trays,
dripping with drawn butter, poured unstintingly;
Bones scattered around like torrents' debris: 5
indigent scavengers' favorite abode and haunt.
Shaykh, son of shaykhs of old noble stock:
Ottoman pashas, hard as nails, are putty in his hands.

مقاصده مع مطير ابن ختلان

١،٥١ الرمال هكالحين يرحلون ولا يوم الا هم شايفين العدو والعدو فاكّين روحهم وهم فاكّين روحهم لكن يتشاوفون بطعوس هالفلاة. وعجلان اجلَد بالقرايا بهذا بام القلبان. وليا يركي على مطير ابن ختلان من الرمال الختلان من عيال عميره. يوم فطنوا ويا مير هكالصّلبي جايهم هاه من اين يا. قال والله من الجبل. قال ما عَيَّنْت نياق عجلان. قال والله نياق عجلان اللّقّحات قاضْبات روحهن والعشايرهن وعيالهن أشوف بهن آه . . . وش نَوحهن. قال ما اودعوهن حِمّاي ابن رشيد يربّعن كل يوم يْصاح عليهن والبل يا صِيح عليه ما تربّع بالخَضار. ياحلالاة يانياق عجلان برّاقات ودلاقات نبي نرازّ بهن العِدْوان.

٢،٥١ ويرسل له مطير ابن ختلان.

راكبٍ من فوق طِـلْق اليمينِ يشـدى ظليمٍ جفّله حِسّ الاوناس
وليـا انهـزم ما تلحـقـه مـارتينِ من العبـد والعـبدة يعَشّي بالاطعـاس

مخار البِرّيت العبد والعبده ورا البريت هنا والاطعاس طعاس قنا وام القِلْبان.

يِلْفي علـى عجـلان ذيب الِكمينِ بيـرَبْعَتـه تَلْقَى التـعاليل جِـلاّس
مـرباعنا وادى المـرا من يمـين نجني به الفِقْعان والعِشب مِحْتاس
وثِغْبان يَـرْهَجِـهن قَـراع الحَنين من غِرّ مِـزْنٍ روّحن قبل الادمـاس

Exchange of Verses with Mṭēr ibn Khatlān

The tribe of al-Rmāl wandered through the desert. Every day, silhouettes of enemy fighters were seen observing them from afar. Still, they would stay away from each other and avoid a confrontation. They kept a close watch in these sand dunes. ʿAjlān was not among them. He had encamped for a long sojourn with sedentary people near Umm al-Gilbān. While there, he was in poetic correspondence with Mṭēr ibn Khatlān, a tribesman of al-Rmāl, descended from ʿAmīrah. One day, they received an unexpected visit from a *ṣlubī*, a member of the pariah tribe of blacksmiths: "Hey, where are you coming from?" "By God, from the mountain." "Didn't you see the camels of ʿAjlān?" "By God," he said, "the pregnant camels of ʿAjlān are holding up nicely, but the mothers with calves, well. . . ." "What's wrong with them?" "The guards of Ibn Rashīd do not let them pasture there. Whenever they draw near, they shout at them to scare them and chase them off. Camels don't like that: if they are being yelled at, they refuse to graze." Goodness! What a pity for ʿAjlān's beautiful camels, the Barrāgāt and Dlāgāt herds. The tribe counted on having those ready in case of hostilities. 51.1

Mṭēr ibn Khatlān sent him these verses: 51.2

Rider of a camel, smooth-gaited, loose-jointed,
  fast as male ostriches startled by human voices;
At full throttle, it outruns bullets of Martini rifles:
  one day al-ʿAbd and al-ʿAbdah, the next at our dunes.[228]

—Al-ʿAbd and al-ʿAbdah are resting places for camel herds at one day's distance from the well of al-Birrīt. The dunes are the sand hills of Gnā and Umm al-Gilbān.

Head for ʿAjlān, hardy wolf waylaying prey,
  regaling companions with entertaining tales.
On spring meadows to Wādī al-Mrā's right,
  we haul in loads of truffles, herbage of all kinds;
Grumbling camels wade into gully puddles
  left by white-blazed clouds before darkness fell.

نرعى بربعٍ كلهم غانمين   فِرسان وان رَكْبوا على قِبّ الافراس
تِفْقان يرمون الشواة السِمين   نزّالة الخرْم المطَرَّف ورا الناس
وانا احمد الله كِلّنا سالمين   نبي من البِرّيت ناخذ لنا راس
وانتم على جال البعَيثة قطين   يذْكَر عليكم من الدواويح مِلْماس
ضَيَّعت نياقك ياالحمار المِتين   من مقْعَدك بين الحبَرتي ودِرْباس
تِذكَر نِقاضٍ عِقْب ما هِن سمانٍ   وعند القفَيعي منزلك باسفل الساس

نقاض يعني هزيلات.

قال انا اخو سِعْدى يقول ياالحمار المتين. ويرِدّ عليه ٣،٥١

راكبٍ من فوق طِلْق اليمينِ   يشدى طَخاة حاديه فَوح نسناس
لا هو ضِعيف ولا بعد هو سمينِ   يرفد الشداد مَكْعَب الحَيل عرماس
وليا تحَدَّر مع خطاة البِطين   يُوهِج كما تُوهِج على العِشّ قِرناس
هِزّ العصا وارْخ الرسن للهجين   لاجل تروّح نجْعنا قبل الادماس
تِلْفي مطير شَوق مُوضى الجِبين   شوق الهَنوف اللي زَهَت زَين الالباس
عند القفَيعي منزلي بالبطين   عند ابن مِطْلَق بين دَلّه ومِحْماس
ورْخَيمي يِلْقَط لنا كِلّ حينِ   وأما العَنب والخوخ والتِين مِحْتاس
والذَود عندي كل يومٍ عَطين   يشرب من البِركة ولا اشْقَى بالامْراس
يا نازل البِرّيت يا طَقْعَتَين   تَنهج وتاتي مِرْدفٍ مِثْل حوّاس
ما اخاف انا من ناقل المارتين   تَراك بقّ ومارتينك تِقِل فاس

Our fellows, camel owners all, the finest breed:
  dashing horsemen on steeds with bulging ribs;
Marksmen, they feast on delicious roasts of game,
  camp without a care in remote empty hills.
Praise God, we are all in sparkling shape:
  full of vigor, we tackle the trek from al-Birrīt.
Glued to al-Bʿēthah, camels couched at the well,
  you met with peremptory treatment, we heard.[229]
Obtuse donkey! Why lay your fine herds to waste
  by settling down between al-Ḥabartī and Dirbās?[230]
Once well-rounded camels were skin and bones,
  al-Gfēʿī banished you to his place's lowest seat.

—*Nigāḍ* means they are very thin, emaciated.

"I am the brother of Siʿdā!" he exclaimed. "He calls me an obtuse donkey!" 51.3
And he dispatched his reply:

Rider of a camel with a smooth, loose gait,
  hurtling along like a scud in a howling gale;
Not thin and worn out nor grown fat;
  lifting a saddle, a fireball of rare stamina.
Put through her paces down a hill,
  she plunges with dizzying speed like a falcon.
Wave the stick, slacken the racer's reins;
  you'll reach a nomad camp as darkness falls.
Go find Mṭēr, love of creamy-chested girls,
  hero of coquettish, sharp-dressed beauties.
I stay at al-Gfēʿī on flat ground ringed by hills:
  Ibn Miṭlag's coffeepots, a pan for roasting beans;
Carefully, pincers pick exquisite dates for me,
  served with assorted grapes, peaches, and figs.
I recline, taking in the view of my couched herd:
  watered in pools, no hassle of pulleys and wells.
Hey, dweller at al-Birrīt, real shithead that you are![231]
  Freeloader, coming and going like Ḥawwās![232]
Don't believe I stand in fear of Martini riflemen!
  Bloodsucking bug, your Martini is a mere axe.[233]

قصايده بالاخوان وسقوط الرشيد

هو بالعراق عجلان يوم يستالون السعود على الرشيد. يا مار فيه طير يقال له قَيس يوغّق بالليل يقولون انه يصوّت لذلول ضَيفه. قال ١.٥٢

يا قَيس قِمْ لامّك عَسى ما تقوم   حَيثك صِغير وتفهم العِلْم يا قيس
يا قيس وين مردّعين الختوم   اللي لهم حُمر النجايب عَواسيس
ما تقل طَقّوا للصِياني بشوم   ولا تقل صوّت للمساكين بِقْعَيس
راحوا كما مِزنٍ نِشَى له رِدوم   مِزنه يزَعّجْنه سِريع النِسانيس
راحوا بحكم اللي بحكمه يدوم   وين الرسول ووين عَدْنان وادريس

ويقول عجلان يوم هو في لاهه وخرجا والتّنَف. ٢.٥٢

الله من برد بَرَى حال عودي   واخَوفتي هذا وَلَد بردنا العام
الله على عجزٍ بهكالنفود   حظّايهن يمرح هَنِيٍّ الى نام

العجز جَزَل الغَضا الجبره.

ويقول عجلان ٣.٥٢

راكب اللي بالنجيره تِشدّ   اللي ليا جا العصر حِلْوٍ مراحه
في مذبَل الشِعبان بالك تغدّي   أودع مَغَدّى فاطرك بالبَياحه

مدبل الشعبان مَطامن الشعبان ذالّ من القوم لا يغتِرّونه.

His Poems on the Ikhwān and the House of Rashīd

ʿAjlān was in Iraq when the Sauds dethroned the Rashīd and supplanted their rule. A bird called Gēs hoots at night: it is said that the bird calls to his guest's camel. He said: **52.1**

Gēs, clear off to your mother, damn you!
  You're still young, Gēs, but you're smart.
Gēs, where are the royal fingers' signet rings,
  wide-ranging scouts on reddish thoroughbreds?
Where the staffs tapping on laden royal trays,
  loud invitations to paupers waiting for food?
Gone like rising towers of cumulus clouds,
  dissipated by northern breezes, swift and stiff,
Their rule doomed by the Lord of Eternal Rule;
  where is the Prophet? Where ʿAdnān and Idrīs?[234]

While sojourning at Lāhah, Kharjā, and al-Tanf, ʿAjlān said: **52.2**

Good Lord, such a cold! It chills my bones!
  Frightening, if it's a child of last year's frost!
God, I yearn for the Nafūd's balsam spurges,
  sleeping, snugly nestled in contented comfort.

—*Al-ʿajz* are bushes of large *ghaḍā* trees.

ʿAjlān said: **52.3**

O rider enthroned on a wooden camel saddle:
  look forward to a pleasant rest in late afternoon.
Beware of dangers lurking in valleys' thickets:
  choose wide plains for your camel's browsing.

—*Midbil al-shiʿbān* is the lower end of narrow valleys. He is afraid of being caught unawares by the enemy in such places.

مسـيرتك تِسْعـة ليـال تعـدّي   والعـاشـرة يحَوش نايف مـراحه

نايف الفرحان امير جبه.

تِلْفِي رجالٍ كِلّهم عَقب جدي   مقـرّين ضِـدّهـم عن قـراحه
تسعة نـزول كلهم عقب جدي   يَرْمي على روس النوازي وضاحه
طلوق ريقك من حلَى ما يمَدّي   وبـرِّيـةٍ ريحـه على الجمر فاحه
الله عـلى دَورٍ لنـا لو يِـــردّ   مَشْتَى النفود وجَضْعَته وانبِطـاحه
مجْعول خرجه ما لاهلها المقـدّي   والتّنف وغـراب الحـدالي ولاهه

خرجا قور دون الشِمْبِل باقصَى الحماد.

بـرده على عِمـري تحدّى تحدّي   والفلج عـندي عامـل له فـلاحه
يا جـا المغَيرب تِقل خـامٍ يقـدّ   يَسْكِرهبوب الفلج والشمس طاحه

قالت مرِتُه فرِيدة بنت شريّان ابن هزيم قعَيميله انت اكيد انك تبي تشَرّق ما انت ٤،٥٢
قاعد بسوريا لأنه دلّى يتطرى بِطين جبة وبطين قنا. قالت عساوه يجيه السيل بطين قنا ولا نجيه ما به الا نَبْته عاذِر وعَلْقا وهالجبال هذي هاللي تشوف نبته مَوز وتِفاح. قال

سِقَى بطين قنـا بسَيلٍ باثـر سيل   عَلْقـاوه وَرْد وعـاذره زِعْفـران
وتفـتّحن فـلوقهـا للنـزازيـل   ونبْت الغَضاة يشادي السِنْديان
مثل الهنوف اللي تِقِضّ العَباهيل   نبتـه حمـاط وخـالطه قحَويان

Brisk of pace, she carries you nine nights long
to your destination, the courtyard of Nāyif,

—Nāyif ibn Farḥān, the chief of Jubbah.

Welcomed by scions of our common ancestors;
warlike, they oust foes from sweet-water wells.
Nine lineages sprouted from our ancestor's sons:
their white camels' silhouettes etched onto the dunes.[235]
Breakfast served, the sweetest tastes are on offer,
aroma of roasted coffee beans wafting from a fire.
God, kindly restore to us golden days of old:
winter grazing in dunes, curled up in soft sands!
To hell, Kharjah; may people get lost on your way!
Joined by al-Tanf, Ghrāb al-Ḥdālī, and Lāhah!

—Kharjā consists of flat-topped rocky outcrops at the far north of the Ḥamād plains. Beyond it lies the land of al-Shumbul, east of the Syrian city of Homs.

Cruel lashes of freezing cold whipped my body;
snow and ice cover the land like plowed fields.
At dusk, a cover of white like shredded shirts,
in the silence of a windless dusk, the sun sinking away.

52.4 His wife, Frēdah, also called Gʿēmīlah, daughter of Ibn Sharayyān ibn Hazīm, said, "Are you sure you want to go east? Wouldn't you prefer to stay in Syria?" She asked because he kept mentioning the flatlands of Jibbah and Gnā. She added, "May the plain of Gnā receive torrents of rain, but without us being there! What does it have to offer us? No more than *ʿādhir* and *ʿalgā* plants, whereas these mountains around us produce bananas and apples." He replied:

May torrent upon torrent flood plains of Gnā:
ʿalgā are roses and its *ʿādhir* costly saffron.[236]
Dunes crossed by dips, open to the Bedouin,
sprout euphorbia bushes like evergreen oaks.[237]
Like smiling temptresses unraveling thick tresses:
a covering of hot weeds, sprinkled with chamomile.[238]

قالت اشْرلنا قِطيفه. هكالحين الملابس قِصيفه والغطا شوَي. قالت اشْرلنا قطيفة عن برد الجماد. قال وَصّيت واحد يشتريه لنا. والله مِشوا وطلعوا من حدود سوريا ما جاهم هالمرسال اللي هو موصي وين القطيفه. قال قِدّام ليا ما طَبوّا حدود السعودية هالحين طَبوّا النبك والقريّات والقرايا هذي. قالت ما هو صحيح انك موصي يشرى لنا قطيفه. قال ٥،٥٢

الله وحـد يا عند اهلنا قطيفـه   مـدٍّ من الله لا شـرانٍ ولا بَيع
ما يِنْتِغَـطّى به فـراشٍ لِطيفـه   والزَمْـل ما تَقْواه لو هي مَـرابيع
يا هَـبّت النَكْبـا هَبوبٍ ذِريفـه   نلوذ بشمّاخ العِكْص عن هل الرِيع

العكص هالنوازي الكبار.

وصل بها الديرة ويوم وصل بهالديرة والى والله هو شَرّاب دخان والى مير بعض الناس كِد دَيّنَوا بعضهم من جماعته وبعضهم مفترقين شوَين وهم كلهم الرمال. والله طَرى على خاطره انه يروح للهذّال. اللي قرّوه ربع حديهم بناخي له بناخي له ما هو بعيد. ويقول ٦،٥٢

واديـرتي زَبْني عن التَـيل والرَيـل   وِمْشَـغّل الدانات ما خَشّ لي راس ١

الدانات القنابل.

جَزْرَة ظما ما يجْرحـه جاري السيـل   ولا يَنْـطَحَـه الا واحدٍ فوق عِـرْماس
اشْـتي بها بالشـبط لوما معي كَيـل   ويمضي شهر كانون ما شِفْت الاوناس
جزّون عنها مِـرْوِحين الشَـماشيل   اللي يطوّون العـمامـة على الراس

"Buy us some carpets!" she demanded. In those days, proper clothes were hard to come by. People went scantily clad. "Buy us some carpets to use as blankets to protect us against the cold of these icy, barren plains!" she demanded. "I have sent a message to someone to buy those for us," he assured her. They packed up and traveled, but after crossing the borders of Syria there was still no sign of the messenger he claimed to have sent. "Where are the carpets?" "Ahead of us," he said. They carried on until they set foot in Saudi territory: the villages of al-Nabk, al-Grayyāt, and other settlements of the northern border region. She said, "Now I begin to understand: you were not telling the truth when you said that you had dispatched someone to buy carpets for us." He replied: 52.5

God is One! Plenty of carpets with our folks,
readied for us by God—no buying and selling!
Such nice coverlets aren't brought and spread:
they can't be carried by camels well fed in spring.
Lashed by razor-sharp blasts of northern gales,
lofty dunes, our hideout from those fanatics.[239]

—*Al-ʿikṣ* are the big sand dunes.

On arrival in his native land, he soon discovered that his tobacco addiction landed him in trouble. In his absence, people of his old homeland had converted to a religious lifestyle—some of them members of his own group, others from different clans, but all of them belonging to the Rmāl tribe. It occurred to him that he might pay a visit to Hadhdhāl, who had been expulsed by a posse of fellow tribesmen, one a relative of his, a quite close relative at that. He said: 52.6

My home, sanctuary from telegraph and rail: *1*
I am not cut out to be a maker of bombs.

—*Dānāt* are bombs.

Island of thirst, not ripped by torrents,
unassailable to all riders of rugged camels:
My winter abode, though I come barehanded;
in fall too, nowhere a single soul in sight.
Escaping riffraff, shirt hems smeared with shit,[240]
blockheads wrapped about with pompous turbans,

جِزِيَتهم بالقَيض عَشَرة مَراحيل   ارْداهن اللي منزله عقب الادماس
ويِذْكَر لنا نِضايض العَود فِرسين   يِذْكُرعلى له وَضحانٍ تغْلس اغلاس

فِرسين فارس السَطِم العَود هجْهوج من جماعته يمكن ما تطالعوا الدَمّ يمكن انهم بالخَمْسه لكن هو حِدى المَدَيْنين اللي يبون يضربونه ليه يَشْرِب الدخان.

لَه مَبْرَكٍ وضحاوه بين الفريقين   يا علّ ما هي وضحانٍ لابن مِرْداس
ياشَين والله حافظك بين جدَّين   وابوك هو حامي وِنِيّات الافراس
وتَشْلي خَدينك بسّةٍ تَلْحس الطين   البسّة النَمْرا اللي تدلغم مع الساس

خدينه واحد ما هو من اهل هالديرة جا لَفُو ودَيّن مع المَدَيّنه والى منه اسْتِحَى لا يضرب عمّه يَنْدِس عليه هالخدين اللي ما هو من اهل هالديره.

الناس من خِلْقَوا رجال ورجاجيل   والفوز للي طَوّع الناس بالناس

اخو الانور يضرب ناس بناس لما صِفَت له.

٧،٥٢ عقب ما حكم عبدالعزيز حايل عجلان اركب له قِعود وهو عند ابن هذّال. الاخوان هكالحين دلّوا يخَبِّصون بالناس ودلوا اللي يشرب الدخان يقولون به ما لابه. واركب له قعود يقول

١ هات الرسن ياسيف واذْن الصعيدِ   من ساس هجنٍ حافظينٍ ضَرابه
ياطا على ياسيف مثل المجيدِ   ويشدى هريف مسلّوعات الذيابه

I put ten days of riding between me and them,
marching at a grueling pace deep into the night.
I was told about the brood of the old man Firsīn:
evil-minded, he trots his white camel in the dark,

—Firsīn is Fāris al-Siṭam, the old man Hijhūj of his group. Perhaps a relative of shaykh Hijhūj, who did not fall outside the *khamsah*, fifth-degree relatives bound by the obligation of blood revenge. In any case, he was one of the religious fanatics with a penchant for administering bastinadoes on smokers of tobacco.

Couching the beast halfway between two camps—
it couldn't be farther apart from Ibn Mirdās.[241]
Ugh, God help you, conflicted by double ancestry,[242]
while your father stands tall shielding the weak.
Toeing your mean mate's line, you lick up the dirt:
a stealthy panther-sized cat slinking along a wall.[243]

—His mate was someone unrelated to the local people. He was an outsider, a religious fanatic. If he felt scruples about giving one of his kinsmen, his uncle, a thorough thrashing, he would wink at his mate who was not one of the local people and who had no compunctions about beating him up.

From Creation Day there were men and real men:
the winner won by cowing people with people.

—Akhū al-Anwar, ʿAbd al-ʿAzīz, set people against people to attain his political objectives.

When ʿAbd al-ʿAzīz had become the new ruler of Ḥāyil, ʿAjlān sent a "camel"—that is, a poem—from his place of residence at Ibn Hadhdhāl's camp. At that time, the Ikhwān sowed dissension and wrought havoc in the area. They would spread all sorts of lies and cast aspersions on people who were in the habit of smoking. ʿAjlān sent these verses, a camel mount, so to speak: 52.7

Grasp the reins, Sēf, bring the camel al-Ṣiʿīd,
racer from ancestry of well-preserved sperm!
Hooves shod with pads round as *majīdī* coins,
trotting, panting like wolves in bursts of speed.

مثل المجيدي يعني خَفافه مقَولمات.

حِطّ الشداد وحط جودٍ صِميد   وبالك تـزوّد حِقّتَينٍ زهـابـه
اخواع هـيقٍ مع صَحاصيح رَيد   هـزّ المـناكب كلها وارتِكى بـه
اخْطاه نِقْض مبَولدات الحديد   خـرْعة حَشا والّا سَلَم من صوابـه
لابن نهيّـر نحّــــره والسويدي   وكلٍّ بَنى له هِجْرةٍ صَكّ بابـه

نِدا ابن نهَيِّر وفِرَيح الحمزي السوَيدي هاجروا بالتيم ودلّوا يا جاهم الضيف ضربوه أول ما هو ينشدونه عن امور دينه والى ما يخَرَج من السُّعالات هذي جابوه ودَبّوه وهو ضيف والضيف ضيف الله من المكرمات.

يبون بالاجـفـر فـلايح وغِـيد   وظَبْي المهـادي قبلهم ما لِقَى بـه
وغَـيّ لهم ذَبْحَة عـيال الفديدِ   وعِـربان نازل شمسهـم وين غـابـه

نازل ابن ثنيان شيخ الزمَيل والفديد من عبده بعد أخذوهم وذبحوا عيالهم ندا ابن نهيّر والاخوان يدوّرون الجنّه.

واغواوه عَرْضة برْجس والفهَيدي   دَوّارة الجـــنّة بـذَبْح القـرابـه

كلهم بالحفَير هكالحين برجس ابن عَردان ابو دِرْزي هذا من السلمان والفهيدي من النِمْصان هو هذا حَيّ الى هالحين صار عند السدَيري بالاضارع كاتب الصِنخ.

حلاة نجد يوم حكم الرشيد   واليوم اشوفـه مـعـرياتٍ ثيابـه

—Shaped like a *majīdī* means that its hoof pads were smooth and round as this coin.

Place the saddle and a small skin with no leaks;
don't forget two cans of provisions for the road.
A mad-paced ostrich, she streaks across plains,
shoulders rocking, wings spread for balance,
Scared to death by bullets whizzing by,
stomach cramped though it escaped unscathed.
Head for Ibn Nhayyir and his friend of the Swēd:
their religious colony, the door slammed shut;

—Ibn Nhayyir and Frēḥ al-Ḥamzī al-Swēdī founded a religious colony, *hijrah*, at al-Tayyim. If a guest called on them, they would give him a beating. First, they would subject him to an examination of his religious tenets, and if he did not extricate himself from the ordeal to their satisfaction, they'd seize him and administer a severe beating. Even though he came to them as their guest! A guest is a guest from God: entertaining a guest hospitably is one of the mainstays of virtue.

Al-Ajfar, hoped-for farm of fields and palms—
earlier, the gazelles of al-Mhādī found it barren—
Excited by the murder of the sons of al-Fdēd—
Bedouin of Nāzil, how sorely they are missed—

—Nāzil ibn Thnayyān, the shaykh of the Zmēl, and al-Fdēd of the ʿAbdah were attacked and their sons murdered by Nidā ibn Nhayyir. That is how the Ikhwān were seeking admission to Paradise.

Awed by violent displays of Barjas and al-Fhēdī,
they seek Paradise by slaughtering their relatives.

—All of them are at al-Ḥfēr now. Barjas ibn ʿArdān Abū Dirzī belongs to the Salmān branch and al-Fhēdī to the Nimṣān. He is still alive today: he is in the company of al-Sudayrī, the governor of al-Jawf Province, in Uḍāriʿ. Kātib al-Ṣinkh is the name of Fhēdī.

Sweetly was Najd ruled as Ibn Rashīd's dominion!
Today, how pitiable! Nakedness dressed up in rags.

وعَنّزت يمّ اللي سِملهم جديد   مِتْمَرْكِي والْعَب على ابو عتابه

يعني الهذال.

وهذا عجلان ابن رمال عند الهذال ويقصد بالاخوان ٨،٥٢

١ متى يجينا طارشٍ فوق مجود   ويخبّرن عن ديرتي وش جرى به
كان هي على ما قيل بسهود ومهود   والا به الاخوان مثل الذيابه
مشيت عشر ايام يبرى لهن سود   وامشي الين الشمس يبدي غيابه
نكّاس للاخوان دودٍ ولد دود   هذاك عفن وينزع الله شبابه
٥ يمسي ويصبح شاربه تقل مجرود   ويِذْبَغ الى شيفت عليه العصابه
يا شيوخ شمر واعسى وجيهكم سود   مضيفكم على يديكم خرابه
برجس بْحِلّة نازل يدوّر الفود   ويدور الجنه بذبح القرابه
حلفت دين ولاحق الدين بشهود   انه فلا عِدّت بدور الصحابه

وصلت القصيده للوحير وهو بالجزيره رد عليه قال ٩،٥٢

١ اقديت ياعجلان ما قلت منقود   هرجك على الخاطر لذيذٍ جوابه
اقبل علينا بدّل الهون بالكود   لا تذبحك ناسٍ تغوّل كلابه
من قوم ختلان الى قوم سلبود   ناسٍ تلاغى واللغى ما يِتْشابه

ما شمر صاروا اخوان لمطير وحرب؟ ما لغاهم واحد؟ ختلان وسلبود شمامره.

I headed for men whose old dresses are like new;
reclining in comfort, I sing my nostalgic tunes.

—He means Hadhdhāl.

During his stay with Ibn Hadhdhāl, ʿAjlān composed these verses on the Ikhwān: 52.8

I'm waiting for a rider on a scrawny, jaded camel 1
to tell me about my tribal land, news of events:
Are things, as one says, going smooth and nicely,
or have the Ikhwān run amok, sowing wrack and ruin?
I marched for ten days and as many nights,
without halting until the sun went down,
To spite the Ikhwān: worms, sons of worms!
execrable rogues, may God cancel their youth!
Morning and evening busy plucking his mustache, 5
upper lip smoothed, he appears with headband on.[244]
Shaykhs of Shammar! Your faces are blackened:
your faults demolished guests' reception rooms.
Barjas is hunting for plunder in Nāzil's camp,
slaughtering relatives to gain admission to Paradise.
I swear a sincere oath, as witnesses can confirm:
this was unheard of among the Prophet's Companions.

Al-Wḥēr was in Mesopotamia when the verses reached him, and he replied: 52.9

Spot on, ʿAjlān, not one word off the mark: 1
delicious verses made to refresh my mind.
Come to us for a life easier and trouble-free:
no wanton murder, no snarling dogs at your throat,
Villains of Khatlān's kin or rabble of Silbūd,
a hotchpotch of foreign twangs and dialects.

—Wasn't the new situation that Shammar tribesmen mixed with men of the Muṭayr and Ḥarb tribes as members of the Ikhwān? These spoke in different dialects. Khatlān and Silbūd were Ikhwān of Shammar.

حـلاة نجـدٍ يوم حـاوي ومردود　　يوم هي ينام قْهـيديٍ من لجى بـه
اليوم لا عِـزٍّ ولا زبن مـضـهود　　والى لفـانا طـارشـه لا هـلا بـه
عسى تـرابـه يقتـلب مـلح بارود　　وعسى مطـرها قـاز عجـل التهـابـه

١٠،٥٢ خلف المظهور ابن غازي من العَلَيّان رد على الاثنين. هم انحاشوا صبّحتهم حرب مع الزغيبي وقوم ابن سعود الاخوان. صبّحتهم بجلديه وذبحوا عيال غضبان ابن رمال واسعر ببيتهم وعقاب ابن عجل هجّ وهجّت شمر مع عقاب ابن عجل. وقصدوا عاد هالقصيد هذا. حنا جانا اللي تثلّب بهذا سويد وعمود والدغيرات ايه اجلدت بهذا. ودلّى يلوفهم الدويش والآخر والآخر وابن سعود. ويجيك ابن سعود ورصّنا وينزل بالقثاميه. ومن القثاميه للنيصيه وحنا نصحب. والدويش ياخذنا خمس وعشرين قطيع ذود هكاليوم للعُلَيّان فقط. أغار من ياطب وخذاه من شطيب وركان. والرجال تحرب بالجويضع والنيصيه. قال خلف المظهور ابن غازي

١ خـلافـذا يا راكـبٍ فوق مجود　　ولد ذلولٍ ناجـبـــــينٍ ضَـرابـه
عـدّوا لُه الحِسّاب بصليـع منـقود　　وابوه من زمـل اللحـاوي نضـا بـه

صليع جمل الراعي اللي يقولون منقود وكاد.

تجويـل ريـلٍ جـفّـله حِسّ بارود　　مـتوكّدٍ من شوف زولٍ عـدى بـه
ما فوقه الا الكور والخـرج وشنود　　والمـيركة من فوق متـنـه زهى بـه
يا جيت لي عجـلان من فوق مجود　　اهرج عليه وعلّمـه وِش جـرى بـه
انتم نهجـتوا ما صـبرتوا على الكود　　وحـنا قـعـدنا بـه على ما لنا بـه

Wonderful was Najd in tribal give and take,
a refuge where one slept in peace undisturbed.
Lusterless today, no shelter for the oppressed;
let no wayfarer count on hearing "Welcome!"
I pray, let its soil turn into saltpeter for powder,
its rains into inflammable gas for combustion.

Khalaf al-Maẓhūr of the 'Layyān clan pitched in with a response to both of **52.10** them. They had made off after being raided by the Zghēbī of the Ḥarb tribe and troops of Ibn Saud, the Ikhwān. The attack occurred at Jildiyyah. Children of Ghaḍbān ibn Rmāl were killed, and his house was set on fire.[245] 'Gāb ibn 'Ijil fled as fast as he could, followed by large numbers of Shammar tribesmen. Under these circumstances, they composed the verses. We were blamed for staying where we were: the tribal sections of Swēd, 'Amūd, al-Dghērāt. They were continuously harassed by al-Duwīsh and many others, the troops of Ibn Saud. Ibn Saud marched on us, pressing us hard. From al-Ǵithāmiyyah, his onslaught reached al-Nīṣiyyah. We offered our submission. That did not stop al-Duwīsh from stealing twenty-five herds of camels, on that same day, just from the 'Layyān clan. He came raiding from Yāṭib and drove the camels from Shṭēb Warkān, while fighting was going on at al-Jwēḍi' and al-Nīṣiyyah. Khalaf al-Maẓhūr ibn Ghāzī said:

Leave that, rider on a scrawny camel mount,
son of a distinguished she-camel, nobly born,
Say camel experts, from Ṣlē''s flawless seed,
pedigree offspring of al-Lḥāwī's Sharārī stud;

—Ṣlē' is the stud camel of the mentioned pedigree.

Zigzagging, it races like an ostrich being fired at,
frightened on seeing the attackers' vague shapes;
Fitted out with saddle, bags, and colorful trappings,
graced with leather padding for the rider's feet.
Brought to 'Ajlān by your rugged camel mount,
speak to him and talk about our vicissitudes:
You made a run for it, not bearing the strain;
we stayed on, enduring what we had to endure.

يقاصر ابن هذّال ويقضي بينه وبين الجربا على الودي

١٫٥٣ عجلان نزَح مع الرمال للروله وبعدين نَهَج مع عَدْوان لاسريا ومن اسريا راح لابن هذّال. نزل عند فهد ابن هذال ابو مَحْروت وجاوره جِيرة طويله حول ثلاث أو اربع سنين وجوّزه بنته جوّز البيق انت يا عجلان زوّجه بنته.

٢٫٥٣ تشاكلوا الجربا وابن هذال تشاكلوا على الودي. حصل مشكل بين عقَيل الجاور الجربا ومحروت ابن هذال على ودي عنزة وشمر. الجربا ياخذ الباج على الدرّابه والملاّحه اللي ينقلون الملح واللي ينقلون البضايع اللي ما هم شمّر وابن هذال يقول الباج لنا. راح ابن هذال للدولة لراعي بغداد قال حنا يآل هذال أقدم العرب وحنا ناخذ على العرب الوَدِي على اهل نجد. قالوا كان العرب يوقّعون لك ما يخالف.

٣٫٥٣ ووصّوا لعقيل الجاور الجربا. جاهم وقالوا له نبيكم توقعون لابن هذال انه هو اقدمكم وانه ياخذ عليكم الودي قبل. قال عقيل حنا ابن هذال ما ياخذ علينا الودي حنا من صيرتنا بالجزيره انا اللي يجينن بديرتي بحدودي انا يا عقيل الجربا اللي يجينن بحدودي آدى الشمري والعنزي اللي يجونن بحدودي وابن هذال الى منه صار بحدوده احد من شمر ما ياداهم يادى عنزة لكن شمر ما ياداهم انا آدى عنزة وشمر بديرتي بالجزيره وابن

As a Neighbor of Ibn Hadhdhāl, He Arbitrates between Him and the Jarbā on the Subject of Tribute

ʿAjlān migrated with the Rmāl to the Rwalah, and from their tribal land he continued to Syria, accompanied by ʿAdwān ibn Rmāl, and once in Syria he made his way to Ibn Hadhdhāl. He took up lodgings with Fahd ibn Hadhdhāl, the father of Maḥrūt, and sojourned with him a long time, three or four years, as his protected neighbor, and married his daughter. Yes, ʿAjlān became a relative of the bey! He was given the hand of the bey's daughter. 53.1

Al-Jarbā and Ibn Hadhdhāl quarreled about the right to levy tribute from the tribes. The dispute started when ʿAgīl al-Jāwar al-Jarbā and Maḥrūt ibn Hadhdhāl each claimed the right to levy protection money from both ʿAnazah and Shammar. Al-Jarbā imposed tributes on road traffic and salt miners: the transport of salt and other commodities. That is to say, on those who were not members of his tribe, Shammar. Hadhdhāl maintained that the tribute flowing into al-Jarbā's coffers was his by right. Ibn Hadhdhāl lodged a complaint with an Ottoman official, the governor of Baghdad. He argued his case at the government's court: "We, the House of Hadhdhāl, represent the most ancient and deep-rooted noble lineage of the Bedouin Arabs, which entitles us to impose tribute on the Bedouin, on anyone coming from Najd." The official said, "As long as the Bedouin recognize your right to do so, it is fine with us." 53.2

They sent for ʿAgīl al-Jāwar al-Jarbā. He duly came and was told, "We want you to recognize that Ibn Hadhdhāl has the most senior rights and that in earlier days he imposed tribute on you." ʿAgīl said, "Not at all! Ibn Hadhdhāl does not collect any tribute from us! Ever since we made our home in al-Jazīrah, it is I, ʿAgīl al-Jāwar, who take tribute from all comers. We impose it on anyone who for whatever reason crosses the borders of my tribal land: from the moment they set foot within my borders, be they from Shammar or ʿAnazah. Ibn Hadhdhāl's case is very different. If someone from Shammar enters his territory, that person does not owe him anything. He may demand tribute from ʿAnazah only. But Shammar—no! As for myself, within the borders of my land in al-Jazīrah I am entitled to collect tribute from ʿAnazah and Shammar tribesmen. 53.3

هذال ما يادي الا عنزة الى جوه شمر ما ياداهم. قال وشو الزَود اللي يزوّدك عليّ. قال والله هذي عادات وله امور قبل. وحصل بينهم كلام.

٤،٥٣ قالوا الدولة انتم شوفوا لكم احد يخلصكم من قالتكم هذي اختاروا لكم احد. قال اختَر انت يابن هذال. قال ابن هذال انا اختار عجلان لأنه من الرمال والرمال كلهم مَنَاهي مناهي حقوق. يوم يختاره انه جار له بزعمه انه يبي يميّل الحق معه. قال وانت يا عقيل. قال انا يا صار ابن هذال مختار عجلان انا بعد ما اقول شين ما يخالف انا راضيه وهذا هو عندك هاته معك وسيروا علي.

٥،٥٣ فِرِح ابن هذال وطلع يم الصَيهد. وسولف على ابوه ابوه مِنَعّمي فهد فهد ابن هذال هذا ولِدُه محروت محروت خَواله التُومان خواله شمر. قال والله يابيه انا هاللون وهاللون سولف عليه. قال ياليتك ما رَدَّيت لعجلان عجلان عنده خبر والخبر يفلّسك ولا ينِطِي ذِمّته لاجل غلاك والا انت اغلى من نص شمّر عليه لكن ما ينطي ذمته. قال والله عاد انا ردّيته لُه. قال يا ولدي ارجع لهم وقولة لقيته رايح لحايل وخلّه تِنفِهق له حدود شهر يما اما تسوّون اصطلاح والا يجيب الله شاهد غير عجلان. والله ما طاع ابوه. وراح يم هله قال ابيك تسير معي يا عجلان يم عقيل الجاور. وراح محروت على سيارته السيارات من اول شويّايه (= شُوَيّات قليلات) ما من الا كان عند احد على ما قال من الشيخان والا هذا ما من سيارات هكالحين. قال يا عجلان ابروح اتمشى انا واياك الباشا عازمك يقول لازم يجي معك عجلان نبيه يونّسنا ونبي

But he has no right to levy anything on Shammar, only on ʿAnazah." Hadhdhāl protested: "What makes you think that you can lay claim to a higher rank in the tribal pecking order?" Al-Jarbā said, "Well, these are old customs rooted in events that happened over a long time." They argued and clashed.

The official said, "The only solution, as we see it, is for you to look for someone 53.4
to assist you in finding a way out of this controversy. You must choose an arbitrator!" And he continued: "Make your choice, Ibn Hadhdhāl!" Ibn Hadhdhāl said, "As far as I am concerned, I'd look favorably on the choice of ʿAjlān because he is one of the Rmāl, and the Rmāl are renowned for having arbitrators with great expertise in judging matters of tribal law." It so happened that at that time ʿAjlān was staying with him as a neighbor under his protection. Ibn Hadhdhāl therefore reckoned that he would be well disposed toward his case. The official said, "And what about you, ʿAgīl?" ʿAgīl replied, "If Ibn Hadhdhāl has a preference for ʿAjlān, I have no objection. It's all right with me. I can go along. This man lives at your place. Bring him with you to pay us a visit!"

Pleased and gleeful, Ibn Hadhdhāl returned to al-Ṣēhad and told his father 53.5
of his feat. Fahd ibn Hadhdhāl, the father of Maḥrūt, was blind. Maḥrūt's relatives from his mother's side were from the Tūmān of Shammar. Triumphantly, Ibn Hadhdhāl painted the tableau of the discussion. However, his father sighed and said, "How I wish you did not try so hard to have this matter referred to ʿAjlān! ʿAjlān knows the history of the case, and what he knows invalidates your arguments. And do not believe that he will jeopardize his honor and credibility for your sake, even though he holds you dearer than half of all Shammar put together. He does not pursue such matters in ways that run counter to his conscience." His son said, "By God, it is too late for that now. I had the case assigned to him." His father said, "Son, go back and tell them that you found that he has left for Ḥāyil. Be quick—ask ʿAjlān to pack up and absent himself for a month or so. During that time, you might arrive at a solution, or if not, perhaps, God willing, another credible witness will take ʿAjlān's place." The son did not follow his father's advice. Instead, he went to see ʿAjlān and said, "Come, ʿAjlān, let's visit ʿAgīl al-Jāwar." Maḥrūt traveled there by car. Back then, automobiles were exceedingly rare. You'd only find them with people like shaykhs. Otherwise, there were no cars in those days. "ʿAjlān," he said, "I feel like going on a jaunt with you. The pasha has invited you. He agreed to see me on condition that I take you along. He wants the entertainment of your conversation, someone well versed in lore. Let's take this jaunt to Baghdad, as he proposed, then come back

ناخذ تاريخه بني نروح نتمشى انا واياك يم بغداد نروح نتمشى على ما قال ونجي. وجا معه. ما علمه بالقصه ما علمه انهم متراضينُه.

٦،٥٣ قالوا لليبق والله راح محروت هو وايا عجلان. قال الشايب لا واحلولاة يا سوالف عجلان وما هم هاللي راحوا جميع. قالوا آه. قال ما يجون جميع يجي كل واحد لحاله. وتشوفون هالشهر اللي دخل – هم باول الشهر – ما يخلص هالشهر الا بيت عجلان اما ببطين جبّة والا ببطين ام القلبان ما يقعد عندنا وهو متزاعل هو ومحروت ولا هو راحل منا ورايح اما للجربا والا لشيخ غيره يَكِفت على هالاخوان هو هاجّ عن الاخوان ويروح يمهم هو ينْغَثّ وانا أنْغَثّ. يقوله الشايب.

٧،٥٣ يوم جوا بغداد ليا مير هذي امرا العشاير كله جالسين. قالت الدولة يا عجلان. قال نعم. قال ابن هذال والجاور عندهم إشْكال بهالقِضية وراضينك تخلصهم ابن هذال يبي العرب يوقعون له انه هو اللي ياداهم قبل والجاور عيّ وتراضوك انت انك تخلصهم. قال والله انا ما عندي خبر من هالسالفه انا رجل صغير ولا انا ابو لشمر وابو لعنزه ولا انا على ما قال من اكبرهم اخلّصهم انا رجل صغير ولا حضرت شي. قال لا هم راضينك لازم انك تخلصهم بمعرفتك.

٨،٥٣ قال والله كان الزعل مدهوم فانا ابعَلّمكم وان كان يبي يصير بخاطر واحد منكم شي والله ما عندي خبر. قالوا لله الزعل مدهوم. ويحتجّون. قال انا عندي كان هم متراضين يكتبون هالحين كل يكتب على ما قال انّه مَقْصَم رِضْمه ما يخالف كان يكتبون انهم يتراضون اني اخلّصهم انهم يخَلْصون ما يخالف بمعرفتي وانا ترى عندي شاهد ابدَلّي به عليكم عاد ان خلّصهم. كِتْبوا ووَقّعوا على ان مِخْلاص عجلان يخلصهم.

٩،٥٣ قال عجلان الحَظّ ما هو حشيش احشّه وينْبِت انا ما انطي حظي احد لا قريب ولا بعيد الجربان ياخذون الباج من وقت فارس إلى صفوق الى عبد الكريم وانت

here." ʿAjlān did not demur: he had not been told what was up, that they had agreed to make him their arbiter.

On being informed that Maḥrūt and ʿAjlān had left, the bey, the old man, said, "Ah, how wonderful, the stories of ʿAjlān! I'll miss them dearly. Didn't all of them leave together?" "Yes," they said. "Mark my words, they will not return together. They will go their separate ways. Before the end of this month—it was the beginning of the month—ʿAjlān's tent will be pitched in the plain of Jubbah or at Umm Gilbān. When he feels aggrieved at Maḥrūt's action, he will be loath to stay here. Not that he will lodge with al-Jarbā or any other shaykh. Rather, he will return to the fold and make his peace with the Ikhwān. He is on the run from the Ikhwān, but after these events he will trace his steps back to them. He feels miserable about the situation, and so do I." These were the old man's words. 53.6

On their arrival in Baghdad, the tribal grandees were waiting, gathered in a large assembly. The Ottoman dignitary called for him to step forward: "ʿAjlān!" "Yes," he said. "Look, Ibn Hadhdhāl and al-Jāwar are embroiled in a dispute and they chose you to disentangle them from it. Ibn Hadhdhāl wants recognition of his traditional right to levy tribute from the Bedouin, while al-Jāwar rejects his claims. All they agree on is that you are the right person to find an amicable solution." He said, "By God, I am not particularly knowledgeable about these matters. I'm an ordinary person who carries no special weight. I am not one of the wise elders of Shammar, let alone ʿAnazah. I do not have the stature to be chosen for such a role. I'm just a little guy. I never played a part in such momentous issues." The official said, "No, you are the person on whom they have settled. We need your knowledge to extricate them from this imbroglio." 53.7

"By God," he said, "if they bury the hatchet, I will tell them. If one of them might resent what I submit and bear me a grudge, really, I'll just keep my mouth shut." "Honestly," they said, "the issue is buried." The opponents presented their arguments. Having listened to them, ʿAjlān said, "I have the key to a solution, but first they must put in writing and sign that they have given their consent and agreed. Each of them confirms in writing that once I have handed them the key to the solution, he pledges to accept it, without holding it against me in any way. That said, I have evidence I'd like to submit for your consideration. Hopefully it will rid them of their problem." They duly wrote and signed a pledge to abide by ʿAjlān's solution. 53.8

ʿAjlān said, "One's good fortune is not like grass, something you cut and it grows again. I am careful not to give others, whether close relatives or 53.9

يا بن هذال ما قطعت للجزيرة انت يوم جِيت الشَّطّ اجْلَدْت ولا عمرك قطعت المخاوض والله انت يا بن هذال تادى عنزه أما شمر فلا لك ودي عليهم والجربا يادى الثنين بديرته.

١٠،٥٣ وعلّمهم بالدليل واستفلج ابن هذال. الدليل قصيدة القريع والقرَيع عنزي. قالوا وشي. قال طول الله عمرك نوّخ لهم فارس الجربا ووداهم بغنَيم غنيم هو هذا على طريق تبوك. قالوا وش لون قصيدة القريع. قال القريع يقول

يا علّ خَيبر هي واهَلها للامحال عن المطر تاخذ ثمانين عام
يومٍ جرى بغنيمٍ ما يِطْرِب البال واللي يعرْف الحيف عاف الطعام
الشمّري نوّخ لنا تقل نزّال خَذى الجمَل ومِرْودمات السَنام
وان كان هذي حالنا ما بقى حال قِضى اللَحم والطَق لحَق العظام

١١،٥٣ قالوا هو صدق القريع عنزي منكم يابن هذال. قال نعم اعرفه والقصيدة معروفه. وخلصهم عجلان بهالقصيده. والله يوم جا من باكر والى هذا محروت جايّك لحاله هاه وين خويك. قال والله اجْلَد يتقضّى. وش صار عليكم. قال والله صار على قولك صار على قولك وعز الله انه ما ظَلَمَ حَظّه انه شهد على بِرّ لكن قال لي لي كلمة مَغثت خاطري عقب ما خلصنا قال وشي يا ولدي. قال يوم عَدّ اللي عنده والى والله المِفْلاج

outsiders, any say in my good fortune, in issues pertaining to my conscience. The shaykhs of al-Jarbā have levied tribute since the days of Fāris, and after him it was the same under Ṣfūg and ʿAbd al-Karīm. As for you, Ibn Hadhdhāl, you have not crossed into al-Jazīrah. When you came to the shore of Shaṭṭ al-ʿArab, you kept to your side of the river. Not once did you make use of the river's crossings to go to the other side. It is correct, Ibn Hadhdhāl, that you collect tribute from ʿAnazah. As for Shammar, no, you do not have an established right to tax Shammar. On the other hand, al-Jarbā takes tribute from both tribes within the borders of his tribal land."

He buttressed his argument by reciting a poem. The outcome was that Ibn Hadhdhāl lost the case. The proof ʿAjlān adduced was a poem composed by al-Grēʿ, a tribesman of ʿAnazah. "Go ahead, recite it!" they invited him. He said, "May your life be long, Fāris al-Jarbā fought a pitched battle against them and imposed a tribute on them at Ghnēm," a place somewhere on the way to Tabūk. "Let us hear the poem of al-Grēʿ!" This is what al-Grēʿ said:[246] 53.10

Drought! Strike hard at Khaybar's tribes:
not a single drop of rain for eight long years!
Events at Ghnēm gave us no cause for joy:
once you've met disaster, food loses taste.
Shammar threw their weight into battle,
seizing full-bodied she-camels and studs.
Our shape of old dissolved at a stroke:
meat gone, knives cut deep and hit the bone.

Those in attendance said, "Isn't it true that al-Grēʿ hails from ʿAnazah, one of your own kin, Ibn Hadhdhāl?" "Yes," he admitted, "I am aware of it and the poem is well-known." The testimony of the verses recited by ʿAjlān resolved the issue for them. Next morning, Maḥrūt reached home, alone. "Hey, where is your companion?" "Well," he said, "he preferred to stay behind and do some shopping to buy household necessities." "How did things turn out?" "By God," he answered, "it went as you predicted, exactly as you said. God Almighty, he did not give short thrift to his luck, he followed the dictates of his conscience. His testimony was that of a righteous man. Only, at the conclusion of his testimony, he said something that's been bothering me." "What is it, my son?" He said, "At the end of his exposé, when it transpired that al-Jarbā had won, someone asked me, 'Can you live with this outcome, Ibn Hadhdhāl?' I said, 53.11

للجربا ما هو لي قالوا لي قنَعت يابن هذال. قلت قنعت. قالوا هذا شاهدك صار عليك. قلت ايه انا اسمع بهاللي يقول

يا طير ابن بِرمان جِبْناك حنا   يا ناقل الحية على راس راعيه

هَسّيت وقلته وسكتّ ما اتْلَيته وقال لي عجلان لا تِكاثر يا بن هذال كان فات خمس بقي ثلاث والله يا يبه اني طلعت من بغداد الى ما وصلت بهذا اني ما ادري وش الارض اللي امشي عليه ما ادري وش الخمس ووش الثلاث.

١٢،٥٣ قال أوووووووه يا غَميضتك والله يقال لك شيخ الشيوخ يا ولدي الخمس والثلاث هذولي سنين المهادي - المهادي من قحطان وراح جلاوي من قحطان وصار عند شمر ودح لجاره ثمان سنين

ثمان سنين وجارنا مجْرِم بنا   ونَرَفّي كما تَرَفّى العَذارى ثيابه

هذا قول المهادي - انت ما صِبَرت مثل صبر المهادي حنا شيوخ الشيوخ ما اودعتنا نتجمل مع ابن رمال واحلولات يابن رمال حَرَمْتَن شَوفته وتعلّلته لى واحسايف والله يا قصرة عجلان وتعللته. والله سكت وهو منكسر خاطره انت يالشايب. يوم بغى ياجب العصر والى مير هذاك الزَول. الا هو الا ما هوب هو. قالوا هذا عجلان. يوم جا الصبح امير يوم قِشع بيت عجلان.

١٣،٥٣ قال فهد ليه عجلان يقشع بيته وش الامر. رح رح يا عبد قل يقول الشيخ فهد ليش تقشع بيتك. قال عجلان للعبد والله انا يوم جيت هلي والى مير والله يحكون الحريم والوِغْدان ان العرب على راي رحيل وقشعت البيت احسب اننا رحيل. قال لا بالله ما هم رحيل. قال سَلِّم لي على الشيخ انا اسمي اللي عاد اللي قشعت بيتي هالحين

'Yes, I accept it.' 'We ask especially,' the other said, 'because you were the one to propose him as witness and yet he dashed your expectations.' 'Yes,' I said. 'It reminds me of a verse I once heard:

> Falcon of Ibn Burmān, we brought you here,
> why did you drop a snake on your master's head?'[247]

"My mind wandered. My recall failed me and I could not recite the entire poem. I fell silent. At that, ʿAjlān sought to comfort me: 'Do not get too worked up about it, Ibn Hadhdhāl. When five have passed, three remain.' My God, Father! From Baghdad until my arrival here I did not see the road I was traveling on for even one moment. I kept asking myself what he meant by the five and the three."

"Aaargh," said his father. "How could you fail to understand the point? And 53.12
you are supposed to be a shaykh of shaykhs! Listen, my son, the five and the three are the years of al-Mhādī—al-Mhādī of Ghaṭān, who sought refuge from blood guilt with Shammar and for eight years showed exemplary forbearance in putting up with his neighbor's lapses:

> Eight years we overlooked a neighbor's sins,
> covering them as women mend torn clothes.

"You were unable to bear with al-Mhādī's equanimity. We are considered a shaykh of shaykhs, but you did not let us treat Ibn Rmāl the way he deserves. Ibn Rmāl is such a wonderful person, and now you have robbed me of his company and conversation. I feel so wretched. I will miss him so much. How can I do without ʿAjlān and his stories!" The old man fell silent, relapsed in his gloom. Around the time of afternoon prayers, they noticed a silhouette moving in the distance. Was it him or someone else? He was told that it was indeed ʿAjlān. Next morning, the tent of ʿAjlān had been taken down and removed.

Fahd exclaimed, "Why did ʿAjlān break up camp? What is the matter with 53.13
him? You, servant, go, go! Tell him: 'The shaykh wants to know why you are taking down your tent.'" ʿAjlān told the servant, "By God, on the day of my return, the women and children told me that the Bedouin had made up their mind to travel. Accordingly, I pulled down my tent, thinking that we'd travel." "No," the other said, "they are not going to travel!" He said, "Convey my greetings to the shaykh. In any case, I have taken down the tent and put our belongings on the pack camels, in keeping with the opinion expressed by

وشدّدنا زملنا على راي هالوغدان وهالحريم لكن انا أبي انقّل ورا هالشفا وانشا الله اما يتقلّطون علي أو نتساير من قريّب. وارحل.

١٤،٥٣ قال البيق سيف يا ولدي يقوله الشايب اركب وانحر عجلان - سيف رجّال لك يا فهد - رح كنك جاي من سَدّ الخلا وخَلّك يوم انه يربط فِرسُه عند بيته والى مير انت ما انت بعيد عنه ان كان هو ليا ربطه جا يَمّ بيت الهذال فالدعوى انشا الله به رجا وان كان انه شَبّ النار ببيته فانت اجلِس عنده وتصَنّت تراوه على ما يتقهوى كود يلعب على الربابة كود يتمثل شف وشو يقول غَدِين انام الليله. والله يقول سيف - عاد يسولف علينا ولد له توظف بطرَيف ولد لسيف بالشركه وجانا بطريف والى مير يجيب امثال عجلان ويجيب سوالفه وقمنا نستانس لسوالفه - يقول وانا اجي واجلس عنده يقول اثاريه عقب ما ربط الفرس يوم انا مِنتَزِح شوي يقول ثاريه قال للمرة لا تطلع النجمه هاللي قدام الصبح ولنا بالأرض علاقه يبي يرحل. يقول يوم شفته شبّ النار يقول وانا اجي واجلس عنده. يقول والله زيّن القهوه هو تقهوى له ثلاث فَناجيل وهو يعَمّر دخان.

١٥،٥٣ يوم عمّر وهو يشرب له فنجالين عقب الدخان وهو يستدْني الرِبابه قال

لولا القدر يا سيف ما جيت بغداد   جيناوه بحكمة عزيز الجلالا
يامل عينٍ ذاربه قلّ الاصماد   قلت اصمِدي وجابته بانهلالا
جيت ابنام وصار للقلب رَدّاد   جيت ابنام وقالت العين لا لا
يا سيف ترطِبّ البغيضين الابعاد   اِرْحل ويِرضِنك بعيد السهالا
والكَبْد عَيَّت تقبل الشرب والزاد   وِقربك على اللي ما يودّك عذالا
ياعين نامي واهجعي قبلك اجواد   راحوا على الرِجلَين مَشْيٍ تتالي

the women and children. But I will move beyond that ridge there, and God willing they will come to me or we will visit. We are not far from one another." And he moved away.

The bey, the old man, said to Sēf, one of his men, "Sēf, my boy, take your camel and ride to ʿAjlān. Make it appear as if you are coming straight from the desert, unaware of what happened, and make sure to be close at hand when he locks his mare in iron at his tent. If, having shackled his horse, he goes on his way to the tent of al-Hadhdhāl, then God willing there is hope. When he lights a fire at his tent, sit down within hearing distance and be sure to prick up your ears. Perhaps, while preparing coffee, he will play a tune on his rebab. Who knows, he might recite some verses. Try to catch the words of his song. Perhaps it will set my mind at rest and allow me to get some sleep tonight." It is told—and we heard it from one of his sons who is an employee at Ṭrēf who came to see us there and treated us to the wonderful entertainment of ʿAjlān's poems and stories—that Sēf said, "When I had come and sat down with him, once he had shackled his mare while I was still at a little distance from him, I heard him tell his wife, 'At the twinkle of the morning star, a little before dawn, I do not want to see even one thread left lying here on our campground.' He was set on traveling. I watched him kindling a fire, then walked over to him and sat down. He prepared coffee, poured himself three cups, filled his pipe, and lit up. 53.14

"When he had finished smoking, he poured another two small cups. Thereupon, he reached for his rebab and sang: 53.15

It was my destiny, Sēf, to come to Baghdad,
  decreed by His Almighty Majesty's wisdom.
Woe is me, tears stream as if from leaky skins:
  telling my eye, 'Hold!' made it gush ever more.
My pounding heart thwarted attempts at sleep;
  'No! No!' said my eyes as soon as I dozed off.
Listen, Sēf! To pack up is wrath's antidote.
  Travel, rejoice at vast lands, at distant horizons!
Mere thought of drink and food revolts:
  staying on as someone unloved is wrong.
Sleep, my eye, rest! Noblemen did so before:
  on foot, one after the other, humbly they went."

قال هذا وما يقول يا عمي. قال ما به حِيله. طلعت الشمس من باكر أويقوا على عربنا. ١٦،٥٣
تقل بينهم لهم مسافة تتقي ناس عن ناس. والله اواقوا على مكان عجلان قالوا والله
راحل عجلان. وهو يصيح الشايب قال أنا عزيت لي ثالث يوم عن سوالف عجلان لكن
اخاف انه يوخذ وهو ما طَبّ ديار شمّر وإلا ليا طب حدود السعودية يامن بوسط
شمر والحكم ضافي عليهم لكن حدود العراق ما عليه حكم.

وهو يصيح. الى بيت محروت متشطّر شوين ويمكن انه نايم ليا وقت طلعة الشمس. ١٧،٥٣
يا محروت يا محروت يالله صِحْ للعرب واركبوا خيلكم هذا الروِي يتبعنكم ليا ما توَسّطون
عجلان من شمر ويامَن لا يوخذ وهو راحل من عندنا. والله ويمشون ليا ما طَبّ لِينه.
يوم طب لينة قال بس ارجعوا.

When Sēf had repeated these verses to his master, the old man said, "The case is lost. At first light tomorrow, betake yourself to our Bedouin and have a look around." They were at some distance and the camp of their neighbors was not visible from where they were. They went, came back, and reported, "By God, ʿAjlān is gone." The old man cried out with grief: "Three long days I had to make do without the stories of ʿAjlān. I fear that he'll be robbed on his way before he reaches the tribal lands of Shammar. Once he crosses the border with Saudi Arabia, he'll be safe in the embrace of Shammar and firm government control. It is a different story on the Iraqi side of the border: no authority whatsoever."[248] 53.16

He called his son. Maḥrūt's tent was pitched at a little remove and at times he was still asleep at sunrise. "Maḥrūt! Maḥrūt! Get up quick! Call our men, jump on your horses, and take along camels loaded with large waterskins! I want you to accompany ʿAjlān until you have safely delivered him to Shammar territory. We must make sure he is not robbed on his way back home." They did as they were told, and on reaching the well of Līnah, ʿAjlān said, "Far enough. You can turn back." 53.17

عجلان يسَيِّر على ابن مساعد

١،٥٤ وارْحَل يما نزل بام القِلْبان هاللي يقول عند القفَيعي نازلٍ بالِبطين. والله وينزل بام القلبان ويوم نزل بام القلبان والى غَضْبان ما هو موجود غضبان يَمّ الرياض. قال من يَنْهَج معي ابي اسلّم على ابن مساعد. قالوا والله ما نجي ابن مساعد ولا ينهج معك الوالي. وينهج معه ضافي ابن ضبعان بناخي له هو عمه عجلان وضبعان عيال بَرْغَش ولد ضبعان هاللي مع عجلان مع عمه عمه بيده.

٢،٥٤ والله يوم جا عند الباب قالوا هذا عجلان ابن رمال يبي يسلم يا طويل العمر. قال خَلّوه يجي. يوم سلم عليه قال جيت يا عجلان. ما هو بهالقصيد مُودِع روحه انه ما يبي يطِبّ نجد آه.

٣،٥٤ قال

يامير جيتك يوم سكر هَبوبي　　ابي النفود اللَيّنة ونْخَلاتي

يعني اول الافِت للرشيد والرشيد سلّموا الامر وصاروا عيال عند ابوهم. له نخل بام القلبان وله ملك.

يامير ما عَيَّنْت حَشْوٍ ذهوبٍ　　حشوٍ غَفال وصوفهن بيّناتِ

جِذْعانٍ هكالحين الرشيد اللي نهجوا كلهم جذعان ابْوَتهم تِذابحوا واجلدوا هالجذعان وراحوا بهم للرياض.

وش هقوتك بيلابسين الخبوب　　هم يضربونَن لو يغَنّن بَناتي

هاللي يلبسون العمايم ويتسمّون بالدين.

Visit to the New Saudi Governor, Ibn Musāʿid

He continued on his journey until he arrived at Umm al-Gilbān, as mentioned, in the low area at the residence of al-Gfēʿī. When he took up his lodgings at Umm al-Gilbān, Ghaḍbān was not present. He was off to Riyadh. ʿAjlān issued an appeal: "Anyone willing to accompany me? I wish to go and pay my respects to Ibn Musāʿid." But they said, "By God, we have no intention of seeing Ibn Musāʿid. There is no one to take you there." He went accompanied by Ḍāfī ibn Ḍabʿān, a cousin. ʿAjlān and Ḍabʿān were sons of Barghash. The son of Ḍabʿān went with his uncle, holding him by the hand, leading him. 54.1

His appearance at the palace gate was announced to Ibn Musāʿid: "ʿAjlān ibn Rmāl wishes to present his respects, may your life be long." "Let him come in," he said. ʿAjlān was ushered in. After the greetings, Ibn Musāʿid said, "So you came after all, ʿAjlān?" Hadn't he made it known in his verses that he had no desire to set foot in Najd again? 54.2

He said: 54.3

Prince, I came to you a chastened man,
longing for soft sands and my grove of palms.

—He means to say, "First, I used to have regard for the Rashīd. Now the Rashīd have abdicated and are like children with their new father."[249] He owned date palms at Umm al-Gilbān.

Prince, didn't you see lost camel calves,
innocent, distraught, clear to every eye?

—The youngsters of the Rashīd family were taken away, all of them. Their fratricidal fathers had assassinated one another. The adolescents were taken to Riyadh.

What to expect from bullies in baggy coats,
beating me with a stick if my daughters sing.

—He refers to the new breed who donned pompous turbans and ostensibly devoted their life to religious practice.

٤،٥٤ قال بناتك ما يقال لهن شي والحشو هذولاك عند ابوهم معزّزين باعزّما هم به حنا ما حناب نحب النشيد لكن انت نشيدك عندنا طريفه. يا والله ما يبي يِبّدي نشيده على ابن مساعد. قال يابو عبد الله والله اني جِيت من جنة دنيا يعني لو انا دَوّار جنة دنيا والله اني ما اجي من هالمحَلّ اللي جيت منه لكن والله اني ما جيت الا عاني لبيت الله وتايب لوجه الله بس هالكلمات هذولي دخالة عن هاللي يتسمّون بالدِين وهم ما همب دَيّنين. سِدّ الباب عن القصيد.

٥،٥٤ قال أنت كبير يا عجلان. قال اي والله كبير. قال وش كِبْرك. قال والله ما ادْري لا نترّخ سنينا انا يوم اتذكر السنين اللي مِضَت علي يا مير ما هي شويه. قال وش كبرك يوم ندبح سِمِيك عجلان. - عجلان رتبة للرشيد بالرياض وسِطَى عليه عبد العزيز وعبد الله ابن جلوي وذبحوه - وش كبرك يوم نَذْبَح سِمِيك عجلان. قال لا لا انا كبير.

Ibn Musāʿid said, "Your daughters should be left alone. And put aside your concerns: those calves, the youngsters, are now lodged with their father, treated with respect, and looked after with the greatest care.[250] True, we have no fondness for song and verse, but your exceptional poems always pique our curiosity." But ʿAjlān was in no mood to recite poems to Ibn Musāʿid. Instead, he said, "Father of ʿAbdallah, I came from a paradise on earth. I mean, were I to seek a paradise on earth, I couldn't find a better spot than where I came from. Honestly, I have come as someone who turns his face to the House of God, a remorseful penitent bowing to his Lord. These verses of mine should be understood, however, as a plea to grant me your protection against those who pretend to be devout, whereas in fact they are not true men of religion in any sense. And by now the gates of poetry have slammed shut." 54.4

Ibn Musāʿid said, "Tell me, have you grown old, ʿAjlān?" "Yes," he said, "it is true, I am advanced in years." "What is your age?" "Honestly, I do not know. We kept no records, but if I try to remember the number of years that went by, then, Prince, yes indeed, they are quite a few." "How old were you when we killed ʿAjlān?" he said, referring to ʿAjlān, the representative of al-Rashīd in Riyadh, who was assaulted by ʿAbd al-ʿAzīz and ʿAbdallah ibn Jluwī and killed. "How old were you when we killed your namesake, ʿAjlān?" 54.5

"No, no. I am just old!"

Notes

1 "Promised meal" (*idbah*): "food given as payment to laborers." In the Arabic edition, the first hemistich of the second verse is missing. It was recited to me by an informant in Ḥā'il who was told by old transmitters that these verses were not addressed to Ibn Saʿūd but to Ibn ʿUrayʿir in al-Aḥsā'.

2 If he died in 1942, he must have lived till he was 106. According to one editor of his poetry, he lived from 1844 to 1942 (al-Ẓafīrī, *Dīwān al-shāʿir Abū Zuwayyid*).

3 The scene repeats itself on the return of ʿAjlān ibn Rmāl from self-imposed exile in the Syrian desert, see §54.

4 Lit. "may your tongue be sound!" (*ṣaḥḥ lsānik*).

5 Ibn Rakhīṣ is the family name of the shaykhs of the Nabhān, the clan to which Abū Zwayyid belonged. Here and elsewhere, the name Ibn Rakhīṣ refers to the shaykh himself.

6 "Always came out the winner": *mā yiflaj hū*, lit. "he is not ruled the loser in a court case"; i.e., his arguments are so cogent that tribal arbiters always rule in his favor. From *falaj*, "to win a dispute submitted to a judge."

7 According to Bedouin customary law, a raider who first touched a camel with his lance acquired title to claim it as his spoil. However, a raid leader (*ʿagīd*) had a mandate to divide the booty among his fellows (*ʿazl*).

8 Explained as "your good luck, *ḥaẓẓik*, must be earned, otherwise one may receive blame, *dhamm*."

9 Lit. "if leaving the well after drinking (*taṣdīr*; i.e., acting upon the counsel) were like heading toward the well (*wird*; i.e., taking the advice)." "Save the day": lit. "there would be no need for a medical doctor (*ṭibīb*)."

10 "Young wolves": *niḍāyiḍ dhīb*; *niḍīd*, explained as a synonym of *silīl* (pl. *salāyil*), "offspring"; *niḍā*, "to bring out (the best), produce."

11 "Slouched against the side": *yathwī bi-ṭarg al-bēt*; *ṭarg*, explained as "the place at the side of a tent, under the overhang of the tent cloth."

12 "Take it!": his nickname was Abū Khdhūh, because whenever a visitor came to ask for something, he would say, "*Khdhūh*": "Take it!"; i.e., from his possessions.

13 The reference seems to be to al-Hādī, a son of al-ʿĀṣī, "the rebel," shaykh of the Shammar tribe in Iraq, so called because he refused to cooperate with the Ottoman-Turkish

overlords and left it to relatives to deal with them. In 1905, al-Hādi was killed in the course of internecine strife. Al-ʿĀṣī passed away in 1925.

14 It is not clear how this reference relates to the transmitter's assertion that the verses are part of a poem dedicated to al-Hādī al-Jarbā.

15 "Spurred by a falcon": i.e., the poem's subject of praise who charges at these tough warriors.

16 The first hemistich is missing.

17 In this composition, perhaps the poet's best known, the staccato repetition of *ḥamrā*, "reddish-brown (she-camel)," is one of Abū Zwayyid's quirks. The preference for a red steed remains strong: the Bedouin of today favor red GMC trucks. The vocative at the outset of the verse, *yā-rākib* (pronounced with affricated *kāf, rāćib*), is the customary address to a rider on camelback ready to carry the poet's verses to its destination. As shown in verse 6, the Shammar consider the Nafūd Desert the northern border of Najd, while Ḥā'il is part of northern Najd.

18 "Daughter of a legend": Turkiyyah ibn Mhēd.

19 Generally understood as a reference to Muḥammad ibn Rashīd, the most powerful ruler of the Ibn Rashīd dynasty, who was rumored to be sterile.

20 This verse infuriated Ibn Rashīd and made him swear to kill Abū Zwayyid; see §10.1.

21 "Rabid monster": *shīb, shībah*, "mythical wolflike animal" (HA).

22 Also the name given to their herds of camels, especially the white ones (Musil, *Rwala*, 262, 420, 550); e.g., in the battle cry "I am the rider protecting ʿAlyā (camels)" (ibid., 526).

23 As the member of an "enemy tribe," he would need Ibn Rashīd's protection to pasture his camels in the tribal area of Shammar.

24 "Fifth degree": *khamsah*, "five," the group of blood relatives to the fifth degree on whom it is incumbent to exact blood revenge if one of their members is murdered.

25 *Ḍēgham* (CA *ḍaygham*, "lion") is the ancient ancestor and the collective rallying cry (*ʿizwah*) of ʿAbdah, to which the Jʿafar section of Ibn Rashīd belongs. Al-Ḍayāghim are the subject of a cycle of stories and verse in the style of the more famous epos of Banū Hilāl (for an Arabic text of recorded oral traditions of al-Ḍayāghim and Banū Hilāl, see Sowayan, *Ayyām al-ʿarab*, 1025–60).

26 A reference to a goat destined for slaughter that dug up the knife that had fallen and disappeared in the dust. Akin to the phrase "give them enough rope to hang themselves," here it is used by the poet to blame himself for not staying longer with Ibn Shaʿlān (al-Suwaydā', *Shuʿarā' al-jabal al-shaʿbiyyūn*, 2:104).

27 This translation is based on communications from Saad Sowayan.

28 ʻGēl (ʻUqayl) is the name for camel traders who mostly hail from the Qaṣīm area. "When the ʻAgejl come to the Shammar they employ many servants and herdsmen. Sometimes they put up their own tents, but not unfrequently they lodge under the tent of some Bedouin" (Musil, *Northern Neǧd*, 135–36).

29 "Futile altercations": *hāt al-lif, ʻadd al-līf*, lit. "give the twig, away with the twig"; similar in meaning to *waddūhā w-hātūhā*, "send it and bring it back"; i.e., "they talked it up and down, back and forth" (Stewart, *Texts in Sinai Bedouin Law*, 2:8).

30 "Gainsayers": *al-jaḥādah*, frequently used in the Qur'an in reference to people who deny the truth of the revelation. The first hemistich is a frequently used opening formula (see, e.g., Kurpershoek, *Arabian Romantic*, 143).

31 As explained, "they run to the right and the left because of exuberance; they only walk straight if they are fatigued."

32 That is, Fate. Cf. "What the dark nights carry in their bellies is unknown, inseminated at dusk, giving birth at dawn" (Kurpershoek, *Arabian Satire*, 89).

33 Saad Sowayan explains that "Only noble men of good means could light a fire to entertain guests and serve them food and coffee."

34 "Damascus goats": *zgēmiyyāt*, explained as "inferior breed of sheep, with an ugly mouth and appearance, and of little use."

35 In his febrile state of mind, ʻAjlān fears that some ill-intentioned men of the Rwalah will circumvent the rules concerning the sanctity of visitors and guests by employing one of his fellow tribesmen of Shammar for the purpose of robbing him.

36 "Didn't I tell you": *ṣādat*, lit. "it hit, caught the game"; i.e., "it happened, my fears came true."

37 As Sowayan explained, when thirsty camel herds converge on a well at the same time and the herders are in a hurry, the well ropes might get entangled, sparking off violent altercations.

38 A battle cry.

39 The stormy relation between Saṭṭām ibn Shaʻlān and Turkiyyah is told by Alois Musil, who made a prolonged stay in the tribe's camp (*Rwala*, 58, 558–59, 593–603).

40 Manhūbah means "snatched away, robbed."

41 Rulers often employed slaves for important and sensitive tasks. Some home-born slaves were accounted slave brothers of the Ibn Rashīd (Doughty, *Arabia Deserta*, 1:655).

42 The scene is reminiscent of Doughty's description of how he found Hirfa, the runaway young wife of Zeyd, a shaykh of the Fgarā tribe with whom he was staying, herself the orphan daughter of a shaykh, when he was asked to persuade her to return: "I found Hirfa, a little shame-faced, sitting in the midst of her gossips; old wife-folk that had been

friends of her dead mother; they were come together to the aunt's booth to comfort her, and there were the young men her cousins" (*Arabia Deserta*, 277).

43 "You piece of dirt": *ya-thiman al-milḥ*, lit. "the price of salt"; i.e., payment for the purchase of a slave.

44 "I will make you go willy-nilly": *tamshīn w-antī mā tshūfīn al-jāddah*, lit. "you will walk without looking at the path," as in the saying *ʿalēk b-al-jāddah law ṭālah*, "you have to stick to the prescribed path, no matter how long it takes" (al-Suwaydāʾ, *Amthāl*, 292).

45 "Twist the promise into your mustache": *iftilhin bi-shārbik*; i.e., "give me a solemn promise."

46 "Don't play such risky games": *la tgaṭṭiʿ al-juwwād*, lit. "do not cut the trails, no shortcuts please"; i.e., "play it straight."

47 *Khaḍīrī*: "someone who does not belong to a known tribe and therefore is not considered eligible to be married to a tribal woman"; in this sense, the term is slightly demeaning (communication from Saad Sowayan). As a blacksmith, a low status occupation, ʿAjab would have fallen within this category.

48 The ladies are compared to thoroughbred horses of the Prophet's companions. Therefore, *ajwāz* ("pairs") probably means that the two forelegs hit the ground at the same time during a spirited gallop.

49 This is Turkiyyah, daughter of Ibn Mhēd.

50 A free translation of a hemistich that many informants were at a loss to explain. The most plausible explanation was, lit., spearheads (*ṣufr*, "yellow, bronze") mounted on shafts (*ʿūd*, "branch, twig, shaft") and fire fueled by kerosene (*gāz*); i.e., in battle he is a lethal opponent and a fireball.

51 "Dearer to me than I am to than myself": *yā baʿad ḥayy*, lit. "may you still be alive (after I and others have passed away)," a Shammar expression of endearment.

52 "I did a lot of work": *ana yābsin rīǧī*, lit. "my spittle has dried up."

53 "Pleasure of conversation": *ytaʿallil*. More than just chatting, it refers to artful storytelling and declamation of poetry that interests and entertains an audience.

54 "Vexed": *ṭāmiḥ*, "a wife thus parted from her husband, but not regularly divorced, is called *ṭāmiḥi*: of this class there are great numbers."

55 "Go ahead": *midd w-ifliḥ*, another way of saying *tifaḍḍal, gil*, "please go ahead, speak!" *Ifliḥ* is also said when inviting someone to start eating (al-Suwaydāʾ, *Amthāl*, 570).

56 "Smooth, rounded": *mithl ash-shuwāshā*, "like Maria Theresa thalers" (sg. *shūshī*); "Maria Theresa dollars, in Arabia are called *riyāl abū shūshe*, in reference to the Empress's being represented on them with her hair brushed up in front" (Musil, *Northern Neǧd*, 3–4); *shūshah* commonly means "bun, tuft" of hair, by analogy with "all that

part of a shrub that is above the ground" (Mandaville, *Bedouin Ethnobotany*, 162; similarly, Lane, *Manners and Customs of the Modern Egyptians*, 29).

57 The rider calms the camel by gently touching it with his feet.

58 *Dibdūb*, pl. *dibādīb*: "thick ornamental tufts made of wool of about twenty-five centimeters length tied to the back, behind or in front of the hump as a sign that the she-camel is of exceptional quality and marked for the procreation of similar high-end camels" (HA, 7575). An "ornamented white she-camel" (*waḍḥā umm dibdūb*) refers to an exceptionally beautiful woman (al-Suwaydā', *Amthāl*, 533).

59 "Supple-necked": *khuḍʿ l-argāb*, lit., "necks held low, bowed," a standard expression of praise for camels, but applied to people it denotes submission.

60 The verse echoes a similar compliment paid to Saṭṭām ibn Shaʿlān; see §4.1.

61 This piece is composed with a single end rhyme instead of the more common separate rhymes for each hemistich.

62 "Shame on me": *allāh yilūm lḥiyyitī*, lit. "God blames my beard," similar to the saying "spit two gobs on my beard" (*tiff ʿalā liḥyitī tiffēn*), an expression of regret (al-Suwaydā', *Amthāl*, 90).

63 When Ibn Rakhīṣ befriended Ibn Rashīd, chief of the Nabhān, he declared his independence from Ibn Thnayyān, the paramount chief of the Zmēl branch of the Sinjārah division of Shammar. Disaffection between Āl Ḍaww and Ibn Rakhīṣ caused Ibn Rakhīṣ to join the Saudi Ikhwān against Āl Ḍaww (for the full story, see Sowayan, *Ayyām al-ʿarab*, 550–58; there is a shorter version, including Abū Zwayyid's poem, in *al-Ṣaḥrā' al-ʿarabiyyah*, 544–47).

64 "He doesn't have to prove anything": lit. "with a blind hand" (CA *makfūf*, "blind"); as explained by Sowayan, "someone higher told him not to do this or that."

65 "Folk of al-Jrāf": *al-jrāf* is the name of the camel markings originally common to all of the Nabhān of the Zmēl of Shammar (Sowayan, *Ayyām al-ʿarab*, 535). As I was informed by Musāʿid ibn Fahd al-Saʿdūnī, the author of *Camel Brandmarks of the Arabian Peninsula, Sedentary and Bedouin* (*Wusūm al-ibl fī al-Jazīrat al-ʿArabiyyah (bādiyah wa-ḥāḍirah)*), *al-jarfah* (pl. *jrifāt*, *jrāf*) is a tribal marking carved with a knife or sharp object into the skin of a camel—in the thigh, neck, cheek, or any other place—unlike the more usual *wasm*, which is branded into the skin with a red-hot iron. Several other Shammar tribes use the *jarfah* instead of a branded *wasm*.

66 Bedouin will not respect the right to asylum of any individual before he has restored "goods stolen or treacherously obtained," something his tribe should force him to do or expel him from their encampment (Burckhardt, *Notes*, 328).

67 To boast of pasturing in or close to enemy lands is a common trope.

68 “Impeccable Hearts”: a moniker of Ibn Hadhdhāl, lit. “Brothers of Batlā, Hearts of Cranes”; *gharānīć*, sg. *ghirnūg*, “long-necked aquatic bird; comely youth.” Nicknames in the same style are *azwāl aḍ-ḍbāʿ glūb as-sbāʿ*, “appearance of hyenas, hearts of lions,” for the Rwalah tribe; *dhabbāḥat al-ḥāyil, naṭṭāḥat al-ʿāyil*, “slaughterers of fat camels, nemesis of aggressors,” for all of Shammar.

69 The reference is to al-Ṭimyāt, the paramount shaykh of the Tūmān, one of the four main divisions of Shammar, and the father-in-law of Ṭārif ibn Shaʿlān. The poet asserts that al-Ṭimyāt will protect Abū Zwayyid from Ibn Shaʿlān.

70 “A mercenary soldier of Eben Rashīd was called *zgurtī*. Prince Muḥammad had kept over four hundred such mercenaries, but the prince at the time of our expedition [1915] kept hardly sixty” (Musil, *Northern Neǧd*, 143); *zgirt*, sg. *zgirtī*, “small trader; irregular troops of ʿGēl [CA ʿUqayl] in Medina” (HA, 4508). Also, *rijājīl*, the men of Ibn Rashīd’s bodyguard or private army who are always in attendance at his court, are sent on errands and perform other tasks at a sign of their master (al-Suwaydāʾ, *Manṭiqat Ḥāʾil*, 566).

71 Booty represented a significant share of state income. Muḥammad ibn Rashīd claimed half of the captured horses, one-fifth of the other animals, and all arms, which were partly redistributed among his private army (al-Suwaydāʾ, *Manṭiqat Ḥāʾil*, 543).

72 The scene has been vividly portrayed by European travelers. See, e.g., Palgrave, *Narrative*, 72–73, 97, and, from the poet’s time, Blunt, *A Pilgrimage to Nejd*, 217–18.

73 “Slaughtered at one’s interment”: *hbāṭah*, “sacrificial animal, a sheep or a goat” (HA, 4108).

74 Poetic self-correction is a trope with a long pedigree. Ibn Mayyādah (d. 754 or 766) saved himself on being confronted by women whose private parts he had insulted as “traces left by little lambs” by asserting that in reality he said, not *ka-āthāri l-ṣighār min al-bahmī* but *ka-athāri l-muqaysirati al-duhmī*, “traces left by dark, mature she-camels” (al-Iṣfahānī, *al-Aghānī*, 2:315–16, 3:159).

75 See Introduction, xix.

76 His eyes are turned to the side of the head, like a locust’s eyes; *ḥawal*, “walleyed, squinting” (CA *aḥwal*).

77 “Charcoal burner,” *faḥḥām*, was considered one of the lowliest jobs, reserved for poor people of humble descent.

78 The poet offers a double plea. He reminds Ibn Rashīd that his father was sheltered from his enemies by the poet’s tribal relatives, and he argues that according to the rules of Islam and custom, he is a “milk brother” of the ruler, since the latter had been breastfed by the poet’s mother.

79 Cutting off a prisoner’s lock is an age-old custom. Like Ibn Rashīd, Miṭlag ibn Jibrīn, the shaykh of the Mufaḍḍal tribe of the ʿAbdah of Shammar, spared the life of an enemy

whom he had sworn to kill and celebrate by slaughtering a camel (*jizūr*), and instead took a knife and cut off a lock of his enemy's hair, saying, "I have forgiven you for the sake of God" (*'afēt 'ank li-wajh Allah*).

80 The Arabic letter *jīm* ج has a bulge. The camel brand called *kaffah* ("scale of a balance") is a circle on top of a cross on the animal's right thigh (al-Sa'dūnī, *Wusūm al-ibl*, 155). The crescent, *hlāl*, is one of the most common brands.

81 The second hemistich is a repetition of §9.3, v. 5, a poem with the same end rhyme.

82 The verses echo Ibn Sbayyil's praise for Muḥammad ibn Rashīd: "[trays] heaped with full-grown sheep, legs interlocked, like a shepherd's flock around the well"; "a word from his mouth unlocks the gates of largesse" (Kurpershoek, *Arabian Romantic*, 95).

83 The verse echoes the concluding line of Ḥmēdān al-Shwē'ir's poem of apologies to Ibn Mu'ammar, in which he stops short of full surrender to preserve his independence and honor as a poet (Kurpershoek, *Arabian Satire*, 87).

84 The Ottoman State is meant. See the Introduction.

85 As the poet did on other occasions; see §10.3.

86 Sowayan cites this poem together with §9.3, v. 1 in the context of the internal struggles of the Nabhān of the Zmēl (*al-Ṣahrā' al-'arabiyyah*, 546–47). "Poisonous leaves": *rihwind*, explained as "a kind of clarified butter distilled from tree leaves in Iraq; it causes an unpleasant burning sensation in the belly, like that of *umm nār*, 'acid.'"

87 Sowayan comments: "He is talking to Muḥammad ibn Rashīd, blaming him for creating discord with the tribe and reminding him that the tribe would be forced to ally itself with Ḥāyil's enemies. The water bucket is a metaphor for the tribe of the poet."

88 Al-Jarādī: explained as Ibn Jarād, the army chief of Ibn 'Alī, the ruling dynasty before Ibn Rashīd, who was hunting for 'Abdallah ibn Rashīd, but took fright when he discovered that Ibn Rakhīṣ had thrown in his lot with Ibn Rashīd.

89 It was explained that the poet reminds (*yiminn*) Ibn Rashīd of past favors received from his kin. In general, *mann* is looked upon with disapproval (e.g., Q Ḥujurāt 49:17, *yamunnūna 'alayka an aslamū*, "They consider it a favor to you that they have accepted Islam"). Reminding someone of favors received is reprehensible, but in this context it might simply be playful teasing.

90 "Hey": *khlāf dhā*, lit. "after, following that," synonym of CA *da' dhā*, "now leave that" (subject), a formula of transition. Perhaps the first section of verse has gone missing. Here the word for "she-camel" is *'admiliyyah*, "peerless, unique"; *bindagin 'admiliyyah*, "tried trifle, an old rifle with which the marksman is so well acquainted that he never misses his aim" (Musil, *Rwala*, 225–26; CA *'adīm*: "being without"). It resembles the more usual *'imliyyah* (CA *'amliyyah*), "sturdy she-camel."

91 After four days on waterless pastures, the camels are led to water on the evening of the fourth day.

92 On finding the well crowded, riders and mounts return to the well whence they came and make do with foul-tasting remnants of water scooped up from the bottom.

93 "Ḍēgham": see n. 25.

94 They are driven by desire to pummel their enemies, not by lust of booty. Cf. ʿAntarah, "I enter the fray, then decline the spoils" (Montgomery, *War Songs: Antarah ibn Shaddād*, 11; al-Mufaḍḍal, *Dīwān al-Mufaḍḍaliyyāt*, 1:56).

95 "Swollen with fury": *ṭanā*, "rage, fury," refers to a moniker of Shammar tribesmen, *ṭanāyā*, "those swollen, red-faced with fury."

96 The Rashīdī war banner (*bērag*, CA *bayraq*) was bloodred, with the profession of faith stitched in gold thread. For about seventy years, from the rule of ʿAbdallah until ʿAbd al-ʿAzīz al-Mitʿib, this function was entrusted to a slave family, al-Frēkh (al-Suwaydāʾ, *Manṭiqat Ḥāʾil*, 449–52).

97 The first hemistich repeats the second hemistich of the preceding line. Saʿūd Abū Khashm was married to Nūrah, the daughter of Ḥmūd al-Sibhān. At the time, clansmen of the Sibhān were shoring up the crumbling power of Ibn Rashīd.

98 "Three legs": *tarfā thalāthin bi-khiṭwah*, "(the mare) folds three legs together as she pushes off with one leg for the jump"; cf. the epithet "single-footed" for outstanding horses in *The Iliad*.

99 It is likely that they were riding in a southeasterly direction, across the empty al-Ḥamād plains toward the Nafūd, and possibly toward the wells of al-Ḥuzūl.

100 "Damned (camels)": *mākhūdhātkum* (CA *maʾkhūdh*), lit. "may they (f. pl.) be taken, robbed"; *mākhūdh*, a rough, somewhat jocular expression, "that damned animal of yours."

101 "Lions": *ḍarāghīm*, an alternative form of *ḍayāghim*, sg. *ḍēgham*; see n. 25. The poet may have had in mind the decline of the Ibn Rashīd dynasty, which would date this piece to after the death of Muḥammad ibn Rashīd.

102 "Blazing plains": *shihb ar-rahārīh*; the color adjective *shihb*, f. pl. of *ashhab*, "gray, dust-colored," frequently occurs with a connotation of menace.

103 In the text, the next verse is exactly the same as v. 14 and has been omitted.

104 Either ʿAbd al-Karīm al-Jarbā or ʿAbd al-Karīm Qāsim. The two were known as *al-kharābtān*, "the two scourges."

105 "Raid leadership is a matter of good fortune and resoluteness. A lucky leader will always have followers desirous to share in his spoils. At that time, it was the belief that some people were blessed with luck." However, "good fortune also depended on

one's devotion to upholding tribal customs and Bedouin values" (Sowayan, *al-Ṣaḥrāʾ al-ʿarabiyyah*, 660–63).

106 The narrator is remembering having heard so from his father, who personally took part in the raid.

107 "His story": this story, which the narrator heard from his father and tells as if his father is the person telling the narrative.

108 *Kurrāth*: a kind of tall, edible grass; a wild onion from twelve to thirty-three inches high (30–110 cm), with pale green leaves, *Allium sphaerocephalum* (Mandaville, *Bedouin Ethnobotany*, 305).

109 "Cunning master": Jifrān al-Maʿaklī, and see §14.1.

110 "End of bad luck": *ʿilm al-Jirdhān bi-sh-sharr*, explained as "the end of evil and the beginning of good things (*atlā athar*: the tail end of bad things); from that moment, the flow of news (*ʿilm*) about their bad luck had come to an end."

111 A Rwēlī is a member of the Rwalah tribe.

112 "Regal": *jīl bi-s-sūg*, lit. "(did not set foot) at the marketplace for a long time"; i.e., the animal is too grand to be put up for sale. "Drawing water": *darb al-maʿāḍib*, lit. "the path of hardship"; i.e., *al-masnā*: the ramp where camels pull up heavy buckets from the well. This is a metaphor for the "nobility" of mobile Bedouin life as compared to the drudgery of settled life at the oases.

113 "Flirter": *ṭimūḥ*, "woman dissatisfied with her husband and eager to attract the attentions of a better man."

114 "ʿAlya camels": *rāʿ al-ʿAlyā*, "owner of al-ʿAlyā (camels)," moniker for the camels of the Rwalah tribe and, by extension, members of the tribe itself. "Any sisters"; i.e., lines of poetry other than these verses.

115 On the fourth day, the droppings of this vanguard are dry enough to serve as fuel for the cooking fires of riders on lesser mounts. That is, these high-quality camels cover the same distance in a much shorter time than ordinary riding camels.

116 "As a venture of this kind is very dangerous, every commander must fix the special reward the spy is to get" (Musil, *Rwala*, 644); see Introduction, n. 23.

117 Likely eighty to ninety camels per herd (al-Musallam, *al-ʿUqaylāt*, 87).

118 Making clarified sheep butter (*gishdah*) is associated with the moneymaking activities of owners of sheep and goats (Sowayan, *al-Ṣaḥrāʾ al-ʿarabiyyah*, 380). A small white butterfly (*ṭēr dhōbah*) may land in the cream to spoil the process (al-Suwaydāʾ, *Min shuʿarāʾ al-jabal al-ʿāmiyyīn*; 3:68; HA, 5722). In Arabic poetry, avarice and cowardliness, *bukhlun wa-jubnun*, go hand in hand (see, for example, al-Ḥakam ibn ʿAbdal in al-Iṣfahānī, *al-Aghānī*, 2:423); see Introduction, xxxvi.

119 "Mangy camel in a pen made of thorny bushes where those infected with smallpox are quarantined": *ajrab b-ʿinnat majdūr*, a standard expression for situations or persons one seeks to avoid (al-Suwaydāʾ, *Amthāl*, 10–11).

120 The second hemistich fits descriptions of the nose, which remains unmentioned. Other versions read *wa-l-khashm maṣgūl*: "the nose is a shiny sword" (al-Suwaydāʾ, *Min shuʿarāʾ*, 2:90; al-Ẓafīrī, *Dīwān al-shāʿir Abū Zuwayyid*, 180).

121 The calf drinks the milk of two she-camels and in consequence its hump is uncommonly big; cf. al-Dindān's verse: "Her hips bulge like the hump of a camel calf, pampered with the milk of two devoted foster mothers" (Kurpershoek, *Oral Poetry and Narratives from Central Arabia*, 1:149–51).

122 "Long-backed": *simḥūg*, pl. *samāḥīg*, "long, tall," said of people, trees, canes, spears (CA *sumḥūq*, "tall," said of a palm tree; ʿUbūdī, *Muʿjam al-uṣūl al-faṣīḥah li-l-alfāẓ al-dārijah*, 6:378–79).

123 The final verses (§17.6, vv. 11–13) heap ridicule on tightfisted owners of small cattle by way of contrast with "noble" camel Bedouin such as the poem's addressee, the shaykh of the Rmāl tribe. The two vignettes, one about a boy encouraged to go raiding, the other contrasting the noble Bedouin with grasping sheepherders, are in praise of the father of Khaznah al-Fiḍīl.

124 *Msās, mrā*: "good pasture" (CA *mara'a*, "to be, become tasty"; in a prayer for rain, "bring us wholesome, fertilizing rain," *isqinā ghaythan marīʾan marīʿan*, Ibn Manẓūr, *Lisān al-ʿarab*, 4,166); the opposite of *wkhām* (CA *wukhām*), "bad grazing."

125 The collected product is called *wadyah*, pl. *widāyā*, as in the saying *wadyatuh bi-sgāh*, "butter collected in his skin," meaning that it is too early to tell what sort of person he is (al-Suwaydāʾ, *Amthāl*, 475). In poetry, it has a negative connotation; e.g., the famous Shammar poet Radhān ibn ʿAngā, "those who devote all their time measuring their sheep's output" (*illī ygawwis wadyatuh kill ḥazzah*) (Sowayan, *al-Ṣaḥrāʾ al-ʿarabiyyah*, 380).

126 The first hemistich is missing. As explained, the miser is out of sorts (*miḥtās*, synonym of *balshān*, "stressed, afflicted"), confused and dazed (*ydāyikh*), because he lives in fear of being bothered by visitors.

127 Mkīdah is pronounced with affricated *kāf*, Mćīdah. Jamʿān al-Ghēthī, a member of the Ghyithah, a subtribe of the Yḥayā branch of the ʿAbdah division of Shammar.

128 *Yā baʿad ḥayyī w-mētī*: "you are dearer to me than all other living beings and those that have passed away together," an affectionate form of address to loved ones, relatives, spouses, friends (al-Suwaydāʾ, *Amthāl*, 522).

129 "Strength": *gaww*, a robust Shammar greeting, and in reply, *yā-halā*, "welcome" (Musil, *Rwala*, 455), also used in Sinai (Stewart, *Texts in Sinai Bedouin Law*, Part 2, 17).

130 "Like this": *hā-l-lōn;* here the narrator must have made a movement with his hands to mimic the quiver.

131 *Misgīnan w-ḥājjin bī*: lit. "you have given me something to drink (a synecdoche for all that is pleasant and good) and you have taken me on a pilgrimage (an even bigger favor)."

132 "Couched": *sijūm,* explained as "alert and silent, as if she is fully aware of what is going on and mentally prepared" (CA *asjam,* "camel that does not roar," Ibn Manẓūr, *Lisān,* 1947). "Fidgets": *tihinwiṣ w-tajwīḍ,* explained as "she utters a bèbèbè-like sound and agitates her body"; *jāḍ,* "to be uneasy, squirm"; e.g., a sick person when being cauterized (al-Suwaydā', *Faṣīḥ al-ʿāmmī fī shamāl Najd,* 157).

133 *Tifāḍīḍ*: explained as "she does not *faḍḍ,* is not wayward when getting saddled, does not try to run off, and does not roar, foaming at the mouth and regurgitating half-digested food" (al-Suwaydā' *Min shuʿarā',* 2:39).

134 Sowayan comments that "when clocks were first introduced to Arabia they were works of wonder, or works of the devil according to some." In 1883, Euting noted the presence of a standing clock in rococo style in the reception room of the Rashīdī prince and later the successor of Muḥammad ibn Rashīd, ʿAbd al-ʿAzīz ibn Mitʿib (*Tagebuch,* 1:188).

135 According to tribal custom and predilection for first-cousin marriage, they had a rightful claim to the daughter of their uncle; see 19.6. "This reservation is called *jīrah.* If the girl does not accept marriage, the first cousin may abdicate from his right after some time. In rare cases, he will not lift his blockade and will prevent her from marrying another man" (HA, 2547).

136 "Brother of Mēthā" is a rallying cry of the poet's Ibn Rakhīṣ clan.

137 "Surahs": *Tabāraka w-ʿAmmā,* popular names for surahs Kingdom, Q 67, Sūrat al-Mulk and Tidings, Q 78, Sūrat al-Naba'.

138 In this verse the cat-like tearing at the camel's flesh (*yanhash*) is explicitly ascribed to jinn. In classical poetry a cat is given this role: "The idea of a camel's speed being stimulated by having a cat, hirr, at her side, which attacks her with teeth and claws, is one which occurs in a number of passages in the ancient Arabic poetry" (al-Mufaḍḍal, *Dīwān al-Mufaḍḍaliyyāt,* 2:107, 155, 229). Lyall doubts the theory of Geyer that the male cat, hirr, is thought of as demonic, a form of the jinn. Compare §15.4, v. 3.

139 "Ages": *ćihhilin bi-l-jlūs,* "left unimpregnated, childless, for a long time"; i.e., very strong camels (CA *kahl,* pl. *kuhhal,* "middle-aged, man of mature age").

140 "Virgin meadows": *al-khaṭāyiṭ wa-l-agfār* (CA *qafr,* pl. *aqfār*); *khaṭīṭah* is an "isolated area of good grazing surrounded by dry vegetation that is of little use," so called if such a grazing patch is narrow and elongated (Mandaville, *Bedouin Ethnobotany,* 95).

141 Such verse still inspired an unruly late-twentieth-century Bedouin poet, Bandar ibn Surūr, who had replaced his camel with a truck. The vocabulary and phrasing remained

unchanged, but the metaphor had overwhelmed the original meaning: "Chivalrous virtue takes undaunted stalwarts, takes what feckless oafs have not: resolve to cross vast deserts and dead emptiness, where cowardly sons of owls fall short."

142 The tough riders and mounts gain time by leaving aside some wells and heading for one farther down the road; see §12.1, vv. 3–4.

143 Similar to Ḥmēdān al-Shwēʿir's "coffee cup in his right hand, hubble-bubble in his left," the ideal state of *kēf* (CA *kayf*), sensual repose (*Arabian Satire*, §17:3).

144 Sowayan comments: "He is talking about an encounter between raiders and owners of the lifted herds, so *ragṭā* here expresses the multitude of raiders wearing different clothes and carrying different weapons."

145 That is, the Prophet Muḥammad.

146 Al-Suwaydāʾ believes these verses were inspired by the internecine struggles in the House of Rashīd that preceded its collapse (*Manṭiqat Ḥāʾil*, 706).

147 Possibly a reference to the internecine strife and murder that brought down the House of Ibn Rashīd.

148 *Taghazzaz lahā sūd*: "for them black (flags) were hoisted."

149 The latter part of the second hemistich is missing and is taken from al-Suwaydāʾ, *Shuʿarāʾ* 1:487.

150 ʿUbūdī, *Muʿjam al-uṣūl*, 11:389, attributes this poem to Khḍēr al-Ṣʿēlīć.

151 "Islam": The poet refers to Sunni Islam. The "Unbelievers" are members of other religions, mostly local Christians or visitors from Europe. As the verse makes clear, members of the Shiʿah sect, mostly traders and pilgrims from Iraq and Persia, are seen as a separate group.

152 *Nlizzih lih ʿalā miltizāzih*; *yilizzih*: said of a dismounted warrior who hugs his horse's neck by way of farewell before a battle, in case the horse gets killed. Similarly, cavalrymen would embrace their comrades before charging the enemy, the "farewell greeting," *salām al-widāʿ* (al-Suwaydāʾ, *Manṭiqat Ḥāʾil*, 492).

153 Accepting payment of blood money instead of extracting revenge is regarded as weakness in the tribal view; *gaṭʿ*, "cutting of throats," if the aim is not booty but revenge (Sowayan, "Customary Law").

154 These lines of gnomic wisdom bear no obvious relation to the other verses or to each other. Perhaps they are the remainder of a lost section. This might be an analogue to "aiming to ferret out secrets of our private affairs," something not be done "in pitch-dark, moonless nights"—that is, when one might be caught unawares.

155 The falcons are of the lesser sort, useless for hunting. When called, they do not return to the hunter but instead try to hide in *shīḥ*, a shrublet (*Artemisia*), which happens to fit the end rhyme.

156 The saying goes *al-gḍā midhallah*, "going to court is a sign of weakness."

157 The implication is that S'ūd Abū Khashm was a commander not less capable than his father, 'Abd al-'Azīz, and uncle Muḥammad ibn Rashīd. In fact, S'ūd's court was in parlous state.

158 The reference is to the Ibn Rashīd prince.

159 "Two good fortunes": *as-sa'dēn mā ytarākabin*, a standard expression; i.e., "one side can be fortunate only at the expense of the other."

160 It is not specified here, but earlier 'Āmish was mentioned as one of the sons of Abū Zwayyid (§1.3). Given Abū Zwayyid's advanced age at this point, his son was more likely to make use of the rifles.

161 'Uṣmalī: "Ottoman," from *'uthmānlī* (HA, 6389); here it refers to a version of the Martini rifle produced by the Ottoman Turks, known locally as Umm Khams, "Mother of Five" (bullets), sent to S'ūd Abū Khashm and first used in the battle of al-Jrāb in 1915.

162 Abū Mish'al is S'ūd Abū Khashm.

163 The enemy is ridiculed because usually "the hareem (women) come riding in their train of baggage camels," while "the sheykhs are riding together in advance," called the *salaf* (Doughty, *Arabia Deserta*, 1:261).

164 *Mirti'ah*, here "weaklings," are Bedouin who pay for the right to graze in another tribe's territory; payment of *rtā'ah* is considered a symbol of weakness. "Poets frequently boast of the strength of their tribes, claiming that they graze their herds wherever there is pasture available without paying" (Sowayan, "Customary Law").

165 His maternal relatives were the Sibhān family, who acted as regents while the prince was still a minor.

166 Mūḍī's brothers: S'ūd's regents and the powers behind his throne (al-Suwaydā', *Manṭiqat Ḥā'il*, 436, 513–14).

167 "Slaves": *'abīd*; these are *al-rijājīl*, the personal troops and bodyguards of Ibn Rashīd.

168 Abū Zayd, the legendary hero of the saga of the westward migration of Banū Hilāl.

169 "Strike sparks": i.e., without it he cannot be creative and sing your praises. "Free me from the debt": lit., "Give me a pass [*bāṣ*] (that sets me free) from the debt." *Bāṣ* originally means passport. Here it probably refers to anything that allows him to get by and pay the debt.

170 "Shaṭṭ": *jāri as-sīb*, lit. "vague line seen at the horizon"; i.e., the confluence of Euphrates and Tigris rivers, known as Shaṭṭ al-Arab, as it appears from afar to camel riders coming from the higher desert ground to the river's southwest; see also §49.15, v. 10. Al-Khurmah is a town at the southwestern end of Najd; Kandahar is in Afghanistan.

171 "Arrogant recalcitrants": *taḥānīb*, lit. "showing a curved back like an angry cat" (CA *taḥnīb*, "crookedness, curving shape").

172 The conceit is that guests are the hosts (*maʿāzīb*, sg. *mʿazzib*), since they are told: "you are *rabb al-manzil*, owner of this house." The rains of late fall and early winter (*dalw*, leather bucket; i.e., the constellation of the Pleiades, so called because it catches "water in a large bailing bucket and then pours it over the scorched land," Musil, *Rwala*, 226) did not come to irrigate the grass seeds (*bdhārih*).

173 The tribes were allowed to stay on their lands as the ruler's subjects as long as they paid zakat to Ibn Rashīd.

174 But in his poem in praise of Saṭṭām ibn Shaʿlān, the chief of the Rwalah tribe, Abū Zwayyid alluded to the fact that Muḥammad ibn Rashīd remained childless because of sterility.

175 Another instance of this popular hyperbole (see §4.1, v. 13, §27.5, v. 41). It is a rejoinder to Abū Zwayyid's claim that women had never given birth to the like of Saṭṭām ibn Shaʿlān, a verse that was particularly irksome to Ibn Rashīd.

176 In late spring and early summer, some nomads used to live in a hut made of palm leaves, *yṣayyir*; also said of a hard-up Bedouin, *ḥaththāl*, forced to make a living in settled country, *yḥathil* (Sowayan, *al-Ṣahrā' al-ʿarabiyyah*, 351).

177 The number of tents with seven poles, such as those owned by paramount shaykhs, is estimated at not more than 2 or 3 percent of all Bedouin tents (al-Suwaydā', *Manṭiqat Ḥā'il*, 583). It might be a legendary touch given by narrators, as al-Hirbīd did not belong to this class.

178 "Forgiveness": *yaṭlibk al-ḥill*; i.e., *al-bayḥah*, "he asks your forgiveness," an expression used on learning of someone's death, to which the response is *allāh yibīḥ fīh* or *minh*, "may God grant him forgiveness."

179 "Servants' heads": *rūs khiddām*; the Bedouin used to have black slaves, to whom the poet compares the slabs of stone blackened by fire.

180 "Plague": *awhām*, sg. *waham*, "cholera" (al-Suwaydā', *Manṭiqat Ḥā'il*, 657).

181 "Our luck remains prostrate": luck, good or bad, is often portrayed in terms related to the movements of a camel.

182 *Nērāt*: "a gold guinea; originally *līrah*, the *lām* changed into *nūn*" (ʿUbūdī, *Muʿjam al-tijārah wa-l-māl wa-l-faqr wa-l-ghinā*, 357).

183 "Hearthstones": *ath-thalāth as-sūd*, lit. "the three black ones"; i.e., the three stones that support the cooking pot, a conventional attribute of the deserted camp scene.

184 A polite interpolation of the narrator, addressed to his audience during recording.

185 *Hāmmah*: "forceful," "a very strong person, camel"; originally "a big, aggressive snake."

186 If the leading she-gazelle is dead, the other gazelles are lost and an easy prey.

187 *Siʿbūb*, pl. *saʿābīb*: "saliva that hangs from the mouth in thin threads (also said of cows)," used for a slouch and good-for-nothing (al-Suwaydā', *Faṣīḥ*).

188 The riddle is about locusts. Before being able to fly, they crawl, walking as if on crutches, a reference to their upwardly protruding jumping legs. Young locusts whose wings are just growing, *dibā*, "are so numerous at times that they crawl in a long chain, urging each other on and even riding one on top of the other" (Musil, *Rwala*, 112–13, 627).

189 If in conversation words for repulsive or unclean subjects come up, one offers an apology; e.g., "far be it from you," *bi'īd mn as-sām'īn*, "at the mention of a dog, donkey, unnamed woman, pair of sandals" (Stewart, *Texts in Sinai Bedouin Law*, 2:8).

190 This is hyperbole: the raiders leave in the morning and in the afternoon of the same day are back at their camp where the robbed camels' young rest after drinking.

191 In poetry, the harsh creaking of wooden doors, big wooden keys, and screaming wooden rollers of the pulley wheels of wells represent everything unpleasant and narrow-minded about village life. In Bedouin opinion, doors are shut in order to keep uninvited guests out, a sign of the worst sin, miserliness (cf. §36.4, v. 11).

192 A note in the source clarifies that the narrator is Ṭlēḥān ibn Mkhallaf al-'Mēm.

193 Each of the poem's similes is developed into a minor excursus on aspects of the *tertium comparationis*. Intricately wrought, this is hardly an apprentice's work.

194 The sheath that envelops the date stalks breaks through the wood with a grating sound and sucks up the "sugar" of the heart of palm (al-Suwaydā', *al-Nakhlah al-'arabiyyah*, 96, 228).

195 The traditional simile for the straight nose of a beauty.

196 Maria Theresa thalers, *ibū al-shūshī, al-faransī*; *faransī*, not "French," but named after Maria Theresa's husband François III Étienne; see §7.2, v. 4 and n. 56.

197 In these two verses, the poet indulges in wordplay on the daughter's family name, al-Jim'ī, the word for fist or clenched hand (*jim'* and the plurals *jmū'* and *ajmā'*) and other words of the same root, *j-m-'*.

198 Another play of words, this time on different coinages and weights: *nērah*, Ottoman gold guinea; *arbā'*, pl. of *rib'*, a quarter of a *ghāzī* (pl. *ghawāzī*), an Ottoman gold coin minted in Iraq (al-Suwaydā', *Manṭiqat Ḥā'il*, 576); *rib' as-sibī'*, "a quarter of a *sibī'*, a seventh"; i.e., "a trifling amount" ('Ubūdī, *Mu'jam al-tijārah*, 168).

199 *Tarthūth* (*Cynomorium coccineum*), a kind of mushroom also called *zibb adh-dhīkh* or *zibb al-ḥmār*, "penis of dog, donkey" (HA, 4663), referring to the plant's phallic form, "a fleshy, reddish, club-shaped, and leafless root parasite that grows to about one foot (30 cm) high" (Mandaville, *Bedouin Ethnobotany*, 329).

200 *Taww ma shadd fazzā'*: "(a girl) whose breasts have just begun to swell and who loudly calls for rescue"; i.e., an innocent enchantress, she appeals to sprightly young men (*jhayyil al-'yāl*).

201 "The expression is literally *ʿatāk al-kōbah*, may you get a skin disease that makes the hair of your beard fall out" (al-Suwaydā', *Amthāl*, 556).

202 The Arabic edition adds a note that the following poem is also ascribed to the poet al-Jhēlī.

203 Wordplay: *Mashwī* means "roasted (meat)"; al-Mashwī is the name of the family of shaykhs of the Shmēlah branch of the ʿAbdah division of Shammar.

204 Al-Shiʿb means "steep gully"; al-Shiʿab is the name of a mountain south of Ḥā'il. Words formed of the root *sh-ʿ-b* occur five times in this line, conveying a sense of harsh urgency (*shaʿʿab*: "to lash").

205 Sowayan comments in a note to the Arabic text: "This is a strange, unique poem, in a meter that is not one of the known meters of Nabaṭī poetry. Perhaps for this reason, there are some irregularities in its long lines that vary from one transmitter to the other."

206 According to the stories, al-Hirbīd was addicted to his pipe.

207 The coffeepot with its cap-shaped lid is compared to an Ottoman-Turkish sergeant (*shāyūsh*; i.e., *shawīsh*) who comes strutting in from town.

208 *Jirjīr*: "arugula" (*Eruca sativa*).

209 Ibn Rashīd's levy on the Bedouin was one riyal, a *majīdī*, for every five camels. Teams of tax collectors, with a scribe and helpers, went out to the tribes at the end of spring to assess the herds. Dodging the tax collection, called *ḥōsh*, carried a penalty of paying double the amount and other punishment at the discretion of Ibn Rashīd (al-Suwaydā', *Manṭiqat Ḥā'il*, 464–65, 555, 577).

210 The ascendancy of the Sibhān family dates from the appointment of Zāmil al-Sibhān to the Rashīdī treasury. It is unlikely that he or one of his relatives would have been dispatched in person to the poet's cattle enclosure.

211 "Ninety" is used here and throughout these corpora as a formulaic number with the general meaning of "many."

212 *Tanfiḍ ʿaskarih*: "raindrops that hit the ground like an army preceded by a rain of bullets" (CA *nafaḍa* "to shake").

213 Explained as "Mikā'īl, the angel of rain, who calls at the clouds as a herdsman calls his camels, to make them follow in his steps, with a sound *urrrhooo*!"

214 As explained, if the porcupine eats the core, *jummār*, of a date palm, the tree dies. They eat from the palms if there are not enough grasses and plants to serve them as food, and they only choose plants that have not been directly exposed to sunlight.

215 Al-Shifā means "a flat top of a long ridge"; it is the name of the country that slopes up to the crest of the al-Tihāmah mountain range. In poetry, "salt of al-Shifā" is another word for gunpowder made by the Bedouin (e.g., Zēd al-Khshēm, a sedentary poet of the Gfār in Shammar Mountain, Sowayan, *al-Ṣaḥrā' al-ʿarabiyyah*, 424).

216 *Khāmid ar-rīḥ*, here translated as "oaf," is the "listless" wind in summer when the grasses have dried up. It is the opposite of *hābb ar-rīḥ*, the animated wind that brings rainclouds and the good things in life, corresponding to *bushrā*, the wind of "glad tidings," as in Q Aʿrāf 7:57.

217 *Mrattināt*: as explained, the Bedouin connect the plural of the Martini gun with *raṭṭan*, "to speak in an incomprehensible tongue, with a rattling sound." *Dharānīḥ*, sg. *dharnūḥ*: "poison." *Ḥallāb al-ablāl*: lit. "milking (the body's) fluids"; i.e., the blood and contents of the abdomen are "milked" by gunpowder.

218 "Faḍlī": the name of an ancestor.

219 "Shalwā falcon": *ṭēr Shalwā*, an expression for a mighty and noble achiever.

220 *Nuṣiy* is a perennial that "thrive[s], with flowers and green forage, well into June," while "annual grazing plants are generally dead and gone by the end of May." *Ḥamāṭ* is a weed that produces an itching sensation, while *khimkhim* is a non-stinging nettle, *Forsskaolea tenacissima*. These plants are part of the Bedouin plant lexicon, which "has carried these names without change for more than 1,100 years" (Mandaville, *Bedouin Ethnobotany*, 74, 92, 234, 262, 336).

221 That is, the Pleiades, a measure of the season since earliest times.

222 Soles: *nʿāl*; as explained, Sājir healed his camel's bleeding soles by cutting a small amount of fat from the hump, melting it (*yaṣharih*) and placing the molten fat inside the hoof of the wounded sole pad. He used this original procedure instead of applying a *rugʿah*, a piece of cloth, to the sole.

223 Lit. "putting aside and bringing" (food). As Sowayan commented: "It is not just about serving food, but also advice that could promote or prevent aggressive action. It means that they are men of authority and sound opinions whose advice and leadership are sought after."

224 The owners have preserved the stallion's sperm. Therefore, they know for certain that the mount was fathered by a camel, not an ostrich, even though it runs like an ostrich.

225 The camel has the brand mark of Htēm, here a reference to a lower-status tribe, the Binī Rishīd (not to be confused with the dynasty of Ibn Rashīd).

226 That is, he does not seek out weaker opponents or booty alone, but goes after the high and mighty to prove his superiority to all and sundry.

227 As explained, the "mouse" (*fārah*) under the skin refers to movements of a sinew that seems to run back and forth above the hocks. The simile evokes the image of a well-trained, hardy camel.

228 These are places near Rafḥā, perhaps small black mountains. Al-Birrīt is a particularly deep well. An expert herdsman allows the camels to rest at the *mikhmār*, one day's easy march from the well.

229 He was approached by the guardians of Ibn Rashīd's reserve of protected grazing and brusquely ordered to clear out.

230 The names are those of Ibn Rashīd's guardians of the protected grazing area.

231 "Shithead": *yā-ṭagʿatēn*, "you are (worth) two farts."

232 "Ḥawwās": explained as the name of *ṣlubī* who takes his seat behind the house or tent, as stated in the maxim "noblemen lining the majlis, the *ṣlubī* out of view at the backside" (*ashrāf bi-l-aṭrāf, aṣ-ṣlubi khalf al-bēt*). He travels seated on the camel's rear, holding on to the rider in front; i.e., he is literally a hanger-on who scrounges from others.

233 The first words of the second hemistich are missing in the Arabic edition. In Ḥā'il, I was informed of the reading provided here.

234 ʿAdnān is the common ancestor of the northern Arabs; Idrīs, according to tradition, was the earliest prophet after Adam and Seth.

235 The reference is to the nine sons of ʿAmīrah, the early ancestor of the Rmāl tribe, famous for its herds of pure white camels.

236 *ʿAlgā*, a yellowish-green shrublet, "is an important grazing plant in some sandy regions"; *ʿādhir* is a perennial bush, "wormwood [. . .] plant characteristic of the red sands of the Dahnā'" (Mandaville, *Bedouin Ethnobotany*, 97, 257–58).

237 "Evergreen oaks" (*sindiyān*) refers to a big tree like the Syrian cedar.

238 Hot weeds (*ḥamāṭ*) refer to "a many-branched shrublet [. . . .] Children use it to play 'itching jokes' on one another," because when rubbed between the hands and applied to the face it produces an itching sensation (Mandaville, *Bedouin Ethnobotany*, 154, 268–69).

239 "Those fanatics": *hal ar-rīʿ*, lit. "the people of the narrow mountain pass"; i.e., the mountainous approaches from Najd to the Hijaz in the area of al-Ṭā'if, usually with reference to Ḥarb, a tribe notorious for shaking down pilgrim caravans on their way to Mecca. Here it has turned into a general reference to men from outside the Shammar tribal lands who were recruited by Ibn Saud to discipline wayward elements of the Shammar tribe.

240 The hems of the shirt stink, in contrast to the Ikhwān's harangues about purity, ritual washings, and the cleanliness of the faith. The poet makes the point that in reality their mindset is dirty: such a person is *ʿafin*, a revolting boor and good-for-nothing.

241 As explained, he is stuck between two countries, his Shammar kinsmen and the Ikhwān who renounced their tribal allegiance.

242 "Double ancestry," lit. "between two grandfathers." The verse expresses revulsion and amazement at the fact that someone with exemplary ancestry turned out such a bad apple.

243 The panther-sized cat is fearsome because he is backed by Saudi state power.

244 The Ikhwān shaved their mustaches in line with a tenet of the Ḥanbalī school of Islamic Law. They held the notion that "those Bedouins who wore the *ʿiqāl* instead of the newly fashioned *ʿimāma* (a thin white turban) were not real Muslims and could be fought" (al-Fahad, "The *ʿImama* vs. the *ʿIqal*," 35).

245 The full story is told in Sowayan, *Ayyām al-ʿarab*, 335–36.

246 In 1837, Khurshid Pasha, the chief of the Egyptian force in Medina, accepted ʿAbdallah ibn Rashīd as the ruler in Ḥāʾil in lieu of the Āl ʿAlī dynasty in exchange for plentiful supplies of pack camels. In consequence, ʿAbdallah and his cavalry attacked ʿAnazah at Ghnēm Mountain southeast of Tayma and despoiled the tribe of hundreds of camels (al-Suwaydāʾ, *Manṭiqat Ḥāʾil*, 355, 395; the story and a version of seven verses are found in al-Rashīd, *Nubdhah taʾrīkhiyyah ʿan Najd*, 72–73). This minor clash can hardly be considered proof in a dispute many decades later between other tribal chiefs over areas of influence in Mesopotamia. But such nitpicking does not take away from the story's broad sweep.

247 Ibn Burmān is a figure from a folktale. One day, the only prey his falcon could find was a coiled-up snake. Released from the air, the viper struck out at Ibn Burmān, who died instantly (a slightly different version is given in al-Suwaydāʾ, *Amthāl*, 266–67). The expression means "rewarding evil for good," though the tale itself does not presume evil intent on the part of the falcon.

248 An anachronism: Saudi Arabia as a country had not yet come into existence and there were no guarded border crossings.

249 The poet soft-pedals his sympathy for the House of Ibn Rashīd and clarifies that he makes a distinction between the rulers of the House of Saud and the hardline Ikhwān.

250 The governor assures the poet that the youngsters are better off under the guardianship of ʿAbd al-ʿAzīz ibn Saʿūd's than they were with their biological fathers. They were kept under close surveillance for the time being in Riyadh. For decades, members of the Ibn Rashīd family were not allowed to return to Ḥāʾil, as I was often told.

Glossary

ʿAbaklī (pronounced ʿAbaćlī) ibn Fāliḥ a shaykh of the Shilgān.

Aba l-Gūr a place near ʿArʿar, on today's border with Jordan.

Abbas I (r. 1848–54) grandson of Muḥammad ʿAlī, the founder of the nineteenth-century dynasty of Egyptian rulers; he was keenly interested in Arabian horses.

ʿAbdah the principal division of the Shammar confederation. It may have migrated from Yemen about seven centuries ago. The ruling families in Ḥā'il during the nineteenth century, Āl ʿAlī and Ibn Rashīd, are both from the Jʿafar section of the ʿAbdah.

ʿAbd al-Karīm al-Jarbā (r. 1835–71) powerful leader of the Shammar tribe in Iraq. He was executed by the Ottoman government and buried in Mosul. His father, Ṣfūg al-Jarbā, was killed by the Ottoman Turks when ʿAbd al-Karīm was not yet ten years old.

ʿAbd al-Karīm Qāsim the military dictator who brought down the rule of the Iraqi royal family in 1958. He and ʿAbd al-Karīm al-Jarbā were known as *al-kharābtān*, "the two scourges, (bringers of) ruin."

ʿAbdallah ibn Rashīd ruler of the Jaʿfar clan of the ʿAbdah division of the Shammar tribal confederation who founded the Ibn Rashīd dynasty in 1835, with its capital in Ḥā'il, after ousting the last ruler of the Ibn ʿAlī family, Ṣāliḥ. On his death in 1847, he was succeeded by his son Ṭalāl. Included in the list of forty poets in ʿAdwān al-Hirbīd's al-Shēkhah poem.

Abū Tāyih the warlike chief of the Ḥuwayṭāṭ tribe (1874–1924), made famous by his portrayal in *Seven Pillars of Wisdom* by T. E. Lawrence ("Lawrence of Arabia").

Abū Zayd nickname of the poet Muḥammad al-Aḥmad al-Sudayrī. Included in the list of forty poets in ʿAdwān al-Hirbīd's al-Shēkhah poem.

Abū Zayd al-Hilālī hero-poet who led the Banū Hilāl on their western migration (*taghrībah*) from Arabia to Tunis.

ʿAjlān ibn Rakhīṣ a shaykh of Abū Zwayyid's tribal section, appointed Ibn Rashīd's governor in Riyadh. He was killed together with numerous members of the garrison during the Saudi reconquest in 1902. That attack was launched by ʿAbd al-ʿAzīz ibn Saʿūd and his cousin ʿAbdallah ibn Jluwī, then the second-most powerful leader of the Saud dynasty and a relative of ʿAbd al-ʿAzīz al-Musāʿid.

Āl ʿAlī a family of the Jaʿfar section of the Ribīʿiyyah branch of the ʿAbdah, who were appointed as governors in Ḥāʾil by the House of Saud. After the destruction of the Saudi capital al-Dirʿiyyah, they acted as vassals of the Turkish-Egyptian overlords. A sedentary family, their writ did not extend to the Bedouin. In 1835, ʿAbdallah ibn Rashīd was appointed governor by Fayṣal ibn Turkī, whom he had befriended on the Saudi military campaigns.

al-ʿAmārāt a major tribe of the Bishr division of the ʿAnazah confederation, centered in the area around Hīt and Karbala in Iraq. In the eighteenth century, the tribe wandered in the northeastern part of central Arabia, joined the Wahhabi troops, and ventured farther north. The tribe's shaykhs are the Ibn Hadhdhāl family.

ʿAnazah one of the oldest and largest Arabian tribal confederations, supposedly named after an eponymous ancestor, ʿAnnāz. About three centuries ago, they moved from their base around Khaybar in the Hijaz north toward Syria and Iraq. Genealogically, they are reckoned among the northern Arabs, Rabīʿah, whereas their hereditary rivals, Shammar, trace their origins to the southern Arabs. Around 1800, a second northward migration of the tribes of ʿAnazah and Shammar occurred, this time caused by Wahhabi pressure. The division of Bishr (Fidʿān, Sbaʿah, ʿAmārāt) pastured along the Euphrates; Ḍanā Muslim (Ḥsanah, Wild ʿAlī, Jlās/Rwalah) pastured more to the west, in Syria. Wars among these divisions were frequent. The only tribe to remain entirely in Arabia is Wild Slēmān. It was not originally part of ʿAnazah and probably joined for political reasons.

ʿAntar ʿAntarah ibn Shaddād, one of the most famous pre-Islamic poets and composer of one of the seven *al-Muʿallaqāt* poems. He is also the hero of a cycle of stories in the Middle East.

al-ʿArfajī Muḥammad ʿArfaj of Āl Abū ʿLayyān (ʿUlayyān), headman of the town of Buraydah in al-Qaṣīm Province.

al-Ashmal nickname of Bnayyah ibn Fāris al-Jarbā. Included in the list of forty poets in ʿAdwān al-Hirbīd's al-Shēkhah poem.

al-ʿAskarī ʿAmʿūm al-ʿAskarī al-Dughmānī of the Rwalah tribe of ʿAnazah. Included in the list of forty poets in ʿAdwān al-Hirbīd's al-Shēkhah poem.

Banū Hilāl Arabian tribes that in 1050 set out from Egypt to invade North Africa, the so-called westward journey (*taghrībat Banī Hilāl*) described by the historian Ibn Khaldūn (732–808/1332–1406), who was the first to give examples of *hilālī*-style "Bedouin" poetry that later became known as Nabaṭī poetry. In more recent times, Banū Hilāl grew into a popular saga, featuring Abū Zayd and other heroes.

Banū Ṣakhr (also al-Ṣukhūr) originally from the northern Hejaz, these nomads and seminomads are the dominant tribe in the hinterland of northern Jordan. By causing trouble for pilgrim caravans, they leveraged their influence with the Ottoman Turks. At the outbreak of the First World War, the only tribe that still paid tribute to the Banū Ṣakhr were the Sharārāt. After the war, they supported Emir ʿAbdallah of Transjordan against raids of the Saudi Ikhwān in 1922 and 1924.

Barjas Barjas ibn ʿIrdān of the Salmān of the Sinjārah division of Shammar. Included in the list of forty poets in ʿAdwān al-Hirbīd's al-Shēkhah poem.

Battle of al-ʿĀmiriyyah the exact date of this tribal battle is unknown, but according to oral sources it probably occurred in the period 1906–11. Tribesmen of al-Rwalah, led by Nawwāf and Mamdūḥ ibn Shaʿlān, and of al-Ḥuwaytāt, led by Abū Tāyih, raided Bedouin of the Zmēl of Shammar, led by Qāsim (Ǵāsim) ibn Rakhīṣ, at the wells of al-Ḥuzūl. Al-ʿĀmiriyyah is a valley in that area.

Battle of al-Jawf battle fought in 1920 that pitted Nawwāf ibn Nūrī ibn Shaʿlān and ʿAwdah Abū Tāyih of the Ḥuwayṭāṭ tribe against Sʿūd, who emerged victorious, one year before the final demise of the Ibn Rashīd rule.

Battle of al-Jmēmā (al-Jumaymā') battle fought in al-Jawf Province in 1910 between the troops of Ibn Rashīd and the ʿAnazah tribes of the Rwalah and the ʿAmārāt. At that time, Sʿūd ibn ʿAbd al-ʿAzīz was about twelve years old and his maternal uncles of the Āl Sibhān family ruled as regents on his behalf.

al-Bāyiḥ a shaykh of the Ǵitāmīs tribe.

ʿBēd ʿUbayd ibn Rashīd, brother of ʿAbdallah ibn Rashīd and the general of the armed forces.

Brēk Brēk al-Asʿadī al-ʿUtaybī, headman of the town of Bagʿā to the east of Ḥā'il, known for his poetic correspondence with Fēṣal al-Ṣwēṭ, the shaykh of the Ẓafīr tribe.

daḥḥah a dance "whereby a girl facing a half circle of men moves a few steps back while playing with a sword. A man in the middle sings while to his right and left others answer each strophe. At the end of the song, the entire line claps its hands, while moving the upper body sideways" (HA). The *laʿb al-daḥḥah* is peculiar to the Bedouin of the Syrian desert and northern Arabia, in particular the ʿAnazah confederation. It served to lift the spirits of tribesmen before a fight or to celebrate victory and recount their feats. Nowadays it is danced at wedding parties and on feast days.

al-Dghērāt a section of the ʿAbdah division of Shammar established on the southwestern side of Ajā Mountain.

al-Dhēmī situated in the area of Sakaka and ʿArʿar in Wadi al-Khirr.

al-Dhirfān one of the sections of the the Zmēl branch of the Sinjārah division of Shammar.

al-Dighmān one of the five subtribes of the Rwalah.

Fahd ibn ʿAbd al-Muḥsin al-Hadhdhāl (1840–1924) shaykh of the ʿAmārāt tribe of ʿAnazah, who camped on both sides of the middle Euphrates, nominally "shaykh of shaykhs" of the entire ʿAnazah confederation (*shaykh mashāyikh ʿAnazah*). He was given the Ottoman title of bey (Arabic: *bēk*). In 1922, he was elected a member of Iraq's Constituent Assembly.

Fahdah daughter of al-ʿĀṣī ibn Shrēm, the mother of Mishʿal. Subsequently, she married King ʿAbd al-ʿAzīz, and their son Fahd was king of Saudi Arabia from 1982 to 2005.

Fajḥān al-Farāwī (1817–97) warrior and poet of the Mṭēr (Muṭayr) tribe, who was rewarded with three horses for his eulogy of ʿAbd al-Karīm al-Jarbā.

al-Fawāʿirah a relatively new tribal grouping established by Ḥasan al-Fāʿūr, who originated from the Faḍl tribe.

Fayṣal ibn Turkī (1785–1865) ruled the second Saudi state in tumultuous times. His first term as a ruler (1834–38) ended with a forced exile in Cairo. On his return in 1843, he ruled until 1865, in alliance with his friend ʿAbdallah ibn Rashīd, whom he had appointed as prince of Ḥā'il in 1835.

Fhēd Fhēd ibn Mʿabhal ibn Shaʿlān of the Rwalah tribe of ʿAnazah. Included in the list of forty poets in ʿAdwān al-Hirbīd's al-Shēkhah poem.

al-Fidʿān a tribe of the ʿAnazah confederation that migrated to Syria and Mesopotamia, where it fought with the migrated Shammar tribes over pasture grounds; see *Ibn Mhēd*. After the First World War, Turkī's son Mijḥim sided with the French occupation of Syria, and his nephew Ḥākim supported the Hashemite king Fayṣal and later the Turkish nationalists.

al-Fighm Khalaf al-Fighm of the Mṭēr (Muṭayr) tribe. Included in the list of forty poets in ʿAdwān al-Hirbīd's al-Shēkhah poem.

'Gāb ibn 'Ijil the chief of the Snān section of the 'Abdah division of Shammar and the Rashīdī prince's father-in-law. In 1920, he recaptured the Jawf oasis for Ibn Rashīd.

'Gēl see *'Uqayl.*

al-Gfē'i the grandfather of Ṭalāl ibn Rmāl.

Ghaḍbān a raid leader of the Rmāl who made his peace with Ibn Saud upon his return from his spell of self-exile in Iraq. He soon joined Ibn Musā'id on his military campaigns in Jordan, making no secret of his dislike of the Ikhwān.

al-Ghūṭah an area to the west of Ajā Mountain; its principal settlement, Mōgag, is the base of al-Hirbīd's tribal group of the Swēd of the Zmēl, and a collection point for tax payments to Ibn Rashīd.

Gnēṭīr ibn Rakhīṣ a famous desert knight and raid leader who specialized in robbing camels of the Ḥwēṭāt and Sharārāt tribes. He was killed by a warrior of the Sharārāt.

'Gūb ibn Swēṭ ('Uqūb ibn Suwayṭ) (d. 1911) a shaykh of the Ẓafīr tribe.

Ḥā'il (Ḥāyil) the capital of northern Najd, the province of central Arabia, situated at almost equal distance from Mecca, Damascus, and Riyadh, halfway between the Red Sea and the Gulf. It is the center of Jabal Shammar, formerly Jabal Ṭayyi', an area of mixed nomadic and sedentary modes of life. Economically, it was primarily orientated toward the Mesopotamian riverine areas of Iraq and caravans plied up and down the old pilgrim road, *darb Zubaydah,* that skirted the southern edge of the Nafūd Desert. Historically, Ḥā'il has been in close interaction, often also adversarial and in competition, with the oases and trade hubs of al-Qaṣīm Province and its major towns of 'Unayzah and Buraydah, a few hundred miles to the south.

Ḥarb a tribe of mostly seminomads and small cultivators, strategically located in the Hejaz where it straddles the pilgrim road between Medina and Mecca. To ensure the safety of pilgrim caravans from Egypt and Syria, their shaykhs received subventions from the Ottoman and Egyptian authorities. Nevertheless, disagreements were common, and tribesmen were notorious for ambushing and plundering the devout travelers at the mountain passes controlled by Ḥarb.

Ḥātim [al-Ṭā'ī] a symbol of prodigious hospitality, the pre-Islamic Bedouin poet Ḥātim al-Ṭā'ī is one of the most widely known ancient figures in Saudi Arabia today. He is especially associated with the region of Ḥā'il, whose inhabitants claim him as one of their own. The tribe may have gone, but the mountain ranges are still called Jabal Ṭayyiʾ.

Ḥaṭṭāb Ḥaṭṭāb ibn Sarrāḥ al-Shammarī, a prominent leader in al-Jawf Province who corresponded in poetry with ʿUbayd ibn Rashīd. He and his son Ghālib were imprisoned by ʿUbayd in 1842 when the province was brought under direct Rashīdī rule.

al-Ḥamāṭiyyah a well at the eastern border of the Nafūd Desert.

Ḥawwās al-Tbēnānī poet specialized in invective poetry and innuendo, especially known for targeting the poet al-Ẓalmāwi of the Shilgān branch of Shammar.

al-Ḥazl (pl. al-Ḥuzūl) wells of the Nabhān and Ibn Rakhīṣ, including Lōgah, in the Ḥjarah region to the northeast of the Dahnāʾ sands, on the way from Ḥāʾil and Jubbah to Karbala, Iraq. They mark the eastern border of the Sinjārah division of Shammar, running from al-Ghūṭah and Mōgag in the west across the Nafūd. This geography almost destined the Sinjārah to excel at long-distance camel raiding.

Hazzāʿ the seventh and last son of Nāyif ibn Shaʿlān, and therefore an uncle of Saṭṭām, and the father of the later leader of the tribe, al-Nūrī ibn Hazzāʿ ibn Nāyif, born in 1847.

Hdēb Hdēb ibn Ṣibīḥ al-Hirbīd of the Harābdah of the Swēd of Shammar. Included in the list of forty poets in ʿAdwān al-Hirbīd's al-Shēkhah poem.

al-Hijhūj ibn Ṭalāl ibn Jārid, a daring raid leader (*ʿagīd*) of the Rmāl tribe of Shammar.

al-Ḥīrah the capital of the Lakhmid dynasty near present-day Najaf in Iraq. It attracted famous pre-Islamic poets like Ṭarafah, ʿAbīd, al-Nābighah, and ʿAdī ibn Zayd.

Hīt a town in the al-Anbar Province of Iraq, built on both sides of the Euphrates River.

Ḥmūd ibn Rashīd an inseparable companion of Muḥammad ibn Rashīd. He acted as a general in the House of Ibn Rashīd.

Al-Ḥrērah a section of the Ṣubḥī branch of the Ṣayiḥ division of Shammar in Iraq.

Ḥsēn Ḥsēn al-Dhnēb of the Swēd of Shammar. Included in the list of forty poets in ʿAdwān al-Hirbīd's al-Shēkhah poem.

Htēm (Hutaym) supposedly *aṣīl*, "pure," tribes would classify the Htēm among tribal groups without "purebred" ancestors. Accordingly, in their usage the word *Htēmī* was an insult, along with the word for an even lower rank, *ṣlubī*, a member of the "pariah tribe" of the Ṣalab. A typical classification would include the Sharārāt, ʿAwāzim, Banū Rashīd (not to be confused with Ibn Rashīd), Ḥuwaytāt, and Banū ʿAṭiyyah, but not the Ṣalab, who are held in even lower esteem in such classifications. Ironically, the camels of these Htēm, the Banū Rashīd and, especially, the Sharārāt, were rated as first-class purebreds and much coveted by the "noble" tribes for long and fast desert journeys and raiding.

Ibn ʿAngā the poet Radhān ibn ʿAngā of the Ghfēlah branch of the Sinjārah division of Shammar was a contemporary of Shaykh ʿAbd al-Karīm al-Jarbā.

Ibn Baggār shaykhs of Shammar who traced their lineage to the ancient tribe of Ṭayy and belonged to the Aslam division of Shammar. In the sixteenth century, they seem to have been on good terms with the sharifs of Mecca. Otherwise, little is known about them.

Ibn Dʿējā Khalaf ibn Dʿējā, a shaykh of the Sharārāt tribe. A legendary figure in the Najdī genre of "martyrs of love." He comes to the rescue of someone who is prevented from marrying his beloved, but too late to save the life of the disconsolate lover.

Ibn Farwān a family of raid leaders of the Ḥabkān clan of the Jirdhān, the biggest section of Āl Bēṭin of the Ghfēlah branch of the Sinjārah division of Shammar.

Ibn Hadhdhāl one of the most respected families of Bedouin shaykhs, already known as such in the sixteenth century. Fahd ibn ʿAbd al-Muḥsin ibn Ḥmēdī, Fahd Bey, was made *qāimmaqām* of al-Razzāzah, near Kerbela in southern Iraq. He was known as a clever and thoughtful leader. After the First World War, he was on good terms with the British in Mandatory Iraq. He died in 1927.

Ibn Ḥithlēn Rākān ibn Hithlēn, shaykh of al-ʿIjmān, who was imprisoned in Istanbul by the Ottoman Turks. The German scholar Julius Euting saw him when he visited Muḥammad ibn Rashīd in Ḥā'il.

Ibn Jibrīn the shaykh of the Mfaḍḍal branch of the ʿAbdah division of Shammar.

Ibn Mʿabhal family of shaykhs of the Mʿabhal section of the Mirʿiḍ, a subdivision of the Rwalah, headed by the tribe's leading family, Ibn Shaʿlān.

Ibn Mashhūr one of the two clans of the Ibn Shaʿlān shaykhs of the Rwalah tribe of the ʿAnazah confederation. In the early nineteenth century, Ibn Mashhūr was outmaneuvered by the other clan, ʿAbdallah. Bad feeling between both branches has continued ever since. For these reasons, many of the Mashhūr joined the Ikhwān in 1925 and followed the extremist rebels in their rebellion of 1929.

Ibn Mhēd (Muhayd) around the middle of the nineteenth century, the house of the paramount shaykh of the Fidʿān of ʿAnazah, Ibn Ghbēn (Ghubayn), was unseated by Ibn Mhēd. Jadʿān ibn Mhēd carried out a daring attack on Turkish-Ottoman troops in 1857, but in the 1870s the Ottoman sultan appointed him as *qāimmaqām* of the Aleppo Bedouin with the title of bey. After his death in the early 1880s, he was succeeded by his son Turkī. Around 1887, Turkī was slain in close combat against the poet Khalaf al-Idhn of the Shaʿlān (who features in the ʿAjlān ibn Rmāl chapter). As a result, the war between the Fidʿān and the Rwalah intensified until mediators, among them Fahd ibn Hadhdhāl (who features in the ʿAjlān and Abū Zwayyid chapters), restored the peace. Ibn Mhēd was legendary for his hospitality and generally known as "he who calls all and sundry to supper."

Ibn Mirdās the nickname of Shāyiʿ al-Amsaḥ, the ancestor of the Shammar tribe of the Rmāl.

Ibn Musāʿid ibn Jluwī ibn Turkī ibn ʿAbd Allāh Āl Saud, ʿAbd al-ʿAzīz (1884/5–1977), from the Jluwī branch of the House of Saud. He entered Ḥā'il on October 30, 1921, as the first Saudi governor to rule the northern capital after the collapse of the Ibn Rashīd dynasty, which he did with an iron hand. He married seven wives, among whom were two from the former ruling families, Ibn Rashīd and Ibn Sibhān of Ḥā'il. He remained governor of Ḥā'il until the end of his life, even after he had retired and gone to live in Riyadh in 1970.

Ibn Rakhīṣ the shaykhs of the Nabhān section of the Zmēl branch of the Sinjārah division of Shammar. In 1837, they sheltered the fugitive ʿAbdallah ibn Rashīd in their stronghold deep inside the Nafūd Desert when the Ibn ʿAlī clan for a short time regained power in Ḥā'il. As trusted allies of Ibn Rashīd, they became influential and declared their independence from the shaykh of the Zmēl branch, Ibn Thnayyān. In 1877, Muḥammad ibn Rakhīṣ appointed Fahhād ibn Rakhīṣ as his governor in Riyadh. Ṣāliḥ ibn Rakhīṣ, a companion of Ibn Rashīd, features in European travel accounts.

Ibn Rashīd the ruling house in Ḥā'il and Jabal Shammar from 1834 to 1921. The name Ibn Rashīd is a shorthand designation for the house, its members, and the ruling emir.

Ibn Rashīd, ʿAbdallah ibn ʿAlī (r. 1834–36, 1837–46) poet, warrior, and statesman who founded the House of Ibn Rashīd. He fled from Ḥā'il when ʿĪsa ibn ʿAlī was reinstated by Turkish-Egyptian soldiers, and went into hiding. This flight and eventual victory became a founding legend of his rule. He was married to daughters of the previous rulers of Jabal Shammar, Ibn ʿAlī, and of Fayṣal ibn Saʿūd. To survive politically, he maintained a balancing act between the House of Saud in Riyadh, the Turkish-Egyptian commander in the Hejaz, and the Ottoman sultan.

Ibn Rashīd, ʿAbd al-ʿAzīz ibn Mitʿib (r. 1897–1906) inherited the unenviable task of safeguarding the far-flung dominions conquered by his brilliant predecessor, Muḥammad ibn Rashīd. During his rule, the influence of the House of Ibn Rashīd waned, while the fortunes of the House of Saud saw a resurgence, starting with the Saudi reconquest of Riyadh in 1902. He was killed in 1906 during a campaign against the seditious al-Qaṣīm Province.

Ibn Rashīd, Bandar ibn Ṭalāl ibn ʿAbdallah (r. 1869–73) started the internecine struggles that expedited the demise of the House of Ibn Rashīd. His father, Ṭalāl, had designated his younger brother Mitʿib as his successor, against the will of his sons. Unable to stomach being sidelined, they shot Mitʿib. Their uncle Muḥammad fled to Riyadh, and on his return killed Bandar and the other progeny of Ṭalāl.

Ibn Rashīd, Ḥmūd ibn ʿUbayd (d. 1908) continued the role of his father, ʿUbayd, as the dynasty's field commander and right-hand man of Muḥammad ibn ʿAbdallah ibn Rashīd. Like his father, he was a prolific poet. He lived to witness the Rashīdī decline and the reckless part played in it by his sons, which made him seek refuge in Medina.

Ibn Rashīd, Muḥammad ibn ʿAbdallah (r. 1873–97) the ruthless and powerful emir of Ḥāʾil and the surrounding area, called the Mountain of Shammar (Jabal Shammar) after the dominant tribe to which the House of Rashīd also belonged. He figures prominently in many descriptions by European travelers and was a vivid presence in popular imagination. His court was frequented by many poets, especially from the northern areas and the northern part of central Arabia. Though not a poet himself, this edition evidences his acute understanding of the art and its importance in his dominions' culture.

Ibn Rashīd, Saʿūd ibn ʿAbd al-ʿAzīz Abū Khashm (r. 1908–20) ascended to the throne at the age of twelve as the only remaining prince of the lineage of ʿAbdallah, the founder of the House of Ibn Rashīd. He was nicknamed Abū Khashm, "Father of the Nose," because of its size. The regency of his in-laws, al-Sibhān, lasted until 1914, but matters of state remained largely in the hands of his maternal grandmother, Fāṭimah, the daughter of Zāmil al-Sibhān. Abū Khashm was killed by his relative ʿAbdallah ibn Ṭalāl ibn Nāyif ibn Ṭalāl ibn ʿAbdallah al-Rashīd in 1920, at the age of twenty-two.

Ibn Rashīd, Ṭalāl (r. 1848–66) remained loyal to the House of Saud in Riyadh and took an active part in some of the Saudi campaigns, while staying on good terms with the Ottoman-Turkish authorities. Under his benign, tolerant, and largely peaceful rule, trade and commerce flourished: he invited traders from Basra and Wāsiṭ in Iraq to Yemen to set up shop in Ḥā'il. Command of the armed forces was left in the hands of his uncle ʿUbayd ibn Rashīd. He committed suicide at the age of forty-five.

Ibn Rashīd, ʿUbayd ibn ʿAlī (d. 1869) cofounder of the Rashīdī Emirate and the strong arm of his brother ʿAbdallah, he was instrumental in putting the fledgling state on a firm footing. He was known for strict adherence to the religious tenets of the brothers' Saudi overlords. His exploits are echoed in his poetry, which has been preserved in many manuscripts and remains popular today.

Ibn ʿRēʿir (ʿUrayʿir) the popular name for the Āl Ḥumayd dynasty of the Banū Khālid tribe, which ruled the eastern al-Aḥsā' Province from 1669 to 1793, when their independence was ended by the Saudi rulers. A later episode of semi-independence ended in 1830, when the Ibn ʿRēʿir were defeated by Turkī ibn Saʿūd and surrendered on honorable terms.

Ibn Saud also Ibn Saʿūd or Ibn Sʿūd family, the principal rulers of Najd and the political leaders of the religious reform movement known as Wahhabism.

Ibn Shaʿlān considered one of the most important families of shaykhs in the period preceding the Saudi conquest of Ḥā'il and al-Jawf. The early ancestor Shaʿlān started out as a poor herdsman. His successors cemented the family's position as shaykhs of the Rwalah tribe, notably Fayṣal, Saṭṭām, and al-Nūrī. Ibn Shaʿlān belongs to the ʿAbdallah division that eclipsed the other division of the Rwalah, the Mashhūr, to claim the leadership. Saṭṭām (d. 1901), a clever desert politician, received the title of pasha from the Ottoman sultan ʿAbd al-Ḥamīd. As in the case of Ibn Rashīd, his succession gave rise to much internecine murder.

Ibn Shrēm (Ibn Shuraym) the shaykh of the Fḍēl branch of the ʿAbdah division of Shammar.

Ibn Smēr (Ibn Sumayr) the paramount shaykh of the Wild ʿAlī tribe. The other leading family, al-Ṭayyār, took command in war and raiding. As guardians of the pilgrim caravan to Mecca, they enjoyed privileged relations with the

Ottoman pasha of Damascus, especially during the fifty years of leadership by Shaykh Muḥammad ibn Dūkhī (d. 1895). His sons lost influence and became affiliated with their major rival, al-Nūrī ibn Shaʿlān.

Ibn Ṭwālah the family of the paramount shaykhs of the Aslam, the southernmost division of Shammar at Jabal Salmā. Often somewhat reserved toward Ibn Rashīd and on good terms with Ibn Saud, they joined Ibn Rashīd on the expedition to reconquer al-Jawf.

al-Jarbā of the Khriṣah division of Shammar, they are the first-known Bedouin shaykhs of Shammar. They led the Shammar tribes that in the late eighteenth century moved from Najd to Iraq after their defeat by the first Saudi state. With Ottoman permission, the Jarbā crossed the Euphrates, entered al-Jazīrah Province, and in 1802 or 1803 reached Sinjār Mountain in the north of Iraq. The area south of Sinjār and the Khābūr River's confluence with the Euphrates is considered Shammar Jarbā area. They were often troublesome for the Ottoman Turks: Shaykh Ṣfūg was killed in 1847 and his son ʿAbd al-Karīm met the same fate in 1871. ʿAjīl al-Yāwar (Turkish for "adjutant, aide-de-camp," 1882–1940, in this edition ʿAgīl al-Jāwar) represented Mosul in the first Iraqi parliament in 1924. His grandson Ghāzī al-Yāwar was the first president of Iraq after Saddam Hussein.

Jārid Jārid ibn Zabin, shaykh of the Rmāl of Shammar. Included in the list of forty poets in ʿAdwān al-Hirbīd's al-Shēkhah poem.

al-Jawf also known as al-Jūbah, a large agricultural area and a town in a depressed plain bordering on its south the northwestern side of the Nafūd Desert and on its north opening to Wādī Sirḥān. Al-Jawf has been a trading town of Shammar, the Rwalah, and the Sharārāt.

Jdēʿ Jdēʿ ibn Qublān ibn Milḥim, shaykh of the Manāhibah tribe of the Ḍanā Muslim branch of ʿAnazah. Included in the list of forty poets in ʿAdwān al-Hirbīd's al-Shēkhah poem.

Jifrān al-Maʿaklī member of the Ṭurēf of the Maʿākilah clan of the Jirdhān, known as expert desert pilots; one of them, Khazʿal, was the pilot of Ibn Rashīd's war banner. A daughter of the leading al-Māyig family of the Jirdhān married Ḥmūd ibn Rashīd, and her sons Mājid and Sālim and daughter Mūḍī were to play a role in the later fortunes of the Ibn Rashīd dynasty. Emboldened by this connection, the Jirdhān, supported by most of the Zmēl and abetted by Ibn Rashīd, rebelled against the Ibn Rmāl shaykhs of the Ghfēlah.

Jimal Jimal ibn S'ēd ibn Libdah of the Ghaṭān (Qaḥṭān) tribe. Included in the list of forty poets in 'Adwān al-Hirbīd's al-Shēkhah poem.

Jrēs Jres ibn Jilbān al-'Ajmī, also called Jrēs al-Yamānī, of the Ḥubaysh of the 'Ijmān tribe, which traces its roots to the Yām tribe in the south of the Arabian peninsula. He is a legendary figure, famous for his hospitality and forbearance in all circumstances. He lived at the time of the eastern Arabian ruler Mājid ibn 'Uray'ir (d. 1829/1830).

Jubbah a village and small oasis at the southern edge of the Nafūd Desert, mentioned in a verse by the *mukhaḍram* poet Namr ibn Tawlab al-'Uklī. Poets present it as a place teeming with wildlife, in particular oryx. Early Arabic sources praise its excellent pastures and remoteness from human habitation. For European travelers coming from al-Jawf, the miniature oasis offered the first vista of green on their way to Ḥā'il, fifty-six miles (ninety kilometers) south of Jubbah. The town was known for the manufacture of wooden camel saddles. Nineteenth-century Bedouin poetry and stories describe Jubbah and the sands of the Nafūd as a natural paradise for camels and Bedouin.

al-Kawāčbah (al-Kawakibah) one of the subtribes of the Rwalah. Unlike the other sections, it traces its origin to the southern Arabs, Qaḥṭān. On their wanderings, they met the Rwalah and their chief married his daughter to the Rwēlī shaykh Fahd ibn M'abhal.

Khḍēr al-Ṣ'ēlīć the chief of the Manāṣīr section of the Āl Ṭwālah, the lineage of the chiefs of the Aslam division of Shammar.

al-Kwēkibī (pronounced al-Kwēčbī) his full name is unknown; the tribal *nisbah* indicates that he belongs to the Kawākibah section of the Rwalah tribe of 'Anazah.

al-'Layyān (al-'Ulayyān) a tribal group of the Khriṣah of the 'Abdah division that left Najd for Mesopotamia.

Khālid son of Saṭṭām ibn al-Sha'lān; his mother was Turkiyyah, daughter of Ibn Mhēd, the shaykh of the Fid'ān division of 'Anazah.

Lōgah an important well of the Sinjārah of Shammar on the way to Iraq.

al-Ma'ākilah a section of the Āl Biṭēn group of the Ghfēlah branch of the Sinjārah division of Shammar.

'Mēr 'Mēr ibn Rāshid Āl Ḍēgham. Included in the list of forty poets in 'Adwān al-Hirbīd's al-Shēkhah poem.

Mghīr ibn Ghāzī Mghīr ibn Ghāzī ibn S'ēd of the 'Layyān clan of the Dghērāt of the 'Abdah division of Shammar. Included in the list of forty poets in 'Adwān al-Hirbīd's al-Shēkhah poem.

al-Mhādī al-Faḍlī, Muḥammad a legendary member of the Għaṭān (Qaḥṭān) tribe or al-Fuḍūl of Banū Lām, remembered for his forbearance toward guests living under his protection. The few verses he left are no more than an adjunct to his legendary chivalry, especially his patience with misconduct of his protected neighbor.

Miḍḥī al-Wḥēr a poet of the Dghērāt of the 'Abdah division of Shammar.

Mish'al (1913–31) eldest son of S'ūd Abū Khashm and his wife Fahdah, daughter of 'Āṣī ibn Shrēm.

Mish'ān Mish'ān ibn Mghēlith ibn Hadhdhāl, shaykh of the 'Amārāt of 'Anazah. Included in the list of forty poets in 'Adwān al-Hirbīd's al-Shēkhah poem.

Miṭlag Miṭlag ibn Muḥammad al-Jarbā, the desert knight killed in the battle of al-'Udwah against Ibn Saud in 1791.

Mrēzīǵ a raid leader and enforcer of Ibn Rashīd (probably a slave).

Mṣīkh Mṣīkh ibn Farḥān of the Rmāl tribe of Shammar. Included in the list of forty poets in 'Adwān al-Hirbīd's al-Shēkhah poem.

Mtāli', Mtāli'iyyāt the remnants of a mountain range running almost parallel with Ajā Mountain. A settlement of the Swēd clan stood there before civil strife destroyed it.

Mūḍī the daughter of Sibhān al-Salāmah al-Sibhān, the mother of S'ūd ibn Rashīd.

Muḥammad ibn Ṣāliḥ ibn Rakhīṣ al-Dimānī known as *rā' al-Ḥzul*, owner of the Ḥuzūl wells, nicknamed al-Dimānī on account of his short stature, and compared to cattle droppings (*dimnah*). Al-Dimānī's father was Ṣāliḥ ibn Rakhīṣ, a close friend of Abū Zwayyid. In protest, the poet absented himself from the court; in time, al-Dimānī was invited back. Ibn Rashīd told Ibn Jibrīn and Ibn Swēṭ that the well of al-Lōgah should be al-Dimānī's.

al-Mu'allaqāt "the suspended poems," a pre-Islamic collection of poems that in the early centuries of Islam were among the most admired long poems of the qasida type. They are so called because the poems, written on cloth in letters of gold, were said to have been hung on the walls of the Meccan Kaaba, but other explanations are also given.

al-Nabhān the tribal group headed by the Ibn Rakhīṣ clan to which Abū Zwayyid belongs. It has a somewhat anomalous position in Shammar genealogy: it originated from the south Arabian Ṭayy, early owners of what is now Jabal Shammar, some of whom joined Shammar and others ʿAnazah.

Nafūd Desert the Great Nafūd, or al-Nafūd, is the second-largest body of sand of the Arabian Peninsula, though it is less than a tenth the size of the Empty Quarter. These two sand bodies are connected by the sand belt of al-Dahnāʿ, which runs more than 870 miles (1,400 kilometers) from the southeastern al-Nafūd to the northern edge of the Empty Quarter. The Nafūd sands, with their rich vegetation after rainfall and plentiful firewood, are considered a Bedouin paradise. At the time of the events described in this volume, al-Nafūd appealed to the imagination of Western visitors and the Bedouin of northern Arabia alike.

Najd generally understood as the central part of the Arabian Peninsula—the plateau area roughly situated to the east of the mountain ranges of the Hijāz, south of the Nafūd Desert and west of the al-Dahnāʾ sands, and including Wādī al-Dawāsir in the south. This large region is subdivided into areas that differ greatly in character. Historically and environmentally, its society has been characterized by contrast between sedentary and Bedouin groups. Nabaṭī poetry is essentially a Najdī phenomenon with roots in classical Arabian culture, a pedigree shared by many of the sedentary and Bedouin tribes in Najd.

Nāyif the headman of Jubbah and Ibn ʿBēkah (ʿUbaykah, pronounced ʿBēćah) of the village Gnā, on the way between Ḥāʾil and Jubbah.

Nawwāf Nawwāf ibn Nūrī al-Shaʿlān (d. 1921).

Nāzil a famous leader of raids, and Musil's guide on his 1915 journey.

Nidā ibn Nhayyir a member of the ʿAbdah division of Shammar, who founded the religious colony of al-Ajfar and was the raid leader of the Ikhwān in the area.

Nimr (ibn ʿAdwān) (1745–1823) a famous romantic poet from al-Balqāʾ district in Jordan. He was admired for his touching dirges after the death of his beloved wife, Waḍḥā.

Nōmān Nōmān al-Ḥsēnī al-Faḍlī of the Ẓafīr tribe. Included in the list of forty poets in ʿAdwān al-Hirbīd's al-Shēkhah poem.

ʿRār ʿRār ibn Shahwān Āl Ḍēgham. Included in the list of forty poets in ʿAdwān al-Hirbīd's al-Shēkhah poem.

Rashīd ibn Nāṣir al-Laylā the longtime agent of the Ibn Rashīds at the Ottoman court in Istanbul. At the outbreak of the First World War, he organized a shipment of arms to Ḥā'il to prop up Ibn Rashīd against Ibn Saʿūd, who enjoyed British support.

Rabdā a well at the eastern border of the Nafūd Desert.

al-Rmāl the shaykhs of the Rmāl section and the chief of the Ghfēlah branch of the Sinjārah of Shammar. Based in the small oasis of Jubbah, the Rmāl are the nomads of the Nafūd sands par excellence.

Rmēzān (Rumayzān) Rmēzān ibn Ghashshām, a seventeenth-century poet of the ruling family of al-Rawḍah in Sudayr Province who was in frequent poetic correspondence with Jabr ibn Sayyār, the kinsman and predecessor of Ḥmēdān al-Shwēʿir.

Rshēd Rshēd ibn Ṭōʿān of the Swēd of Shammar. Included in the list of forty poets in ʿAdwān al-Hirbīd's al-Shēkhah poem.

al-Rwalah having left their basis in Khaybar some centuries ago, the Rwalah moved along the north side of al-Nafūd Desert from Taymā in the west, across al-Jawf, and as far as the well of Līnah in the east. Their pasture grounds included Wadī al-Sirhān and the southern part of the Syrian Desert. Rivalry between the Ibn Shaʿlān and Ibn Rashīd defined prickly relations with Shammar. After 1922, some sections of the Rwalah that had embraced Wahhabism no longer crossed into Syria. Together with three allied tribes, the *maḥlaf*, the Rwalah form a group known as the Jlās. A single person of the tribe is called a Rwēlī, and the tribe's war cry is "I am the rider of al-ʿAlyā from the Rwalah," al-ʿAlyā being the first mother of the tribe's herds of white camels.

Ṣaʿab Ṣaʿab al-Ṣdēd of Shammar in Iraq. Included in the list of forty poets in ʿAdwān al-Hirbīd's al-Shēkhah poem.

Sājir Sājir al-Rifdī, a desert knight and the shaykh of the Salgā section of the ʿAmārāt of ʿAnazah. Included in the list of forty poets in ʿAdwān al-Hirbīd's al-Shēkhah poem.

Ṣalab singular *ṣlubī*, a member of the pariah tribe of handicraftsmen who used to accompany the Bedouin tribes on their migrations. Renowned as skilled hunters, they dressed in the hides of the game they killed and rode donkeys, not camels. They shod the Bedouin's horses, repaired their metalwork, and performed other manual jobs, but otherwise lived a life completely separate from them.

Ṣāliḥ ibn Rakhīṣ "the old warhorse"; together with Ḥmūd ibn Rashīd, he was an inseparable companion of Muḥammad ibn Rashīd. The shaykhs of

Ibn Rakhīṣ had given refuge to the founder of the dynasty, ʿAbdallah ibn Rashīd.

Āl Sarrāḥ of Shammar a branch of the Jarbā lineage belonging to Āl Muḥammad; it settled in al-Jawf, in the northwestern part of Saudi Arabia.

Saṭṭām ibn Ḥamad ibn Nāyif ibn ʿAbdallah al-Shaʿlān (d. 1904) shaykh of the Rwalah, one of the most powerful chiefs of the far-flung ʿAnazah confederation. The Ibn Shaʿlān shaykhs were often considered near peers of Ibn Rashīd and were referred to as princes by European travelers.

Saʿūd the House of Saud, the ruling house of Saudi Arabia. One of the early poets of note was the imam Turkī (the First) ibn ʿAbd Allāh ibn Muḥammad Āl Saʿūd.

al-Sbaʿah a tribe of the Bishr division of ʿAnazah, less powerful than the Fidʿān. Known for their camels and horses, their market town is Ḥamāh in Syria. In fall, they pastured their animals in the Syrian steppe and desert.

al-Ṣēhad Ṭār al-Ṣēhad is a steep scarp that encloses on the north the flood plain of Wādī al-Khirr; *ṣēhad* means "sandy vastness."

Shammar the tribal confederation after which the area around Ḥā'il is called Jabal Shammar (it is also called the Two Mountains, i.e., Ajā and Salmā). As early as the seventeenth century, Shammar families began wandering toward Mesopotamia, while the thrust of ʿAnazah was toward Syria, as far as Aleppo. The area between the Euphrates and Tigris rivers is the northern heartland of Shammar. Genealogically, Shammar belongs to the southern Arabs, Qaḥṭān, of Ṭayy, while ʿAnazah is north Arabian, ʿAdnān.

al-Sharārāt a tribe in northern Arabia that in Bedouin opinion belonged to the lower-status tribal group of Htēm (Hutaym) because its members paid protection money to other tribes and to the Ibn Rashīd princes in Ḥā'il. They enjoyed renown as hunters and were skilled breeders of excellent riding camels. After the establishment of Saudi rule, their status improved and many of them attained positions of privilege at the Saudi court in al-Jawf and elsewhere.

Sharīf the family of the Great Sharifs of Mecca.

Shaṭṭ al-ʿArab the confluence of the Euphrates and Tigris rivers before they exit into the Gulf.

Shāyiʿ al-Amsaḥ a legendary ancestor of the Rmāl tribe of Shammar whose lore in poetry and narratives has been transmitted in oral tradition. His poetry shows the influence of Banū Hilāl epic poetry and probably dates from the seventeenth century. His chivalry and hospitality made him an avatar of the legendary Ḥātim al-Ṭāʾī, who lived in the same area and is celebrated by Shammar and other inhabitants as the epitome of their land's excellence.

al-Shēkhah a name given to poems considered a "shaykh" among the other poems (it is female because of the gender of the word for poem, *giṣīdah,* CA *qaṣīdah*). ʿAdwān al-Hirbīd's al-Shēkhah names forty poets. Several other poems are called al-Shēkhah because of their importance to a tribe, e.g., poems by Mighim al-Ṣagrī, Mishʿān al-Hadhdhāl (mentioned in al-Hirbīd's al-Shēkhah), and Muḥammad al-Dasm for ʿAnazah.

al-Shilgān a tribe of the Zmēl branch of the Sinjārah division of Shammar.

al-Sibhān from humble roots, the family married into the House of Ibn Rashīd and rose to become regents for minor princes, and the power behind the throne, in the final decade of its existence.

Sinjārah one of the four divisions of Najdī Shammar. Its territory and wells stretch from al-Ghūṭah district in the west through the Nafūd sands to the wells of the water-rich area of al-Ḥuzūl in the east. This edition's three poets belong to three different branches of Sinjārah: Abū Zwayyid is from the Nabhān of the Zmēl branch, headed by Ibn Rakhīṣ; al-Hirbīd is from the Swēd of Āl Thābit branch; and ʿAjlān of the Rmāl, headed by Ibn Rmāl, of the Ghfēlah branch. Though Sinjārah were the most "Bedouin" of Shammar, many of them owned permanent water holes and palm groves. They were known as independent-minded raiders with a particularly rich tribal and Bedouin lore.

al-Sirḥān probably named after Wādī Sirḥān. They are neighbors of Banū Ṣakhr in the southern reaches of Ḥawrān in southwestern Syria. In 1925, they lost most of their camel herds to attacks by the Saudi Ikhwān.

Sʿūd Abū Khashm Abū Mishʿal. Included in the list of forty poets in ʿAdwān al-Hirbīd's al-Shēkhah poem.

al-Ṭayyār Kanʿān al-Ṭayyār, shaykh of the Wild ʿAlī tribe of ʿAnazah. Included in the list of forty poets in ʿAdwān al-Hirbīd's al-Shēkhah poem.

al-Tbēnānī the poet Mbērić al-Tbēnāwī; the family of Tbēnāwī (pl. Tibānā) belongs to the Shrēḥā branch of the Dghērāt of ʿAbdah.

Al-Thāyah a place to the north of Sakaka.

Thmēl a place near ʿArʿar, today on the border with Jordan.

al-Tīh the herds of the Ḥwēṭāṭ (Ḥuwayṭāt) tribe in northwestern Arabia.

Ṭrād Saṭṭām ibn Shaʿlān's son by Mahā, sister of Ḍbēʿān ibn Khashmān of the Sirḥān tribe; a number of poems noted by Musil were recited to him by Ṭrād, who learned them from his mother.

Turkiyyah, daughter of Ibn Mhēd a remarkable and strong character, she had married Saṭṭām ibn Shaʿlān from love. She intervened forcefully after Saṭṭām's death to stop al-Nurī ibn Shaʿlān from capturing the litter with the tribal emblem. In 1910, she was present at the battle of al-Jmēmā, the subject of a poem by Abū Zwayyid. Her sons were often called "the children of Turkiyyah."

Ṭwayyah a well near Mōgag.

ʿUbayd (ʿBēd) ibn Rashīd brother of ʿAbdallah ibn Rashīd, the first ruler of the dynasty. He died in 1869.

ʿUqayl also ʿUqaylāt (ʿGēl, ʿGēlāt), camel traders mostly from al-Qaṣīm who bought up camels and, in much smaller numbers, horses all over Arabia. They drove the animals through Syria to sell them in the markets of Egypt and Iraq. They were intermediaries or agents who received the money to buy the camels from a wholesale dealer. The chief of the camp where the trader put up tents was also his host, insofar as he protected him as his guest but did not board him. The Bedouins as a rule sold their camels for cash. The purchased animal was marked with the ʿGēlī mark. To protect themselves against raiders, the ʿGēl paid to have a "brother" in every large clan: the brother was obliged to restore every camel stolen by another member of his clan.

Wādī al-Khirr a riverbed that terminates at the Euphrates and upcountry comes close to al-Ḥazl (also al-Ḥuzūl), the wells of the Sinjārah division of Shammar.

Wahhabi used in reference to the doctrines and practices preached by Muḥammad ibn ʿAbd al-Wahhāb, and later established as the foundational principles of the Kingdom of Saudi Arabia, it is perceived as a pejorative term in its native country. In Saudi Arabia, the movement is called Salafī: a return to the religious practices of the *salaf*, the early generations of Muslims. With respect to doctrine, its adherents call themselves "those who profess the unicity of God" (*al-muwaḥḥidūn*).

Bibliography

ʿAbdallāh ibn Sbayyil. *See* Kurpershoek.

Blunt, Lady Anne. *A Pilgrimage to Nejd*. 2 vols. London: Frank Cass, 1968. First published 1881.

Burckhardt, John Lewis. *Notes on the Bedouins and Wahabys*. London: H. Colburn and R. Bentley, 1830. Reprint, Cambridge: Cambridge University Press, 2010.

Dhū l-Rummah, *Dīwān Dhī l-Rummah*. Edited by ʿAbd al-Qudūs Abū Ṣāliḥ. Beirut: Muʿassasat al-Īmān, 1982.

Doughty, Charles M. *Travels in Arabia Deserta*. 2 vols. London: Jonathan Cape, 1936. Reprint of the third edition, New York: Dover, 1979.

Euting, Julius. *Tagbuch einer Reise in Inner-Arabien*. 2 vols. Leiden, Netherlands: E. J. Brill, 1896–1914.

Al-Fahad, Abdulaziz H. "The *ʿImama* vs. the *ʿIqal*: Hadari-Bedouin Conflict and the Formation of the Saudi State." In *Counter-Narratives: History, Contemporary Society, and Politics in Saudi Arabia and Yemen*, edited by Madawi Al-Rasheed and Robert Vitalis, 35–76. New York: Palgrave Macmillan, 2004.

Goldziher, Ignác. *Abhandlungen zur Arabischen Philologie*. 2 vols. Leiden, Netherlands: E. J. Brill, 1896–99.

Hess, J. J. The Hess Archive (referred to in the text as HA). Unpublished. Archive of the Institute of Asian and Oriental Studies, University of Zurich. A dictionary of handwritten cards with lexical notes on nineteenth-century Bedouin language, primarily from the ʿUtaybah and Qaḥṭān tribes in Central Arabia, kept at the Institute of Asian and Oriental Studies of Zurich University.

Ḥmēdān al-Shwēʿir. *See* Kurpershoek.

Ibn Manẓūr. *Lisān al-ʿarab*. Cairo: Dār al-Maʿārif, n.d.

Al-Iṣfahānī, Abū l-Faraj. *Kitāb al-Aghānī*. 24 vols. Cairo: Maṭbaʿat Dār al-Kutub al-Miṣriyyah, 1927–94.

Jacob, Georg. *Altarabisches Beduinenleben*. 1897. Reprint of 2nd ed. Hildesheim, Germany: Georg Olms Verlag, 1967.

Kurpershoek, Marcel. *Oral Poetry and Narratives from Central Arabia*. 5 vols. Leiden, Netherlands: E. J. Brill, 1994–2005.

Kurpershoek, Marcel, ed. and tr. *Arabian Satire: Poetry from 18th Century Najd; Ḥmēdān al-Shwēʿir*. New York: New York University Press, 2017.

———. *Arabian Romantic: Poems on Bedouin Life and Love; ʿAbdallāh ibn Sbayyil*. New York: New York University Press, 2018.

———. *Love, Death, Fame: Poetry and Lore from the Emirati Oral Tradition; Al-Māyidī ibn Ẓāhir*. New York: New York University Press, 2022.

Lane, Edward William. *Manners and Customs of the Modern Egyptians*. London: Everyman's Library, 1966. First published 1836.

Mandaville, James. *Bedouin Ethnobotany*. Tucson: University of Arizona Press, 2011.

Al-Māyidī ibn Ẓāhir. *See* Kurpershoek.

Montgomery, J. E., ed. and tr. *War Songs: ʿAntarah ibn Shaddād*. New York: New York University Press, 2018.

Al-Mufaḍḍal, Abū ʿAbbās ibn Muḥammad aḍ-Ḍabbī. *Dīwān al-Mufaḍḍaliyyāt*. Edited by Charles James Lyall: vol. 1, *Arabic Text* (1921); vol. 2, *Translation and Notes*. Oxford: Clarendon Press, 1918–21.

Al-Musallam, Ibrāhīm. *Al-ʿUqayliyyāt*. Cairo: al-Dār al-Thaqāfiyyah, 2006.

Musil, Alois. *The Manners and Customs of the Rwala Bedouins*. Oriental Explorations and Studies 6. New York: American Geographical Society, 1928.

———. *Northern Neǧd*. Oriental Explorations and Studies 5. New York: American Geographical Society, 1928.

Nolde, Eduard. *Reise nach Innerarabien, Kurdistan und Armenien, 1892*. Braunschweig, Germany: Vieweg, 1895.

Palgrave, William Gifford. *Narrative of a Year's Journey through Central and Eastern Arabia*. London: Macmillan, 1865.

Al-Rasheed, Madawi. *Politics in an Arabian Oasis: The Rashidi Tribal Dynasty*. London: I. B. Tauris, 1991.

Al-Rashīd, Ḍārī ibn Fuhayd. *Nubdhah taʾrīkhiyyah ʿan Najd*. Edited by Wadīʿ al-Bustānī. Riyadh: Dār al-Yamāmah, 1966.

Al-Saʿdūnī, Musāʿid ibn Fahd. *Wusūm al-ibl fī al-Jazīrat al-ʿArabiyyah (bādiyah wa-ḥāḍirah)*. 2nd edition.ʿUnayzah: self-published, 2012.

Sowayan, Saad Abdullah. *Nabaṭī Poetry: The Oral Poetry of Arabia*. Berkeley, CA: University of California Press, 1985.

———. *The Arabian Oral Historical Narrative: An Ethnographic and Linguistic Analysis*. Wiesbaden, Germany: Otto Harrassowitz, 1992.

———. *Al-Shiʿr al-nabaṭī: Dhāʾiqat al-shaʿb wa-sulṭat al-naṣṣ*. Beirut: Dār al-Sāqī, 2000.

———. *Fihrist al-shiʿr al-nabaṭī*. Riyadh: self-published, 2001.

———. *Al-Ṣaḥrā' al-ʿarabiyyah, thaqāfatuhā wa-shiʿruhā ʿabra al-ʿuṣūr, qirā'ah anthrūbūlūjiyyah.* Beirut: Arab Network for Research and Publishing, 2010.

———. *Ayyām al-ʿarab al-awākhir: Asāṭīr wa-marwiyyāt shafahiyyah fī l-tārīkh wa-l-adab min shamāl al-jazīrah al-ʿarabiyyah maʿa shadharāt mukhtārah min qabīlat Āl Murrah wa-Subayʿ.* Beirut: Arab Network for Research and Publishing, 2010.

———. "Tonight My Gun Is Loaded: Poetic Dueling in Arabia," *Oral Tradition* 4, nos.1–2 (1989): 151–73.

———. "A Poem and Its Narrative by Riḍa ibn Ṭārif al-Shammarī." *Zeitschrift für arabische Linguistik* 7 (1982): 48–73.

———. "Customary Law in Arabia: An Ethnohistorical Perspective." http://www.saadsowayan.info/Publications/pub_E_13.pdf.

———. "Studying Nabaṭi Poetry." http://66.39.147.165/articles/Studying_Nabati_Poetry.pdf.

Steinberg, Guido. "Ecology, Knowledge, and Trade in Central Arabia (Najd) during the Nineteenth and Early Twentieth Centuries." In *Counter-Narratives: History, Contemporary Society, and Politics in Saudi Arabia and Yemen*, edited by Madawi Al-Rasheed and Robert Vitalis, 77–102. New York: Palgrave Macmillan, 2004.

Stewart, Frank Henderson. *Texts in Sinai Bedouin Law.* 2 vols. Wiesbaden, Germany: Harrassowitz, 1988.

Al-Suwaydā', ʿAbd al-Raḥmān ibn Zayd. *Al-Amthāl al-shaʿbiyyah al-sā'irah fī manṭiqat Ḥā'il.* Riyadh: Dār al-Suwaydā', 2007.

———. *Faṣīḥ al-ʿāmmī fī shamāl Najd.* 2 vols. Riyadh: Dār al-Suwaydā', 1987.

———. *Manṭiqat Ḥā'il ʿabra al-ta'rīkh.* Riyadh: Dār al-Suwaydā', 2009.

———. *Min shuʿarā' al-jabal al-ʿāmiyyīn.* 3 vols. Riyadh: Dār al-Suwaydā', 1988.

———. *Al-Nakhlah al-ʿarabiyyah adabiyyan wa-ʿilmiyyan wa-iqtisādiyyan.* Riyadh: Dār al-Suwaydā', 1993.

———. *Shuʿarā' al-jabal al-shaʿbiyyūn.* 5 vols. Riyadh: Dār al-Suwaydā', 2013.

Al-ʿUbūdī, Muḥammad ibn Nāṣir. *Muʿjam al-tijārah wa-l-māl wa-l-faqr wa-l-ghinā.* Riyadh: Dār al-Thalūthiyyah, 2012.

———. *Muʿjam al-uṣūl al-faṣīḥah li-l-alfāẓ al-dārijah.* 13 vols. Riyadh: n.p., 2008.

Von Oppenheim, Max Freiherr, *Die Beduinen.* 5 vols. Wiesbaden, Germany: Harrassowitz, 1939–.

Watts, David, and Abdulatif H. Al-Nafie. *Vegetation and Biogeography of the Sand Seas of Saudi Arabia.* London: Kegan Paul, 2003.

Al-Ẓafīrī, Muḥammad Muhāwish. *Dīwān al-shāʿir Abū Zuwayyid, ḥakīm Shammar wa-shāʿiruhā.* Dammām, Saudi Arabia: Dār al-Adab al-ʿArabī, 2015.

Further Reading

ʿAqīl, Abū ʿAbd al-Raḥmān ibn, al-Ẓāhirī. *Dīwān al-shiʿr al-ʿāmmī bi-lahjat ahl Najd*. 5 vols. Riyadh: Dār al-ʿUlūm, 1982–86.

Ashkenazi, Touvia. "The ʿAnazah Tribes." *Southwestern Journal of Anthropology* 4, no. 2 (1948): 222–39.

Geiger, Bernhard. "Die Muʿallaqa des Ṭarafa." *Wiener Zeitschrift für die Kunde des Morgenlandes* 19 (1905): 323–70.

Habib, John S. *Ibn Saʿud's Warriors of Islam: The Ikhwan of Najd and Their Role in the Creation of the Saʿudi Kingdom, 1910–1930*. Leiden, Netherlands: E. J. Brill, 1978.

Al-Ḥaqīl, ʿAbd al-Karīm ibn Ḥamad ibn Ibrāhīm. *Alfāẓ dārijah wa-madlūlātuhā fī al-Jazīrah al-ʿArabiyyah*. Riyadh: Maṭābiʿ al-Farazdaq, 1989.

Hess, J. J. *Von den Beduinen des innern Arabiens*. Zurich: Max Niehaus Verlag, 1938.

Hinds, Martin, and El-Said Badawi. *A Dictionary of Egyptian Arabic: Arabic-English*. Beirut: Librairie du Liban, 1986.

Holes, Clive. "The Language of Nabaṭi Poetry." In *Encyclopaedia of Arabic Language and Linguistics On-Line Edition*, edited by R. De Jong and L. Edzard. Leiden, Netherlands: E. J. Brill, 2012.

Huber, Charles. "Voyage dans l'Arabie Centrale, 1878–1882." *Bulletin de la Société de Géographie* 7, no. 5 (1884): 304–63, 468–530.

———. *Journal d'un voyage en Arabie (1883–1884)*. Paris: Société Asiatique et la Société de Géographie, 1891.

Ibn Khamīs, ʿAbd Allāh ibn Muḥammad. *Al-Adab al-shaʿbī fī al-jazīrat al-ʿarabiyyah*. 2nd ed. Riyadh: Maṭābiʿ al-Farazdaq, 1982.

Ibn Mandīl, Mandīl ibn Muḥammad, Āl Fuhayd. *Min ādābinā al-shaʿbiyyah fī l-jazīra al-ʿarabiyyah, qiṣaṣ wa-ashʿār*. 4 vols. Riyadh: Maṭābiʿ al-Farazdaq, 1981–84.

Ibrāhīm, ʿAbd al-ʿAzīz ʿAbd al-Ghani. *Najdiyyūn warāʾa al-ḥudūd: Al-ʿUqayliyyāt wa-dawruhum fī ʿilāqat Najd al-ʿaskariyyah wa-l-iqtiṣādiyyah bi-l-ʿIrāq wa-l-Shām wa-Miṣr (1750–1950)*. 2nd ed. Beirut: Dār al-Sāqī, 2014.

Imruʾ al-Qays. *Dīwān*. Beirut: Dār Bayrūt, 1986.

Ingham, Bruce. *Bedouin of Northern Arabia: Traditions of the Āl Ḍhafīr*. London: KPI, 1986.

Al-Jāsir, Ḥamad. *Al-Muʿjam al-jughrāfī li-l-bilād al-ʿArabiyyah al-Saʿūdiyyah, Shamāl al-Mamlakah: Imārāt Ḥayil wa-l-Jawf wa-Tabūk wa-ʿArʿar wa-l-Qurayyāt*. 3 vols. Riyadh: Dār al-Yamāmah, 1977.

Al-Juhaymān, ʿAbd al-Karīm. *Al-Amthāl al-shaʿbiyyah fī qalb al-jazīrah al-ʿarabiyyah.* 10 vols. Riyadh: Dār al-Ashbāl al-ʿArab, 1982.

Ingham, Bruce. "The Pool of Oaths—A Comparative Study of a Bedouin Historical Poem." In *A Miscellany of Middle Eastern Articles: In Memoriam Thomas Muir Johnstone*, edited by A. K. Irvine et al., 40–54. Harlow, UK: Longman, 1988.

Kurpershoek, P. Marcel. "Two Manuscripts of Bedouin Poetry in Strasbourg National and University Library and the Travels of Charles Huber in Arabia." *La Revue de la BNU* (Bibliothèque Nationale Universitaire de Strasbourg) 17 (2018): 92–103.

Lane, Edward William. *An Arabic-English Lexicon.* Beirut: Librairie du Liban, 1980. First published 1863.

March, Jenny. *The Penguin Book of Classical Myths.* London: Penguin, 2008.

Al-Mutanabbī, Abū l-Ṭayyib. *Dīwān Abī l-Ṭayyib al-Mutanabbī bi-sharḥ Abī l-Baqāʾ al-ʿUkbarī.* 4 vols. 2nd ed. Cairo: Maṭbaʿat Muṣṭafā al-Bābī al-Ḥalabī, 1956.

Philby, H. St. John. *Saʿudi Arabia.* Beirut: Librairie du Liban, 1968. First published 1955.

Reynolds, Dwight Fletcher. *Heroic Poets, Poetic Heroes: The Ethnography of Performance in an Arabic Oral Epic Tradition.* Ithaca, NY: Cornell University Press, 1995.

Sowayan, Saad Abdullah, ed. *Al-Thaqāfah al-taqlīdiyyah fī al-mamlakah al-ʿarabiyyah al-suʿūdiyyah.* Riyadh: The Circle for Publishing and Documentation, 1999.

Al-Tibrīzī, Abū Zakariyā Yaḥyā ibn ʿAlī. *Kitāb Sharḥ al-qaṣāʾid al-ʿashr.* Edited by Charles J. Lyall. Calcutta: Asiatic Society of Bengal, 1894. Reprint, Farnborough, UK: Gregg Press, 1965.

Al-ʿUbūdī, Muḥammad ibn Nāṣir. *Al-Amthāl al-ʿāmmiyyah fī Najd.* 5 vols. Riyadh: n.p., 1979.

———. *Muʿjam al-anwāʾ wa-l-fuṣūl.* Riyadh: n.p., 2011.

———. *Muʿjam al-azwāj fī al-turāth.* Riyadh: Dār al-Thalūthiyyah, 2017.

———. *Muʿjam al-ḥayawān ʿind al-ʿāmmah.* 2 vols. Riyadh: Maktabat al-Malik Fahd al-Waṭaniyyah, 2011.

———. *Muʿjam al-kalimāt al-dakhīlah fī lughatinā al-dārijah,* 2 vols. Riyadh: Maktabat al-Malik ʿAbd Al-ʿAzīz al-ʿĀmmah, 2005.

———. *Muʿjam al-malābis fī al-maʾthūr al-shaʿbī fī al-manṭiqat al-wusṭāʾ min al-Mamlakah al-ʿArabiyyah al-Suʿūdiyyah.* Riyadh: Dār al-Thalūthiyyah, 2013.

———. *Muʿjam alfāẓ al-maraḍ wa-l-ṣiḥḥah.* Riyadh: Dār al-Thalūthiyyah, 2015.

———. *Muʿjam wajh al-arḍ.* Riyadh: Dār al-Thalūthiyyah, 2014.

Wallin, Georg August. *Travels in Arabia.* Cambridge, UK: The Oleander Press, 1979.

Al-Wuhaybī, ʿAbd al-Laṭīf ibn Ṣāliḥ ibn Muḥammad. *Al-ʿUqaylāt, maʾāthir al-ābāʾ wa-l-ajdād ʿalā ẓuhūr al-ibl wa-l-ajyād.* Riyadh: Obeikan, 2017.

Al-Zawzanī, Abū ʿAbd Allāh al-Ḥusayn ibn Aḥmad ibn al-Ḥusayn. *Sharḥ al-muʿallaqāt al-sabʿ.* Beirut: Dār Bayrūt, 1982.

Index of Poems, Editions, and Manuscripts Used for This Edition

This edition is based on poems and narratives recorded on audiotapes, mostly from elderly transmitters who heard them from sources closer to the nineteenth- and early-twentieth-century oral compositions and traditions, as explained in the Note on the Text. A number of poems by Khalaf Abū Zwayyid are found in the manuscripts listed below. The poems have been ordered not by rhyme letter, as is customary for classical Arabic poetry, but according to their place in the body of the text. The great majority of poems and lines of verse are an integral part of the narrative text and therefore cannot be dealt with separately. The poems are referred to by their number in the text of this edition. The shorthand references in bold at the start of each source listed below indicate where a particular poem can be found in the manuscript. These references are followed by the number of verses of the poem in that edition or manuscript. The first line of each poem in manuscript is given below. In most of the poems, the meter corresponds to the classical *al-ṭawīl*, called *al-mashūb* in Nabaṭī poetry.

The translation is based on the following pages of Sowayan, *Ayyām al-ʿarab al-awākhir*, in the order used for this translation: for Abū Zwayyid: pages 395–96, 591–624, 697, 846, 933–35 ; for ʿAdwān al-Hirbīd: pages 191–220; for ʿAjlān ibn Rmāl: pages 403–12, 756–57. Annotated versions of a substantial number of the poems, sometimes with a brief indication of the occasion on which they were composed and general introductions, are found in al-Suwaydā', *Min shuʿarā' al-Jabal al-ʿāmiyyīn* (1988) 2:9–122 and its later edition (2013): 1:352–495 for Khalaf Abū Zwayyid; 3:85–141 and 3:1789–1848 (2013) for ʿAdwān al-Hirbīd; and 3:1770–1785 (2013) for ʿAjlān ibn Rmāl. The poetry of Abū Zwayyid is also available in a 2015 edition by Muḥammad Muhāwish al-Ẓafīrī.

For the best description of all known manuscripts containing Nabaṭi poetry, and the challenges such manuscripts pose to researchers, see Sowayan, *Al-Shiʿr al-nabaṭī*, 196–206. The Manṣūr al-Ḥusayn al-ʿAssāf (**Assaf**) manuscript as well as the al-Dāwud (**Dawud**) manuscript can be found on the website www.saad-sowayan.com.

Lāfī ibn Shabbāb al-Shurayyiṭī's *Makhṭūṭah li-shuʿarāʾ al-Jabal wa-shuʿarāʾ min Najd* (**Shurayyiti**), based on notes by ʿAbd Allāh ibn ʿAlī ibn Sālim al-Dāwud and collected by al-Shurayyiṭī.

The following ten poems by Khalaf Abū Zwayyid are found in the collections of these manuscripts:

§2.2, pp. 6–8:

دخِـيل خِـذ من والِدكِ لك مسـاله   مسـالةٍ ما يفـهمه كـل رجـالــــ

Dawud 117, 12 vv.; **Shurayyiti** 117, 24 vv.

§2.4, p. 10:

أبـديت انا هولاس قـلبي بقيـلي   ما هن هواليس القلوب الهبايل

Dawud 243, 14 vv.

§2.5, pp. 12–14:

بـرّقت بالدنيـا وانا قبـل غـافـل   ثـري له موارد ومسـاقي وقليـب

Dawud 243, 21 vv.

§4.2, pp. 22–24:

يا بو زويـد يا جَـذَيّ المـراقيب   يا وجـحـه ذيبٍ دانخ له روبـه

Dawud 244, 12 vv.

§5.5, pp. 30–32:

يالله يا عـالمِ خفيّـات الاسـرار   عـليـم ما تخـفى عـليك الجحـاده

Shurayyiti 118, 11 vv.

§13.2, pp. 76–78:

يارَبّ ياعـايـد من المـزن بالسـيل   عايد على روض المَحَل عقب الاصداد

Dawud 244, 15 vv.

§17.5, pp. 104–6:

القلب يِبْرِم بالهواجيس ويدير من جادلٍ جَتْنا طوارف طروشه

Dawud 241, 17 vv.

§24.2, pp. 142–44:

يامـلّ قَلْبٍ فيه عَذْلٍ ومايل لكنّ به غِلّ وغاشيه سلال

Shurayyiti 117, 24 vv.

§25.2, pp. 146–50

يامـلّ قلبٍ به هواليس وِهْموم همٍّ لِجا بالقلب من كِثْر ما رَيت

Dawud 192, 24 vv.; 240, 25 vv.; **Assaf** 157, 25 vv.

§25.3, pp. 150–52:

يا راكبٍ حمرا جِليله من القُود وَجْنا عَثافر من مِزابير الاوراك

Dawud 242, 16 vv.

Index

dishonesty, §5.5, §6.2, §18.7, §31.6. *See also* falsehood
disputes, §11.1, §17.1, §53.7
disreputable, §31.10
divorce, xxix, §6.3, §13.2, §20.1, §23.4, §46.1, 372n54
Dlāgāt (camels), §51.1
doe, §7.2, §10.4, §19.5, §21.1, §31.10, §34.1, §39.3, §41.1
dogs: barking, §18.3, §25.9; herding, §31.11; hunting, §16.7; mad ruckus of, §7.2; "penis of dog" mushroom, 383n199; rabid, §4.2, §37.3, §50.4; snarling, §52.9; starving, §31.10; unclean, 383n189; wolf-faced, §4.2
donkeys, §25.1, §32.6, §32.7, §32.10, §51.2, §51.3, 383n189, 383n199
doom, §7.2, §12.1, §29.1, §30.5, §52.1
Doughty, Charles M., xxvii–xxviii, xxxiv, xlix n3, lii n36, liii n44, 371n42
doves, §19.5
downfall, §31.5
dreams, xix, xxxiv, xxxvi, §13.2, §17.6, §30.5, §35.3
drinks, §24.2, 379n131
droughts, xx, xxxvii, liv n56, §13.2, §16.1, §33.1, §48.9, §53.10
al-Ḍubbān, §40.2
dullards, §2.4
dustups, §49.1, §49.17
duty, §25.3, §25.5, §25.7, §31.9
al-Duwīsh, §52.10
dwellings. *See* houses; tents

Eben Rashīd. *See* Ibn Rashīd (dynasty)
eggs, §20.1
Egypt, xxix, xli, liii n41, §31.4, 387n246
embers, §5.5, §25.5, §32.6, §42.2, §49.15, §50.4
encouragement, §1.4, §5.2, §14.2, §31.2
enemies: to ally with, 375n87; blood of, §29.1; camels, §8.1, §17.4; camp, §13.2; caught unawares by, §52.3; charging, 380n152; enemies' bane, §49.19; fending off, §17.6; fighters, §51.1; fighting, §11.2, §24.1, §27.5, §28.1, §42.1, 376n94; foes, §23.1, §25.5, §48.2, §49.8, §50.5; herds, xx, §10.4, §16.3; infested with, §49.8; inside the house, §25.2; kissing an enemy's hand, §11.2; lands, §49.12, §49.15, 373n67; lying in wait, §2.4; made offensive by, xix; nemesis, §28.1, §48.8; plunge into grief, §12.1; pressed by, xxiii; protection against, §49.11; prowling, §49.19; ridiculing, 381n163; shamefaced, §24.2; sheltered from, 374n78; show mercy to, §31.5; spare the life of, 374–75n79; terrified, §44.3; on their minds, §32.3; tribes, §4.1, §16.3, 370n23; unhurt, §48.2; where no enemy treads, §4.2
entertainment: conversation as, §53.5; of guests, §42.3, 371n33; happy, §42.2; poetry as, xxi, xxiii, xxxvi, §33.4, §44.1, §51.2, 372n53; songs as, §49.11
Euphrates, 381n170
European travelers/visitors, xiii, xxiii, xxvii, liv n58, 374n72, 380n151
Euting, Julius, xxvii, liii n43, 379n134
Eve (biblical figure), §3.1
evil: breeding grounds, §5.5; days, §22.1, §25.4; end of, 377n110; evildoings, §8.1; evil-minded, §52.6; fate, §30.3, §30.4; gossip, §7.2; harbinger of, §49.18;

fihrist, xvi
fire: blackened by, 382n179; burning, §24.2; cooking, §6.3, §15.4, §17.6, §30.4, §35.3, §40.5, §42.2, §52.3, 377n115; embers, §5.5, §25.5, §32.6, §42.2, §49.15, §50.4; fireball, §5.5, 372n50; flames, §28.1, §43.2; furious, §25.5; Hell's, §27.5; jump into, §7.3; lighting a, §32.10, §53.14, 371n33; set on, §23.4, §48.5, §52.10; Shammar's, §12.1; smoldering, §45.1; sparks, §27.5, §28.1; of war, §11.2; welcoming, §50.4
firearms, xiii, §19.5, §27.4
Firsīn (Fāris al-Siṭam), §52.6
First World War, xiv
flames, §28.1, §43.2
food: for animals, §32.7, §43.1, 384n384; appetite, xxxii, §48.7; beans, §35.3; bread, §6.3, §50.2; breakfast, §15.4, §43.2, §52.3; butter, xxxvi, §17.6, §25.5, §32.3, §32.5, §48.2, §50.6, 375n86, 377n118, 378n125; crushed wheat, §50.6; dinner, §2.5, §4.1, §6.3, §6.7, §13.2, §19.3, §31.10, §32.10; (dried) cheese, §17.6, §25.5, §31.3; drinks, §24.2, 379n131; eating, §12.1, §31.1, 372n55; edible *kurrāth* grass, §14.3; fat, §17.6, §25.5, §31.3, §31.6, §31.10, §31.13, §42.2; feasts, §48.9, §49.19; feeding guests, §12.1, §29.1, §32.10, §36.4, §42.1, §48.2, §49.2, §49.14, §50.5, 371n33; from fields, §25.8; grapes, peaches, and figs, §51.3; honey, §28.1; invisible, §5.5; invitations for, §52.1; lack of, §18.8; loses taste, §53.10; lunch, §9.3, §10.1, §16.4, §32.1, §50.2; meals, §1.2, §31.6, 369n1; meat, §10.4, §31.6, §31.12, §49.9, §49.11, §53.10; morsels, §25.9; plentiful, §32.1, §48.9; refusing, §40.3; regurgitating, 379n133; revolting, §53.15; rice, §32.1, §32.2, §50.6; roasts, §6.3, §10.4, §31.1, §32.10, §42.2, §49.19, §50.5, §51.2, 384n203; in search of, §13.2; serving, liv n58, §4.3, §49.19, 371n33, 385n223; sheep, §49.8, 375n82; spilling from their mouths, §32.10; sugar, §34.2; supper, §10.1, §31.10, §50.4, §50.6; thought of, §21.1; for wolves, §32.7. *See also* coffee; dates; hunger; milk
fools: blockheads, §52.6; dazzled, §27.5; dimwits, §2.4, §16.7, §24.2; dullards, §2.4; erring, §25.7; folly, §31.9; foolish babble, §25.7; foolish escapades, §25.2; foolish urges, §31.9; greatest, §31.12; idiots, §24.1, §32.11; merciless, §31.5; not being, §19.6
forgiveness, §9.3, §30.3, §49.7, 382n178
fortune, §5.5, §14.4, §25.4, §25.8, §25.9, §49.8
foxes, §2.5, §13.2, §25.1, §27.5, §48.1
François III Étienne, 383n196
Frēdah (daughter of Ibn Sharayyān ibn Hazīm, G'ēmīlah), §52.4
freeloaders, §51.3
Frēḥ al-Ḥamzī al-Swēdī, §52.7
Frēḥ (son of 'Assāf al-Hirbīd), §49.15
al-Frēkh, 376n96
friends, xx, xxi, xxxv, xxxvi, §§2.1–2, §2.4, §2.5, §4.1, §6.2, §14.2, §15.1, §16.1, §18.7, §18.9, §25.3, §25.5, §25.7, §27.5, §28.1, §31.3, §31.4, §31.5, §31.6, §31.8, §31.10, §32.11, §38.1, 372n42, 378n128
Fugarā (tribe), xxviii

horses (cont.): horsemen, xxxiv, §6.2, §10.4, §32.10, §34.2, §40.7, §51.2; jump on your, §53.17; mares, xxxv, lv n74, §2.4, §3.1, §6.3, §6.4, §6.5, §6.7, §7.3, §12.1, §18.8, §25.2, §29.1, §34.2, §38.5, §40.2, §50.2, §50.5, §53.14, 376n98; pedigree, §6.3, §6.7, §25.2; prance and trot, §31.10; seized, §44.2; sorrel, §18.8, §34.2; spirited, §40.10; as spoils, 374n71; stallions, §27.5, §29.1; steeds, §6.7, §10.4, §25.2, §27.5, §42.1, §51.2, 370n17; studs, §2.4, §4.1, §25.2, §29.1, §34.2; thoroughbred, xxxi, §29.1, 372n48; warhorses, xiv, §27.5, §49.8. *See also* stalwarts

hospitality: from desert lords, xxiii; hospitable, §2.5, §15.2; hosts, xix, xxv, §4.3, §5.3, §5.5, §19.4, §24.2, §28.1, §29.1, §31.10, §31.13, §42.2, §49.19, 382n172; lavish, xxxi

hostility, xxxvii

House of Hadhdhāl. *See* Ibn Hadhdhāl

House of Ibn Rashīd. *See* Ibn Rashīd (dynasty)

House of Saud. *See* Ibn Saʿūd (dynasty)

houses: big and imposing, §7.3; booth made of palm leaves, §30.1; of hair, §10.4; have around in your, §37.1; in Jubbah, §32.5; masters/owners, §28.1, 382n172; seat behind the, 386n232; set on fire, §52.10; shacks, §31.1, §32.1; spring, 382n176; tobacco in the, §42.5. *See also* tents

Ḥrērī tribesman, §9.1

Ḥsēn (poet), §49.19

Htēm, §50.5, 385n225

al-Hūj, §33.3, §33.6

hunger: fasting, §34.2, §40.8; hungry, §43.2; lack of food, §18.8; in search of food, §13.2; starving, §23.4, §31.10, §32.10, §34.2, §42.2

hunt: bounty hunters, §4.3; with dogs, §16.7; with falcons, xvi, §6.7, §12.1, §27.5, §32.7, 380n155, 387n247; game, §31.1, §31.10, §45.2, §49.3, §49.4, §49.9, §49.11, §49.15, §49.19, §51.2; gunman, §31.5, §35.3; hunters, xvii, §27.5, §31.5, §45.2, §49.3, §50.5, 380n155; jolly, §49.5; marksmen, §§40.9–10, §48.8, §48.9, §51.2; prey, §4.2, §6.7, §7.2, §12.1, §25.2, §27.5, §32.7, §36.4, §45.3, §51.2; quarry, §4.3; saluki hunting dogs, §16.7. *See also* falcons

husbands, xxviii, xxxvii, liii n44, §6.3, §7.1, §23.3, 372n54, 377n113

al-Ḥuzūl, §10.4, §11.1, 376n99

al-Hwērī (tribe), §14.3, §14.5

al-Ḥwēṭāṭ, §49.12

hyenas, xxxii, §18.3, §23.3, §32.10, 374n68

hyperbole, xxxii, xxxvii, liv n60, 382n175, 383n190

al-Hzēm, §50.2, §50.6

ibexes, §31.1, §45.2, §45.3, §48.8, §49.3

Ibn ʿAlī, xxv, xxvi, §11.2, 375n88

Ibn ʿAngā. *See* Radhān ibn ʿAngā

Ibn Baggār, §§48.3–4

Ibn ʿBēkah, §47.1

Ibn Burmān, §53.11, 387n247

Ibn Ḍēgham, §12.1

Ibn Dʿējā (poet), §49.19

Ibn Ghāzī, §2.3

Ibn Hadhdhāl, xix, xxiv–xxv, xxviii, xxxv, xxxvi, §7.2, §7.3, §10.1, §52.7, §52.8, §§53.1–3, §53.2, §53.7, §§53.9–10, 374n68

quarrels, §5.2, §5.4, §9.1, §9.3, §49.17. *See also* fights
Qur'an, xxx, §48.2, 371n30

Rabdā, §8.1, §10.4
rabid, §4.1, §4.2, §37.3, §50.4, 370n21
raconteur, §18.7
Radhān ibn ʿAngā, §19.2, 378n125
Rāḍī ibn Fārān, §29.1
Rafḥā, 385n228
raids: by ʿAnazah and Shammar, liv n56; bloody, §30.3; capture, xlix n7, §32.10; champion raiders, §33.6; death-defying raiders, §39.3; expeditions, xxxvii, §10.2, §14.1, §16.3, §17.6, §§32.4–5, §32.8; by Ibn Rashīd, liv n59; leader (*ʿaḡīd*), lii n31, §2.1, 369n7, 376–77n105; lucky raiders, xxxi, lii n35, §16.3; lucky raid leader (*miḥrām*), §33.6, 376–77n105; mounts for, §25.8; pilfering, §6.8; plunder, xxxi, xxxii, lv n74, §10.2, §15.1, §16.4, §17.4, §32.3, §49.8; raided and stripped bare, §33.4; raiders, xviii, xxiii, xxxiii, xxxiv, xxxvi, xlix n7, §2.1, §2.3, §9.1, §10.2, §13.2, §14.2, §16.5, §16.7, §17.1, §17.5, §27.5, §49.11, 369n7, 380n144, 383n190; raiding, xx, xxxi, xxxv, l n11, 378n123; raiding party, xxxvi, §9.1, §13.1; raid leaders, §16.3, §16.6, §23.1, §23.3, §50.1; robbers, §32.11, §40.3, §40.7, §49.12, §49.15, 371n35, 371n40; for sport, §32.10; taking part in, 377n106. *See also* spoils
rail, §52.6
rain: of Arcturus, §30.5, §40.2, §49.10; chances of, §49.12; clouds, §29.1, §48.1, 384n213, 385n216; curtains of, §40.3; fall (autumn), §49.8, §49.10, 382n172; hail, §36.4; on Ḥayyah's eyes, §48.2; heavy, §9.3, §35.3, §48.1; Mikāʾīl (angel of rain), 384n213; morning, §33.6; not a single drop of, §53.10; Pleiades rains, §28.1; plentiful, xvi, liv n56, §13.2; pools of, §§18.1–2, §49.19, §50.1; pouring, §24.2, §40.3; protection from, §31.3; raindrops, 384n212; rain-fed grazing/pastures, §15.2, §17.6, 378n124; rainwater, §28.1, §30.4; refreshed by, §40.2; relief by, xxxvii; scattered, §17.5; showers, §18.1, §40.10; soaked by, §31.3; spring, xxiii, xlix n4, §30.1, §40.2, §49.10; sprinkles of, §18.1, §18.4, §19.5, §34.2; steady drum of, §47.1; torrents, §10.4, §27.5, §32.10, §44.3, §47.1, §48.1, §50.6, §52.4, §52.6; water from the sky, §42.1; winter, §49.10, 382n172
Rājī ibn Ṭōʿān, §48.2, §48.3, §48.5, §§48.6–7, §48.9
al-Rakhīṣiyyah, §1.3
ransom, §11.1
ʿRār (poet), §49.19
Rāshid al-Hijlī, l n15
Rāshid al-Hirbīd, §48.1
Rashīd ibn Nāṣir al-Laylā, §27.3, §27.4
ravens, §33.4
rebabs, §32.1, §53.14, §53.15
refuge, xiv, xxiii, §9.3, §11.2, §17.6, §25.3, §27.5, §31.6, §43.2, §49.11, §52.9, §53.12
regret, §5.3, §9.3, §20.1, §25.4, §48.10
religion: Christians/Christianity, xxvii, liii n40, 380n151; devout, §54.4; Islam, xxvii, §25.5, §40.8, 374n78, 375n89, 380n151, 386n244; Jewess, §40.8; Muslims, §9.3, 386n244; and naming, liii n40; in poetry, xxvii;

جامعة نيويورك أبوظبي

NYU ABU DHABI

About the NYUAD Research Institute

The Library of Arabic Literature is a research center affiliated with NYU Abu Dhabi and is supported by a grant from the NYU Abu Dhabi Research Institute.

The NYU Abu Dhabi Research Institute is a world-class center of cutting-edge and innovative research, scholarship, and cultural activity. It supports centers that address questions of global significance and local relevance and allows leading faculty members from across the disciplines to carry out creative scholarship and high-level research on a range of complex issues with depth, scale, and longevity that otherwise would not be possible.

From genomics and climate science to the humanities and Arabic literature, Research Institute centers make significant contributions to scholarship, scientific understanding, and artistic creativity. Centers strengthen cross-disciplinary engagement and innovation among the faculty, build critical mass in infrastructure and research talent at NYU Abu Dhabi, and have helped make the university a magnet for outstanding faculty, scholars, students, and international collaborations.

About the Typefaces

The Arabic body text is set in DecoType Naskh, designed by Thomas Milo and Mirjam Somers, based on an analysis of five centuries of Ottoman manuscript practice. The exceptionally legible result is the first and only typeface in a style that fully implements the principles of script grammar (*qawāʿid al-khaṭṭ*).

The Arabic footnote text is set in DecoType Emiri, drawn by Mirjam Somers, based on the metal typeface in the naskh style that was cut for the 1924 Cairo edition of the Qur'an.

Both Arabic typefaces in this series are controlled by a dedicated font layout engine. ACE, the Arabic Calligraphic Engine, invented by Peter Somers, Thomas Milo, and Mirjam Somers of DecoType, first operational in 1985, pioneered the principle followed by later smart font layout technologies such as OpenType, which is used for all other typefaces in this series.

The Arabic text was set with WinSoft Tasmeem, a sophisticated user interface for DecoType ACE inside Adobe InDesign. Tasmeem was conceived and created by Thomas Milo (DecoType) and Pascal Rubini (WinSoft) in 2005.

The English text is set in Adobe Text, a new and versatile text typeface family designed by Robert Slimbach for Western (Latin, Greek, Cyrillic) typesetting. Its workhorse qualities make it perfect for a wide variety of applications, especially for longer passages of text where legibility and economy are important. Adobe Text bridges the gap between calligraphic Renaissance types of the 15th and 16th centuries and high-contrast Modern styles of the 18th century, taking many of its design cues from early post-Renaissance Baroque transitional types cut by designers such as Christoffel van Dijck, Nicolaus Kis, and William Caslon. While grounded in classical form, Adobe Text is also a statement of contemporary utilitarian design, well suited to a wide variety of print and on-screen applications.

Titles Published by the Library of Arabic Literature

For more details on individual titles, visit www.libraryofarabicliterature.org

Classical Arabic Literature: A Library of Arabic Literature Anthology
Selected and translated by Geert Jan van Gelder (2012)

A Treasury of Virtues: Sayings, Sermons, and Teachings of ʿAlī, by al-Qāḍī al-Quḍāʿī, with the **One Hundred Proverbs** attributed to al-Jāḥiẓ
Edited and translated by Tahera Qutbuddin (2013)

The Epistle on Legal Theory, by al-Shāfiʿī
Edited and translated by Joseph E. Lowry (2013)

Leg over Leg, by Aḥmad Fāris al-Shidyāq
Edited and translated by Humphrey Davies (4 volumes; 2013–14)

Virtues of the Imām Aḥmad ibn Ḥanbal, by Ibn al-Jawzī
Edited and translated by Michael Cooperson (2 volumes; 2013–15)

The Epistle of Forgiveness, by Abū l-ʿAlāʾ al-Maʿarrī
Edited and translated by Geert Jan van Gelder and Gregor Schoeler (2 volumes; 2013–14)

The Principles of Sufism, by ʿĀʾishah al-Bāʿūniyyah
Edited and translated by Th. Emil Homerin (2014)

The Expeditions: An Early Biography of Muḥammad, by Maʿmar ibn Rāshid
Edited and translated by Sean W. Anthony (2014)

Two Arabic Travel Books
Accounts of China and India, by Abū Zayd al-Sīrāfī
Edited and translated by Tim Mackintosh-Smith (2014)
Mission to the Volga, by Aḥmad ibn Faḍlān
Edited and translated by James Montgomery (2014)

Disagreements of the Jurists: A Manual of Islamic Legal Theory, by al-Qāḍī al-Nuʿmān
Edited and translated by Devin J. Stewart (2015)

Consorts of the Caliphs: Women and the Court of Baghdad, by Ibn al-Sāʿī
Edited by Shawkat M. Toorawa and translated by the Editors of the Library of Arabic Literature **(2015)**

What ʿĪsā ibn Hishām Told Us, by Muḥammad al-Muwayliḥī
Edited and translated by Roger Allen **(2 volumes; 2015)**

The Life and Times of Abū Tammām, by Abū Bakr Muḥammad ibn Yaḥyā al-Ṣūlī
Edited and translated by Beatrice Gruendler **(2015)**

The Sword of Ambition: Bureaucratic Rivalry in Medieval Egypt, by ʿUthmān ibn Ibrāhīm al-Nābulusī
Edited and translated by Luke Yarbrough **(2016)**

Brains Confounded by the Ode of Abū Shādūf Expounded, by Yūsuf al-Shirbīnī
Edited and translated by Humphrey Davies **(2 volumes; 2016)**

Light in the Heavens: Sayings of the Prophet Muḥammad, by al-Qāḍī al-Quḍāʿī
Edited and translated by Tahera Qutbuddin **(2016)**

Risible Rhymes, by Muḥammad ibn Maḥfūẓ al-Sanhūrī
Edited and translated by Humphrey Davies **(2016)**

A Hundred and One Nights
Edited and translated by Bruce Fudge **(2016)**

The Excellence of the Arabs, by Ibn Qutaybah
Edited by James E. Montgomery and Peter Webb
Translated by Sarah Bowen Savant and Peter Webb **(2017)**

Scents and Flavors: A Syrian Cookbook
Edited and translated by Charles Perry **(2017)**

Arabian Satire: Poetry from 18th-Century Najd, by Ḥmēdān al-Shwēʿir
Edited and translated by Marcel Kurpershoek **(2017)**

In Darfur: An Account of the Sultanate and Its People, by Muḥammad ibn ʿUmar al-Tūnisī
Edited and translated by Humphrey Davies **(2 volumes; 2018)**

War Songs, by ʿAntarah ibn Shaddād
Edited by James E. Montgomery
Translated by James E. Montgomery with Richard Sieburth (2018)

Arabian Romantic: Poems on Bedouin Life and Love, by ʿAbdallāh ibn Sbayyil
Edited and translated by Marcel Kurpershoek (2018)

Dīwān ʿAntarah ibn Shaddād: A Literary-Historical Study
By James E. Montgomery (2018)

Stories of Piety and Prayer: Deliverance Follows Adversity, by al-Muḥassin ibn ʿAlī al-Tanūkhī
Edited and translated by Julia Bray (2019)

The Philosopher Responds: An Intellectual Correspondence from the Tenth Century, by Abū Ḥayyān al-Tawḥīdī and Abū ʿAlī Miskawayh
Edited by Bilal Orfali and Maurice A. Pomerantz
Translated by Sophia Vasalou and James E. Montgomery (2 volumes; 2019)

Tajrīd sayf al-himmah li-stikhrāj mā fī dhimmat al-dhimmah: A Scholarly Edition of ʿUthmān ibn Ibrāhīm al-Nābulusī's Text
By Luke Yarbrough (2020)

The Discourses: Reflections on History, Sufism, Theology, and Literature—Volume One, by al-Ḥasan al-Yūsī
Edited and translated by Justin Stearns (2020)

Impostures, by al-Ḥarīrī
Translated by Michael Cooperson (2020)

Maqāmāt Abī Zayd al-Sarūjī, by al-Ḥarīrī
Edited by Michael Cooperson (2020)

The Yoga Sutras of Patañjali, by Abū Rayḥān al-Bīrūnī
Edited and translated by Mario Kozah (2020)

The Book of Charlatans, by Jamāl al-Dīn ʿAbd al-Raḥīm al-Jawbarī
Edited by Manuela Dengler
Translated by Humphrey Davies (2020)

A Physician on the Nile: A Description of Egypt and Journal of the Famine Years, by ʿAbd al-Laṭīf al-Baghdādī
Edited and translated by Tim Mackintosh-Smith **(2021)**

The Book of Travels, by Ḥannā Diyāb
Edited by Johannes Stephan
Translated by Elias Muhanna **(2 volumes; 2021)**

Kalīlah and Dimnah: Fables of Virtue and Vice, by Ibn al-Muqaffaʿ
Edited by Michael Fishbein
Translated by Michael Fishbein and James E. Montgomery **(2021)**

Love, Death, Fame: Poetry and Lore from the Emirati Oral Tradition, by al-Māyidī ibn Ẓāhir
Edited and translated by Marcel Kurpershoek **(2022)**

The Essence of Reality: A Defense of Philosophical Sufism, by ʿAyn al-Quḍāt
Edited and translated by Mohammed Rustom **(2022)**

The Requirements of the Sufi Path: A Defense of the Mystical Tradition, by Ibn Khaldūn
Edited and translated by Carolyn Baugh **(2022)**

The Doctors' Dinner Party, by Ibn Buṭlān
Edited and translated by Philip F. Kennedy and Jeremy Farrell **(2023)**

Fate the Hunter: Early Arabic Hunting Poems
Edited and translated by James E. Montgomery **(2023)**

The Book of Monasteries, by al-Shābushtī
Edited and translated by Hilary Kilpatrick **(2023)**

In Deadly Embrace: Arabic Hunting Poems, by Ibn al-Muʿtazz
Edited and translated by James E. Montgomery **(2023)**

The Divine Names: A Mystical Theology of the Names of God in the Qur'an, by ʿAfīf al-Dīn al-Tilimsānī
Edited and translated by Yousef Casewit **(2023)**

Bedouin Poets of the Nafūd Desert, by Khalaf Abū Zwayyid, ʿAdwān al-Hirbīd, and ʿAjlān ibn Rmāl
Edited and translated by Marcel Kurpershoek **(2024)**

The Rules of Logic, by Najm al-Dīn al-Kātibī
Edited and translated by Tony Street (2024)

Najm al-Dīn al-Kātibī's al-Risālah al-Shamsiyyah: An Edition and Translation with Commentary
By Tony Street (2024)

English-only Paperbacks

Leg over Leg, by Aḥmad Fāris al-Shidyāq (2 volumes; 2015)
The Expeditions: An Early Biography of Muḥammad, by Maʿmar ibn Rāshid (2015)
The Epistle on Legal Theory: A Translation of al-Shāfiʿī's *Risālah*, by al-Shāfiʿī (2015)
The Epistle of Forgiveness, by Abū l-ʿAlāʾ al-Maʿarrī (2016)
The Principles of Sufism, by ʿĀʾishah al-Bāʿūniyyah (2016)
A Treasury of Virtues: Sayings, Sermons, and Teachings of ʿAlī, by al-Qāḍī al-Quḍāʿī, with the **One Hundred Proverbs** attributed to al-Jāḥiẓ (2016)
The Life of Ibn Ḥanbal, by Ibn al-Jawzī (2016)
Mission to the Volga, by Ibn Faḍlān (2017)
Accounts of China and India, by Abū Zayd al-Sīrāfī (2017)
A Hundred and One Nights (2017)
Consorts of the Caliphs: Women and the Court of Baghdad, by Ibn al-Sāʿī (2017)
Disagreements of the Jurists: A Manual of Islamic Legal Theory, by al-Qāḍī al-Nuʿmān (2017)
What ʿĪsā ibn Hishām Told Us, by Muḥammad al-Muwayliḥī (2018)
War Songs, by ʿAntarah ibn Shaddād (2018)
The Life and Times of Abū Tammām, by Abū Bakr Muḥammad ibn Yaḥyā al-Ṣūlī (2018)
The Sword of Ambition, by ʿUthmān ibn Ibrāhīm al-Nābulusī (2019)
Brains Confounded by the Ode of Abū Shādūf Expounded: Volume One, by Yūsuf al-Shirbīnī (2019)
Brains Confounded by the Ode of Abū Shādūf Expounded: Volume Two, by Yūsuf al-Shirbīnī and **Risible Rhymes**, by Muḥammad ibn Maḥfūẓ al-Sanhūrī (2019)
The Excellence of the Arabs, by Ibn Qutaybah (2019)

Light in the Heavens: Sayings of the Prophet Muḥammad, by al-Qāḍī al-Quḍāʿī (2019)

Scents and Flavors: A Syrian Cookbook (2020)

Arabian Satire: Poetry from 18th-Century Najd, by Ḥmēdān al-Shwēʿir (2020)

In Darfur: An Account of the Sultanate and Its People, by Muḥammad al-Tūnisī (2020)

Arabian Romantic: Poems on Bedouin Life and Love, by ʿAbdallāh ibn Sbayyil (2020)

The Philosopher Responds, by Abū Ḥayyān al-Tawḥīdī and Abū ʿAlī Miskawayh (2021)

Impostures, by al-Ḥarīrī (2021)

The Discourses: Reflections on History, Sufism, Theology, and Literature—Volume One, by al-Ḥasan al-Yūsī (2021)

The Book of Charlatans, by Jamāl al-Dīn ʿAbd al-Raḥīm al-Jawbarī (2022)

The Yoga Sutras of Patañjali, by Abū Rayḥān al-Bīrūnī (2022)

The Book of Travels, by Ḥannā Diyāb (2022)

A Physician on the Nile: A Description of Egypt and Journal of the Famine Years, by ʿAbd al-Laṭīf al-Baghdādī (2022)

Kalīlah and Dimnah: Fables of Virtue and Vice, by Ibn al-Muqaffaʿ (2023)

Love, Death, Fame: Poetry and Lore from the Emirati Oral Tradition, by al-Māyidī ibn Ẓāhir (2023)

The Essence of Reality: A Defense of Philosophical Sufism, by ʿAyn al-Quḍāt (2023)

The Doctors' Dinner Party, by Ibn Buṭlān (2024)

About the Editor–Translator

Marcel Kurpershoek is a senior research fellow at New York University Abu Dhabi and a specialist in the oral traditions and poetry of Arabia. He obtained his PhD in modern Arabic literature at the University of Leiden. He has written a number of books on historical, cultural, and contemporary topics in the Middle East, including the five-volume *Oral Poetry and Narratives from Central Arabia* (1994–2005), which draws on his recordings of Bedouin tribes. For the Library of Arabic Literature, he has edited and translated *Arabian Satire* by Ḥmēdān al-Shwēʿir (2017), *Arabian Romantic* by ʿAbdallāh ibn Sbayyil (2018), and *Love, Death, Fame* by al-Māyidī ibn Ẓāhir (2022). In 2016, Al Arabiya television broadcast an eight-part documentary series based on the travelogue of fieldwork he had undertaken in the Nafūd desert of northern Arabia for his book *Arabia of the Bedouins* (in Arabic translation *The Last Bedouin*). In 2018, Al Arabiya broadcast his five-part documentary on Najdī poetry. He spent his career as a diplomat for the Netherlands, having served as ambassador to Pakistan, Afghanistan, Turkey, Poland, and special envoy for Syria until 2015. From 1996 to 2002, he held a chair as professor of literature and politics in the Arab world at the University of Leiden.

Milton Keynes UK
Ingram Content Group UK Ltd.
UKHW041115190324
439540UK00004B/27/J

9 781479 826155